BRITAIN'S RAILWAYS

- THE REALITY

by

E.A. Gibbins M.C.I.T., M.I.L.T.

Published by :

Leisure Products
11 Bedford Grove
Alsager
Stoke on Trent
ST7 2SR

British Library Cataloguing in Publication Data

A catalogue record of this book is available from the British Library

ISBN   0 9535225 0 4

The 1947 Transport Act was phrased in bureaucratic language and civil-service-speak. (see example on page 27). In simple everyday language it should have read as follows:

NATIONALISED RAILWAYS

An Act to ensure that British Railways are whipping boys
for Government & inefficient industry.

Sec.1: Unlike shipping, railways will not be restored to pre-war condition by Government as they are not essential in peacetime.

Sec.2 To please the electorate, fares will not be allowed to catch up with inflation, but should fall further below inflation.

Sec.3 Rail freight charges will be held below inflation to provide hidden subsidies to inefficient industry, to enable them to compete with foreign industry.

Sec.4 Tortuous legal proceedings will be held to decide fares & charges, and to delay any modest increases. Fortunes will be made for lawyers which may equal those gained when railways were required, in the 19th century, to plead before Parliamentary Committees for the right to build and run railways.

Sec.5 To enable road transport to poach all profitable rail traffic, railways will be tied to outdated laws that compel them to convey unprofitable traffic, which hauliers do not want.

Sec.6 Taxpayers' money will not be used to buy railways from their owners, nor to subsidise rural lines, although they have no economic future.

Sec.7 British Railways will pay a high price for the 19th century wagons owned by *powerful interests* which really are completely worthless. A handful of assets provided at Government expense purely for purposes of war, although of little or no peacetime use, will be purchased by British Railways, at an unjustifiably high price. Railways will be saddled with assets that deteriorated under Government wartime control, will take out costly loans to buy new assets, and will not be allowed to modernise until road transport has done so.

Sec.8 Agencies will be created to block or delay any attempt to close uneconomic lines, as these may be required in the next war. Rural communities will be grateful for their continued existence in case bad weather closes local roads.

Sec.9 Railways may be exploited by vested interests and trade rings, who may increase prices without fear that rail charges will be likewise increased.

Sec.10 Irrespective of the effect on costs, standards of safety on railways must be of a much higher standard than those tolerated for their competitors.

Inspired by MP, Mr. A..J. Champion, who said, in 1955, a better title for the Rural Transport Bill might be: *A Bill to make it more difficult to close a branch line, no matter how little used, to give power to a Tribunal never designed for that purpose, to give Directions without making provision for the finance to enable it to ensure the carrying out of that Direction.* (Hansard vol. 547, col. 757)

Dedicated to Irene with all my love and gratitude
for her understanding and her tolerance
of the disruptions caused to our family life
by many years of railway "On Call" duties and extended working hours;
and
for her encouragement in my post-retirement research.

The author wishes to thank those who assisted his research:

Public Record Office, House of Lords Record Office,
British Library, Keele University Library,
National Railway Museum, Office of National Statistics,

Alsager, Birmingham, Crewe, Ellesmere Port,
Hanley, Kidsgrove, Liverpool, Manchester, Norfolk & Somerset libraries;

and also Newton Abbott, Widnes & Winchester libraries for access to their railway collections;

Central Rail Users Committee
and many others.

The author also wishes to thank those who
assisted in the preparation of his economy & productivity schemes at
Crewe, Doncaster, Leicester, Rugby, Sheffield, Stoke-on-Trent & Sunderland

those who were affected or displaced by those schemes
for their co-operation in implementation

and to place on record that these and other economy schemes
did not affect the dedication of staff, especially during adverse weather,
to keep trains running safely

CONTENTS

Introduction

It is now seen that BR - state owned British Rail - was not as bad as it was painted. The *reality* is that the subsidy has now soared, and that quality and safety have declined. The perceived image of BR managers was of incompetence due to the "losses", which were a direct result of Government policies that held fares and charges below inflation, blocked closures of rural routes, delayed investment, enforced higher wages than BR could afford and imposed interest bearing loans to *compensate* for ensuing deficits! A series of Acts of Parliament retained principles which it should have been obvious to any unbiased mind were preventing BR from acting like the private sector businesses they were supposed to emulate. No industry, subject to such policies, however skilled its managers, could have avoided insolvency. Published BR complaints were not compared to the private sector, which published *no* data - implying no complaints - but experience shows that they sell inferior products, give poor service, are out of stock and recall unreliable or unsafe products.

It came as a shock to those now running railways, that they bear no similarity to table-top railways, nor the preserved railways on which some enjoy playing engine drivers; and that the standards of performance demanded by users completely eclipses that which they tolerate from other transport and industry. Promises to improve punctuality by "getting drivers to drive faster" - when trains were running at maximum safe speed - were common. It came as a bigger shock to discover that BR managers had been running a tight ship, and that the scope for economy was severely constrained. Panic economies: sacking experienced middle managers, supervisors and drivers - led to cancellations, poor maintenance, unsafe practices and other failures.

Retrospective claims that assets were decrepit were bandied about to explain worse performances This book reveals modernisation did not cease 40 years ago, as some would have the public believe. Indeed, in many respects BR practice was in advance of that in other industry. Had the newcomers taken over railways in 1948, they would have known the meaning of *decrepit stock*, which was a direct result of the period of ruinous wartime Government control. Post-war Government Directives blocked modernisation, and even prevented restoration to pre-war standards for ten years after the war, in order to give priority of materials and resources to industry, which repaid them by losing a world lead in *every* field. Worse, Government turned a blind eye to blatant non-compliance of its materials control Directives, when excess numbers of road vehicles were built for the home market from the same materials. This was not, as is popularly believed, because Government money was needed to restore railways. British Rail inherited funds from their predecessors and there was also £150m of maintenance cash held in a Trust Fund. Government had iniquitously gained £1bn from enforced discounts in charges for Government rail traffic, and from an unwarranted *share* of profits mugged from railway revenue, (see page 18) - a robbery not perpetrated on any other industry, many of which - especially road transport - profited very nicely from the war, (see "*Square Deal Denied*"). Even worse, post-war Government ensured that there would be no profits to invest in railways, by devising a bureaucratic system that held fares and charges below the raging inflation in costs - precipitated by incompetent and timid industrialists who were unable to apply their minds to improving productivity. Unreliable rolling stock and other equipment supplied by the private sector caused cancellations, delays, loss of revenue and increased costs, for all of which, BR was blamed.

Including nationalised railways in the BTC - an unwieldy bureaucratic conglomerate dreamed up by civil servants - was a major factor in the decline of railways. BR was denied independent financial status, which was exploited by politicians, *competitors* and the public to prevent BR achieving viability. Given that inland transport was formed into a conglomerate, it should have been headed by one of the four Chairmen of the main line railway companies, each of whom was experienced in running rail, road haulage, hotels, canals, ships and buses. Some 85% of assets[1] taken over by the BTC had been under the control of these Chairmen. Government's first two appointees as Chairman

---

[1] 70% of total assets went under the Railway Executive, the rest were transferred to the other Executives.

were accustomed to acquiescing to Ministers: "*Your obedient servant*" was the standard end-phrase in Reports to Ministers by the first two Chairmen - a retired civil servant and a retired general. Only two of the ten Chairmen of the BTC and Railways Board appointed in 47 years of nationalisation, by the Minister, were professional railway executives. Civil servants heading the BTC did not delegate any real authority to the professionals appointed to the Railway Executive - a most inappropriately named body - since it was denied *executive* powers.

Criteria of success in other industries, when applied to BR, was regarded as failure. In other industry, a *demand in excess of supply equals success, supply in excess of demand equals bankruptcy*. Perversely, overfull trains were regarded as failure, despite no advance warning of intention to travel. Overfull airplanes are not so regarded, passengers, who have booked in advance are "bumped-off", (see page 150). A hotel asked for a room in the peak at a week's notice produces a patronising response. A BR apology for an inability to provide a seat in the peak with five seconds notice creates hysteria and sarcasm. Industry *avoids excess stock, which increases costs*. Excess stock [seats] on BR is an irretrievable loss, in the private sector, it is a delayed profit. Contrary to popular opinion, longer trains will not end standing. Commuters broke into a cardiac inducing gallop to catch a train, rather than wait minutes, and were critical it was not elasticated. Many stand near to a door, due to the obsession to be first off. Standing passengers were injured in the Cannon Street accident in 1991, when 200 seats were unoccupied at the rear.

One could answer critics off- but not on-duty. Their minds were closed to explanation or analogy: "Don't confuse me with facts - my mind is made up". Neither were they willing to accept that it "was only human error" - an excuse paraded frequently by the private sector. Abject apologies and compensation was the minimum demanded, even if their conduct had contributed to the cause of a complaint. Any other response often led to a letter to MPs, thence to the BR Chairman, and down to the misguided manager whose reasoned reply was deemed unacceptable. Many in BR believed that the best reply was the abject apology - even to complaints of having to stand in train for which no prior notice of user had been received, when the passenger had the same option as by bus or air, of travelling on the next service. An analogous complaint of lack of stock by retailers was met with: "*its uneconomic to carry stock to satisfy everyone*".

No industry could have succeeded against a backdrop of the unconstructive and unbalanced criticism that faced BR. For some inexplicable reason, BR was expected to become UK's **first** perfect industry - having no defects, no delays, no complaints with prices continually below inflation. It was safe to predict that BR would be the second, as there would never be a first, all front line critics not excepted. Any claiming first place, must prove it remained as far below inflation as BR from 1948, and open its books on complaints, including records of returned and recalled products. Were any other company subjected to so many *Watchdogs*, they would take full page advertisements to boast of the minute ratio of complaints to customers which BR experienced. (see page 105).

At some stage, it must *surely* have dawned, even on ideological politicians, that *no* industry could prosper without control of its own prices and investment. There must have been some soul searching as to a solution. The most obvious - conceding equality of commercial freedom sought by pre-war railways, and in the 1950s and 1960s by BR - must have crossed even the most obtuse minds. But the corollary was that such a concession would leave the condemning finger pointing at ministers and government. That could not be contemplated, hence privatise railways, concede almost total freedom, retain a pale semblance of interference, which would gradually disappear, and give them even more money to keep open electorally sensitive lines. It will be, *at least* 30 years before any papers, which reveal options considered, are released and by then the interest will be dead. Meanwhile this book reveals that the subsidy to the private sector was grossly inflated above that needed by BR to run a service that was improving, and contrary to current political spin, expanding. Even worse, the newcomers have asked for and been given extra subsidies above those for which they contracted, and warned of closure if no more money was forthcoming. No meaningful benchmarks were established against which private sector railway performance could be measured.

Abbreviations

ATOC	Association of Train Operating Companies
BR	British Railways, later shortened to British Rail - state owned from 1948.
BREL	British Rail Engineering Ltd
BRB	British Railways Board [1963-97]
BRS	British Road Services, [a BTC subsidiary until 1962]
BTC	British Transport Commission [1948-62]. Controlled railways, road transport, canals, etc.
CBI	Confederation of British Industry
CIGS	Chief of the Imperial General Staff
col	column
CSO	Central Statistical Office, later re-named Office of National Statistics - [ONS]
CRUCC	Central Rail Users Committee renamed Rail Passengers Council [RPC] in 2000.
CTCC	Central Transport Consultative Committee - "Rail Watchdog" - renamed CRUCC in 1993
CWR	Continuous welded rail
d	pence [pre 1971 coinage; one old penny written as 1d, was equal to less than 0.5p]
DMU	Diesel Multiple Unit
DoT	Department of Transport
EMU	Electric Multiple Unit
HGV	Heavy Goods Vehicle - later replaced by LGV.
HMRI	Her Majesty's Railway Inspectors [under the MoT; originally "the Railway Inspectorate"]
H&SE	Health & Safety Executive. HMRI is now under this Executive
HST	High Speed Train
LGV	Long Goods Vehicle.
LMSR	London Midland & Scottish Railway
LNER	London & North Eastern Railway
LPTB	London Passenger Transport Board
LRPC	London Regional Passengers Committee. A Rail "Watchdog"
LSE	London & South East passenger sector - later renamed NSE
LT	London Transport
LT&S	London, Tilbury & Southend line
M&EE	Mechanical & Electrical Engineer
MoT	Minister of Transport [includes Secretary of State for Transport]
MoWT	Minister of War Transport, [1941-1946]
NBPI	National Board for Prices & Incomes
NCL	National Carriers Ltd - a subsidiary of NFC - formerly BR Sundries Division
NFC	National Freight Corporation
NRES	National Rail Enquiry Service. Replaced the telephone enquiry bureaux operated by BR.
NSE	Network SouthEast - BR's Passenger Business Sector for south east England
OPRAF	Office of Passenger Rail Franchising - A highly remunerated body set up by Government
PRO	Public Records Office
PSO	Public Service Obligation Grant -for losses on lines Government required to be kept open
PTE	Passenger Transport Executive [controlled by a PTA - Passenger Transport Authority]
PSV	Passenger Service Vehicle [now re-named Passenger Carrying Vehicle - PCV].
RPI	Retail Price Index
RUCC	Rail Users Consultative Committee - now renamed Rail Passengers Committee
SRA	Strategic Rail Authority - another highly remunerated body set up by Government
TOPS	Total Operations Processing System. BR's real time computer for controlling rolling stock.
TUCC	Transport Users Consultative Committee - "Rail Watchdog"; became RUCC in 1993
vol	Volume
WPI	Wholesale Price Index

SOURCES

Sources are shown in the text. The main sources are as follows:

BRB minutes	PRO: AN167/1 to 167/9
BTC minutes	PRO: AN85/1 to 85/16
Cabinet Minutes & Papers	PRO: CAB
Charges Review, 1946	PRO: MT6/2704, closed to 1997
Inland Transport Statistics in Great Britain	Munby & Watson (referred to as "Munby").
Marshall Aid	PRO: MT6/2830, closed to 1999 - seen 1995
Parliament, Debates & Answers	Hansard - Commons, unless shown as Lords
Railway assets	BTC/BRB Accounts, Railway Yearbooks, HMRI
Railways, Finance & Future	PRO: MT47/275, closed to 1972
Railway Passenger Duty - ended 1929	PRO: MT47/128, closed to 1986
Special Advisory Group (Stedeford Committee)	PRO: MT124/361, 124/547, 132/80-88
Square Deal - Cabinet & Dept of Transport	PRO: CAB 60[38], 18[39], 24/286, MT6/2876,
- LMS Railway Company	PRO: RAIL424/27
- Railway Companies Association	*"Railway Crisis"* & *"Fair Play for Railways"*
Transport Advisory Council 1937 Report	PRO: CAB Minutes 1938; CAB23/92, 24/274
Transport Bill, 1952	PRO: MT62/138, closed to 1983
Transport Tribunal - Proceedings (Hearings)	Manchester Central Library : PP380.1622.T1
- Annual Reports	House of Lords - Unprinted Papers
War compensation paid to railways	PRO: MT47/263, closed to 2000 - seen 1995
Wartime Control - Cabinet	PRO: CAB65/18, 66/17
- DoT	PRO: MT6/2604, 47/276-278, closed to 1991/2
	47/279, closed to 1999, released 1972
- LMSR	PRO: RAIL424/15, 424/16, 424/18
- Other	White Papers : CMD 6168, CMD 6314
Wartime requisition of private owner wagons	PRO: MT6/2611, closed to 1991, released 1972
War traffic	The Railway Companies Association

Secondary sources: Titles and authors are shown in the text, except the following, where the author's name is used. A suffix number identifies the book concerned for certain authors.

Barnett, C. *"The Verdict of Peace"* - Barnett/1	Joy, S. *"The train that ran away"*
Barnett, C. *"The Lost Victory"* - Barnett/2	Keesings Contemporary Archives
Bell, R. *"History of Railways 1939-45"*	Pearson A.J. *"Man of the rail"* - Pearson/1
Elliot, Sir John *"On & off the rails"*	Pearson A.J. *"Railways & the nation"* -Pearson/2
Henshaw, D. *"The Great Railway Conspiracy"*	Savage, C.I. *"Inland Transport at War"*

British Transport Review is referred to as the BTC Review

Glaister, Burnham, Stevens & Travers *"Transport Policy in Gt Britain"* is shown by its title

[ ]	Encloses text that was in brackets in the quoted source, or was implied, or for clarification
( )	Encloses the source of documents or cross reference to a page or Table N° within this book
Page	refers to a page in the source quoted. **page** cross refers to another page in this book

Italics in the text are inserted by the author.

Chapter 1 Prologue

No railway could be built, except on private land, without an enabling Act of Parliament which specified charges to be made for its use. Profits were restricted by the Construction of Future Railways Act 1844. The Railway Clauses Act 1845 stated that all must pay the same in like circumstances. The Railway & Canal Act 1854 compelled railways to provide reasonable and equal facilities to all without undue preference. The Regulation of Railways Act 1873 obliged them to publish rates and keep them available for public inspection at stations. The 1888 Railway & Canal Traffic Act created Railway & Canal Commissioners with power over charges for merchandise traffic.

The Cheap Trains Act 1883, required railways to provide workmen's trains between 6.0 pm and 8.0 am at fares not exceeding 1d per mile and gave powers to order provision. The Railway & Canal Act 1894 required railways - not canals - to justify rate increases, so that Railways had to plead their case in public before a Tribunal. The Railways [Private Sidings] Act, 1904 - not repealed until 1962 - obliged railways to provide reasonable facilities for anyone wishing to have private sidings.

When there was no competition, these conditions were just. However, in the 1920s road haulage ruthlessly exploited the Acts to capture railway traffic. (see pages 7-8).

Military Use of Railways

Having not contributed to railway costs, but compelling them to fight through Parliament, paying huge legal fees in the process, the Better Regulation of Railways Act 1842 was enacted to provide for conveying troops at prices to be settled between Government and railway companies. Under the Future Railways Act 1844, railways must charge a maximum of 1d [0.5p] per mile for each soldier. *The concept of agreeing charges had ended.* The Regulation of Forces Act 1871, gave Government powers to take-over railways on a temporary basis. Compensation was to be agreed between both parties - in the event of difference, to be settled by arbitration under the Land Clauses Act 1845. This was replaced by dictating "next to nothing" terms in two World Wars, (see below & page 13-17).

The Cheap Trains Act 1883 also provided for military movements at reduced rates - up to 150 personnel at 75% ordinary fare; if more than 150, the balance at 50% ordinary fare. The 75% rate also applied to families entitled to travel at public expense, and, later to private journeys.

At the start of the Great War in 1914, railways were taken over under the 1871 Act, and retained for four years after war ended. *All* military traffic was carried free. Munitions workers - among the best paid - were given half fare or free tickets. Despite inflation, freight rates were frozen, and fares little altered. Industrial prices were allowed to rise. Coastwise shipping rates doubled and canal charges increased, causing diversions to railways. In 1917, armed forces and other Government personnel made 29.6m free journeys, rising to 62m in 1918. They secured a good bargain, having only to guarantee 1913 net receipts in return for free transport of men and materials on an unprecedented scale. Government increased rail wages to match inflation, and in 1919, conceded wage rises and an eight hour day against companies' wishes. A 1911 Act allowing railways to raise charges promptly to match increased wages, was suspended. Inflation rose by 241%. In September 1920, the MoT set up the Colwyn Committee to look into compensation due to railways under the Act. There was no need for it, the 1871 Act provided for arbitration by the Railway & Canal Commission - *a court of law*. Colwyn was a kangaroo court - the judge was appointed by the defendant: Government; the plaintiffs: rail companies were excluded! The Committee urged "*that settlement should not be based on a tenacious insistence on documentary rights*", implying that **Agreements** be ignored to the disadvantage of railways, not Government. The Committee saw £150m as the compensation due. In 1921, Government said they would pay £60m in satisfaction of all claims under the agreements. Media reports said it should be up to £400m. After the war, maintenance was so far in arrears that it was a barrier to development for a decade after control ceased in 1922. (see "*Square Deal Denied*").

As examples of the increased wartime workload of railways, for which no adequate reward was gained "in 1915, 13.9% more traffic - excluding Government traffic whose volume was not recorded

- was carried than in the most prosperous pre-war years". (Midland Railway AGM). "In 1917, the Midland Railway conveyed 6.4% more freight and 12.2% more passengers, excluding Government traffic. Railways were the *only* industry which did not pay higher dividends or interest in the war. Chancellor Bonar Law did not invest in rail shares, but in shipping shares. Rail dividends were unchanged against a 120% rise in the cost of living. Staff got increases but not shareholders". (PRO: Rail 491/12). Rail profits had been pegged by Government at pre-war levels. Applying the traffic percentages to total pre-war railway profits of £51m, would have added £6-8m to each of the six years that railways were controlled by Government, not counting their traffic carried free of charge.

Post War Reorganisation

In 1918, Churchill advanced a case for nationalising railways as 'it may be expedient to run them at a loss if they developed industry and stimulated development'. (Times 11.12.18).

Government set up Committees to determine the *minimum* increases necessary to return railways to viability, after falling behind inflation, *whilst keeping an eye on the effect on coastwise shipping*! They recommended higher freight rate increases and lower fares increases than railways proposed. This made railways more vulnerable to unregulated road haulage and protected coastwise shipping.

The 1920 Railways Bill planned to merge 120 companies into Groups to prop up rural railways that had been over-worked and under-paid in the war, and avoid *any* closures. "The fundamental principle of Grouping was that more prosperous lines should help balance losses on badly paying lines". (Savage, Page 12). The Bill referred to "*extending the Charter of the companies*", entitling Government to participate in surplus revenue to assist backward districts and develop light railways. Companies pointed out that maximum charges were not "Charters" but restrictions upon charging powers that, otherwise, would be limited only by their reasonableness. *This limit did not apply to industry.* The Railways Act, 1921, merged companies into four Groups - the "Big Four" and set up the Railway Rates Tribunal - a Court of Law - to decide all rates not merely maxima as hitherto. It promised profits no less, nor no greater than in 1913 without adjusting for inflation.

The allocation of goods into Rate charges bands was decided by the Rates Advisory Committee set up by the Government. Their General Classification of Merchandise, listing every item known to man, was described by the companies: "as a "*Nonsense Novel*", because it prescribed, for example, that in sending fish products, you had to separate oysters from periwinkles and from crabs because all go at different rates. Goods - say shoes, packed in different containers - hampers, sacks, casks or cases go at different rates". Nominally, there were 21 classes but with sub divisions there were 66. The companies said that Classification was applicable only where there was a monopoly.

The different rates systems applied by road and rail, and outdated laws applicable only to railways, initiated a loss of traffic from rail to road. Despite this, Government did not revise laws that enabled hauliers to "cream off" higher value traffics which subsidised low value rail traffic. Under 1845 and 1854 Acts, Railways had to offer equal facilities to all at the same price. Road could, and did, discriminate. The 1873 Act compelled railways to open rate books to **all**, allowing hauliers to know by how much to undercut rail charges. They did not need to make blind tenders.

The Railway Rates Tribunal

The 1921 Act specified a Charges Scheme, unique in industrial legislation, to be devised by this Government appointed Tribunal - a Court of Law, that took seven years to implement a monopoly based strait jacket, by which time, railways had ceased to be a monopoly! Under the Act, "standard charges" would be the only permitted charges, with no variation up or down, except for "exceptional charges", which only varied *down* from Standard. Agricultural products were given concessions. Charges "*will be sufficient with efficient and economical working and management, in the opinion of the Tribunal, to yield equivalent to the Standard Revenue in 1913 of constituent companies*" - £51m - which the Act specified that railways forcibly amalgamated by the Act should be able to earn. No other industry had profits pegged in perpetuity. It was required to review and adjust charges annually to ensure that Standard Revenue was earned, taking account of whether railways were run efficiently and economically. If not, it would not authorise an increase: "If the Tribunal find that the revenue obtained, or which could with efficient and economic management have been obtained exceeds Standard Revenue, they shall modify charges to effect a reduction of Net Revenue in subsequent years equivalent to 80% of such excess". This would return the excess to users through lower charges. Its obligation to adjust charges, to achieve Net Revenue, was never carried out, despite the fact that in no year was it achieved. There was no reason to prevent them from increasing low and decreasing high rates to fulfil the statutory objective and end unfair competition. *"The source of the railway problem was being left with unremunerative traffic. The solution is to rationalise the rates system. Heavy industry would have to cease being subsidised by lower rates"*. (DoT Memo, August 1943, PRO: MT47/275).

The 1961 Special Advisory Group said: "The Tribunal was inflexible and railways were placed at a disadvantage in meeting competition from a growing road haulage industry". (PRO: MT132/82).

In the eleven years preceding the Second World War, the shortfall totalled £171m. Railways were promised Standard Revenue in exchange for statutory rates control. Government got its part of the deal, railways got the "Unsquare Deal". The basis of the 1928 Charges Scheme was that traffic in lower classes was subsidised by profits from higher classes, **claimed** to be in accordance with the principle: *"What the market will bear"*. After 1894, (see page 5), railways could not increase charges to test what the market would bear. That could not be ascertained by asking customers - no one else does that. Obviously, customers would always demand still lower prices.

Bonavia[1] says that "the average receipt per ton mile of minerals and heavy merchandise was 0.96d [0.4p] with a wagon load of 9.8 tons giving 9.4d [3.9p] per wagon mile. Other merchandise receipts were 2.0d per ton mile, with a wagon load of 2.5 tons, giving 5.6d [2.0p] per wagon mile. Coal showed earnings of 10.8d [4.4p] per wagon mile". Costs and other factors affect this comparison:-
- coal and mineral wagons returned empty, thereby halving their revenue per wagon mile.
- coal/mineral wagon turn-round was twice that of a goods van (see Table 9), reducing it further.
- coal/mineral train speed was half that of a fast freight - incurring higher manpower & loco costs
- coal wagons were stopped ten times as often as railway owned wagons due to hot axle boxes, (see page 50), and caused costly delays to other traffic, inflating traincrew and other rail staff costs.

These alter the comparison in favour of merchandise traffic, even allowing for handling costs on that portion of traffic not unloaded in public and private sidings by consignees.

Hauliers charged a discriminatory rate for every job, after exercising a legal right to check rail rates, and creamed-off 16% of merchandise by 1937 and 26% by 1938, compared to 1927. The basis of the 1928 Rates Book was unaltered until 1957. Hence, its vulnerability to "creaming-off" was undiminished throughout that time.

The margin for undercutting rail is illustrated by the 1928 rate for traffic conveyed 100 miles: that for class 21 being nine times that of class 1, whereas the cost of carrying, ton for ton would be broadly the same. Before road competition, goods were, in aggregate, carried at a profit - low rated traffic being subsidised by high rated traffic. When road began to "cream-off" top layers offering 10% below the rail rate, rail lost profitable traffic which was subsidising low rated traffic.

Railway companies could offer rates between 5% and 40% below Standard - *to all users equally*. Sir Wm. Wood, Vice President, LMSR, informed the Rates Tribunal in 1939 that *"Railways were told that packed confectionery and packed explosives are carried at the same rates by road and that the same must apply to rail, although the rail rate for explosives is, at 50 miles, double the rail rate for confectionery. No suggestions were received from consignors that the converse should apply and the rates for traffic in lower classes increased to the level of road rates"*.

---

[1] *"Railway Policy between the wars"*, Page 142.

In 1925, against railway company advice, the Tribunal reduced wagon demurrage rates, an action detrimental to wagon utilisation. The consequences were disastrous for profitability over the next 50 years, and counter productive in the 1939-45 War when traffic increased by 50%, (see page 17).

"From 1921 to 1929, £490m was spent on roads against £180m received from licence and petrol duties. Railway capital was £1,100m, of which £800m had been spent on the permanent way. Railways paid municipal rates which funded roads. Anyone with a vehicle could operate on roads and choose the cream, leaving the rest for railways". ("*Fair Play for Railways*").

Four Ineffective Government Inquiries into Inequality

After years of railway protests about unfair competition, a Royal Commission on Transport was set up in 1928, to consider problems arising from the growth of road transport. It said: "Parliament fixed a maximum profit for railways" - unlike hauliers - "if this was exceeded, four-fifths of the surplus must be given back to the public as reduced charges". It made three Reports covering PSV licences and limited hours for drivers, enacted in the 1930 Road Traffic Act; proposed *another* Inquiry into rail and road freight competition, and advocated a permanent Advisory Committee.

In 1932, the Association of British Chambers of Commerce called "for removal of disabilities and restrictions which made it difficult for railways to compete with road transport". The National Organisation of Trade & Industry criticised the Commission "for failing to deal with the division of function between rail and road. It must eventually deprive trade and industry of alternative means of transport, destroying the reasonable competition which is their safeguard". (Keesings 281A & 528K).

Government's **second Inquiry** - the Salter Conference - recommended a Committee to advise the Minister on road licensing and the division of goods between different modes and that road haulage should pay towards the cost of building and maintaining roads. It recommended that railway bridges carrying roads should be the responsibility of road authorities and paid for by the new licences. The Road & Rail Traffic Act 1933 introduced road goods licences and created the Transport Advisory Council. Heavy bridge costs are still borne by railways today. Gilbert Walker ("*Road & Rail*") completely ignored the issue of bridge and level crossing costs. (see also the footnote on page 9).

The **third Inquiry** - by the Transport Advisory Council - recommended, in July 1937, in a Report: "*Service & Rates*", that all transport should be rate controlled, which Government accepted but did nothing, apart from discussing it at a Cabinet Meeting in February 1938, when the MoT said he had looked to the Council for a more complete and scientific scheme.

In 1938, as Government had not enacted similar controls on hauliers, railways launched a "Square Deal" Campaign proposing that statutory control of rail rates be abolished to put them on a par with hauliers - for rates to be confidential and traffic at "cost plus" - as applies to all businesses. In November, they submitted proposals to remove legal restrictions on freight charging powers, saying that they had made representations for 15 years, adding: "*The extreme urgency is apparent*".

The DoT accepted that railways were disadvantaged by the law, but that equal freedom would end subsidies to agriculture and industry paid via Freight Rebates and legally enforced rail rates; leading to Government subsidies. "If the demand was rejected, railways would reduce wages - causing a strike, close lines required in wartime, or be bankrupted because reserves were almost non-existent: any of which would embarrass Government". They emphasised "the importance of railways in peace and war. Judging by the progress made in rail and road co-ordination, it is probable that the process will be interrupted by the advent of a Labour Government which will nationalise transport. By this time rates may have fallen below cost, and transport will need a subsidy. Railways should have powers to modify rates within the present Standard. This would not bring equality, but gives time for a permanent policy to be worked out". (PRO: MT6/2876). Preventing low rates being increased, but '*permitting higher rates to be decreased*', was no help, and would still bring ruin.

On 1st December, Railways told the DoT: it "took six months to obtain an increase in charges from the Tribunal by which time the boom was over". A simple Act on one piece of paper was needed to repeal specified Parts and Sections of seven Acts. *The 1937 application to raise rates resulted in a sixteen day Inquiry and six months delay, despite proof that prices of trade and industry had increased, without hindrance. That delay would have cost £4m or 2.5% of net revenue.*

On 8th December, the MoT asked companies "to specify particular features in the system that were exceptionally galling". They said "we are not seeking a little relief, which may help keep up an unequal battle through another round, but equality with other transport". He admitted that "*road had creamed-off traffic which subsidised low rated rail traffic,* but did not think Parliament would agree to freedom. By law, he was bound to refer it to the Transport Advisory Council". Had the law changed, rail would not have lost core traffic. Freedom was blocked until 1962. (see pages 114-115)

In December 1938, the Council of the London Chambers of Commerce stated that railways are seriously handicapped by the unequal treatment of different forms of transport and called for legislation to free railways at an early date. (Times, 15.12.38).

On 12th December, the MoT asked the Council to consider the problem, as there was a prima facie case for relaxing statutory regulations. The DoT file (PRO: MT6/2876), shows the remit for this **fourth Inquiry** required retention of control over maximum rates, classification and publication of Standard and Exceptional Rates. *Railways would still be tied by the restraints which lost traffic.*

The Advisory Council Chairman said: "*It is no wonder Railways took the action they did. It was the Minister's fault for doing nothing tangible for so long on the 1937 Rates Report*". A Sub Committee stated that co-ordination could not be effected between transport systems whose charges are based on widely differing principles. By 1937, railways had lost £32m in merchandise receipts after adjustment for reduced traffic caused by changes in the structure of industry. Between 1926 - the earliest census of road goods vehicles - and 1937, the number of road goods vehicles rose by 86%, and their unladen weight by 73% - much greater than justified to meet a rise in production of 46% between 1924 and 1937. The use of trailers further increased available carrying capacity.

The MoT said "railways are essential in peace and war. They wanted freedom to quote rates which would be contrary to 100 years' experience[2]. No solution could be found which did not include control and provision for appeals. Given complete discretion, they could refuse to carry a colliery's coal if a single ton of coal is carried by road[3]. Railways were handicapped by antiquated controls. Under the present system, machinery was brought by road from the North, and empty crates returned by rail at exceptionally low rates based on the assumption that profitable traffic had passed by rail[4]. Government's objective was co-ordination". (Cabinet Minutes, December 1938).

On 14th January the Council Chairman wrote to railways: "difficulties with publication and shipping, should not be insuperable". The MoT wrote to the Chairman - who favoured freedom to alter rates - "I dislike giving an opportunity to alter rates of their own volition". *This was supposed to be an independent Inquiry, whose **advice**, he was required by law to obtain!* Coastwise shipping said that "protection against railways was lessened by unregulated road transport". In a further letter to the Chairman, the DoT wrote: "We must insist on publication of Standard Charges & Exceptional Rates as provided by the 1921 Act. Railways should have powers to modify on giving due notice, but if that increases charges, and a trader objects, the modification should not have effect until determined by the Tribunal". *This gave railways nothing.* The MoT was represented at the Inquiry, and could have spoken openly. Clearly, Government was not willing to make concessions[5].

In February 1939, Lord Stamp, LMSR President, told the Glasgow Chamber of Commerce: "There is no restriction in the Square Deal for competitors or customers. It seeks to give railways the same freedom as competitors. Industries who have no control by outsiders over their own prices think the railways should have hardly any power to raise charges without first having to do what no

---

[2] Without competition! Little wonder, the UK fell behind with such blinkered thinking.
[3] This was nonsense - the submission was for merchandise traffic, which they were losing, not coal.
[4] This was tantamount to fraud by senders.
[5] Clearly, Walker was mistaken in believing that the railway demand was met. He refers ("*Road & Rail*", Page 108) to "complaints between the railways and their apologists". This smacks of bias against railways.

other trade in the country is required to do - get the permission of the Tribunal. The need for the Square Deal was now or never - if out of date laws were not changed the railways would succumb".

Walker pointed out that most firms can discriminate between customers, if knowledge of lower prices charged to favoured customers can be kept from the others. (*"Road & Rail"*, Page 193).

Road interests orchestrated a media campaign to discredit the Square Deal, but did not offer to exchange rail and road rate constraints - road being controlled and rail free. Hauliers claimed that they were constrained by law, because an application to set up business was subject to opposition from other transport. Railways needed an Act of Parliament to set up or extend their operations!.

The Council reported on 24th March. On *the* key issue - publication of rates - they made no recommendation. Railways were prepared to accept publication if applied to all transport. Only one, of ten bodies at the Inquiry, objected to ending publication. The Council said that material relaxation of statutory control of rail charges was necessary, but because of the ultimate [Government] objective of co-ordination of transport, recommendations were regarded as for not more than five years or such shorter period as may be necessary to establish adequate co-ordination. They said that freedom was incompatible with Freight Rebates. *This railway subsidy to industry would fall on Government.* Railway companies said that the "proposals did not meet the basic demands of the railways". The claim that the proposals would facilitate co-ordination was dismissed by Walker: "none of the measures suggested by the council can or will promote that end". (Walker, Page 194).

The DoT edited the Council's Final Report, interfering in what was supposed to be an independent Inquiry. DoT papers show that paragraphs and statistics were deleted from the Draft Report that supported the case for freedom, and proved that road transport capacity had increased well above production indices, although the 1933 Act was designed to prevent excess capacity. (*"Square Deal Denied"*, Pages 110-111). These statistics were the clearest confirmation that road transport had "creamed-off" traffic. The President of the Railway Rates Tribunal secretly urged the MoT:

> A Bill should specify that railways may make charges not exceeding those they were entitled to make at the passing of the proposed Act. The Tribunal would decide the reasonableness of a rate if a trader objected. There would be no presumption that existing rates were reasonable".

Existing rates had been set by the Tribunal after traders' objected. Railways would gain nothing "The prospects of railways gaining benefit get slighter as proposals become encompassed by safeguards and stipulations. Rates will be constantly under review by railway-cum-trader committees and associations with a right of appeal to a Tribunal". (Modern Transport, February 1939)

It has been the received wisdom that the war put off action to implement the Square Deal. Walker argued that if railways could cover costs there was no case for freedom. (Page 194). He failed to see that the trend was leading to a situation when revenue would not cover all costs, and vast freight only assets would be valueless. Like other contemporary observers, he assumed that the Council's proposals would pass into legislation. Of course, he was unable to see DoT papers (PRO: MT6/2876, closed for 50 years), which reveal that Government had no intention of conceding railway demands, nor the Council's pale substitute. Whitehall played "*pass the parcel*" until war came. In May 1939, the MoT told Cabinet that "It does not seem possible to accept that railways should be put on the same footing as other transport". He added that he needed "to determine points not covered in the Report which must be settled before a Bill could be prepared". *As the DoT had edited the Report, there could be no points to determine. The file contains no list of points nor of any action.*

Government quickly passed complex Defence Laws. Four weeks before the war, they passed the 50 page British Overseas Airways Corporation Act, which did not control *their* charges. The railway claim required a one page Act. There was never any hope that an industry, so disparate as road haulage would establish a common rates structure to facilitate co-ordination. War did *not* preclude action - the War Cabinet busied itself with *civil service leave* and post war plans: a national health service, housing, etc. A charges Act could have been passed in 1939 or prepared for post-war application, for this problem would not disappear but would get worse. Government was thinking ahead of the need for post war exports to repay war debts. Ensuring that railways did not continue to lose traffic to road due to unfair legislation would release road vehicles for export. Giving railways freedom to decide their own prices in line with industry, especially suppliers, would have enabled them to adjust charges up or down to remain solvent. Instead, Government controlled railway charges for $2^1/_2$ years after the War ended, and in 1947 enacted that railways devise Charges Schemes to submit to a Court of Law to control monopoly powers lost 29 years earlier! ("*Square Deal Denied*").

Railway Freight Rebates

The Local Government Act, 1929 relieved industry, agriculture and railways of 75% of local rates, to reduce production costs. Under the Railway Freight Rebate Acts, the corresponding railway relief, including that for *their* factories, was paid to the Railway Rates Tribunal to subsidise coal, iron, steel and agriculture via railway freight rebates on charges of prescribed traffics.

"Railways' relief is to be passed to industry via Railway Freight Rebates. Those industries bene-fited twice, railways, not at all". (LMSR 1936 AGM). Railway Returns to the MoT show £35m rebate was paid on selected traffics up to 1938, 70% on coal traffic which produced 36% of freight receipts

In 1949, the BTC asked for the Scheme to be wound up, stating that "20% was used for rebates on livestock and milk, and the rest subsidised coal and merchandise by coastwise shipping", *which was empowered to object to lower rail rates*! Between 1948-50 the total rebates credited to the scheme averaged £3.8m pa. BTC had to continue rebates on milk and livestock, at 12.5%, pending the in-troduction of the new Freight Charges Scheme. The Scheme was wound up in January 1951.

A DoT Memo, August 1943 stated: "The Railway Freight Rebate scheme was designed deliber-ately as a subsidy to heavy industry". (PRO: MT47/275).

Unemployment Legislation

For decades, railways called for the abolition of Passenger Duty - a tax levied only on railways since 1842. Road transport had no comparable tax, and did not pay to use roads. In 1929, to cut un-employment, the Chancellor offered to abolish the tax if they bought privately owned wagons and replaced them by larger wagons. Railways said that such wagons were useless unless collieries built facilities to accept them. The Chancellor changed direction, but insisted that tax repeal must create employment by being invested in projects that might otherwise be uneconomic. The Federation of British Industries asked the MoT to compel railways to place orders with industry rather than in railway workshops! The tax was repealed in 1929, and railways had to capitalise the duty running at £370,000 pa to finance capital projects worth £6.7m. (PRO: MT47/128, closed for 50 years).

To cut unemployment, Government allocated £100m to roads, but offered a *loan* to railways to spend with UK industries! Under the Development [Loans, Guarantees & Grants] Act 1929, grants could be made to defray, *interest payments* on Loans under the Act for unemployment works, which would not have been undertaken without financial help. *An interest free loan - to be repaid*!

The Railway Agreement Act 1935 provided a Treasury loan of £27m at 2.5% repayable in 16 years. Railways paid the same interest rate paid by the Treasury, so it didn't cost the State a penny. Sir Josiah Stamp said "the LMSR will only borrow from Government if it is economic and will pro-duce a return, not for relieving unemployment". *Any other business would do likewise.* "The interest rate paid was a gain of 1% compared to commercial rates". (Times 26.11.35). The loan was repaid to the Government 16 years later by the BTC. (BTC 1951 Report, Page 65). It helped employment and the war effort, but Government wanted their pound of flesh!

The LNER received Government aid to electrify suburban lines Both they and the MSW were undertaken grudgingly. (Henshaw, Page 27). This was to aid the unemployed, not railways.

Second World War: 1939-45

Having not contributed a penny to railways and prevented them from making adequate profits to fund improvements, Government again sequestrated railways to contain war costs. Because the UK had been left without means to prevent bombing of railways, the MoWT funded 98 miles of main line, sidings and bridges at a cost of £13.08m, (Bell, Page 128) to provide alternative routes across the Thames, and in key industrial areas. They were eclipsed by £1 billion of railway assets, had no peace-time value and the companies told the MoWT that they would not wish to buy them after the war. (PRO: AN3/7). He funded 2,500 ore wagons of 22 ton capacity and 10,000 mineral wagons of 16 ton capacity, during the war to replace worn out privately owned wagons, that their owners failed to replace. (Bell Pages 96 & 101). Wagons had a potential post-war use - *until production fell*. Neither Bell nor Savage - Government's official historian - mention the costs of the wagons. Tracing expenditure on wagons built at Government expense during the war, was not facilitated by the vagueness of MoT file titles in the Public Record Office. 2,500 ore wagons built by private wagon builders at Government expense cost £420 each - total £1.05m, for delivery by early 1941, but some were undelivered by mid 1942. (PRO: MT6/2739). Records show that only 9,000 other wagons were built at Government expense and these cost £2.5m. (PRO: MT6/2734). Costs were higher than if built in rail workshops, and the MoT admitted that Ordnance Factories wagons cost £40 more than from wagon builders. (PRO: MT47/223). Ordnance factories were building wagons, whilst rail workshops were making armaments! (Bell, Pages 201-212). Those wagons, "costing £350-400 each, were fitted with cast iron door fasteners which broke easily, rather than forged steel which is cheaper, and were being stopped in transit for defects". (Hansard, vol. 444, cols. 791,798). BR built wagons in 1948, after heavy war-time inflation - at an average £350 each! (BTC 1948 Report, Pages 246 & 313).

In 1949, he demanded that BR pay for those wartime Works[6] and wagons claiming that they cost £23m and were now valued at £18.3m. In peacetime, £23m would depreciate to about £17.5m, but would be less after heavy war use. The initial cost was really £13.08m plus £1.05m, plus £2.5m - total £16.63m. Depreciated for wartime use would have reduced the cost to about £12m.

According to the official History, (Savage, Appendix X), half of all infrastructure works were for emergency diversions and the heavy intake of USA armies and materials. Of the remainder, a significant proportion was for freight facilities to handle military traffic and diverted coastwise shipping traffic, which would have no post-war value. The Big Four told the MoT that war time Works would be of no post-war value. They offered to buy a small proportion of the Works, but the MoWT refused to agree unless they accepted all or most. The railway companies then withdrew their offer to buy a small portion of the works. (PRO: MT6/3473, 24.6.42, MT6/3474, 24.3.43).

BTC Comptroller R. Wilson and BTC Chairman Sir Cyril Hurcomb - both formerly at the MoWT - accepted the figure of £18.3m on behalf of the BTC. (PRO: AN85/18). Professionals on the Railway Executive were not consulted. It was a typical tight-fisted Treasury ploy. Had railways not been nationalised, Ministers and mandarins such as Hurcomb knew that the Big Four would have refused to buy them or "dictated the price they will pay post-war, which if not accepted, would leave Government with assets at scrap value, worth less than the recovery and restoration of land". (PRO: MT6/2735). The price would have fallen steeply. In view of the vast profits skimmed out of railways during the war, (see page 18), the assets should have been transferred to British Rail, free of charge. Government was happy enough to *give* war factories to industry after the war. Also, an MP said the Minister is assisting in the biggest racket in relation to second hand motor vehicles - the price paid to Government is much less than charged to the public by dealers. He was dissatisfied with the reply and the refusal to quote figures publicly to the House. (Hansard 21.3.45, vol. 409, col. 810).

Talks on wartime control of railways began in 1937. DoT Memos referred to "*Compensation we are prepared to give*"; "*anticipations of 1914 that receipts would diminish, during Control were falsified*". Despite this, in 1938, Browett, Permanent Secretary, disagreed with rail claims that they would be in a position to earn in excess of Standard - "*this view seems to be fantastic*". In the file a Board of Trade letter in October 1937 stated: "Railways were overburdened in the last War". (PRO: MT6/2604). A Government Committee had forecast 25% more coal, which was bound to go by rail.

---

[6] In 1938, Government allotted £1m to build & equip a Rolls Royce factory. ("*Sentinel Story of the War*", Page 52).

In March 1938, the Railway Companies Association stated: The 1921 Act imposed an obligation on the Tribunal to ensure attainment of Standard Revenue. It was not achieved due to losses to road and shipping. It would be earned easily in war as both will be crippled. Railways ask that Standard Revenue be paid, objecting to Government participation in earnings already limited by Statute.

On 20th July, the DoT told railways that Government proposed variable compensation - a minimum fixed on pre-war profits plus a share of profits over pre-war. They could "not accept railways profiteering during an emergency". This was withdrawn when railway chairmen retorted that a 4.7% return (see page 14), was not profiteering, a contractor would want 5%, and said that Standard Revenue had not been achieved due to Government inaction. No other industry had profits so restricted and further restriction during intensive use was illogical. Government would not accept the basis suggested, but said that there should be a partnership between Government and railways. Railway lawyers argued that in a partnership, unlike this one, profits are divided *after*, not before tax. The LMSR harboured doubts about Government sincerity on charges, and observed that reducing passenger facilities to handle Government and other freight traffic would cause loss of revenue. Clearly, blocking the "Square Deal" kept the cost of sequestration down.

Government's Draft Agreement stated:."Government are prepared to give a definite undertaking that rates, fares and charges will be raised promptly to meet variations in costs". Railways objected to Government sharing in revenue. Government "considered it equitable that they should share to the extent proposed", but advanced no justification. (PRO: MT47/276). From 1937 to 1946, the only railway increases were subject to two Public Inquiries in 1940, with invasion threatened!

The Prices of Goods Act 1939 permitted businesses, not railways, to increase prices to reflect cost increases. The *Permitted Price* was the *Basic Price,* at 21st August, plus the *Permitted Increase*: costs of materials, manufacturing operations, transport, wages, salaries, pensions, benevolent and welfare schemes, administrative and establishment expenses, premises, customs duty, advertising, loan interest and bad debts. Independent arbitration would hear appeals. There is no proof that wartime firms conformed to law on prices. Indeed, increases in inflation indicate that many did not.

On 1st September 1939 the MoWT took control of all railways under the Emergency Powers [Defence] Act 1939. The railways were to be run by a Railway Executive Committee composed of top management of the main railway companies. Before the war, Sir Ralph Wedgwood - Chief General Manager of the LNER - was appointed chairman of the REC, by the MoT, when it was set up in anticipation of war. He retired from the LNER, soon after war began. The MoT wished to keep him as chairman, whilst adding his LNER replacement. Other members were on "five figure salaries" paid by railway companies, but the Treasury opposed Wedgwood being paid on that basis, nor even £7000 as advocated by the MoT, "as he had a substantial pension and should be willing to work for nothing in the national interest", unlike the Treasury's Third Secretary - on £3000 pa (see Imperial Calendar, 1941) - who wrote this letter opposing payment. He offered £1700 at most. (PRO: T161/888). There was other evidence of Treasury meanness, (see pages 11-12). Wedgwood resigned in July 1941. The salary of his successor - Sir Alan Anderson, who was not a rail executive - was not disclosed, and he was allowed to retain earnings from five directorships. (PRO: MT62/23). The reason for Wedgwood's resignation was not revealed. He had written to Sir James Milne in November 1939, that he would resign if his loyalty to railways was in conflict with his role on the REC. (PRO: Rail 424/23). In July 1941, the Big Four were told that the current - unfair - Control Agreement was to be replaced by a more miserly and penny pinching one.

On 7th February 1940, three years after talks began, the Control Agreement[7] set out sequestration terms. "Appropriate charges" were to be made for Government Traffic - implying on the low not the high side, confirmed when Government said it had "*negotiated*" reductions of 10-33$^{1}/_{3}$% for freight traffic. Agreed Charges for industry, with high volume, were based on average rates, not average

---

[7] In 1941, it was arbitrarily replaced, and the 1940 "Agreement", was known as the "First Control Agreement".

less $33^1/_3$%. Government enjoyed up to 50% reduction on fares for military and other Government travel. Railways did not need to cut charges - there was no capacity by other transport. The freight terms contravened the 1854 Act on Undue Preference and the 1933 Act on Agreed Charges.

Receipts would be pooled - with £43m pa going to railways, including the LPTB. From £43m to £68m pa would be shared equally between Government and railways. At this level, the railways' share would not exceed Standard Revenue of £51m. Railways would get a return on capital of 3.3% to 4.7%. All over £68m pa would go to Government. Costs of restoring war damage, up to £10m pa would be charged to working expenses, i.e. before profits were shared. The Agreement could be revised if both parties agreed that there was a change of a major character. The railways' first opportunity to recover sixteen years of being short changed by Government inertia, was blocked.

Lord Stamp told LMSR shareholders at the AGM in March 1940: "Railways were taxed three times - by Government taking 50% of net revenue, by withholding all revenue over the Standard Revenue, and by Excess Profits Tax. No other industry was so heavily penalised".

On 23rd April 1940, the MoWT told Parliament: In the absence of the Control Agreement, railways and the LPTB would have been earning £55.2m, and the Rates Tribunal would have had to sanction the increase. (Hansard, vol. 360, col. 136).

Adjustments in railway working costs are not distinguishable from the "cost plus" in operation for pricing Government contracts with industry. The clamour against proposed fares increases might be more validly directed against the whole system of Government contracts. (Times 16.8.40).

In September 1940, Churchill directed the Chancellor and MoWT "To aim at limiting the Pool to £40m, and avoid any increase in charges". A DoT Memo warned of "problems at the end of Control, if charges were not maintained at an economic level and railways handed back in an insolvent condition. If not handed back, are they to be subsidised permanently, or is a national system to commence with sudden and unpopular increases?" (PRO: MT47/276). A month later, the Chancellor and MoWT reported: "It is our view that railways be maintained in a healthy state. Proposed increases do no more than offset increases in wages and other costs that railways incur through no fault of their own. Whether, after the war, they are brought under Government or returned to their owners, difficult and costly problems will arise, as they did at the end of the last war. If they are not run on an economic basis during Control, Government would face a large and continuing subsidy or heavy increase in charges on the cessation of Control. The existing Agreement, which recognises that railways are entitled to a reasonable and modest reward is sound. We recommend charges be increased and the Agreement preserved, modified in respect of war damage".

DoT Memos referred to First War problems and added: "Government decided, this time, railways be kept solvent. Subsidising industry and travel by static rates involved risk of bankruptcy. Higher charges do not increase profit, but reimburse money paid out. When war began, railways had a right under the 1921 Act to have charges increased, not merely to cover cost increases, but to increase profits. It is unfair to saddle railways with increased costs without increasing charges - that way lies bankruptcy or subsidy. Nationalisation of railways already dependent on subsidy, will perpetuate dependence on the taxpayer, since no Government will willingly increase charges as the first result of public ownership. Railway charges are only one element in inflation, and if artificially held down by subsidy, inflation will continue, and the subsidy will continue to increase accordingly".

In November, 1940, the MoWT stated that the only change in the Rental Agreement related to the War Damage element. (Hansard vol. 365, col. 1771). Clearly, that was not the case.

Sir Leonard Browett, Permanent Secretary, told the MoT in January: "Rail charges are dragged in at the tail of the spiral rather than contribute to it". A later Memo stated that "rail increases are less than general price levels and much less than coal, iron, steel and timber, which were between 60% and 100% over pre-war compared to a proposed rail increase to 31% over pre-war. Government liabilities for requisitioning Private Owner Wagons has been carried by railway earnings, saving the taxpayer £millions". *They were paid £88m during the war.* "Once the economic stability of railways is interfered with, it will be difficult to restore. This means: if they revert to their owners after the war, a substantial lump sum payment, plus compensation for loss of earning power and big increases in charges; or if nationalised, a severe and unfair handicap on the new Railway Authority. Disadvantages of frozen charges include less responsible use of railways by Government", as in the First War. Browett advocated "maintaining the present Agreement unless *politically* impossible". (PRO: MT47/277). That, and a Treasury ploy to attribute it to War Damage, identify the real agenda.

In April 1941, despite his recommendation, (see page 14), the Chancellor said "Government policy was to restrict prices to hold down inflation. Transport costs were an important factor in determining general price levels and it was a question of how far he might help in averting further increases in railway rates and fares". *No change was imposed on private owner wagons, nor other transport.*

On 20th June 1941, the DoT told the railways that it was agreed that the present Agreement should terminate. Sir Wm. Wood [LMSR], said it had not been agreed, adding that the first twenty weeks net revenue of 1941 was a 100% improvement on 1940. He said that Government proposals on maintenance were unsound, and if Government were trying to subsidise users they should pay the Pool for it. The DoT did not refute these comments nor produce evidence to the contrary. Railways told the MoWT that the existing Agreement was not liked by Railways nor honoured by Government, which was going back on its word. The MoWT said it was not a fair way of putting it. Hurcomb told railway chairmen: "Government may consider amalgamation or reorganisation after the War". It was a warning to toe the line or risk nationalisation. (PRO: MT47/276). The threat of nationalisation caused the Big Four to prepare a case against it in April 1943. (PRO: Rail 424/29).

A War Cabinet paper LP [41] 138, August 1941, stated: "It was impossible to freeze gas, electricity and water prices, which must be allowed to rise by 30% or more over *present* prices". *The rejected level of rail increases was 31% over 1939 prices.*

In 1941, Government established a Trust Fund into which was paid money chargeable to expenditure not spent due to lack of materials or labour. It was not a gift, but part of chargeable expenditure. By the end of 1946, it amounted to £147m plus interest of £5.26m. As average costs in 1935-1937 were £42m pa, £147m was $3^{1}/_{2}$ years' expenditure at pre-war levels - a formidable backlog to arise from eight years of Government Control. The inference was that this Fund would be handed to railways after the war to restore their assets. In evidence to the Transport Tribunal in 1951, Reginald Wilson stated that "*Trust Funds did not belong to the companies - they might prove excessive because of falls in the levels of repair and renewal costs, which some people seemed to think were likely at the time. The excess would have been returned to the Government*". (Q.3803). The prospect of such costs falling after the war could not have occurred to any businessman, only to civil servants. Any other industry would have banked its temporarily unusable cash until resources were available. It was yet another devious ploy by the Treasury to hang on to railway profits.

As part of a Stabilisation Policy, the Chancellor sought "to avert further increases in railway rates and fares". *His attention focused on rail, the only sector already rigidly controlled, not on road, canals, shipping or industry.* "Compensation for war damage to public utilities provided that the State and undertaking pay half each, which they decided to impose on railways". *As Government did not share the profits of other Public Utilities, this was irrelevant.* "The Policy involves substituting a fixed remuneration". *Stabilisation of rail rates was embraced in the 1921 Act which required the Rates Tribunal to reduce rates if the 1913 Standard Net Revenue was exceeded. This reduction applied to no other industry, all of which were increasing prices - otherwise the RPI and Industrial Price Indices could not have outstripped rail fare and rate indices during the War.* (see page 17).

The MoWT told Cabinet, on 21st July 1941: "The new terms represent a reasonable payment to the railways during the Control Period. Railway chairmen agreed that new policies made it necessary to modify the present agreement. Government failure to act on the Agreement to raise charges had cost railways £13m and in 1941, railways could earn under the Agreement as much as £57m". *Railway Chairmen had denied that it was necessary to modify the Agreement.* (see above).

Having imposed an "Agreement" limiting railways to a maximum £51m in 1940, the Memo says: "Government regard £39.4m - the pre-war average - as favourable to railways". This was known in

1940, hence does not justify abrogation of the "Agreement", which was less than railways' entitlement under the 1921 Act. Laws were to be obeyed by railways, not by Government. The Agreement could be altered if both parties agreed there were major changes - but railways did not agree.

The MoWT told the companies that the Government proposed to substitute a fixed rental for the existing Agreement, because there were - unspecified - "major changes" affecting it. Railways were confident that revenue would rise. Government made it clear that the Agreement would be changed and pressured the companies with talk of a National Emergency. Railways gave way, but asked for Standard Revenue of £51m plus £4m for LPTB. "The Treasury would not go above £41.7m". This was raised to £43m, which the MoWT had told the Cabinet he was prepared to offer. Railways wrote that this "in no way represented the existing or potential earning capacity of the undertakings, they regarded it as an accommodation to meet Government in time of a National Emergency".

The Railway Companies wrote to the MoT: "We have never agreed that the proposals are a major cause entitling a revision. 1940 receipts before war damage were £44m; and the lag between cost and price rises cost £13.8m. We forecast average net revenue not below £47.25m if no increase is made in wages, prices or charges. We are only willing to accept a Rental because of the Emergency"

"Sir Ernest Lemon, LMSR Vice President, said that the revised terms would have to be accepted, despite it being unfair, because of the threat of nationalisation if the companies refused the terms. Sir James Milne, of the Great Western, resigned from the Railway Executive Committee because of the terms. Wedgwood expressed uneasiness due to the proposed compensation terms". (Pearson/1, Pages 85,90). Wedgwood, Chairman of the Committee, also resigned. (see page 13).

The media criticised the change. "Railways were subject to a double limitation on revenue, unique and inequitable. Railways are doing a good job - due to their foresight and maintaining a good system. After the War, they should be put back in a position where they can earn enough to carry on the good work. Stabilisation means a subsidy". (Times, 15.8.41; Financial News, 18.8.41).

"Railways could not accept £43m as representing existing revenue earning capacity. It is an accommodation to meet Government representations in the National Emergency. The Minister told Parliament that but for the restrictive effect of the First Control Agreement, railways would have earned the Standard Revenue. Railways did not hold out for £55m to which they were entitled, "fearing a bad Press" and "disliking the prospects of litigation or the tender mercies of the House". (LMSR Board Minutes, August 1941). Railway Chairmen stated at AGMs that they had no choice but to accept the £43m. (Railway Gazette 22.5.42 Page 585). So much for a "strong rail lobby". (see page 108).

These facts undermine reports (e.g. T.R.Gourvish: "British Railways 1948-62", Page 4), that "railways had accepted all too readily the uncertainty of war profits for the security of guaranteed net revenue"

On 30th August, the MoWT implemented, backdated to 1st January, a fixed £43m Rental - 3.3% on capital - £4.7m to LPTB and £38.3m for main line railways - £13m below the 1921 Act figure. He said on 25th October "Government had assumed the risk of profit and loss in exchange for £43m pa Rental". This was the "Second Control Agreement". Railways were used to subsidise industry and the war. Government had only assumed the risk of profit. (see page 17).

Railways had said in 1939, "there was no risk of loss, if they were not used to subsidise other activities, Government having solemnly promised to increase charges to maintain revenue and offset increases". War damage ceased to be a charge and the railway proportion fell on the companies, whose 50% share was estimated at £2.5m pa, to be met from the Rental, giving £40.5m net, instead of up to £56m. Net revenue for 1941 was £65.1m, despite no increase in fares or charges.

The real reason for replacing original ungenerous payments by the new miserly arrangement was not that publicly advanced - "a general stabilisation of prices". Government was playing to a gallery of traders and users protesting about rail price increases - all of whom had legal authority to cover increased costs by increased prices - and did so! "None but the least reasonable advocate of nationalisation would claim that the new *Agreement* was unduly generous". (Economist 6.9.41)

Overt Government profit was £127.5m, (see Table 1); hidden gains were greater. (see page 18).

Year	Receipts £m	Expenditure £m	Other debits £m	Net revenue £m	Rental £m	State profit £m
1940	248.0	205.2		42.8	42.8	
1941	293.8	226.6	2.1	65.1	43.0	22.1
1942	343.4	251.7	2.6	89.1	43.0	46.1
1943	381.7	272.2	3.9	105.6	43.0	62.6
1944	394.4	301.2	2.9	90.3	43.0	47.3
1945	383.9	317.0	4.4	62.5	43.0	19.5
1946	360.7	325.2	3.3	32.2	43.0	-10.8
1947	355.6	367.2	4.7	-16.3	43.0	-59.3
Total	2,761.5	-2,266.3	-23.9	471.3	343.8	127.5

Table 1: Source - Keesings 4515A, 6404C, 7138C, 7925C, 9323F

Due to lack of materials and war damage, train speeds were cut. Passenger services were cut by the MoWT to give preference to war traffic - passenger & freight. A typical munitions factory had 426 trains weekly for 222,500 passenger journeys. 6,500 workmen's trains ran weekly to Government factories. In 1943, railborne coal was up 12.5% over pre-war. Other freight, including war materials, was up 79%. In 1944, railways ran 178,263 trains with war materials - one third of the total for the war. After D-Day, Government traffic included food and supplies for liberated civilians.

In April 1944, the railway companies pointed out that the extension of the war area put a greater burden on them and pleaded, in vain, for a bigger Rental. This "Change of a major character" eclipsed Government's concept of a "major change". Given the vastly increased workload handled without additional rolling stock and with fewer staff, they should have emerged from the war in a wealthy condition, but instead faced ruin, entirely due to Government anti-rail policies. A Select Committee reported in April 1944: "The revised Agreement proved favourable to the Exchequer".

The MoWT did not accept there was a major change, but in November 1943, he said railways were carrying 50% more" - effectively free of charge - "without additional rolling stock and with staff depleted by armed forces' claims." ("*Coming of Age*" - a railway booklet - Page 53). Railways were carrying 50% more freight and 100% more passengers by 1943. (Savage, Page 589). Meanwhile, in 1943, shipping rates had increased in January - liners by 20% retrospectively to 1st January 1942, and deep sea tramp shipping by 25% retrospectively to 1st November 1942 (Keesings 5873A).

Sequestration was unjustified, as railways had not been funded by Government, whose inertia had lost substantial revenue. Railways had integrated freight working before the war. Operations remained in railway hands from top to bottom. It needed only a Directive to give priority to war traffic. Government did not take control of, nor seize a share of the profits of 60,000 road hauliers, (see page 20). Neither did they do so in respect of industry - notably coal - which profited from the war.

Post War Control

In May 1946, the MoT said revenue did not cover the Rental. Rail costs were up 70% on pre-war, rail charges 16²/₃%, because Government had "determined charges without obligation to adjust to working costs". No increase was made after 1940. Government forgot it had "assumed the risk of profit *or loss*" and authorised an increase in fares to 33¹/₃% and freight rates to 25% above 1939 - increases justified in 1941. (see pages 14,15). Had charges kept pace with costs, a surplus of £154m would have accrued to Government in 1946, instead of a £10.8m loss, (see Table 1).

In September, Government asked the Rates Tribunal acting as a consultative committee to advise on closing the gap between rising costs and Rental. Under the 1921 Act, the Tribunal would have had to approve increases to lift profits to £51m. Their *secret* Report of a 25 day Hearing (PRO: MT6/2704) was "Closed to 1997". Industries, local authorities and others objected to *any* increase. The MoT said: "If every commodity and service had increases comparable to railways, we would be in a happier position". Objectors said that low rail charges kept down prices, assisted employment and helped industry to maintain their position - i.e. profits. Much of the "last $5^1/_2$ days was devoted to the interests of Coastwise Shipping". They recommended lifting fares by 35%, and freight rates 30% over 1939, from January 1947. "Workmen and Season tickets should not be increased due to a critical period for industry" - *this was a subsidy by privately owned railways*. The MoT delayed action, but had to increase charges by 55% over 1938, in November, as costs continued to rise.

There were two equitable ways to treat railways during the war - to control prices and profits under the 1921 Act or to treat them on the same terms as all other industry.

In the first scenario, the Act required charges to be increased to produce £51.4m pa Standard Revenue for 1940-47: £411.2m. A surplus over £51.4m was earned 1941-45. Under the Act 20% of that surplus - £31.1m - was payable to railways giving a total of £442.3m. They got £343.8m.

In the second scenario, prices would have been subject to the 1939 Prices of Goods Act. Wartime costs were £2,266m (Table 1). Average pre-war costs of £158.5m pa for eight years, equals £1,268m. The Permitted Increase in prices would have produced an extra £998m, viz: £2,266m less £1,268m. Railways would have been restricted to £40m pa profit - the average for 1935-37. The balance would have been subject to Excess Profits Tax, but, in line with the Chancellor's 1941 Budget Day promise to industry, they would have been "*refunded 20%, after the war, for reconstruction and adjustment. The aim was for it to be spent on replacing obsolete or unsatisfactory machinery etc.*". (Keesings 4564A). The Chancellor said the Bill provided for a 20% rebate after the war as a *statutory* right. (Keesings 5357A). It would have returned £200m, redressing some of the heavy wear and tear caused by excessive war traffic and restored some assets to pre-war condition - as applied to others, especially shipping, (see page 21). Had "Square Deal" demands been conceded, railways would, inevitably, have been subject to the 1939 Prices Act, and tax refunds. The Chancellor explained that the aim of the tax was *to take the profit out of war and, that increased production required by war would not become the means of enrichment as it did in the last war*. In that war, railways *alone* were prevented from profiting from war, by having their business sequestrated and prices and profits frozen. Uniquely, their profits were not to exceed those of pre-Great War levels, in perpetuity!

Instead, Government doled out the unique third scenario. Railways received £343.8m (Table 1). Of this, 11% was paid to the LPTB and £0.5m pa to minor railways, leaving main line railways with only £306m for eight years' sequestration. Government covertly gained that £998m plus an overt £127m, (Table 1). Deducting 11% for LPTB, the £1 billion balance, due to mainline railways, consisted of profits and discounts to Government from holding down prices it paid to industry due to frozen rail rates and traffic diverted to rail from other modes, in effect free of charge! This was in addition to tax, Excess Profits Tax and Government traffic charged at 50% below public fares and up to $33^1/_3$% below public freight rates. Heavier wear and tear warranted higher rates. Their discriminatory policy left BR behind the start line as post war inflation took off. If charges had increased in line with costs as with other industries, rail charges at the start of nationalisation would have been much higher, creating a greater surplus to finance modernisation.

War Damage and Abnormal Wear & Tear

In 1939, Government "promised compensation at the highest scale at the end of hostilities", later reduced it to 50%, and then told railways to pay their share of war damage from the "Rental" - not from the working costs, whilst Government covered its share from fat sums they gained. In contrast, compensation for other industries was decided by independent Tribunals. By Treasury Order in 1949, Government, as its share, paid £24.8m of the Railways claim for wartime damage, adjusted for inflation. As at 1948, the claim was to be uplifted by 118%, amended in 1949 - when the claim was paid - to 100%. (PRO: MT47/263). *As prices were still rising the inflation factor should have increased, not decreased.* Government blocked the repair of some war damage for up to ten years after the war, by which time the value of compensation had fallen even further, so that less was achieved from it. "The cost of commodities in general use had risen 145% over 1939". (BTC 1949 Report, Page 64).

In 1939 the War Office *demanded* 800 locos for use overseas, were given 443, plus others hired for government use. Railways had to hand over 2,088 wagons for military use in the Middle East. By 1945, 12% of wagons were under repair: three times the 1940 figure[8], due to retention of over-age wagons and a shortage of materials and labour. No coaches were built during the war. Over 1,000 were converted as ambulance trains and trains for military leaders. In 1945, a further 330 were transferred to Europe. The Government were told that 25% of coaches were under repair, and this would cause great difficulty, but they insisted. (Bell, Pages 100,110-111,196-198). Railways had to hand over 6,000 wagons for military use in France in 1939 - they fell into German hands. (Pearson/2 Page 85). Ministers had the gall to criticise railways for wartime and post-war traffic delays! On 15th December, 1945, the MoWT told Parliament that passenger miles were 70% above 1938, and train miles up 24% causing overcrowding, due to shortage of coal and coaches. He neglected to admit that it arose from wartime sequestration. Passengers suffered, blamed BR and transferred to road.

Gratitude for Railways' Wartime Efforts

After the First World War, Ministers and military leaders expressed gratitude for the vital part played by railways in the conduct and winning of the war. The 120 separate railways were then forcibly amalgamated into four Groups, and the rates that they could charge were subject to legal control. Their profits were, uniquely in UK industry, to be held, in perpetuity, at 1913 levels, without adjusting for inflation! In 1939, Government swept this aside to reduce profits *below 1913 levels*

In 1943, the MoWT said "railways have earned the gratitude of the country. No other transport could have moved the masses of men and materials required by modern warfare". Prime Minister Churchill expressed "gratitude to every railwayman who has participated in this great transport effort which is contributing to final victory". He repaid that gratitude by denying equal freedom to railways and enacting laws designed to transfer rail traffic to road. (see page 26). Owners were criticised, (see page 49), for the poor state of assets, which were put into that condition by Government policy and the heavy war workload for which railways were grossly underpaid. Rail workshops were heavily engaged on producing weapons and ammunition instead of rolling stock - 32% of their labour was deployed in this way[9]. Words were no substitute for restoration of assets worn out by excessive war demands, which should have been funded by Government using vast sums creamed from railways. (see page 18). Others were treated more favourably. (see pages 20-22 & 54-55).

In 1944, a Select Committee stated: The revised Agreement proved favourable to the Exchequer. It paid tribute to the immense contribution to the national effort made by railways, and that no corresponding financial advantage accrues to them or investors in railways. In contrast, it criticised the road haulage organisation set up in 1943: for uneconomical use of vehicles and higher prices, and recommended re-examination and adjustment of road freight charges. (Report Paras. 7,18,35,37).

Critics claim that Directors lost interest after the war[10]. They began planning *during the war*, but, up to nationalisation, were under Government control. A secret DoT plan was prepared for post-war unification undermining a Big Four plan reported in the media. In 1946, the LNER Chairman stated that work on electrification was suspended in 1939. "If the necessary priorities for labour and materials are received, the scheme will be operating in two years. But for the war, suburban routes would have been electrified - orders had been placed with manufacturers for new electric trains before the war". (Railway Gazette, 3.1.47). "There were huge sums for deferred maintenance and abnormal wear and tear to spend when Cabinet permits". (Railway Gazette, 10.1.47). "Ministers have forbidden or made it impossible to restore assets to the same good condition they were in at the start of the war". In 1947, the Southern Railway had plans for electrification and improved stations, but the

---

[8] In 1939, the figure was approximately 3.7%. (PRO: MT6/2636).

[9] *"The LMS at War"*, by George C. Nash, Page 4. The value of this work was £39m. (Bell, Page 213).

[10] See *"The Great Railway Conspiracy"* by Henshaw, Page 37.

MoT was in complete control of railways - and investment. They had been **allowed** to approve a £1.2m signalling scheme on the London-Brighton line. (Railway Gazette, 29.11.46).

Other Transport & Industry in the Second World War

Privately owned railway wagons [POWs] were, for historical reasons, used mostly on short hauled coal traffic, arising from the Railway Clauses Consolidation Act 1845 which entitled "Owners of engines, carriages or wagons to use any railway on payment of controlled tolls". (1845 Act, Sec. 92).

Government decided to take over 640,000 of these wagons - 90% of which were in the coal trade - in 1938 to facilitate a forecast wartime movement of 25% more coal. They were requisitioned under the Emergency Powers [Defence] Act. They were not fit for long hauls (see page 50), on which many were used - in lieu of coastwise shipping - had frequent breakdowns and were so slow that they occupied tracks for almost twice as long as other freight trains. Railway companies said that there were powers in the Ministry of Transport Act, 1919, to compulsorily purchase these wagons, but the DoT said *"there would be strong opposition from powerful interests"*. Their owners were powerful. In contrast, the Big Four and their directors in Parliament were obviously not. (see pages 13-18).

The Compensation [Defence] Act "provided for a fair rate of hire, together with the cost of making good any damage, to be decided by a special Tribunal". This applied to private owner, but not railway owned wagons and other railway assets! There was no special Tribunal for railways.

During the War, railway companies were told to take over and organise movement and repair of POWs from wagon companies, and pay them wagon hire and repair costs from main line railway revenue. The railway companies objected to the arrangements[11], saying the wagons should simply be common user - on similar lines to the 1914-18 War. *Railways did the work, free of charge, Government took the profit - another change of a "major character"*, without paying a penny.

Compensation for 640,000 private owner wagons was subject to *agreement* with owners, unlike that for railways. The DoT estimated that £5.75m pa compensation would be payable for requisitioning such wagons, to which must be added liability for repair and maintenance of about £4.5m pa. They were valued at £48m by the DoT in 1939. The Hire Charges compare generously - 11.9% return on capital - with a return on railway company assets, which included 664,000 goods wagons, of 3.3%, (see page 14), and included free use of railway manpower. Railways carried out 10% of all repairs in rail depots free of charge to the Government. (PRO: MT6/2611 & *"Square Deal Denied"*)

The DoT file (PRO: MT6/2611) on the wagons - endorsed "closed until 1991" - was released in 1972. *Had they known the facts, railway shareholders would have been justifiably aggrieved.*

Road haulage - 60,000 "A" & "B" Licence Hauliers, with 150,000 vehicles were not taken over in 1939. Nor were 350,000 "C" Licence vehicles which were operated by 140,000 traders.

In September 1939 the MoT told Parliament: "316,000 Road Transport vehicles had been organised in **700** regional groups"! (Keesings 3634B). *Government could not liaise with four railways!*

That same year, Government pooled all road and rail insulated units. The road transport industry contributed 1,241 road vehicles, and railways 6,317 vans and 2,354 containers on flat wagons. Hauliers were fully paid for their work; railways, before 1940 were paid 50% of the revenue therefrom, and after 1940, did it for nothing due to the "Rental" ceiling.

On 30th September 1939, the MoT *suggested* payments for requisitioned road vehicles, after consulting Road Transport representatives! *Railways were told what they would be paid.* On 21st October 1939, the MoT warned hauliers, if the voluntary pooling system was unsuccessful, they would have to be under Government control. Consideration was given in January 1941 to a Government Road Haulage Scheme on a voluntary basis under the MoT. The warning was unheeded. "Road Transport pools formed at ports have forced rates up, causing the MoT to draw attention to high

---

[11] An MoT *peacetime* study had forecast savings from pooling, by ending sorting for each colliery. It did not envisage wagons travelling the long distances experienced in wartime due to transfer of long distance coal from ship to rail.

rates. Regional Transport Commissioners do not seem to have checked the tendency of hauliers to increase rates. Steps may have to be taken to combat the inclination inherent in human nature, to take advantage of Government Departments". ("*Modern Transport*", February 1941). The National Director, Association of Road Operators urged hauliers "to keep rates at a reasonable level". ("*Modern Transport*", May 1941). In July 1941 a Standing Joint Committee was set up comprising eight Road Haulage organisations - to negotiate rates on behalf of members with Government".[12]

The MoWT said "Road Haulage pools have not hesitated to push up rates to an undesirable degree". In October 1941 he again drew attention of the tendency of road rates to increase. In November 1941, increases in road rates were approved to reflect Sunday working costs for drivers.[13]

"The rise in road rates was out of all proportion to increased costs". (Modern Transport, 28.2.42). The MoWT had announced Government's Road Haulage Scheme in January 1941. In August 1942, "*Modern Transport*" pointed out, that "not until March 1942, did the first chartered vehicle turn a wheel under the compromise partnership scheme, evolved between Ministry and Road Haulage", which was intended to embrace 2,500 vehicles - a fraction of the road fleet.[14]

A Select Committee reported in April 1944 of complaints by industry of unexplained increases in road rates. "Protesting firms said charges were absolutely ridiculous". (Report Para. 32 f).

In 1945, the Fawkner Committee rejected as "impractical, a railway style Classification of Merchandise and rates structure for road transport". (Modern Transport, 24.11.45). Experts said in 1939, that a common rates structure was vital to co-ordination. ("*Square Deal Denied*", Page 85).

Canals owned by railways - 34 canals, 995 miles - passed into Government control, on the outbreak of war. Three weeks later, the MoT told Parliament: "To ensure best use of canals, *an Advisory Committee* has been set up"! MoWT took control of 24 other canals - 1,000 miles - and certain leading canal carriers in July 1942. Whilst Government creamed profits from railways, Government had to *subsidise* independently owned canals - which may explain the delay in their take-over. Railways subsidised their own canals, which they had, by law, to retain and maintain. In May 1944, "*Modern Transport*" stated: "On the whole, canals came out of it [Government Control] financially, better than railways, as the annual payment can be increased upon an increase in efficiency of working". *Only Government gained from improvements in railway efficiency and productivity.*

Aircraft were, initially, hired by the Air Ministry to transport men and supplies, because a penny pinching Government failed to provide enough aircraft and took over 100 aircraft at valuation - *a better deal than railways received.* They were subsidised before the war, (Hansard vol. 338, cols 44-46).

Agriculture "at the beginning of the war, farmers had 50,000 tractors; at the end there were 200,000: all paid for by Government. They were given Grants for this, and Grants for that". (Channel 4 programme, Testimony Film, "*Land Girls at War*", 19.6.00).

Shipping had been subsidised before the war, (e.g. Hansard vol. 338, cols. 44-46). After the war, the industry was paid all costs and compensation for lost ships. Government "would return them to owners in the same good order as when taken over". *This contrasts with the lack of action by Government to restore railway assets - including ships - to the condition they were in 1939.* The requisitioning of coastwise shipping placed an extra load on railways, for which they gained nothing, but ran from 1940 to the end of the war in August 1945, 46,000 "Convoy trains" of coal from East coast collieries, previously carried by sea. In November 1941, the MoWT accepted ship requisition terms were low and made allowance for higher building costs. The schedule of charges

---

[12] In contrast, Government demanded 33% discount on frozen rail rates and took a huge slice of the profits!

[13] No allowance was made for railways' increased Sunday working and overtime to handle their traffic increase.

[14] Three years after sequestrating railways, Government was compromising with hauliers over 1.6% of the fleet.

approved by the MoWT for coastal tramp shipping, in 1946, was up to four times pre-war rates, contrasting sharply with increases he approved for railways which were only 25% above pre-war. Payment for lost railway ships - 130 were sequestrated - were to be thrown into the Trust Fund and received in the light of "existing relevant liabilities". It was subsequently defined to mean that if that asset was not required in future, they would not be recompensed for its loss. (see page 15).

"The rate of Government hire of shipping is to cover owners' costs, provide for depreciation, and give a reasonable return on capital. For liners, the return will be worked out for each ship at 10% pa on an agreed basis of value. This allows 5% return on capital and 5% depreciation. Under the ship-building loans scheme £4.8m was approved". (Keesings 4195N 6.6.40). This was more generous than the 4.7% sought by railways and far more than the 3.3% which they received. (see pages 13,14). Shipping hire rates were retrospectively increased in 1942 and 1943.

Within days of the outbreak of war, shipping shares rose, Cunard doubled, stimulated by [profits] experience in 1914. Railway shares fell ! (Modern Transport 19.9.39, 23.9.39).

Docks & Ports Railways were criticised for wagon shortages at ports, when no advance information was given of arrivals, much less, the contents of ships. Independently owned docks were given 90% compensation for wartime damage compared to only 70% for railway owned docks. The difference for the BTC owned Hull Docks alone was £0.25m. (TUCC North East, minute 273, 24.11.58).

Industry did not improve wagon turnround despite Government pressure. Increased traffic required faster turnrounds, since, apart from retaining 50,000 wagons due for scrapping, few were likely to be built, as workshops were put on war production. Railways unloaded wagons on Sundays to speed turnround - industry did not. The MoWT doubled detention charges, and reduced the "free period" for unloading or loading to 24 hours. Traders would not pay, saying free periods were inadequate - they did not get 24 hours to unload lorries! The Minister capitulated and increased free periods. Traders were still dissatisfied and refused to pay on the new basis with £5m unpaid. He backed off, introducing a "List of Circumstances" for claiming a reduction in detention charges. They were *excuses* for not unloading wagons, which continued after the war. In 1948, the BTC was told that there was "no prospect of getting outstanding arrears of wartime demurrage". (PRO: AN85/21). In contrast, Government demanded repayment of a pre-war railway loan. (see page 11).

Whilst railways carried 50% more traffic for which they were not paid[15]. steel production fell 4%, and imported steel rose 132% compared to pre-war. (Iron & Steel Statistics Bureau). "Factories were only beginning full production in 1941. (J. Colville "*Downing St. Diaries*", Page 343). Long before, railways were carrying more traffic - imported and diversions from coastwise shipping and roads.

Under the Compensation Defence Act 1939, [Sec. 7], Tribunals were to decide compensation for war damage to industry. Railways were excluded from arbitration. [Sec. 12].

Industry profited pre-war as military spending increased: "Sub contractors are reaping a rich harvest".[16] In March 1939, there were 3,500 sub contractors to the aircraft industry[17]. Many contracts gave 33% profit. (Hansard vol. 345 col. 349). Coal mines - 1135 companies - should have been taken over before railways, which with shipping and industry depended on coal. At the start of the war, 60% Excess Profits Tax was imposed on the amount by which war profits exceeded pre-war profits and increased to 100% in 1940, (Keesings 4079D). Before 1940, industry kept 40% of war profits, and were refunded 20% of Tax paid after the war. Only railways did not profit from the war.

Len Deighton[18] revealed unofficial strikes, go slows and bloody-minded attitudes in industry during the war, and that by 1944, lost working days were three times 1938 levels.

---

[15] Increased traffic was a disbenefit, as assets wore out faster. Responsibility for privately owned wagons was an extra unpaid task not a saving for railways as some wagon owners claimed. ("*Alsager: the places & the people*", Page 206)
[16] "*The Life of Neville Chamberlain*", by K. Feilding, Page 292.
[17] Correlli Barnett refers to this fragmentary factor in UK's uncompetitive aircraft industry ("*The Lost Victory*").
[18] "*Blood, Tears & Folly in the Second World War*"

End of Hostilities

During and after the 1914-18 war, Government froze rail charges, but in 1921 had to approve a 200% increase over 1913 to avoid bankruptcy because inflation was up 241%. A similar policy in the 1939-45 war without similar post-war action, created inevitable losses. Government wasted no time helping other transport. A meeting chaired by Sir Cyril Hurcomb, on 15th June 1946, released road transport from pseudo control, leaving railways, which unlike road contributed huge sums to the Treasury, controlled for another 18 months, obviously in expectation of more unearned income for the Government, from controlled rail rates. It was not due to impending nationalisation, as road transport was also to be nationalised. Unlike railways, they were subject to independent arbitration. The LNER Chairman, told the 1947 AGM that the Government's arbitrary compensation terms for nationalisation, "*would bring a blush of shame to the leathery cheeks of a Barbary pirate*".

The 1944 HMRI Report stated: "The effects of longer hours in traffic, heavier loads and insufficient staff to repair and service engines had a marked effect on their condition, and increases in failures in traffic adversely affected efficiency". By October 1945, 12% of wagons were Under & Awaiting Repair - three times that of 1940. (see page 19). In contrast, road haulage, from the higher rates they imposed or "negotiated" with Government, bought a new post-war fleet. (see page 55). Railways had 35,000 track miles and renewed 1,400 miles of track pa before the war. With little or no renewals during eight years of Government control, this equalled arrears of about 11,000 track miles. Under the USA Marshall Aid Plan[19], Government assessed post-war needs of railways: 400,000 tons of rails = 2,680 track miles, 1,000-1,500 locos, 6,000 coaches; and road: 80,000 lorries. Road hauliers got over 80,000 *annually*, but rail needs were severely curtailed. (see pages 52-55).

In August 1946, the MoT told Parliament: 10 railway ships were still under requisition, of which four were undergoing reconditioning to return to commercial service. In contrast, the SS Queen Elizabeth ended war duties on March 6th and by 7th September was in civilian service.

After the Essential Works Order was lifted in August 1946, nearly 5,000 footplate and 13,000 permanent way staff left in six months because wages in other industries were 68% above 1939, whilst railway wage rates had been restricted to 54%. So much for stabilisation of costs in industry. Government, which controlled railways, had held rail wages lower than industrial rates.

Government pre-war policies were driving privately owned railways towards bankruptcy. Due to wartime policies, nationalised railways began with worn out assets, and they were not permitted to match prices to rising costs. At the root of rail's declining share in freight, with its disastrous effect on finances, was the iniquitous disparity of pre-war Government policies on road and rail rates, regulations, legal constraints, and Government's uncommercial wartime and post-war attitude on charges. Running assets literally into the ground, Government gained enough to buy railways outright, leaving BR free of debt. *Then* the State *could* have claimed that it owned BR. Instead, they paid not a penny, decreed that BR should buy itself out of revenue, but prevented them from doing so by imposing a wholly unnecessary and dilatory court of law which held prices *below* the RPI, whilst costs rocketed on materials and railway wages were forced up by Government interference, (see page 131). In no other industry, has a take-over taken place, in which the predator pays for its acquisition over 30 years out of revenue, nor is one likely to do so, especially if prices are to be decided by a court of law. It cannot be claimed that nationalisation was necessary because of the dilapidated state into which railways had been put by Government control. The "cotton industry's equipment was out-of-date, but Government offered them 25% of the cost of new equipment as an outright gift and rejected nationalisation". (Economist, 21.12.46).

The Minister stated: "transport[20] is to be the basis of a 10% cut in passenger services compared to last year. Coal and industry will take priority over passengers this year, especially next winter". (Hansard 10.3.47, vol. 434, col. 964).

---

[19] American post-war aid. UK was given $3,585m; far more than any other country. (PRO: MT6/2830, originally closed to 1999, but released in 1994). None of the American Aid was used to restore Britain's railways.

[20] He really meant "railways" - no cut was imposed on bus and coach operators.

Railways, still under Government control, were nationalised *without arbitration.* "Terms were arbitrarily announced in 1946". (Keesings, 8267A). One author wrote[1] that S.W. Hill arbitrated in rail nationalisation. The LNER Chairman described the terms as piracy. (see page 23). In the Debate on nationalisation, in December 1946, Anthony Eden stated: "Lord Leathers [MoWT] told me that in the war, the USA sent experts on three occasions to inquire into railway working and see if they could send help. They told Leathers that they were so impressed with the management and the way the railways were run, that they had absolutely no suggestions to make". (Hansard vol. 431, col. 2065). This is in marked contrast to visits by USA industrialists who were very critical of UK coal and steel industries which they said were too small and ought to be amalgamated into large units.

"The organisation of the BTC and the Executives was entirely the work of civil servants and bore every sign of bureaucracy". (Elliot, Page 67). Over the ensuing years, Government tinkered with the organisation. It ignored issues needing to be addressed - notably freedom to manage, but created a unique system to control BR fares and charges, ensuring they remained below inflation created by industrial price and wage pace-setters. All other State bodies, including BRS owned, like BR, by the BTC, were free to charge as they wished - none had to apply to a Court of Law to increase prices

- **Civil Aviation Act 1946**: British European Airways, British South American Airways and British Overseas Airways were to provide services "at reasonable charges".
- **Coal Industry Nationalisation Act 1946:** Make supplies available at such prices as may seem to *them* best calculated to further public interest. Revenue to be sufficient to meet all outgoings properly chargeable to revenue account, including reserves, on an average of good and bad years.
- **Electricity Act 1947**: Prices to be charged by the Central Electricity Generating Board as may be fixed after consultation with the Electricity Council.
- **Gas Act 1948**: Boards to satisfy, so far as it is economical to do, reasonable demands. Limits on charging were swept away. Boards may prescribe different tariffs and fix prices to be charged.
- **Iron & Steel Act 1949**: Provide products at prices as may seem to the Corporation best calculated to satisfy the reasonable demands of users.

Government's First Organisation : Integration

The 1947 Transport Act created a British Transport Commission which took over railways, LPTB and canals[2], and embodied principles, which precluded railway viability:-
- The BTC to provide an efficient, adequate[3], economical, integrated inland transport and ports.
- The BTC "*shall form one undertaking*" which precluded making BR independently accountable. Co-ordination could have been achieved with the BTC as a Holding Company, and BR as a self accounting subsidiary. Burying BR in a cumbersome Transport Commission was a serious error.
- Assets were bought by fixed interest loans[4], which were to be redeemed and interest paid from revenue. BR had to fund 70% of these payments and "Central Charges" averaging £50m pa, the rest shared by London Transport, Waterways, Ships, Road Passenger, BRS, Docks and Hotels
- The BTC had to *pay its way taking one year with another*[5]. Prolonged legal Hearings to consider submissions to alter charges were exploited by those who objected to BR attempts to catch up on inflation, but increased their own prices. "*It was not at all clear over what period Accounts must balance*".[6] (Butterworth's Legislative Service, Supplements 49 & 50).

---

[1] Henshaw, "*The Great Railway Conspiracy*", Page 67
[2] 85% of assets acquired had been owned by the railway companies, including canals, ships, hotels, docks & haulage
[3] In 1968, the MoT stated that "no one has succeeded in defining an adequate service". (Cmnd 3836, Page 34).
[4] National Bus Co. said all its capital was debt, repaid by taking out loans. (1977 Select Committee Report Para 288)
[5] In November, 1991, the Financial Times said the purpose of BR was to provide a social service - clearly, it wasn't.
[6] Tribunal & Government decisions prevented the objective being achieved. (see Chapter 15 & Appendices A & B).

- The BTC, not the Executive, had to apply to the Transport Tribunal - a Law Court - to increase rail charges. As suppliers had no such obligation, it could *only* lead to insolvency. Statutory rail charges enabled hauliers to cream-off traffic from BR lumbered with war-worn wagons to compete with post-war built lorries. (see pages 52-55). Nor could it be claimed that the BTC was a monopoly, as some public haulage remained and "C" Licence vehicles - carrying a trader's goods were increasing. Hauliers, shipping and canals were protected against low rail rates. (see page 112).
- A Railway Executive[7] was set up with six geographical regions, which paid no regard to the existing structure. Civil servants created an organisational nightmare with *penetrating lines*[8] responsible to two managements! The civil service dominated BTC replaced General Managers of the former companies by Chief Regional Officers[9], who had no overall Regional authority.
- Control of fares & charges limited wages that could be offered within the Duty of the BTC to pay its way. Staff turnover reached 20% pa by 1951, increasing training costs. Rail wages were low because Government held wartime rail wages below those of industry. (see page 23).
- Closure of uneconomic routes[10] was delayed by newly created bodies - CTCC & TUCCs - required to consider and recommend any matter, affecting services and facilities which has been subject of representation by users[11], or appears to be a matter to which consideration should be given, or is referred to them by the MoT or BTC. *They had no role for competitors, even on the same routes.*

As if these handicaps were not enough, the MoT appointed civil servants, with no business experience to key positions[12]. The first Chairman was Sir Cyril Hurcomb, a retired civil servant, who forced through the inequitable terms of wartime Control. Sir John Elliot, formerly Southern Railway General Manager, and one time journalist, wrote (Page 90), that "Hurcomb was *out of his depth where business experience was essential*". "Hurcomb was *a safe bureaucratic mediocrity, whose entrepreneurial experience and engineering knowledge were nil.* (Barnett/2, Page 223). He was in receipt of "a substantial pension", which probably eclipsed Wedgwood's but was not expected to offer *his* services free. (see page 13). His salary was nearly six times that which the miserly Treasury offered to Wedgwood. At its first meeting, Hurcomb stated that the "Executives would act as the Commission's agents". (PRO: AN85/1). A structure of functional lines was imposed, which was unsuited to railways. "Railway Executive delegated powers were strictly limited to operating, maintaining and unifying railways", and they were to "assume the former role of General Managers whilst the BTC would carry out the Board's role". (PRO: AN85/17). The BTC then proceeded to act like General Managers and even took decisions hitherto taken by Departmental Heads! Imported bureaucracy was quickly evident. BTC minutes show that they called for copies of Executive minutes. It showed an unwillingness to delegate authority. They took decisions on minor matters: "Approved lease of 516 square yards of railway land at Aberystwyth to coal merchants at £52 pa"; "Approved at Highbridge of right of way over station approach at £5.5.0d pa [£5.25]". (PRO: AN85/5).

When Chairman Hurcomb, despite years at the Ministries of Shipping and Transport, where he *must* have seen the "*Square Deal*" submission, allied papers and the Transport Advisory Council Reports, (see pages 8-10), said he could not see how railways had been embarrassed by Undue Preference, (see page 5), Blee gave examples, saying he wanted the same charges freedom as competitors. He was told by the Chairman that he was asking for the impossible. (PRO: AN6/10).

---

[7] "The defect of the Executive organisation arose from BTC decisions. It appeared to be Government's intention that the Executive would be largely autonomous, which was not the BTC view". (Pearson/2, Pages 100,123).

[8] The concept of penetrating lines was finally eliminated in 1957. (BTC 1957 Report, Page 19).

[9] Sir John Elliot stated that they were not - as some authors have claimed - General Managers. (PRO: AN6/1)

[10] A 1940 DoT post-war plan envisaged a Corporation free to decide rates, with uneconomic requirements imposed by the State, paid for by the Government. (PRO: MT47/275)

[11] Later, they successfully pressed for non-users to be allowed to object! (see "*The Railway Closure Controversy*").

[12] A secret Committee appointed by the MoT in 1960 said there were too few rail professionals. (PRO: MT56/412). Elliot also criticised imported "unsuited civil servants and ex-trade unionists" to the BTC. (Elliot, Page 68).

Until 1953, the Railway Executive [BR] was run by men who had run railways before and during the war, and with no extra rewards had produced a quart of wartime movement from a pint pot. If freed from the suffocating influence of the monolithic BTC and Government interference, BR would have achieved no less than in wartime. The Executive set up regular - 6-day a week - morning telephone conferences: Executive with Regions, Regions with Districts - to address problems: loco availability, delays, accidents, and to expedite traffic and empty wagon movements.

Some limited *co-ordination* was achieved between bus and train. (BTC Officers Conference 7.4.49). Attempts to *integrate* passenger transport as required by the 1947 Act in two trial areas - North East and Isle of Wight were blocked by councils and MPs. (BTC Review April 1950). Freight integration, impeded by the slow process of buying up haulage businesses, was ended by the 1953 Act. Hence, there was no case for BR remaining part of a Commission when that integration was abandoned.

In December 1946, an MP said that the Executives should be independent. He was told that there would be a high degree of political interference. (Hansard, vol. 431, col. 2080). The mind boggles at the prospect that there could have been *more* interference than occurred over the next 50 years.

Professor Gilbert Walker said: "The 1948 BTC organisation was the least promising form of business organisation yet devised by man". (quoted in Savage, Page 183).

Government's Second Organisation : Disintegration - Stage 1

"Reorganisation proposals put to the MoT at the end of 1951, in response to a directive, had still not been discussed by May". (BTC 1952 Report, Page 1).

A Draft Bill in April 1952 proposed total freedom for the BTC, but Prime Minister, Winston Churchill told Cabinet: he *would not accept the BTC should be free even with the approval of the Tribunal to adjust rail rates without intervention by Government or Parliament.* This was not surprising, as Government had a few days earlier overturned a *legal* judgement by the Tribunal. (see page 170; see also Churchill on railways - page 6). The Draft envisaged an MoT representative on the BTC reporting to him. The Secretary of State for Economic Affairs said that *this would destroy any semblance of even semi-independence.* Clearly, the BTC was not intended to be independent[13].

The Bill [tabled in December 1952] for the Transport Act 1953 was preceded by a White Paper, "Transport Policy" (Cmnd 8538), dated May 1952, which said: 'The BTC will be given latitude to vary Charges Schemes so as to improve the ability of railways to compete with other transport. Within prescribed limits they will be free to raise or lower charges with subsequent approval by the Tribunal, subject to the overriding power of the MoT'. A unique form of freedom. Suppliers and competitors had no "*prescribed limits*", no Tribunal and no Minister with "*overriding powers*".

The DoT file on the Draft Bill states: "The main principle is that road haulage should be allowed to expand to the extent that may be justified by demand and BR should effect economies to offset the loss of traffic". (PRO: MT62/138). That was only valid if Government foresaw that BR could not avoid traffic loss, due to statutory rates control. The BTC pointed out that "it had barely completed road haulage take-overs under the 1947 Act to integrate transport". Clearly, pre-war Tory Government claims that their objective was transport co-ordination, (see page 9), to avoid conceding the "*Square Deal*" - equal commercial freedom for privately owned railways - were empty words.

"Charges Schemes would provide for maximum charges giving flexibility"[14]. They would "*contain provisions precluding unduly low BR charges designed to undercut competitors and drive them out of business*". Road charges designed to drive BR out of business were not precluded! To match cost increases, "*the BTC would have power to make temporary increases up to 10%, which must be across the board, not discriminatory*", and seek approval of the Transport Tribunal to those

---

[13] Ministers made decisions: The Cabinet "authorised the BTC to submit a fares application to the Tribunal and to issue a press statement (Minutes Mch 1951). The Cabinet authorised the BTC to reduce working hours to a level still higher than industrial levels, (PRO: CAB128/35). Gave directions on wages, closures & fares. (Chapters 12 & 15).

[14] Flexibility demands no maxima - as applied in any industry except railways, even when privately owned.

increases which were needed to catch up on inflation[15]. Hauliers did discriminate. The BTC drew attention to 19th century laws from which competitors are free - while a new disability is introduced giving hauliers power to object to lower charges, whilst they undercut rail charges as they please.

The Act retained restrictive concepts: *operating as one undertaking, taking one year with another*[16], *Charges Schemes*: ritual appearances in a Law Court to beg permission to increase prices when suppliers made unfettered increases. The Act allowed the BTC to apply to the Tribunal for an Order amending a Charges scheme, to match cost increases, by not more than 10%, up to which the Tribunal may give temporary authority. BR could not recover past losses. Consequently, fares would fall further below inflation. The BTC then had to apply to the Tribunal for permanent authority. Maximum charges were controlled "in the public interest". The concept was bureaucratic nonsense[17]. This Act perpetuated provisions of the 1921 Act protecting coastal shipping and canals against *unfair competition* by BR, but gave no protection to BR against unfair competition. Traders desiring to send merchandise by rail *in circumstances in which that merchandise cannot reasonably be carried by other means of transport* were protected against *unreasonable charges*. Interpreting *reasonably* must have been a lawyer's dream. There was no protection for BR against unreasonable prices by suppliers. "*Heads BR lose, tails they do not win*".

Sec. 20 [4] of the Act had a high fog index: "For the avoidance of doubt ... the power of the Tribunal to alter a charges scheme includes power so to alter a scheme that it extends to charges to that it would not otherwise extend or does not extend to charges to which it would otherwise extend".

Sec. 24: "In default of agreement between the BTC and the Secretary of State", armed forces' fares "shall be at such rates as may be determined by the Tribunal".

"The Act made a move towards a different conception - the railway as a commercial enterprise". (Hansard vol. 546, col. 1353). The MoT said the Act would give freedom to develop the principles of enlightened private enterprise. (Hansard, vol. 555, col. 1320). He failed to name *one* company that did not decide its prices, reject unprofitable business, close loss making branches and decide its own investment. The Act denationalised road haulage. MPs called for denationalisation of railways. (Hansard vol. 499 col. 1041), and a group was formed to promote it. (Railway Gazette, 21.7.50). Government would have had to implement the "*Square Deal*" (see page 8), refund 20% of Excess Profits Tax - including 20% of the £1bn skimmed off by Government, (see page 18) - as to other industry, and *adequately* compensate railways for *excessive* wartime wear and tear. Fare rises to match inflation implemented by railways returned to the private sector would have been attributed to market forces. Instead the Act abolished all Executives except London Transport leaving the BTC to directly run the rest, instead of abolishing the BTC and retaining the Executives as integration was to cease[18]. Impractical geographical Regions created by civil servants were retained. Abolition of the Railway Executive has been "justified" by critics on the grounds that it was intransigent. Elliot - who was there at the time - sees the boot as being on the other foot. The BTC called for costly plans to be prepared when it knew that no money was available - a typical time consuming civil service paper exercise. Hurcomb was trying to tell the railways how to do their job - down to limiting the length of trains - a task for which he was ill-equipped and mixing policy with management. (Elliot Pages 82,84).

---

[15] They never succeeded in catching up - see Appendix A.

[16] Churchill "did not consider BR should be obliged to recover from revenue all costs including capital investment". (PRO: CAB). *But his 1953 Act required all costs to be covered.* In 1956, a DoT Memo stated : We shall have to find a new formula to replace '*taking one year with another*'. (PRO: MT132/32). Forty years later, it was still the formula.

[17] It was criticised by Beeching, then a member of the MoT's secret Advisory Group. (see page 29).

[18] The Executive was run by men who ran pre-war and wartime railways. It had no pricing powers, but was responsible for costs, making economies *every* year, despite Government forcing up wages that were 66% of costs, and suppliers increasing the rest. "Much credit is due to the Railway Executive for the smoothness with which the work of unification was effected". (1956 DoT Draft of White Paper, PRO: MT132/32). *The sentence was not published.* The Stedeford Committee criticised abolition of the Executive (PRO: MT132/85). "BR are paying their way and subsidising London Transport. They saved £15m pa since 1947". (*Railway Gazette* 1953, Page 583). It was 5% of costs

There were reports that Churchill blocked proposals to replace Hurcomb as Chairman of the BTC, by a career railwayman, and selected Sir Brian Robertson, a retired General, said to have a *distaste for commerce and a distinct dislike of the breed of businessmen.*[19] He took personal decisions on railways, e.g. he personally decided not to back managers who sought an end of the statutory duty to issue Day Returns in the peak. (PRO: AN85/12). He created, to sit between him and Regional General Managers - a General Staff - through which passed all communications. The BTC had concluded that a "three tier structure: Commission-Executive-Regions was no longer suitable" (BTC 1953 Report Page 7) and replaced it by a *three tier structure*: Commission-General Staff-Regions. "The General Staff was a military concept drawn from a War Office publication: *The Conduct of War*. It was not popular at BTC HQ, nor in the Regions and was an unnecessary barrier". (Pearson/2 , Page 125-6).

Responding to a directive to "decentralise", the BTC created six Area Boards - one in each Region - the members were selected from outside industry and served part-time. (BTC 1955 Report, Page 1).

The Economist criticised retention of BR's common carrier obligations. Ministers "*could not see how obligations bear so hardly on railways, which would not turn away traffic, just as hauliers do not, although they have no common carrier obligation*". Hauliers refused empty crates, and traffic to remote areas. BR could not refuse nor price up to cover costs. Government was given facts on this. (see page 9). The MoT wrote to the Prime Minister: *Had talked to the Economist, who said the Bill was unjustifiable unless we were relieved railways of all obligations - common carrier, prohibition of undue preference, and see out-and-out competition. This would lead to outlying and sparsely populated districts paying more for rail services than towns.* (PRO: MT62/138). This was only true if hauliers rejected such traffic, leaving BR with no competition. Government did not want *out-and-out* competition despite claiming that denationalising haulage was supposed to achieve that. Canals became a rail burden, as there was no other significant BTC revenue to cover their losses.

In 1955, John Boyd-Carpenter, MoT, told the Mansion House Association: "railways were no longer a monopoly and could rightly ask to be given freedom which other industries had in marketing their products". (Railway Gazette, Page 345). *He did not grant freedom.* (see also page 172).

MPs were told "The BTC believes that it should be free to run on business lines, and that the financial structure [fixed rate interest] should receive consideration". (PRO: MT115/279, 12.6.59).

The Special Advisory Group noted that "Executive powers were delegated by the BTC and approved by the Minister. Abolition of the Executive changed the nature and balance of the BTC and not for the better. The BTC has an effect on the initiative, judgement and sense of responsibility of railway managers. The Executive was a body of professionals exercising control down functional lines rather than an instrument of general management. Among fifteen [on the BTC], there were only two professionals. They said that Area Boards are not in a position to carry out the responsibilities borne by Directors, and should go. Prohibition of BTC manufacturing other than for its own use has worked against advantageous exploitation of land and property. The BTC should have power to develop land for associated transport purposes including carparks. We note that the 1953 Act abolished undue preference, equality of charging, publication of freight rates and charges, and obligations in respect of exceptional rates and agreed charges[20]. We do not think that BR should need Tribunal authority on charges. There is no case for retaining the 'reasonable facilities' clause within the meaning of the 1854 Act. The obligation to consult coastal shipping is unwarranted. There are no grounds for a Tribunal controlling fares. Some part of the deficit is due to delay in raising charges. Fares are low. There should be no need to refer to the Tribunal even in London. It should be abolished. There is some case for appeal on freight charges for coal and heavy minerals to the CTCC. There should be no form of appeal on fares even post facto". (PRO: MT56/412).

---

[19]*The Paperclip Conspiracy*, Page 178, by Tom Bower. The MoT said Churchill picked Robertson as Chairman, as he had missed the post of CIGS because he had not commanded an army in the field during the war. (Elliot Page 87).

[20] No change was effective until a new Freight Charges Scheme was prepared, argued over by lawyers and objectors and considered by the Tribunal. Freedom only came in 1962, and then the Minister could still interfere (see page 170).

Government's Secret Review

Ministers initiated Inquiries into BR finance and organisation but did not implement recommendations which would have been beneficial to BR finances and standards of service.

In 1960 Tory MoT, Ernest Marples, set up the Special Advisory Group - the Stedeford Committee - to report on BTC finance and organisation. Its members were: Sir Ivan Stedeford, Chairman Tube Investments; Dr. R. Beeching, Technical Director ICI; C.F. Keaton, Joint Managing Director Courtaulds; H. Benson, Partner of Cooper Bros.; D. Serpell[21], DoT and M. Stevenson, Treasury. Marples was asked why he had appointed four businessmen with no knowledge of railways to advise on the re-organisation of the BTC, when the BTC had already reported on it, and its plan accepted by the MoT who had appointed several top businessmen[22] as part time members of the BTC. (Hansard, vol. 621, col. 1347). He gave no answer. The Group's conclusions were not disclosed to Parliament nor the BTC, and were only released in 1991. The papers contain many criticisms of Government, which explains why their Reports were kept secret. The Inquiry did not affect State Security and should not have been kept from taxpayers, much less from MPs.

The Group criticised the BTC taking on the Railway Executive's role in 1953: "A change which was not for the better - there was no real general management of the railways as a whole - the Executive which exercised that role had been abolished by Government". Stedeford "completely lacked confidence in the BTC organisation". Government had retained "the unitary nature of finances and other statutory restrictions on commercial operations", which the Group said was "one of the major causes underlying the defects of the BTC structure both as regards management and finance". The Treasury told the Group that "if the BTC was to split into separate Boards, any surplus accruing in one should be used to offset losses in another" - retaining the *unitary nature of finances*, which the Group criticised. Beeching said: "railways should be run mainly by professional railwaymen". There were two among the 15 members of the BTC[23]. Beeching also said: "The 1947 Act modified by the 1953 Act lays upon BTC responsibility to provide railway services for Great Britain, due regard being had to efficiency, economy, safety of operation, the needs of public, agriculture, commerce and industry. In a commercial organisation - judgements[24] of what is efficient and adequate are strongly conditioned by what is economic and profitable". They were impressed by the thorough, detailed technical investigation of the Modernisation Plan, approved by Government, (see page 57), but had doubts about financial grounds. They told the MoT that these criticisms will not be given to the BTC, *preventing it from defending itself by blaming legislation and Government policies.*

The Tribunal President admitted to the Group, that his actions held down revenue and caused BR losses, and that he had applied principles not set out in the Acts. Of 1953 Act changes in Tribunal powers, the Group said there remained a weakness in that the accelerated procedure could only be used if the BTC proved costs had increased - it could not be used to replenish depleted reserves.

The Group stated that at least "*some part of the deficit can be put down to delays in securing authority for fares and charges increases, and that the level of fares is inordinately low in relation to the general movement of prices since the war and railway passenger receipts make an inadequate contribution to running railways. BR and London Transport ought to pursue a commercial fares policy both as regards commuters and ordinary passengers without delay or reference to a statutory Tribunal*". They advocated abolishing the Tribunal, not the watered down arrangement, enacted in 1962. "*The Tribunal is a symbol that all proposals for increases in fares, rates and charges are unreasonable until proved justified. It is inimical to any imaginative and positive approach by BR staff*". The BTC criticised price control. (BTC 1955 Report, Pages 6,7,11).

---

[21] Serpell conducted a review into railway finances in 1982. (see page 142).

[22] Three - Barker, Sinclair and Hanks - were Chairmen or Managing Directors of top companies.

[23] BR paid 70% of BTC Central Charges: Capital Redemption and Loan Interest, incurred 68% of all costs, had 70% of the total staff. (see BTC 1961 Accounts). Effectively, railways were 70% of the BTC.

[24] Shareholder interests precede customer interests, and both are subjugated to the interests of directors & managers.

The Federation of British Industries and the Chairmen of the CTCC and the Scottish and Welsh TUCCs advocated to the Group that BR should be free to decide its own prices. The Association of British Chambers of Commerce told the Group: it *"favoured subsidies for social and uneconomic services paid by taxpayers and supported by freedom of charging"*.

Dr. Beeching *"had strong views on TUCCs, CTCC and the Tribunal and that the procedure resulted in the least possible benefit to the BTC coupled with the worst possible public relations. The Tribunal had allowed increases in fares which provoked public criticism but were too small to have any real impact on financial results"*. His criticisms pre-dated appointment as BR Chairman.

The Group stated that it was necessary to speed up closures, as the machinery was too slow - *two years after it was "accelerated"* - and listed changes which the BTC said were essential to viability:

- Pricing freedom.
- Removal of legal obligations to provide facilities which traders used as a minimal convenience whilst making maximum use of road transport. *BTC proposed this to the MoT two years earlier.*
- Ending the requirement to consult coastal shipping on freight charges.
- The right to develop land for car parks and other purposes.

The BTC *"would prefer to be free to run the business as they judge, but doubted whether such freedom would ever be accorded"*. (BTC minutes. 13/176, 12.5.60). The DoT opposed removal of restrictions, notably on rates for bulk freight - the field in which BR had volume, and were concerned about freedom on season rates for commuters because of "a possible effect on road congestion". *They did not advocate money changing hands from highway to railway budgets.*

The Group were critical "that road haulage was free to charge and carry as it will, whilst BR was under an obligation to consult coastal shipping about charges and be at risk of reference to the Tribunal. If shipping needs protection, it should not affect the legitimate commercial freedom of BR". They criticised "statutory prohibitions on the use of land and property, the lack of powers to develop car parks: Sec. 2 [2] of the 1947 Act prohibits the BTC from practices which would make good use of land and property. They need to be able to develop land themselves and should have power to develop car parks"[25]. *Government had created a body to provide integrated passenger services but prohibited from providing essential ancillary facilities.* Government ignored the Group's advice.

Government's Third Organisation : Disintegration - Stage 2

Whilst Government abolished its own creation - the bureaucratic BTC, external bureaucracy and interference remained: the Tribunal, Consultative Committees and the MoT.

The Transport Act 1962 split the BTC into separate Boards: BR, London Transport, Transport Holding Co., etc.; repealed the concept of Charges Schemes, but required BR and LT to seek Tribunal authority for increased fares in the London Passenger Transport Area[26], where the objective of an *adequate service* continued. The Area, shown in London Transport's 1963 Report, applied also to BR, and included the LT&S. The Act permitted BR or LT to announce an increase of up to 10%, to meet increased costs, but they then had to apply to the Tribunal for a confirming Order!

The 1962 Act repealed the 1845 Act directive to afford private siding facilities and the 1854 Act "reasonable facilities" clause. The Tribunal's freight charges role and reasonable charges protection for traders ceased. BR never had protection against suppliers. The meaningless concept of *paying its*

---

[25] In April 1960, MP Tony Benn asked "why not give the BTC a one clause Bill allowing them to develop its land as carparks. Cripps proposed it in 1932 in reference to the LPTB Act and was supported by the present Prime Minister". (Hansard, vol. 621, col. 1390). This would have enabled BR to offer an improved service to tempt motorists from their cars. Fares below inflation were not enough, motorists needed parking close to a station to minimise walking.

[26] In the 1950 Fares submission to the Transport Tribunal, London Area fares were £74.5m. The BTC 1950 Annual Report shows LT: £56m, leaving £18.5m as BR fares. That was 17.4% of BR fares of £106.6m - a significant part of revenue still controlled by the Law Court. Whilst technically "free", it imposed a knock-on limit on provincial fare increases to avoid widening the gap at boundary stations, to lower London Area fares which lagged behind provincial fares, (see page 92).

way taking one year with another continued. Changes came too late to reverse losses to road caused by 40 years of Government inertia on rates. Shipping could still object to BR rates, but BR could not object to other transport rates. The MoT may make Grants up to £450m to meet a deficit. It did not cover the £1115m lost due to external control of charges (see page 176), delayed closures and losses on lines kept open by him. The 1953 Act was repealed except Sec.24, which dealt with Armed Forces' fares, *ensuring continuing protection for Government.* The CTCC/TUCC role on fares and charges was ended, their closure role reduced to reporting on hardship, and that in regard to passenger services reduced to cessation of services and Quality of Service. Under the 1962 Act, BRB will not be regarded as common carriers. (BT Review, April 1963, Page 115).

Belatedly, Government which had taken out the wrong level of management in 1953, leaving the monolithic BTC in place, as an even more unwieldy organisation, nine years later, put BR on an independent footing, after the horse had bolted. Well, nearly independent - Government still withheld essential powers. There were still controls on fares, interference with freight rates and rationalisation, with BR still required to cover losses on unprofitable services from other revenue, and no change in the favourable conditions under which competitors operated. (see pages 186-187).

Dr. R. Beeching was appointed Chairman of the new British Railways Board[27]. A BBC radio programme on 27th February 2003, said he was "brought in as an *outsider* to put BR right". BRB's predecessor, the BTC was led by outsiders from Day One, (see pages 25,28); both brought in more outsiders. Beeching himself believed BR should be run by professionals. (see page 29). He appointed Regional General Managers as Chairmen of the Area Boards and senior railway officers to these Boards, and was "greatly encouraged by the manner in which they carried out their duties". These "Boards were hitherto composed almost entirely of part time members, [from outside industry] but now have a strong infusion of Regional management". (BRB 1963, 1964 & 1966 Reports). This demonstrates that he - an outsider - believed that BR would benefit by reducing external guidance.

Beeching failed to insist on pricing freedom, quick closure of loss making lines and an end to protection for shipping, which the Stedeford Committee said impeded viability. It was said that he introduced the title "Manager". From 1953, Regions had General Managers; and District Commercial [Goods and Passenger] Managers. From 1955, Districts merged into Divisions, headed by a Manager, embracing Commercial, Operating and Motive Power functions. After Beeching left, Area Managers replaced station masters, goods agents and shed masters. My Area based at Leicester was responsible for 90 route miles, displaced twelve such people and had fewer administrative staff.

"Beeching failed to shake the belief of managers that the nation wanted a comprehensive system irrespective of cost". (Joy, Page 92). He was *the* boss! They *knew* the nation wanted it on the cheap.

"The political decision not to proceed with the full implementation of the 1962 Act has already been taken, although the new [1968] Act will not be effective until 1969". (BRB 1966 Report, Page 6).

Government's Fourth Organisation : Disintegration Stage 3

The 1968 Act created the BRB and Boards for other transport. It set up the National Freight Corporation [NFC] to control BRS, Freightliner and BR Sundries: traffic of less than one ton by freight train, and *all* BR cartage. "It complicates what was a straightforward exercise with common ownership of all types of vehicle needed to carry out a job". (BRB 1970 Report, Page 2). The Sundries Division became National Carriers Ltd, [NCL]. BR Area Managers had to hire back - at prices inflated to give a profit - the same vehicles previously owned by BR, to deliver parcels [passenger train traffic][28]. A stated option to hire cartage from elsewhere was constrained by caveats and delays. Freightliner, created by BR to compete with road, was transferred just when traffic had increased

---

[27] "Dr. Beeching had to be paid double his predecessor's salary, but it was the same as Lord Stamp who ran the LMS before the war". (Pearson/2, Page 102).

[28] As Area Manager at Leicester, I successfully demanded vehicles of a lower capacity than provided, to cut costs that the NCL was charging us. Even so, we still paid more than hitherto, due to the profit element. It was bureaucratic nonsense. and led to NCL drivers influencing traffic by NCL, so BR lost revenue as well as facing increased costs.

threefold. "The relationship between BR and the NFC is a complex mixture of customer, supplier, competitor and partner". (BRB 1969 Report, Page 2). Perversely, Sec. 50 [5] of the 1968 Act, not only transferred to a new Waterways Board, *existing* powers to operate road vehicles as feeders to canals, but gave *new* powers to provide road transport! The Act required BR *to pay its way taking one year with another*. It created the Railways & Coastal Shipping Committee to preserve protection for shipping against unfair railway rates! Neither shipping nor BR had protection from road nor canal rates. BR had no protection against low shipping rates. Geographical Regions were retained.

The Act set up Passenger Transport Authorities [PTAs], for conurbations to provide rail, road and waterway services and stated that losses caused by enforced retention of loss making services should be seen as a social cost, not a BR deficit and paid for - on a route specific basis - by the State that wished to keep them, (but see page 139). Each PTA had an Executive [PTE], to manage its transport. The first were set up in Manchester, Birmingham, Liverpool and Newcastle-upon-Tyne. (BRB 1969 Report, Page 19). Statutory pricing freedom was promised in 1952, in the 1953 Act, in the 1962 Act, and finally given in the 1968 Act, only to be replaced by more political control. (see pages 94,177).

"The inherent capabilities of railways are not fully exploited due to the frequently changing statutory position, and different Government views on integration and competition". BR was "disappointed that the 1968 Act did not substitute equity for some or all of interest bearing debt. It is not appropriate to finance a business with capital wholly of fixed interest. A Select Committee stated that Ministers must be concerned with the efficiency with which industries carry out policies and financial, economic and social obligations imposed on them. But they must not do the managers job for them. Information should not be sought because of its inherent interest, or to discover whether *everything* is being done properly". (BRB 1968 Report, Pages 2,5-7).

BR maintained its European lead in the container revolution. Career railwayman, Mr. J. Ratter, was appointed Chairman of Inter-Container Co. set up by 15 countries. Freightliner was not yet out of a commercial development stage and into the profitable field. The impending organisational change was a distraction. Freightliner was now under the control of the National Freight Corporation [NFC]. The time is ripe for a massive marketing drive. (BRB 1968 Report, Page 3).

"Neil Carmichael, JPS to the MoT: It can be said that BR objectives are virtually identical with private industry except that they will provide certain social services but only if they are paid for doing so". (BRB 1968 Report, Page 1). The private sector did not provide free services, hence the word *except* is superfluous. In two areas, BR remained different - they did not have freedom to decide fares without political interference, nor make investment decisions where the rate of return would have been regarded as adequate in the private sector. Ministers still had to flex their muscles.

Changes in the Management Chain

The basic structure began as BTC-Executive-Region-District-Station/Yard/Depot. General Managers, abolished in 1948, were restored by the 1953 Act - with control of the six Regions: Eastern, London Midland, North Eastern, Scottish, Southern, Western - but the bureaucratic BTC remained - with its "General Staff". The departmental structure below General Managers began to change from 1957 to a more business focused structure: "Traffic Department District Offices - Operating, Commercial and Motive Power - were merged to form Traffic Divisions". (BTC 1957 Report, Page 15). Its objective was to improve inter-departmental liaison and make more economies. Common functions: personnel, works and finance were merged. Each Region and Division retained a Control Office, providing 24 hour control of the railway - which had proved their value from their inception. (see also pages 38,46). Below Divisional level, the existing structure at station/depot level was largely unaltered in the BTC era, except where one station master took responsibility for two or more adjacent stations or a goods agent took over a nearby small depot, leading to economies,

The number of Regions was reduced in the late 1960s, when the Eastern and North Eastern Regions were merged with Headquarters at York. Administrative savings of £1.15m pa were forecast, involving elimination of some 1,500 posts. (BRB 1966 Report, Page 31).

Chapter 3   Business led organisation

Outside consultants said that existing costing principles and methods used by Board and the way in which they were applied were sound. The present system compares favourably with other large businesses. In the field of investment criteria, BR was sound. (BTC 1967 Report, Page 28).

In anticipation of a requirement of the 1968 Act, to submit a reorganisation scheme for MoT approval, the BRB entrusted to consultants McKinsey & Coy Inc., the task of examining Board and the top management structures of railways. (BRB 1968 Report, Page 4). It became known as the "Field" organisation. The Company's proposals for organising the undertaking were submitted to the MoT in 1970. It created a Chief Executive [Railways] and "will restructure the organisation of BR under him". (BRB 1970 Report, Page 3). The new three-tier structure was eventually spelled out:

- A Chief Executive, replacing the practice of the Chairman embracing that role.
- Seven or eight geographical multi-functional Territories replacing five Regions and 20 Divisions
- Area Managers[1] at "ground level" - replacing Station/Yard/Depot Masters, etc.

A Chief Executive was appointed in 1969. Divisional Managers continued to replace ground level 'management' with Area Managers - the theory being that with these in place, the business would continue to function, with minimal disruption when the major change occurred of replacing Regions and Divisions with Territories. Area Management proved to be a huge success: embraced operating, commercial, traincrews and minor engineering functions, and were delegated powers hitherto the preserve of Divisional levels. A new system of budgets - devised in-house, enabled them to control expenditure and secure a new tranche of economies. It opened up an opportunity to merge common tasks of the different departments. BRB executives developed and agreed new job structures for base grades with the unions, through Pay & Efficiency Deals, which facilitated job mergers. By bringing a fresh look, Area Managers were able to secure economies, not only in Operating but also in engineering expenditure - notably in loco maintenance and wagon repairs at small depots.

The Territorial leg was not implemented. On paper, it looked good, cut staff, and could have been made to work. However, all such changes were subject to Joint Consultation[2] before implementation. It was usual, with changes affecting more than one function, to send the Operating Department in to bat first - as they had more practice in conducting Joint Consultation meetings due to the perennial stream of operating economies implemented over many years. For some reason, the Personnel Department went in to bat first, and were caught on one foot, when union spokesmen queried disparities in proposed establishments of the seven Territories. What they had discovered, was that in some Territories, the ratios of HQ personnel organisation to staff in the field were significantly different. No explanation was forthcoming from the management side chairman, nor changes offered to redress the differences, and the Territory concept was abandoned[3]. With the benefit of hindsight, the Territory organisation would have been short lived, as it would have been displaced by the fundamentally different - "Business Sector" - organisation, devised in-house. In many ways, the Territory was a variation of the Regions/Divisions as both were geographical, which did not best lend themselves to the management of train services that crossed boundaries.

The 1974 Act returned Freightliner to BR, and provided for Grants to companies to encourage transfer of freight to rail for environmental or other reasons. Local Authorities delayed schemes. (see page 126). BR Workshops were constituted as a company trading as British Rail Engineering Ltd and began exploiting manufacturing powers given under the 1968 Act. (BRB 1970 Report, Page 4).

---

[1] The Area Management concept was devised by BR and progressively implemented from the early 1960s. By the 1970s, some were merged, after Area Managers made economies in staffing, enabling them to control wider areas.
[2] Introduced in 1956, it successfully secured changes without disruption. When the Health & Safety Act was passed, a "Roadshow" comprising TUC and CBI members toured the country in 1975-6 explaining the need for such practices!
[3] A union spokesman told me that had Operating proposals been discussed first, it would have been difficult to argue as there was no obvious "ratio" to exploit.

Managers of Divisions and Regions were charged with bottom line responsibility for improving the results on designated routes - Divisions in respect of services wholly or mainly within the Division, and Regions for other services. Data produced by computer set out costs and earnings.

The Government Contract

The 1974 Railways Act provided for an all embracing Public Service Obligation Grant [PSO], in place of route specific funds for loss making lines retained by Government for socially necessary reasons. In December 1974, the MoT directed the BRB, from January 1975, to operate its passenger system so as to provide a public service which is comparable generally to that provided at present. (BRB 1977 Report, Page 4). In 1988, this Directive was replaced by one based on 1988, and this continued through to the eve of privatisation. (BRB Reports, 1988/9, Page 30 & 1993/4, Page 1).

The "Contract Price" - the payment for meeting the PSO - "is calculated each year on the basis of the budget produced by the BRB. Payments from PTEs are deducted from the estimated cost of operating the system to arrive at the contract price for fulfilling obligations imposed by the MoT. Once a price is agreed by Government, variations are only made on the basis of certain specified factors, e.g.: national emergencies, major disasters, Government intervention on prices or changes in the obligation. A subsequent development was the application of Cash Limits. The Limit for the PSO is fixed by reference to the 1975 level adjusted for inflation. A new change was to publish financial results of four sectors: InterCity, LSE, PTEs, Other Provincial Services. (BRB 1977 Report, Page 15). Later the PTE and Provincial Services were merged to form one Sector. In 1980, Government introduced External Finance Limits - cash limits on public expenditure, (Cmnd 6440). So far as BR concerned, this embraced the PSO, external borrowings and leasings. (BRB 1980 Report, Page 15). This placed limits on loans which could be raised for investment.

In 1975, the MoT set a short term PSO limit, at no more than that for 1975 in real terms, and in 1976, added that it would remain at that level in subsequent years. In 1977, he required a reduction of £20m in the PSO, by the end of the decade, and called for a further reduction from 1979/80 onwards. (BRB 1977 Report, Page 4). In 1987, a substantial BR surplus caused the Minister to require a further reduction in the PSO of 25%. (BRB 1987/8 Report, Page 4). In 1983, the MoT wrote to the BRB noting forecast reduction of the PSO to £700m in 1986, and £635m in 1988, that Government required them to reduce to £635m by 1986 at 1983 prices. It was not to be achieved by closures. Rationalisation of BREL capacity[4] must be completed as soon as possible. (BRB 1983 Report, Page 5). Government said that, after 1986/7, InterCity would be ineligible for PSO[5]. (BRB 1986/7 Report, Page 3). BRB forecast that NSE will break even by 1992/3. The MoT called for a further reduction of the PSO for the Provincial Sector by £20m below the reduction of 12% made by BR for 1992/3.

The MoT wrote to the BRB Chairman in December 1989 of the "success of the BRB in meeting the objectives[6] set in October 1983". (BRB 1989/90 Report, Page 31).

Despite inflation, and recessions, BR beat the Contract Price set by Government, by £6.4m. (BRB 1976 Report, Page 3). In a year of recession, BR beat the contract price with Government by £27m. (BRB 1977 Report, Page 3). Thereafter, with an odd exception, BR regularly beat the Contract[7] or stayed within Government Cash Limits, as BRB Annual Reports reveal:

- 1978: The Contract price was beaten by £8m, £56m below the cash limit set by Government.
- 1979: The Contract Price was beaten by £14m. The railways cost the taxpayer 17% less in real terms in 1979, than five years ago, despite a massive increase in the fuel bill.
- 1980: The Contract was exceeded by £6m.

---

[4] This had been blocked by Government in 1967. (see page 177).

[5] InterCity no longer receives any Grant. (BRB 1987/8 Report, Page 4).

[6] Which begs the question - why privatise? His praise contrasts with John Major's criticism - see footnote, page 35.

[7] This contrasts sharply with some publicised Government contracts, where prices seem to be routinely exceeded and delivery dates unfulfilled.

- 1981: Stayed within the cash limit.
- 1982: Exceeded the cash limit by £40m.
- 1983: Surplus of £7.8m, stayed within PSO.
- 1984/5: The PSO was some £50m lower than 1983 in real terms.
- 1985/6: The PSO requirement was down 14% compared with 1983.
- 1986/7: The PSO was 2.1% below target. Beat the target by 25% in the last three years.
- 1987/8: Made a surplus of £291m - prompting a further reduction in the Contract price.
- 1988/9: The PSO was 29% less than last year.
- 1989/90: The PSO reduced by 7% on last year.
- 1990/1: The PSO is down 40% in real terms below 1983.[8]
- 1991/2: The PSO was 34% below 1983.
- 1992/3: The PSO was 21% below that of ten years earlier.
- 1993/4 [9] : The PSO was 20% below 1992/3.

"BR to improve productivity and make most efficient use of resources to minimise direct pressures of costs on fares. The MoT requires an annual report on unit cost trends". (BRB 1989/90 Report, Page 32). *This was the Board's role. Without freedom, BR could not be held responsible for losses*[10]. The MoT wanted to make decisions, but absolve himself from the consequences.

BR must not use its market position[11] to raise fares unreasonably. (BRB 1983 Report, Page 4). "Government reneged on its agreement to let BR raise commuter fares". (Economist 30.3.91, Page 28). There were similar media reports in 1993, of interference: "The BR Chairman laid proposals before the MoT who must decide whether to approve increases". In response to inquiries as to the legislation governing such powers, the DoT said: "BR set individual fares within a Framework & Policy set by Government". This confirms that freedom - promised 40 years earlier - was illusory. (see page 175). Being unable to establish exactly what is set out in the elusive "Framework & Policy", or to obtain sight of it - perhaps for 30 years - one can only conjecture hypothetical scenarios:-
- BR wished to increase fares across the board by a standard percentage, but the "Framework & Policy" limited them to a lesser percentage - to avoid political fallout.
- Responding to market forces, BR wished to raise some fares by a greater percentage than others, but the "Framework & Policy" precluded that - to avoid political fallout.

In either case it would seem reasonable that the MoT should either:-
- Compensate for protecting the public from market forces, as would apply if inflation busting car insurance had been capped by Government, or,
- Specify economies as the Attorney General told the Cabinet on 22nd March 1955. BR managers implemented economies, that did not jeopardise safety. This was an ongoing exercise. It would be a risk area for Ministers to specify additional economies, *especially if they staked their jobs on it*.

The Benefits of Business Sectors
The Monopolies & Mergers Commission unequivocally confirmed that BR is acting in the public interest and were impressed with managers they met at all levels. (BRB 1980 Report, Page 9). They also said that BR managers are totally dedicated to the railway with a high degree of pride in the service which came before financial reward in importance. (Rail Policy, 1981, Page 17).

In 1981/2, BR was re-structured into business sectors, based on markets served, distinguishing between "commercial railways": Freight, Parcels and Inter City, and "social railways": London & South East and Provincial Services. "Restructuring of our businesses in 1981/2 was warmly

---

[8] John Major wrote of having to repay BR's excessive spending. ("*My Autobiography*", Page 665). Government was paying BR to provide services which Government *itself* judged were in the national interest. (see page 42).
[9] The last year in which BRB had full responsibility for railways. As subsidies were to continue - why privatise?
[10] No private sector Board could be held accountable for bankruptcy if it could not decide its own prices.
[11] In contrast to the private sector that does not hesitate to do so. BR had less than 10% of the transport market.

welcomed by our customers". (BRB 1982 Report, Page 8). The concept was initiated by Robert Reid[12] - a career railwayman - to replace the geographical and functional basis originally imposed by civil servants and politicians, who were reluctant to admit that it was ineffective. They had tried to convert Regions into accounting centres, which businessmen drafted in to the main and Regional Boards said was impractical. London & South East and Provincial passenger services. were re-named Network SouthEast [NSE] and Regional Railways in 1986 and 1990 respectively. These new business sectors brought a new eye into project development and modernisation, in that they had to approve that schemes would meet their needs. It led to economies that would have been missed under the previous regime. The Divisional tier of management was removed, saving 6,000 posts. (BRB 1984/5 Report, Page 4). Ownership of trains, stations, track and signalling transferred to the appropriate businesses, dispensing with the Regional management level. (BRB 1990/1 Report, Page 11)

From 1987/8, InterCity had sustained profitability for six years up to privatisation, even in reces-sion, despite political limitations on BR freedom, in comparison with which, subsequent interfer-ence pales into insignificance. NSE showed a big improvement in viability in the three years preced-ing privatisation, and in its final year received no subsidy. The subsidy for the Provincial Sector was falling. Despite continued interference, BR was moving towards viability. The time was opportune to get BR into the private sector quickly, before they disproved political ideology. As a result of these organisational changes and also in consequence of improvements made in standards of travel comfort through new design and improved maintenance techniques and projects developed by BR, passenger volume increased, and would expand even more in the years ahead[13]. BRB Reports give many examples of these achievements. (see also Chapter 10).

Contrary to political views, BR services were not cut at "*the whim of the Operator*", but on the basis of viability, by marketing managers in the Business Sectors, as applies in the private sector.

BR chairman Sir Bob Reid[14], a former oil executive said "BR is poised for a decade of expansion as demand and environmental pressures enhance the case for public transport. My predecessor - Sir Robert Reid - fostered a businesslike approach to running a railway, more than halving the subsidy, and doubling investment, shifting emphasis from support to self help. He hands over a railway that has met its principal objectives over the last six years. The railway has renewed most of its asset base and has the underlying strength to meet the challenge of an expanding market". He stated: "We are better than many people think", and: "The past year has been one of constant upheaval. It is to the credit of railway people that service and quality have been maintained whilst coping with the major privatisation workload". (BRB Reports, 1989/90, 1991/2, 1994/5).

An obituary to Sir Robert Reid, stated that Reid had created the business sector concept, and that "The re-organisation created Europe's only genuinely profitable long distance passenger network - InterCity". (Daily Telegraph 18.12.93).

Transportation Systems & Market Research Ltd. [Transmark]

In 1970, the BRB stated that it had been receiving an increasing number of requests from overseas for advice and assistance, including from the World Bank and individual foreign railways, as well as UK clients including shipping companies. These were met by secondments. In January, BR set up Transmark, a separate unit with a small corps of BR professionals, but continuing to draw exten-sively on the expertise available within BR for specific assignments. Its work included:-

1971: Studies of cross-channel traffic. Two projects for the International Bank for Reconstruction & Development; a five year contract in Brazil, plus work in Africa and Asia.

---

[12] Previously BR Marketing Director, hence origin of market based, he was C.E. from 1980, and Chairman in 1983.

[13] Without doubt, these and other developments triggered increasing traffic that would gradually reduce Government support. No one can determine to what extent these changes, rather than any introduced since, were responsible for current traffic levels. One post-privatisation development that will reverse the trend is their imprudent reductions in essential manpower and the fragmentation which gave the unions negotiating leverage that did not exist before.

[14] Not to be confused with his predecessor - Sir Robert Reid.

1972: Launched less than three years ago, it has orders in six countries stretching to the end of 1974
1973: Work in hand for seven railways in eight countries. Orders at home have trebled.
1974: Continued to expand on a profitable basis handling 25 projects in 23 countries.
1975: Work in 25 countries included a £7m contract for Iran. Advised USA Dept of Transportation on a plan for Amtrak & the North East corridor: Washington-New York-Boston. Transmark asked to lead a consortium of British firms to bid for constructing a railway across Venezuela.
1976: 36 projects in 22 countries. Sales of BRB licences include bogie design to the USA, computer programmes to South Africa and overhead electric design to Australia.
1977: 47 projects in 31 countries, including the first for the Asian Development Bank, EEC, and Canada. Projects include marketing, paved track in Australia; and co-operation with the Coal Board, P&O and Davy International on a mining, railway, port and shipping project in Sumatra.
1978: Awarded Queens Award for export achievement in 1978. 69 contracts in 29 countries.
1979: 74 projects in 29 countries, including a three year contract with the Federal RailRoad Administration in the USA on development of passenger and freight services in the USA.
1980: 94 projects in 31 countries. Work continued in Australia on HST based on the BR design.
1981: 91 projects in 27 countries. The Australian XPT based on BR HST made its debut.
1982: 91 projects in 29 countries. USA Federal RailRoad contract was renewed for a further three years. A big railway project in Brisbane, involving Transmark, opened in time for the Olympics.
1983: 102 projects in 34 countries. Transmark owns 40% of Davy-BR International consultancy.
1984/5: 128 projects in 36 countries. Another joint company formed - Cole Sherman Transmark - won contracts in Canada. Jointly with London Transport, undertook studies in the USA.
1985/6: Existing contracts were extended. 125 projects in 33 countries, include two World Bank studies. A joint consultancy was set up in Australia with Australian consultants.
1986/7: 137 projects in 32 countries included a two year contract in Botswana. Two licensing agreements to provide BR rail clamp locks and structure gauging developed by BR Research.
1987/8: 148 projects in 30 countries cover Signal & Telecomms, marketing, licensing BR's high speed train geometry technology and overhead electric measuring instrumentation. A Cairo Metro contract was renewed for the seventh year. New studies relating to the proposed Channel Tunnel.
1988/9: Contracts for the World Bank and UK Overseas Development. 170 projects in 27 countries.
1989/90: 190 projects in 25 countries. More work for the World Bank and Overseas Development. UK work included studies for PTEs in West Yorkshire and Manchester, and the Channel Tunnel.
1990/1: 195 projects in 25 countries, bringing to 80 the number of countries Transmark has worked in. Sold BR's computer seat reservation system under licence to Australia. Over 50 UK contracts.
1991/2: Over 200 projects in 30 countries on six continents. Expanded UK work. Advice also to Netherlands railways on plans for expansion.
Transmark was privatised in 1993. In its 22 years, it had tackled every aspect related to railways: train design electrification, operating, maintenance, signalling, training, marketing, stock control, and transport integration. It had worked in over 80 countries, as well as in the UK for other businesses. It was profitable. Crucially, the expertise that it was selling, was that of the railway professionals who had learned their craft on BR, and were mostly seconded for a year or so for such work.

The Logical Course to BR Viability
To continue to reap the benefits flowing from the new successful Business Sector structure, and put BR firmly on a comparable basis with other industry, the following changes were justified:
• Full commercial and managerial freedom, promised in 1952, but still undelivered 40 years later[15].
• Maintenance costs of bridges over railways - estimated £400m pa - to be borne by road users.
• All level crossing costs - not merely 50% - funded by the highways' budget. (see page 130).

---

[15] The CTCC - so often critical of BR stated: "Government does not have to involve itself in managerial issues, it chooses to do so, although it has consistently claimed that it does not". ("*New Opportunities for Rail Passengers?*").

- The Exchequer to fund bridges to replace crossings to cut road traffic delays and avoid collisions.
- State funding of footpath diversion as applies with motorway building.
- Costs of fences on rail boundaries to be paid by owners of adjoining land, as applies to roads.
- Infrastructure, asset and labour costs, incurred to avoid road building or reduce commuter journey times overtly funded by the State not paid as so called "subsidies", designed to look like losses.
- Costs of preserving historic structures to become an Exchequer responsibility.
- Air, road & sea transport also compelled to improve safety *now*, despite the cost, to reduce deaths
- Road transport drivers' hours reduced to those required of BR, *and enforced*, with effective action taken by authorities to ensure that all road transport becomes much safer.
- "Watchdogs" replaced by self regulation as in the private sector or extended to cover air, sea, road and travel agents. TUCCs never had a role for *all* transport, as some believe, not even for all public sector transport - municipal buses and state owned air transport were always excluded. In 1993, they were re-named "*Rail Users Committees*", but given no role for railways privately owned *before 1993*, nor for privately owned catering or car-parks serving *rail users*.
- Government's wartime gains from railways were £750 billions at 1991 prices (see page 83). Railways were due to, at least 20% of that under the wartime Excess Profits Tax provisions, (see page 22). This should have been put into BR. They should also refund losses from delayed and below inflation fare and freight rate increases, blocked and delayed closures and interest paid on enforced loans. Even after deduction of past subsidies, there would be billions left in BR hands.

The Illogical Course

Instead, Government pursued the *Illogical* solution. (see Chapter 4), and reversed past successes. It changed the remit from maintaining the present services and reducing the subsidy, to increasing both traffic and the subsidy. It was claimed that the change was to break the BR monopoly - which Ministers admitted BR had *never* had (see pages 28,129,172). By 1993, BR had less than 10% of the inland passenger market. Government tried to claim that privatisation and fragmentation was enforced by Brussels. The much quoted EEC Directive 91/440 did not require it. (see page 46).

In January 1992, the Sunday Times attributed the origin of the idea of a track owning authority to the Adam Smith Institute, which was set up in 1977. The LNER advocated it in 1946 in "*The State & the Railways*", BR revived it in its 1974 Report. Neither envisaged fragmentation of operations.

Contracting out had been tried by BR, notably in carriage cleaning at Aberdeen and Leeds. BR supervisors had had to be kept to inspect vehicles to ensure they were satisfactory before entering service, and many were rejected. It had been expected that costs would fall, but they had increased.

The keystone of BR operations was its Control Office organisation. A Control received a constant stream of reports from yards, collieries, signalboxes, stations, depots, traincrew supervisors, engineers, etc., together with automatic computer data from various sources. Within a defined area, it controlled locos, crews and trains and was required to disseminate to all concerned, instructions and reports affecting accidents, safety, train running, connections, diversions, to organise short notice special trains for passenger or freight, and road transport in place of delayed or cancelled trains. It would be informed immediately of all unusual incidents which may affect services or safety and of an accident blocking a line. It would then initiate an established "call-out" procedure which would bring experienced operating managers, engineers, breakdown trains and men, quickly to an accident site, and set up diversions to maintain a service. Over the years, the Control organisation was streamlined in consequence of the development of PSBs, TOPS, new technology and communications and economy measures. (see pages 70,146). Train reports from PSBs were automatically input to Controls, and also into TOPS for general use. After 1994, Control was fragmented for the worse.

The last BR train ran on 31st March 1997. Thereafter, all trains were run by franchisees, but some reports still appear of *BR* delays! The media reported that the first train run by the private sector was a bus! Since then, the incidence of buses replacing trains has expanded. (see page 84)

Chapter 4   An illogical organisation

BR was privatised for ideological reasons[1], and to secure short term capital for the Treasury, which was too blind to see that the taxpayer would be paying an arm and a leg in return - in perpetuity. Had it been privatised as one entity - as applied with other privatisations - it could have been a success, given an end to interference by politicians and civil servants whose railway expertise was zilch. Privatisation obscured - before it became apparent that, despite interference - the Business Sector organisation was bearing fruit. As it would have been apparent, even in privatised garb, that the existing structure was successful, and hence, that BR was being unnecessarily privatised, it was wise to create a different format. A reversion to the Big Four formula would have had some merit. Instead, impractical dreamers came up with a winner - a winner that is for the City, accountants, and especially, lawyers who have since the earliest days and until the demise of the Transport Tribunal in 1968, waxed fat on railway law. The format devised was based on a belief that "if one company operated all services on one line, there would be no incentive to improve services", (*"Transport Policy in Great Britain"*, Page 128); a damning indictment of the private sector.

Politicians sought to justify privatisation: "Our experience of privatisations is that they work, have led to improvements in efficiency, innovation, and responsiveness to customer needs". (DoT booklet *"Britain's Railways: A New Age"*, 1994). Unlike railways, they remained under the same managers and were not split. Freightliner managers planning a buyout[2], were taken off their jobs, so that "they had no advantage over other bidders". This never happened in other privatisations. The easiest utility to split was BT. The Hull service, which was still independent when BT was privatised, proves the case. Gas and Airports could have been split. Gas and BT are nearer to a monopoly than railways have been since 1919. Water remains a monopoly. The privatised utilities - even when in the public sector - were never subject to the price controls and political interference that dogged railways. (see pages 24,173). They are not successful from a user viewpoint. (see page 165).

If past success guarantees future success, why did industry lose a world lead (see pages 152-4), in so many fields? To prove success, required the same political and judicial interference and social burdens, but there are fewer. Comparisons are invalidated as they benefit from changes essential for successful privatisation, which would have helped to make BR viable (see pages 37-38). That would have required politicians to admit that 50 years of interference was the problem. Obviously, no politician would do so. Media reports stated that some £600m or more was spent on privatisation, that could have been used to improve BR. The subsidy paid to franchisees is higher (see pages 182-4).

It was promised that BR would be allowed to bid for franchises. That was undermined by the power of the Regulator to reject lower BR bids[3]. It was promised that management buyouts would be encouraged. However, some were rejected. It will be 30-50 years before the papers relating to bids are released to the public by the Public Record Office. It is likely that they will show bids accepted from outsiders that have proved impractical and led to bail-outs. Too many buyouts running profitable services may have proved that political interference was the root of BR problems.

There was a belief that privatised railways would attain the 100% standard not achieved by *any* industry. Without changes that would have benefited BR, privatisation in any guise was bound to fail. Fragmentation ensured a worse service. In the privatisation debate, an MP said that the Swedish Railways Chairman told him that Government proposals were insane. (Hansard vol. 216, col. 772). The President of JR East, Japanese Railways said: "I have been to England, looked at the way they are trying to privatise BR, and know it will fail". (Railwatch, Dec. 1993). BR was unfavourably compared with these countries. The Minister had said that "Japan and Sweden were among countries that were following the same path as the UK". ("Britain's Railways: A New Age", 1994).

---

[1] The intention was to entitle this Chapter "The Ideological Organisation", when it was clearly Illogical.

[2] Their bid succeeded, and the management buyout company has expanded under career manager Alan Galley.

[3] Chiltern Railways - run by career manager Adrian Shooter - is one of the most successful passenger companies.

John McGregor, Secretary of State for Transport said: "Privatisation is no criticism of BR or its past achievements, which have been considerable. BR's recent record on productivity, service, safety and punctuality is impressive and it is known to run one of the most efficient railway systems in Europe". ("Britain's Railways: A New Age", 1994, Page 1). It begs the question: "Why change?"

The taxpayer believed that privatisation would end the subsidy, which arose from Government policies. (see Chapter 15). Taxpayers would be surprised to learn that the "new set-up will not save the taxpayer money. Government admit that the overall cost to the taxpayer will be a significant increase. Much of it will be needed to offset the additional costs of splitting up. The MoT admitted that the profitable InterCity East Coast line will need a subsidy". (Scottish TUCC 1993/4 Report). The DoT said that BR's East Coast £40m profit will become a £50m loss. (Daily Telegraph, 9.3.94). A study predicted East Coast profits of nearly £40m after seven years! (Sunday Times 28.4.96).

Railtrack was formed as a separate State owned division on 1st April 1994, and became a plc on 20th May 1996. "Government wrote off £1.5bn of Railtrack debt prior to sale. A Labour Government would find it impossible to reverse privatisation. Compared to BR, which was subject to constant ministerial interference, the new operators will have an easier task". (Economist 3.2.96, Page 29)

A former BR manager says that a management buyout bid, based on the realities of current knowledge, was underbid by bus operators, who later lost their franchise, when, having found no scope for easy productivity cuts, slashed staff, only to find there were not enough traincrew left to run the advertised service upon which their subsidy was based! They had to pay fines for cancellations.

Barrier staff at many stations were removed leaving passengers with no information when CCTV fails. Contracting out maintenance, is a risk and cannot be deferred, like road repairs. Thousands of trains were cancelled due to staff cuts. Now the SRA states that the lowest bid should not be the sole factor in awarding a franchise. Existing bus dominated franchisees will benefit, when had the policy applied in 1995, franchises would have been awarded to realistic management buyout bids.

Hopes advanced by politicians, whistling in the dark, to keep their spirits up included:
- "Competition will be introduced, promoting improvements in efficiency[4] and quality of service. Subsidy will continue, but will be allocated clearly, so that the public can see where it is going[5]". ("Britain's Railways: A New Age", 1994, Page 3). Unlike buses, a train company could not block-in competitors nor race ahead picking up passengers. Government knew where the money was going until their 1974 Act introduced the PSO block Grant to replace route specific subsidies that applied under the 1968 Act (see pages 178-181). They would also be aware that BR had a management control system[6] setting out cost and revenue of all services, and led to economies?
- "Investment will flood in from the City". It was assumed that the private sector had so much cash that it was waiting to spend it in railways. This is the same private sector, that failed to invest in modernisation and expansion, so that the UK now imports ships, lorries, aircraft, buses, cars, and many other products. UK industry focuses on acquisition, where it seeks to strip assets, and build up *gross* turnover to justify telephone number salaries, bonuses, and share options to those who negotiate deals. When deals go sour, because acquisitions have been over-priced, they plead international recession or the rate of exchange. UK industry is not noted for its interest in investing in UK operations. The policy of investing abroad, or through acquisitions is the lazy - and as it has proved - risky way of expansion. In the private sector everything that goes wrong is due to external problems, and everything that goes right is due to entrepreneurial skill.
- "*To end* [unspecified] *restrictive practices*". Some practices required for safety, may *seem* restrictive. Practices which most hampered viability came from external sources. The MoT spoke of

---

[4] The same Minister stated (Hansard vol 218, col 154), that "Railways had improved considerably in recent years, it had a tendency to ask for more taxpayers' money" - *but the BR subsidy had been falling year after year* - "A regime not fundamentally changed since nationalisation" *when it had changed drastically.* See also the footnote page 148.
[5] The public saw that "£1m of profit went in bonuses to six Railtrack Directors"! (Hansard vol. 275, col. 902).
[6] BR had budgets from the 1960s, and later, Profit Planning & Cost Centre Analyses for each location and route.

privatised rail staff operating "away from the constraints of a Rule Book", which is the corner-stone of safety, **containing not one word on demarcation**., and has been developed over 150 years with the help of the HMRI - his *own Railway Officers* - the only people in Whitehall with real railway knowledge. Thankfully experienced drivers ignored him: "*Traincrews go by the book and avoid potential tragedy*". (RailNews Feb 1999). Nevertheless, safety standards have fallen. (see pages 195,196). The BR Rule Book was confused with Union Rule Books that decimated industry.

- "*To reverse a 40 year decline in passengers*". There were 1.84m passenger miles per route mile in 1993/4 compared to 1.07m in 1948 - a 72% **improvement** in productivity. (see BTC/BRB Reports). A private sector company making improved use of fewer assets would be praised. Moreover, Government policy limited growth by directing that the subsidy be continually reduced, whereas now, they cannot give away enough to prop up the private sector, with the new objective of increasing use of railways - which has not been a Government policy since World War II. Despite that, BR had been expanding its passenger business. (see pages 97-100).
- "*To get freight back*". It was lost due to Government policy. (see pages 112-117). The MoT claimed freight goes by road due to a "*just in time*" requirement. Empty shelves and instructions to return in weeks for goods needed *now*, prove the UK is a *long* way from just-in-time delivery. "The freight facilities scheme will be broadened. A new grant will be introduced to contribute to access charges. The allocation for the next three years is £43m". ("Britain's Railways: A New Age", 1994).
- "*To end union power*". It ended long ago, (see pages 140-147). Fragmentation restored it in separate arenas - first with Railtrack. Significantly, media and public sided with unions and criticised Railtrack. Board Room greed increases union demands. Different pay rates for the same job created dissent as ex-BR managers foresaw. "BR managers were effective at dissuading staff from industrial action. Today's managers seem not to have the same skills". (Modern Railways March 2002)
- "*To cut fares*". Full fares have risen more, (see pages 47,162), "cheap" tickets are *secretly* limited.
- "*To improve services & reliability*". No industry gives a 100% service. The public has been disappointed or brainwashed. Improvements funded by bigger subsidies are no big deal.
- "*To eliminate complaints*". No industry is free of complaints. Some create an illusion of being free by replacing defective goods and not revealing statistics. Complaints have increased. (see page 161)
- "*To end the railway culture*". This gem was not translated. To BR managers, it meant putting safety on a higher plane than other transport or industry and that essential engineering and operating expertise *cannot* be learned externally. That is confirmed by a report that a Chief Executive of Railtrack stated that "punctuality and safety were our *number one* priority". (Daily Telegraph, 5.7.03). That is *two* priorities - which experience shows are often mutually incompatible. The "*Private sector culture*" is: astronomical salaries, tax free perks, immoral share options, telephone number pensions, mind boggling severance payments for failure and price rises above inflation.
- "*To change bureaucratic structures*". Civil Servants created the 1947 organisation, "it bore every sign of bureaucracy". (Elliot, Page 167). Government approved the much criticised 1953 structure, and imposed the 1962 organisation. Career railwayman Robert Reid initiated the successful Business Sector organisation. (see pages 35-36). Now, "bureaucracy is worse, and managers less skilled". (*Railway World*, March 2002, Page 43). Government has created a structure worse than the one that they created in 1948, requiring a most complex structure of contracts. (see pages 42,48).

In November 1995, a Minister said that the passenger has two guarantees he never had before:
- Key fares will not rise in real terms over the next three years,
- trains in a contract will not be withdrawn in the franchise term. (see "fewer services" page 42)

An MP retorted that an all-Party Report on privatisation stated that it would cost £700m pa to maintain the same level of service as exists at present - not one extra service or train. (Hansard, vol. 267, col. 917-8). Mrs. Dunwoody [Chair of Transport Select Committee] asked "what will happen if a franchise is surrendered. The Minister replied that the Franchising Director is required under the 1993 Act to secure continued provision of service generally by transfer to another company. Staff would transfer. If any staff essential to safe operation did not transfer, arrangements are in place to ensure they would quickly be replaced with suitably skilled staff.[7] Regrettably, passengers find that the "key fares" apply to someone else or require a crystal ball to determine when to travel cheaply.

Passengers would *lose* an important guarantee. The MoT had directed BR to provide a service comparable with that provided in 1988, and that direction was in force in 1994, on the eve of privatisation. (BRB 1993/4 Report, Page 1). Until 1988, the directive was to maintain services at the 1975 level, hence the 1994 level was effectively that of 1975. The MoT also required BR to progressively *reduce* the subsidy, (see pages 34-35,181). The new regime was given licence to *reduce* services, and given *more* subsidy (see pages 182-184). This was justified on the grounds that they would not wish to reduce, but would increase services. In that case, retention of the existing Directive would not have tied their hands. Some companies have run more services, but services are now being cut because too many trains on some lines are causing delays. It took some time for that penny to drop. Worse still, in 2003, the SRA invited potential franchisees to submit plans to replace trains by buses.

The Bill to privatise railways was only approved after the Government conceded the retention of reduced fares for senior citizens and students. (Daily Telegraph 5.11.93). This was surprising - the public had been led to expect that the private sector would be cutting fares, but, clearly there was doubt that they would even maintain the reduced fare offers provided by BR!

Forecast Consequences, Problems and Risk Areas

In contrast, to Ministers' pious hopes, former BR managers warned:

Closures: services will be withdrawn that are less lucrative, not necessarily loss making - a common private sector practice. If closure is blocked, more subsidy will be demanded.*

Competition: will be limited[8].

Connections: will not be maintained with other companies' trains, to improve punctuality[9].

Delays & cancellations: will not be "due to incompetence", but "circumstances beyond our control"* - private sector's exclusive excuse, translating into improved statistics[10].

Fares Those expecting fares to fall, except short term, were in for a rude awakening. Fares lagged behind the 1948 based RPI for the first 30 years, and nine of the remaining sixteen (see Appendix A) Those missing a train will need another ticket to replace the invalid original*.

Fewer services: A service, below BR levels was justified as "*the first time that minimum service levels have been stipulated*". The MoT had specified BR's level (see above). No minima was needed if they respond to *any* demand, which BR was criticised for not doing. On 24th March, 2001, Crewe staff were told not to sell cheap tickets to Liverpool, where an international soccer match was being held, because trains were full. BR would have been told it was incompetent not to have found extra trains. Now, in 2003, it has been announced that there will be a reduction in services.

Fragmentation: Disputes over delays, accidents*, compensation, paths[11], fares, refunds and shared facilities will ensure a rewarding future for accountants and lawyers*. 100 companies will play *pass the parcel* and claim failures and problems are *due to circumstances beyond our control.* A most astonishing revelation (BBC Radio 4, 21.6.03), is to learn that contracts for track work are let separately for plain line track and for points. The opportunity for inter-face error is frightening.

---

[7] The training period for new staff recruited for key jobs would cause serious changeover problems. Even base grade staff require training to equip them to work safely in this unique environment.

[8] Some franchisees were not allowed to run new services, because another company objected! A Virgin brochure states that fares on certain routes could not be reduced, "because another company is responsible for setting fares".

[9] I have often missed a connection which leaves as my inbound train arrives at Crewe - unknown in BR days. At other times, having caught a train due to depart, and warned staff that others are coming, the train leaves without them.
* These prophecies have been fulfilled.

[10] To improve punctuality, some train journey times may be increased. (Daily Telegraph 17.1.02). This will reduce track capacity, leading to fewer trains on the route. BR would have been savaged for making such a change.

[11] The introduction of trains which are much faster than others on a route will cut the number of available paths.

Leaves on the line. Offending trees will be cut down[12]. Worse problems will arise from weeds on the line, judging by growth on some routes. (see also page 102).

Price restraint: The Regulator will block *"unreasonable increases"*. Franchisees will not have to justify fares in a Court of Law as applied until 1968. If they are denied increases and no extra subsidy follows, their options are closures or liquidation[13]. That cannot improve services. Moreover, OPRAF states that the regulation is not of *all* fares, but only selected or token fares. A promise to cap fares was unnecessary - private sector railways were expected to reduce fares! Clearly, Ministers feared that they would apply market forces[14]. Ministers could have won popularity by capping car insurance to benefit the 90% who do not use rail.

Profits: will come from higher fares, ancillary charges, shorter trains* and withdrawing less lucrative, not necessarily loss making, services* - a common private sector practice.

Safety: standards are well above other transport, especially road, hence, the State* will be asked to fund improvements, *in the National Interest*. (see Chapter 16).

Snow: will cause delay* when it is found machines are not justified for five days pa, (see page 101).

Subsidies: Franchisees will be back for supplementary payments when they can't make ends meet*.

Through booking: Broken connections will reduce the value of through tickets.

It was not forecast that Railtrack would depend wholly on outside contractors. This is *not* analogous, as some claim, to contracting out maintenance of machines and buildings - or even more absurdly of contracting out car servicing, (BBC Radio 5.3.03 "After Beeching"). Car servicing is placed with trained mechanics. No one outside railways had expertise in maintaining 125 mph track. Contracting out maintenance is akin to contracting out the operation of a production line - the infrastructure *is* Railtrack's production line. Moreover, contracting out maintenance in big companies is not that prevalent. Shipbuilding, steel, engineering, motor and other major industries employed in-house maintenance as the scale of it required on-the-spot attention. The delay in welding broken rails, now experienced, did not occur under BR. The structure of privatisation showed that Railtrack would contract out renewals and maintenance, but not that it would leave itself completely without technical control, so that it did not know whether work was being done at all, much less to a safe standard - and safety was *the* key element in Railtrack's product. An impression was given that the industry was set for a better future: "Railtrack will buy in around £1bn worth of maintenance and renewal annually from the infrastructure service units being set up". (DoT: "Britain's Railways: A New Age", 1994, Page 12). The casual reader would see this as big bucks - more investment than under BR. Annual Reports for BR's last two years show that investment totalled £2.5bn; and track and signalling maintenance £1.2bn. The former included £680m on rolling stock, leaving a balance for £1.8bn on infrastructure, which added to maintenance produces an annual average of £1.5bn. When account is taken of the fact that the much trumpeted "£1bn bought-in" would include profit margins for the contractors, sub contractors and sub-sub contractors etc., the warning bells should have been ringing. Warnings appeared when Railtrack abandoned the practice of renewing track according to a forecast life span, which varied according to volume, weight and speed of traffic using it. This practice was pursued by BR, its forebears in the private sector and the rest of Europe. The terms "pinch points" and "sweating the assets" were bandied about. These were explained as being a businesslike approach to avoid replacing assets until it was absolutely necessary. The previous practice involved replacing rails before they were worn out, and cascading them, after checking their condition, onto low speed branches or sidings. What Railtrack did not explain - and no one in

---

[12] Railtrack was said to be cutting down trees in conservation areas to tackle the problem. (Daily Telegraph, 23.7.94). A study revealed that to avoid the problem of leaves on the line and trees being uprooted onto railway lines, the acreage of trees to be cut down would cover an area three times the size of Liverpool. (Scottish RUCC 2001/2 Report).

[13] In fact, they are being allowed to increase fares above inflation, are given more subsidy **and** allowed to cut services!

[14] As they did.

* These prophecies have been fulfilled.

the DoT nor the H&SE appears to have asked, is: "how will they *know* that a rail is about to crack under the strain of extended use". Had rails in BR days been left as long, it would have been difficult to detect a defect, on the last day of the safe life of a rail - despite the regime of ultrasonic checks by track recording cars, hand held ultrasonic devices and regular visual inspection by patrolmen. Railtrack made it impossible, by cutting the use of track recording cars, some hitherto attached to trains, for which they would doubtless, have to pay train companies, and reducing the frequency of inspections. This was not due to sudden replacement of men by machines. (see page 85). Worse, following fatalities to contractors' patrolmen[15], they were required to walk along the cess - a "footpath" along the formation - making it difficult to inspect the far rail of the nearer track, much less, the other track. An incident on the West Coast line was reported early in 1997, and discussed on Radio Stoke, in which hundreds of pandrol clips - which hold rails in place - were loose or had fallen out. In my 40 years with railways, there was no report of a similar incident. On the contrary: "the pandrol clip was a breakthrough. There should be no working loose as was the case with some fastenings. On exceptionally busy lines, track might require renewal at 12 year intervals; but on average the life was 18 years. Prestressed concrete sleepers will last 50 years". (Institution of Civil Engineers: "Developments in Railway Traffic Engineering", 1967, Pages 6-7).

BR began laying trial lengths of CWR[16] [continuous welded rail] in 1956. By the end of 1959, 200 miles had been laid. From 1960, this important aspect of modernisation accelerated with hundreds of miles laid each year. Most BTC/BRB Annual Reports record the mileage laid. In 1986/7, BR reported that 59% of the 20,000 track mile system was CWR. By adding to this, track miles laid, as recorded in Reports up to 1991/2[17], brings the total to 12,611 miles. Hence, in the 32 years from 1960, the average was 394 miles pa. Network Rail say, as at February 2003, 14,000 track miles were laid with CWR. This means that, in the 11 years from 1992/3 to 2002/3 inclusive, 1,389 miles was laid - an average of 126 miles pa. That period includes two years under BR in which some CWR was laid, although the two Annual Reports do not itemise it. Had there been none laid in those two years, Railtrack/Network Rail would have laid, at the most, 154 miles pa. CWR resolved the problem of rail end failure arising from the thumping that joints experienced, extended the life of rails, improved the riding quality of trains and gave rise to much faster train speeds.

It is claimed "that decades of under investment had bequeathed too much *bumpy* track".[18] (Economist, 21.9.96). Pre-privatisation TUCC Annual Reports make no mention of bumpy track, as they would have done, given a tendency to miss no point of criticism. Given such a situation, Railtrack should have been laying CWR at a faster - rather than a slower - rate than BR

Some claim that under Railtrack: punctuality improved, more trains ran and more passengers carried. Railtrack cannot claim credit for the latter - Government moved the goal posts from cutting to increasing the subsidy so as to increase rail traffic. Railtrack policy in not renewing track as often, cut possessions, giving more train "paths", which should help punctuality. Punctuality has been "improved" by closing four track sections of line for engineering work for months, where under BR, two lines were kept open. Trains are replaced by buses which do not appear in statistics. It is claimed that this policy is necessary because bigger machines are used and it is safer for staff. BR engineers recognised that their job was to interfere with trains as little as possible, and hence used machines that enabled a route to remain open. The change in practice for staff safety is necessary because staff have been employed with no experience of working on railways.

---

[15] A leaked report stated that outside contractors are not given enough training. (Economist 19.8.95, Page 29).

[16] Originally referred to as Long Welded Rail. "London Transport was the pioneer of CWR before the war. It was laid in lengths, never less than a quarter of a mile, and up to 3 miles". (BTC 1960 Report, Page 31).

[17] BRB Reports for 1992/3 and 1993/4 showed less detail, and no CWR mileage was mentioned.

[18] On business or leisure, I travelled thousands of miles annually and would have taken action by stopping the train to report a track fault, or after BR's mobile phone system was set up, by arranging for action to safeguard following trains - but never did so. My first experience of bumpy track was, a few years after privatisation, being thrown off balance near Reading - a track hitherto noted for the highest quality - having never lost my balance on a train before.

Alternative Options

One option was to assess what infrastructure BR needed to cut heavy road freight, beginning with dangerous goods - in view of adverse safety checks. Government could have invested a fraction of its roads' budget into lifting bridges to cater for piggyback trains. That would have resolved the problem of poor maintenance and unsafe driving of HGVs, and cut HGV imports. A Transport 2000 report showed 50% of long distance HGVs would be saved by doubling rail freight.

An illusion was created that BR, with under 10% of the market, was a monopoly. If Government could not bring itself to give BR full commercial freedom - and thereby tacitly admit that political interference had been the source of BR problems - and wished to bring those mysterious principles of enlightened private enterprise into railways, (see page 27), there were other options:

- A competing railway could have been built, without constraints on gauge and speed inherent in 150 year old routes, on French principles with straight routes and no crossings, provided that the NIMBY factor which blocked the Chunnel link, could be overcome. If the French had had to tunnel half of their routes, their high speed lines may never have been built. It is not clear why motorways are not underground to eliminate their intrusive noise and pollution. A new high speed passenger railway would attract traffic. Owning its' infrastructure has benefits. It has disbenefits, because when trains are delayed or lines blocked, they will be unable to blame someone else. It would be embarrassing when 21st Century technology also proves to be less than 100% reliable.
- Loss making lines kept open by Ministers should have been privatised first. That would have been a *real* challenge to show how to operate without a subsidy. Instead Government franchised first, with subsidies, Inter City and NSE services that were profitable under BR. The subsidy doubled immediately before privatisation, providing an "administrative profit" of 20.3%. (see page 183). The BR subsidy was the forecast deficit, which was falling, and any excess was repaid. (see pages 34-35). Former Chancellors must be turning in their graves. A contract for a reducing subsidy is worthless if a company goes bankrupt. Some have been given more subsidy to prevent that.
- 6,940 miles of closed track - including some main lines - which objectors always claimed could be profitable (see *"Blueprints for Bankruptcy"*, Page 185), could have been sold to the private sector.
- Part of BR could have been sold, the rest left in the public sector. That would have been a wiser course - facilitating comparisons, and if privatisation failed, making it easy to revert to BR. If privatisation succeeded, that remaining under BR could have been privatised. That would be a risk too far - for the Party with implicit belief in the infallibility of the private sector!

Some consequences of fragmentation

Now that it is obvious that fragmentation *has* caused serious problems, politicians claim it is only apparent *"with the benefit of hindsight"*. Many BR managers forecast it[19]. It caused pay leap-frogging, inter-company poaching of trained staff, and led inevitably to disputes. During wage negotiations between Railtrack and the National Union of Railwaymen in 1994, a disagreement arose as to what was offered. It was said that an unauthorised offer was made by a junior manager. Under BR, junior managers did not advance views at negotiations, only the management side Chairman did so. Hence, under BR, such a dispute could not have occurred. Two issues were exaggerated:

Walking time: payment for which was insignificant and falling with modernisation, being largely limited to relief staff travelling to manual signalboxes, some of which can only be reached on foot. Such payment is not unique to BR - those in other activities are paid when on company business.

Cashless pay: unsurprisingly, staff were reluctant to change, in view of the risks - fewer banks, limited hours, unreliable cash machines, inability to get at their money, misprinted cheque cards, "computer errors", standing orders not paid or paid twice, money credited to wrong accounts, or cash taken by the bank from an account without legal authority. The practice was not unique to BR. Research by APACS found that 17% of wages were paid in cash.

---

[19] This was prophesied in 1993 in *"Blueprints for Bankruptcy"*, and repeated by me on Radio Stoke in April 1993.

During the ensuing dispute, publicity regarding the operation of half of the network by a third of the workforce was flawed, as 12 hour shifts were being worked, which is unsustainable and dangerous over long periods. Contrary to media opinion, most signalmen did not oppose modernisation. If the private sector had achieved as much change with their unions as BR did, there would still be engineering and shipbuilding, a bigger car industry and no balance of payments problem. There is more to signalling than "*pressing a few buttons*" as some seem to believe. Railways cannot be operated with fewer signalmen without major investment, and experience shows that the return on this investment is low. Those arguing that "computers will solve all" reveal the most dangerous ignorance. Programming computers to permit two trains in a section: e.g. for engineering purposes, or for one train to assist a failed train invites catastrophe on other occasions. Computers are not 100% reliable as shown by air accidents, near misses, and breakdowns in business and commerce.

Failure of the electric supply, led under BR, to diesel locos replacing electric. Now, delays occur as diesels are owned or leased by other companies. Diversionary routes are not used in emergency as readily, due to cost factors. Whilst they were supposed to be winning traffic from road, they now send locos for repair by road to avoid track use costs, and tell staff to use cars as it is cheaper!

The BR system of integrated Controls was swept away by the new regime. Railtrack, the 25 Train Operating companies and rolling stock maintenance companies each introduced Control Offices which destroyed the integration which hitherto existed and was a key factor in subsequent failures in safety reporting - such as that which contributed to the horrific Southall collision - ended the maintenance of connections and the organisation of speedy diversions when lines were blocked by accident or extreme weather. Good communications and long experience ensured close liaison between Controls covering the system. Controls also kept local radio informed.

BR had "Contingency Train Plans" - implemented at short notice if a route was blocked. They set out diversions, trains running to stations either side of the blockage, trains making extra calls, trains combined, cancellations and bus or taxi links. We did not pause to consider the cost - nor whether BR was culpable. Pre-planning ensured a structured format to a reduced service. Passenger information staff had copies, and were told when a plan came into operation. It required a central authority to direct changes to schedules and hence must have been abandoned after 1994. The plans worked well. When a bomb warning occurred at Crewe on 25th March 1997, I phoned to find what services were running from Stafford and they said none "because the line is blocked at Crewe". NRES didn't know about the "Independent Lines" via which north-south trains could have been diverted. Neither did they realise that trains from London, on reaching Stafford would turnround and provide a southbound service. I did, and took a relative to Stafford where a service was available.

Politicians claimed that fragmentation was unavoidable under EEC Directive 91/440 - but that left it to Governments to decide - the only requirement was to split infrastructure *accounts* from train operations accounts, and allow cross border access. Such a split is no different to that applied by conglomerates and Holding Companies with the Accounts of their subsidiaries.

Each unit's charges are calculated to enable it to be a self sustaining commercial company, earning profits to fund new investment and provide for shareholders. This has led to much higher charges for many items than had been attributed to them while BR was still a single corporate entity. Government now pays much higher grants. There was a reduction in staff fatalities, but the staff most at risk - track staff - were then not counted as they were contractors' staff. (BRB 1994/5 Report).

Half of all railway companies are losing money. North East Area trains had a subsidy of £200m and lost £19m. Arriva had inherited a shortage of drivers from the previous franchisee that had cut staff levels from BR's 3,000 to 2,100 - trains were cancelled due to driver shortage. They would revert to the former level. Prism said economies are few and far between. (BBC Radio, File on Four 20.1.02). Arriva reinstated two thirds of its cancelled West Yorkshire trains on February 25, and aims to restore full service by June. The SRA reported 1,000 trains per week cancelled during Summer 2001. [RailNews March 2002]. Whilst some companies cut staff, the SRA and allied bodies were increasing staff numbers! The SRA has more staff than the BRB, but runs no trains.

A Minister said (BBC Radio 15.10.02): "It must be right for taxpayers to pay part instead of all the subsidy". What he overlooks is that private sector railways are said to be spending £3 to achieve what cost BR £1 - so if taxpayers paid one third, it is no better, nor no worse. The reality is they are paying half: "Passengers may be required to pay more of the true costs of rail travel with less from the taxpayer. At present, £3.4bn paid in fares accounts for half of the operating costs[20]. A total of 44% of fares are regulated, including season tickets and savers". (Times 19.7.02). The SRA stated that it has been forced to prop up several train companies with extra subsidies this year. It says London & South East commuters pay too little for season tickets. Commuter travel accounts for 47% of all rail travel, but only 27% of total fare income.

Predictably, Inquiries into accidents, hitherto held within days are delayed for years, whilst track clearance takes weeks not days. Col. D. McMullen - Chief Railway Inspector [HMRI] to the Minister of Transport - told an Engineers conference: "It would be intolerable to bring in a large number of people running their own trains". (Developments in Railway Traffic Engineering, Page 67).

In time, "the wheel will be rediscovered", and all activities brought in-house as early pioneers did. Government may enforce mergers as they did in 1921. This will cut out staff employed to argue about delays, inter-company payments and accidents[21], and various new supervisory bodies.

Revelations

On the whole, the media is now philosophical about closures and *very* understanding regarding external problems which had also affected BR performance. They now concede that road safety is much worse than rail safety - something BR had been saying for years.

Critics cannot admit that BR did anything to attract passengers. Current publicity implies that Senior Citizens and Bargain First are new, when BR introduced them in 1975 and 1978. They trumpet plans for Parkway stations, without conceding that BR created them in 1972. Asked to acknowledge this, a critic said that they were done on the cheap with minimum facilities. And so they should, as critics forecast failure, saying nothing short of free travel would tempt motorists to rail. The inference is that the private sector throws money at such projects. Little wonder there is so little industry, if they throw money at speculative ventures. Motorists using rail require minimum time between car and train. Provision of new facilities implies that they are waiting for late trains!

In 2002, ATOC justified above-inflation fares increases as "they are demand led" - by which they meant if demand goes up, so do prices, to increase profits and create equilibrium with supply - in accordance with long standing economic theory. BR was criticised retrospectively by newcomers for having done so in the 1980s. (Rail 11-24 Dec 2002). Evidently, what is accepted practice in the private sector, is not deemed acceptable in the public sector, despite the promise of the MoT in 1956 that he would show BR how to apply private sector principles. (see page 171). It was announced by the Strategic Rail Authority, in 2003, that fares, notably seasons, will increase above the rate of inflation under SRA plans to relax fare capping. The SRA "believes that fares must rise to force people to book and travel outside the peaks".

These fare increases are not to be accompanied by cuts in the subsidy to levels below those paid to BR prior to privatisation, as would be expected from the 'enlightened' private sector. (see pages 183-184). Subsidies are increasing, and will continue to increase.

Virgin Trains' Chief Executive said the industry should eat humble pie and re-recruit lost talent. (Institute of Logistics & Transport journal "*Focus*", May 2001). "Railtrack is short of railway engineers and is to bring back permanent way Inspectors. A new training school is to be funded externally". (Modern Railways, March 2002). Many former managers have returned as consultants.

"Management will be free to cut costs[22], improve efficiency and introduce new services to meet customer services. Regulation will be introduced to promote competition and prevent anti-

---

[20] In the five years preceding privatisation, fares were 80-85% of operating expenditure. (see BRB 1993/4 Report)

[21] A report in the Financial Times on 4.6.01 stated that 300 people were employed for this purpose.

[22] Managers had been cutting costs since Day One (see Chapter 13), Ministers had not been taking notice.

competitive behaviour, to protect the customer as well as operator interests. Key rail discount cards will be preserved[23]". (DoT publication "*Britain's Railways: A New Age*", 1994, Page 4).

An Industry in Decline?

Critics say that BR was in decline to justify bigger subsidies to the private sector, and to explain increasing business. Yet, critics say that BR was told by Government to increase fares to dampen [rising] demand. Annual BR Reports reveal an expanding market and increasing investment. (see pages 97-100). Recession apart, it wasn't in decline when it was privatised, but it is moving that way now. Newcomers need not worry as they are protected against decline: the Franchising Director said that subsidies could be increased in the event of passengers falling! (Daily Telegraph 18.5.95).

Sir Bob Reid - BR's Chairman when privatisation was mooted - wrote (BRB 1991/2 Report, Page 4): the five key criteria against which [privatisation] proposals should be judged are:
- They build on our success in the last decade.
- Improve service to the customer and ensure benefits of a nation-wide network are still available.
- They allow the railway to compete vigorously in domestic and international markets.
- Must meet the needs of operational integrity with arrangements to protect the safety of operations.
- They must provide for uninterrupted investment in the railway.

These criteria are inadequate, having a subjective, rather than an objective basis. They are not measurable. More meaningful criteria would be measurable benchmarks. (see page 161).

"A wide range of access agreements, property leases and other contracts are required by each [of the 25] Train Operating Companies, [TOC]. On 1st April 1994, passenger rolling stock was transferred to three new leasing companies [ROSCOs]. The contractual agreements for leasing trains to TOCs involved extensive negotiations on 51 leases as each lease had to be individually agreed between each ROSCO and TOC". (BRB 1994/5 Report). It was well on the way to fulfilling my prophecy (see "*Blueprints for Bankruptcy*"), of a rewarding future for railway accountants and lawyers! It was soon evident that privatisation reversed BR's achievements, treating some passengers worse than in the darkest days of BR, destroying the nation-wide network concept, failing to maintain the safety of the travelling public as carefully, and that much investment was still to come from the taxpayer. Whereas, BR provided advice to hundreds of foreign railway administrations in 80 countries (see page 36), the newcomers publicised that they sought advice from abroad. It is a fact, that former BR managers have been discreetly engaged as consultants to solve problems. This was not publicised, and hence the high profile publicity to the use of consultants from abroad to solve problems that would have been easy tasks for sacked BR managers.

"In years to come, I believe that 1996/7 will be seen as the turning point in the history of the UK railway industry". (Railtrack Chairman, 1996/7 Accounts, Page 5). Regrettably, it was a downturn!

When Government wound up Railtrack, the company said that the Minister would learn that the change would make little difference to an infrastructure with rails that were 40 years old. The public may have taken that to mean that *all rails* were 40 years old. That was not the case. Some may be found in lightly used lines[24]. The system under BR was renewed more frequently than now. (see page 87). One source stated that Railtrack renewed rails on average every 125 years, (see page 164), so 40 years would have posed no concern. The current practice of prolonged closures of major routes for renewals[25] - where BR carried out work without closure, or for shorter periods - is having a major impact on reliability. They will have to close again for renewals in the future.

In 1999, Midland Mainline boasted of re-instating direct London-Barnsley trains - axed ten years earlier by BR as loss-makers. (BBC File on Four). In 2000, there were 31 trains over seven days. By 2003, they had fallen to a total of 17 over six days. Such a token service will soon again be "axed".

---

[23] Wisely, no assurance was given that their prices and conditions would not change. (see page 161).

[24] A BR manager visiting north Scotland a few years ago, was told by a BR civil engineer that some bullhead rails on a branch line, were nearly 40 years old. As "they hadn't been turned yet" they had some serviceable life left.

[25] It has been claimed that this is due to H&SE requirements, but this was denied by an H&SE source.

Chapter 5

It has been widely acknowledged, (see page 16), that the Big Four railways had reached a high peak of operational efficiency before the Second World War, despite their unjust treatment by Government in respect of the limitations imposed on their competitive position. (see pages 7-11).

"During the War, the railway system, its equipment and rolling stock was subject to workloads well in excess of design and kept in use long after normal renewal dates. It had been impossible to provide resources to maintain railways except to the very minimum to keep them running, whilst they were subjected to the increased strain imposed by heavy war traffic and wartime operating conditions". (MoT 1956 Paper: "*Proposals for Railways*", Cmnd 9880, Page. 4).

In 1944, railways appealed in vain to Government to adjust the basis of the Rental and maintenance provisions, which were out of line with heavy wartime traffic. (see page 17). Little wonder the MoT said that "*railways emerged from the war with most of their equipment out of date and all of it run down*". (Cmnd 9880). Having sequestrated railways, Government had a moral, even a legal, duty to return assets to the condition in which they seized them. Had they repaid gratitude voiced by Ministers, (see page 19), they would have put them into *better* condition as a reward for wartime efforts. In contrast, competitors used wartime profits to obtain new road vehicles in excess of Government policy, (see pages 21,54,55). Shipping, which had been subsidised before the war, and treated generously during the war, was restored to pre-war condition, (see page 21).

By Government directive, railway maintenance and renewals were deferred during the war, below pre-war levels, despite traffic rising by 50%. Cash not spent thereon was placed in a Trust Fund, (see page 15) It was depleted by payments to Auditors - a cost that would not have arisen had the funds been left in railway company reserves, as fees paid for auditing company accounts would have embraced this cash along with other reserves. Sums that needed to be spent during the war should have been 50% higher to cope with the heavier workload. BR inherited a system that was very rundown. When BR was allowed to draw on the Fund, its value had fallen sharply due to inflation.

BR's Inheritance

The phrase "a rag-bag of assets" has been attributed to Chancellor Hugh Dalton. In fact, he said "the railways are a very poor bag of assets[1]: the permanent way is badly worn, the rolling stock is in a state of great dilapidation, railways are a disgrace to the country". (Hansard vol. 431, col. 1809). He overlooked that railways were subject to excessive use under Government control [1939-47], and that the companies had not been allowed to maintain them to pre-war standards. During the debate, an MP demonstrated a woeful lack of research in regard to railways, that others have demonstrated: "Railways only got investment by borrowing £26m at 2.5% from Government". (col. 1832). In fact, from amalgamation in 1923 to the start of the 1939-45 war, excluding maintenance, they invested £313.8m capital in track, rolling stock, workshops, plant, etc. (Munby, Table A6). In the same debate, another MP claimed that "Government war [rail] traffic cost 75% more than traffic between civilian consumers". In fact, Government had dictated that its traffic would be conveyed at *lower* rates than civilian traffic (see page 14), on top of which, Government skimmed back the entire extra wartime revenue after 1940, (see pages 17,18). Had he referred to hauliers skimming the Government, he would have been 100% right. (see page 21). Another MP goofed likewise in respect of the inadequate £60m paid to railways for their use in the 1914-18 war (see page 5) claiming that it was a subsidy. (Hansard vol. 493 col. 306). It was not the last such political error.

Unlike Europe, which used its American Aid to restore its railways and infrastructure, the UK Government gave priority, over restoring railways to the condition in which they acquired them, to the "Empire", housing, and industry - notably the aircraft, cotton, textile, shipping and motor indus-

---

[1] In 1948, MP Anthony Eden reminded Dalton of his jibe when Dalton said BR was providing a cheap service. (Hansard vol. 457, col. 706). Eden said: "Not bad for a rotten bag of assets".

tries, which repaid them by losing foreign and domestic market share. (see Table 10). Little wonder that critics found cause to compare BR unfavourably with European railways. (see page 149).

On 1st January 1948, the BTC had to buy, under the 1947 Act, from "powerful vested interests". (see page 20), 544,000 independently owned wagons mostly over 40 years old and in poor condition, at a price - £43m[2] - dictated by Government. It was a bad purchase - 55,000 had to be scrapped in 1948! Some 347,000 were repaired in 1948 - BR: 260,000, private wagon repairers: 87,000. That left 26% fit for traffic. These 0.5m wagons, of 19th century technology, were included as assets when they were liabilities - 27% were still in use, causing delays, ten years later. They should have been left in private hands, until BR built modern wagons to replace them.

A study, in 1944 by the railway companies, into converting grease box wagons to oil axle boxes[3] noted that instead of oil axle-boxes on railway company wagons, 76% of privately owned wagons had grease lubricated axle-boxes which often ran hot - "hot-boxes". They ran hot ten times as often as oil boxes. They were lubricated by animal fats. In cold weather, the grease solidified if a wagon stood for a short time, whilst when running in hot weather, they sometimes caught fire. When a wagon was on fire, trains on all lines had to be stopped - to avoid risk to passing trains - causing serious delays. The speed of the wagons was such that two trains took up the paths of three trains of oil axlebox wagons. Trains conveying grease box wagons could only run half the distance of fast freight trains before being stopped for safety checks. Hence, transits were slower and additional manpower was required to examine and re-grease the wagons when they stopped. Sidings were needed for such examinations. Conversion would cost £6m, and should be done after the War.

About 1912, the standard wagon became 10 tons and was lifted after the 1914-18 war to 12 tons, with oil axle boxes[4]. In 1923, Government again directed that all new wagons should have oil axle-boxes. (PRO: Rail 1098/39). Government files dealing with the requisitioning of private owner wagons in 1939, showed that many were pre-1904. Owners built few wagons during the war. Of the railway companies' wagon fleet in 1939, 67% had been built since 1918, compared to 30% of the private fleet. (Munby, Tables A25.2 & A26). The North Eastern Railway - one of the few to supply its own coal wagons - from the early 20th century, built *20 ton* bottom discharge wagons for shipment coal.

"Ex-private owner wagons were stopped for repair twice as often as railway company wagons". (BTC 1949 Report, Page 84). Due to the excessive time that wagons were kept under load by collieries, industry and traders, the slow transits caused by their poor condition, and, especially, the failure of industry to supply sufficient steel and other materials, BR was compelled to keep large numbers of these museum pieces in use until 1957. "Some 43,800 grease boxes were in use at the end of 1956". (BTC 1956 Report, Page 36). The maximum speed for privately owned coal wagons was 20-30 mph[5], grease axle box wagons were at the lower end.

Interest on the Loan - to be paid by BR - raised to buy them continued for 25 years. Dr. Joy criticised *"BTC's inexplicable decision to pay £43m for the fleet. BTC rushed to take them over"*.(Joy, Page 77). Government announced their acquisition eight months *before* the Act was passed to create the BTC, and long *before* Members of the BTC were appointed! The BTC approved construction of 16 ton capacity mineral wagons at £375 each[6]. (BTC minutes 4.9.52). £43m would have bought 115,000 such wagons, equating to 170,000 10-12 ton private owner wagons, whilst faster transits arising from higher speed, fewer breakdowns and minimal time out of service for repairs would have more than doubled their annual capacity. Economies would have arisen from fewer repair and examination staff, fewer delays to other trains. As coal wagons spent most of their time in a static

---

[2] Compensation for these wagons had no regard to the condition of wagons, but was based on a normal rate of depreciation. If wagons were not kept up to normal standard, the BTC was paying more than their worth.(PRO: MT47/223)

[3] Railway companies study Feb 1944. (PRO: Rail 1098/39)

[4] C.E.R. Sherrington, *"Economics of Rail Transport"*, vol. 1 Pages 214-5. This means that all under 12 tons capacity at the time of nationalisation were pre-1919.

[5] T.B. Hare, *"Practical Railway Operating"*, Page 24.

[6] The price in 1948 would have been less. Price indices were up to 49% higher than 1948 - see Table 8.

condition: empty waiting loads, loaded at collieries waiting orders, loaded at destination - effective detention charges could have made up the balance. It made no more sense to nationalise them, than tank wagons which remained in private hands. But, Government had a hidden agenda. They tried for decades to pressure private owners to modernise and failed. They enacted legislation in 1919 to buy them out, but did not implement it. Bringing them under the control of BR would achieve their objective without using taxpayers' money, since BR was expected to fund their purchase from revenue. Such a course would ensure replacement by modern wagons which in its turn would create employment. A ministerial belief that coal wagons could be widely used for other traffic was misplaced. They were unsuitable for merchandise and ought not to have been used for any other traffic. The principal other use to which they were put was to convey scrap metal from the premises of industrial coal consumers. The scrap was almost never completely unloaded. Consequently, wagons arrived eventually in colliery sidings, and frequently had coal loaded on top of the scrap. This caused damage if the scrap was not discovered before being fed into furnaces.

Pre-war railways replaced about 4.1% of their wagons pa. In the first five years of nationalisation, BR was only allowed to replace wagons at a rate of 2.5% pa. Coupled with the higher numbers undergoing repairs as a result of heavy wartime use, it is no surprise that road haulage, which was allowed to expand its fleet, (see page 55), succeeded in poaching substantial flows of rail freight.

Another inherited burden was lines that had struggled to avoid bankruptcy in the era of the horse. The 1921 Railways Act was designed to avert the post-Great War closure of bankrupted minor railways, and preserve rural transport without cost to Government. The major railways were given the option to merge with loss makers, or lose everything by nationalisation. (see "Square Deal Denied"). Scarce and precious resources - albeit on a minor scale - had to be spent on such lines, to keep them operationally safe, whilst main lines were crying out for every penny.

Dr. Dalton also ignored that the Government had forced railways to place cash allocated for maintenance and renewal in a Fund controlled by Government which had been ironically entitled a "Trust Fund". *Trust* was the last emotion that railways had towards UK Governments - and with very good reason, in view of its treatment of railways in regard to their competitive position and disclosure that the Fund did not belong to the railway companies, (see page 15). Evidently, Government did not think it had skimmed enough out of railways with its wartime £1bn (see page 18) and its pre-war exploitation of railways to subsidise UK industry (see pages 7,11), which was a duty of the Government, if industry could not stand on its own feet. Responding to Dr Dalton, the LNER Chairman said that if the railways were a disgrace, it was nothing to do with railway managers. He pointed out that there were huge sums for deferred maintenance and abnormal wear and tear which they had at their disposal to spend when Cabinet permits. (Railway Gazette, 10.1.47, Page 58).

The LNER Chairman told the 1947 AGM: "Ministers have forbidden or made it impossible for us to restore assets to the same good condition they were in at the start of the war". He said that compensation terms for nationalisation arbitrarily decided by Government would "bring a blush of shame to the leathery cheek of a Barbary pirate. Ministers have not advanced any logical argument for the basis of compensation. He can hardly be serious in asserting that the price at which a small fraction of shares change hands is a fair and correct basis for valuing the undertaking as a whole"

The Southern Railway Chairman said the MoT was still in complete control of railways. They had plans for electrification, new ships, improved docks and stations. They had been *allowed* to approve a £1.2m London-Brighton line signalling scheme. (Railway Gazette, 29.11.46, Page 605). Modernisation begun just before the war, was completed by BR: "London-Shenfield electric service opened, despite difficulties in the supply of men and materials", (BTC 1949 Report, Page 71); Manchester-Sheffield/Wath electrification opened for freight & passenger, (BTC 1954 Report, Page 34).

The first BR electrification plan was the LT&S. (BTC 1949 Report, Page 72). Their claim to be the "Misery Line" was a Freudian slip. It was the Miserly Line, as users opposed increases on the cheapest fares on BR, whilst demanding that their line be modernised at the expense of others.

Delays to modernisation

In 1948, the BTC stated: It would be premature to tackle railway modernisation until progress was made on the acquisition of road transport[7]. Rail assets were not fully maintained during the war. It has not been possible within limits laid down [by Government] to restore the stock of carriages and construct modern goods wagons which are the first requirements of railways, and without it much uneconomical expenditure on maintaining out of date rolling stock must be continued. The general level of investment which has been prescribed by the Government has been largely governed by the availability of the principal controlled material - steel. Both allocation and delivery have been matters for grave concern. Excessive wear and tear arising from minimum maintenance standards since 1939[8]. Arrears of war damage, large numbers of temporary speed restrictions due to condition of track and bridges, which with poor quality of coal causing loss of steam pressure and locomotive failures had undermined standards of service. The Summer service operated with 4,000 fewer coaches than pre-war - 3,000 smaller fleet due to war damage losses etc.[9], plus 1,000 more than pre-war under repair after excessive wartime usage. Due to a lower steel allocation, new rolling stock building had to be cut back. To make up some of the shortfall 355 coaches which had been condemned had to be repaired[10] and kept in service for 2-8 years. Wagons under & awaiting repair were 16.6% in September 1947, due to wartime material shortages, but had reduced to 9.8% by December 1948[11]. Poor quality and uneconomical sizes of timber used in wagon repairs during and since the war placed a heavy burden on repair capacity. It will be years before the pre-1939 repair figures are achieved. Shortage of nuts and bolts impeded output throughout the year. Hopes of overtaking [war] arrears within a short time were 'modified' by the 1948 White Paper on Capital Investment that supplies of materials for the permanent way must be reduced to current needs, about the same as pre-war without overtaking arrears. Materials shortage especially, steel, timber and electrical cables governs the rate of tackling arrears. (BTC 1948 Report, Pages 29,30,75,77,110,111,119).

In February 1948, the BTC minuted that it had asked the MoT to authorise more coaches. Trains are overcrowded - in 1947 passengers were 30% above pre-war, 1948 will be higher. They noted "the Government's Economic Survey restricted rail investment: '*Arrears of track renewal to be overtaken only to the extent necessary for safety*'". (Cmnd 7647, Page 51). It would cause speed restrictions[12], waste money, lose revenue and help competitors who got more vehicles than specified, (see pages 54-55).

In 1949, the BTC stated: It has been possible to do little more than keep pace with current maintenance and overtake to a very modest extent, railway arrears accumulated during and since the war. Steel allocation to BR for 1949 was one million tons. It proved impossible to obtain more than 810,000 tons. At Government request, BTC prepared expenditure estimates - **1950**: £100.2m; **1951**: £114.8m; **1952**: £123m. Government reduced these to £95m for **1950**, rising to £100m in **1952**. Due to steel shortages, the 1949 service was run with 3,000 fewer coaches than pre-war. Wagons under repair were almost three times pre-war levels due to the poor condition of private owner wagons which need repairing nearly twice as often as former railway company wagons. (BTC 1949 Report, Pages 17,18,84,85,88). The 1950 investment amount was later reduced again to £92m, despite warnings that it would seriously impair efficiency. Powers to raise capital for investment were put in abeyance. *Capital would have been funded by the BTC*. In 1949, Government reduced the planned £123m for 1952 to £100m and by 1952, to less than £84m despite rising inflation:-

---

[7] They were still pre-occupied with road transport acquisition in 1949. (BTC 1949 Report Pages 10-12). This excuse lacks credibility. They were involved in acquiring *road haulage* which had no bearing on modernising *rail passenger* long distance and commuter services. Either they lacked the skill to handle two projects simultaneously, or were bowing to Government pressure. Acquisitions had not been completed by 1952 (see page 26).

[8] Repairs and renewals were deferred by Government directive, because industry could not produce enough steel.

[9] Including some sent to war zones by Government acting as though they owned them!

[10] The practice continued over the next 4 years on 40 years old coaches at a cost of £0.6m (see BTC Reports 1949-52)

[11] The pre-war figure was under 4%.

[12] Para 134 of the Government Paper stated that speed restrictions will accentuate wagon shortages.

Year	steel rails	steel plate	copper plate	copper tubes	brass bars	sleepers
1950	216	207	316	278	520	416
1951	278	244	359	308	536	659

Table 2 - Cost of materials; 1938 = 100; Source : BTC 1951 Report, Page 45

For BR "to be up-to-date requires expenditure which it is hopeless to expect can be found from revenue. In the war, millions were spent on additional lines not needed in peace-time". (see page 12). "Maintenance costs should fall on the Defence Minister, not on users". (CTCC 1950 Report, Page 6)

The BTC stated: "Such projects as electrification are practicable only if capital resources are available. Public transport counts itself fortunate if the ration of capital allowed[13] is sufficient to patch and maintain existing apparatus, let alone permit large schemes of capital improvement. Accounts are in balance, but there are no reserves to meet rising costs of replacing assets". (BTC 1950 Report, Page 40). Hurcomb told Elliot "to bring electrification costs to a Treasury meeting. Hurcomb said: 'I doubt if we will get much' - nor did we. R.A. Riddles [Member for M&EE, Railway Executive, formerly with the LMSR], was not in favour of a rush for diesels because of their poor reliability record. He favoured electrification but knowing the cost was out of question said there was no point in wasting time working up detailed costs". (Elliot, Page 85).

The MoT told the Cabinet in March 1951: "Government refusal to allow railways to carry out much of the capital investment which they thought to be necessary resulted in an accumulation of higher costs". Cabinet thought the BTC "should use its maintenance reserve to meet the wages deficit". (Cabinet minutes). *A sure road to ruin. Government had caused that deficit.* (see page 131).

In 1951, the BTC stated: "Control on expenditure [for renewals and certain maintenance] by Government continued in addition to control on materials supply. Government reduced the investment requirement from £114m to £95m, then to £81m. The actual investment was £76m. Under-spending was due to material shortages. The steel shortage reduced new rolling stock builds: planned - locos 447, coaches 2,764, wagons 45,190; built - 340, 1,923 & 37,796 respectively". The BTC pointed out that "Until BR can be assured of sufficient steel to carry out maintenance and renewals no return to pre-war speeds is practicable. Only 96 bridges repaired, two thirds of the programme due to steel shortages. (BTC Report Pages 1,112,113). *Bridges not repaired would necessitate speed restrictions.*

In 1952, Sir John Elliot, Railway Executive Chairman told the London Rotary Club that BR would get only 65% of the steel required for the 1952 wagon construction programme and none for coaches. They would have to retain a high proportion which were obsolete and uneconomical. In April, he told Cambridge District Station Masters: "We shall not have the steel, and so will have 2,000 aged coaches, old, shabby and unfit for modern traffic this Summer. (Times, 13.3.52 & 28.4.52).

The BTC continued to draw attention to its investment problems: "The steel shortage affected replacement of rolling stock. Government allocated 20% below needs. Deliveries did not reach the reduced allocation, hence output was at half railway workshops' capacity. Compared to 1951, new building by BR and contractors was down - locos: **12%**, coaches: **48%**, wagons: **24%**. BR had to repair life expired coaches that were 40-50 years old. Since 1949, BR spent £0.6m on such repairs, to keep them in service for four years and is having to continue this wasteful practice. Government will limit investment to £76.6m for BR". (1952 Report, Page 3). It had been set at £123m (see page 52)

In 1953, the BTC stated: "The explanation [of arrears of development], lies in past restrictions and shortages of materials. The position is more serious in relation to rail than road transport, not only as regards rolling stock but civil engineering works. Maintenance arrears due to intensive use made of railways during the war have hardly yet been made good. Short of steel and other materials. Discouraging and disruptive effects of constantly changing limits upon capital investment combined to hinder progress. Still having to 'make do and mend'. Arrears accumulating of loco and rolling stock building. Steel shortage is the cause". (BTC 1953 Report, Pages 22,23,28).

---

[13] "Capital allowed" were interest bearing loans Government allowed the BTC to obtain - its sole source of capital.

The BTC 1954 Report showed that railways were still hampered in operating an efficient system: "Although progress on repairs is at the highest level since the war, BR is still having to keep old vehicles in use. *War arrears were still not cleared by the end of 1953*. Old rolling stock and structures are outdated and over expensive to maintain. A condition to undertaking this bold plan [modernisation] is that the enterprise must not be allowed to get into a position of irredeemable balance meantime". (Pages 8,30,31,33). *Government created that situation*, (see pages 166-178).

The MoT White Paper *"Proposals for Railways"*, (Cmd 9880), included a BTC Memorandum: "Controls over capital investment are likely to depress their competitive power for some years. Restrictions on replacement of out of date rolling stock, buildings and equipment have been severe and have led to excessive maintenance costs. Delays in overcoming war arrears meant that the funds inherited to finance arrears at 1947 prices proved inadequate at prices ruling at the time work was carried out. Competitors' equipment was up to date. It is significant that most Western European nations gave priority [in the use of American aid] to railway reconstruction in their post war plans". (Pages 12,13). *Waste arises from keeping out dated equipment in service. The MoT did not contradict or dissociate himself from the BTC statement.*

Post-war (1946-7) passenger traffic was 32% higher than pre-war. The Big Four's new build in 1938 - for a smaller demand - was over 3,000 pa. Government restrictions on the use of BTC's *own* capital, reduced the passenger coach building programme. BR inherited 57,000 coaches, with an average age of 21 years, compared to 18 pre-war. To revert to an 18 year age profile, 3,200 pa needed to be built. The 3,000 coaches lost in wartime (see page 52), had to be replaced. The DoT had had in mind, restoring the fleet in five years, (PRO: MT6/2830). That required a build of 3,800 pa: 3,200 + $^1/_5$ of 3,000 = 19,000 over five years. In 1948, the BTC planned to build 3,600, but it was cut to 1,200. The total build 1948-52 was only 7,508. The BTC was not allowed to raise the annual building programme to the required level. In comparison, PSVs were built above planned figures.

"Despite steel shortages, wagon output included 41,739 sixteen ton wagons, permitting the withdrawal of 87,300 twelve ton capacity grease box wagons [formerly owned by non railway companies], leaving 239,600 former private owner wagons". (BTC 1955 Report, Page 31). *The residue were all of low carrying capacity - twelve tons or less.*

From 1948 to 1952, the real value of increased investment in industry was 20% compared to 2% on railways. Investment in roads and road vehicles was 3.5 to 4 times rail levels. New road vehicles in 1952 were 84,000 compared to 87,000 in 1951. (BTC Review December 1954).

The BTC calculated that they were due £56m for abnormal wear and tear under the enforced "Agreement". As in the earlier war, government sought to reduce the bill, by various ploys including pressuring the BTC to adopt superfluous war works and wagons. (PRO: AN85/18). The claim for abnormal wear and tear was settled in 1949 for £46m. Little opposition to the MoT was likely from BTC Chairman, Sir Cyril Hurcomb, who, when at the DoT, had led the iniquitous Rental talks.

The £1 billion seized by Government from railways in wartime, should have accrued to owners, who would have been able to keep assets in good order. Government had a moral duty to use these immoral gains to restore railways to their pre-sequestration condition. By the time of privatisation, invested wisely, that sum would have grown to over £750 billions. (see page 83).

Government's Inequitable Control of Resources
In the first nine months of 1948, 710 locos were exported despite serious shortages. BR was allocated fewer materials than needed, (see pages 52-53), but the supply of new road transport vehicles exceeded Government limits. In addition hauliers were buying up ex-Army vehicles. (see page 12).
Government Economic Surveys: Road transport for the home market.
1947 Cmd 7268, Page 30: The PSV fleet is now *59,200, only two years after the war* - it was *52,000* pre-war. Private cars are up from zero at the end of the war to 75% of pre-war production.

1948 Cmd 7344, Page 4: *8,000* PSVs supplied in 1947, to be limited to *6,000* in 1948. Goods vehicles in 1938: *500,000*; 1945: *450,000*; 1947: *650,000*. 100,000 were supplied in 1947 - to be limited to *50,000* in 1948. Two years after the war, the goods fleet was 200,000 more!

1949 Cmd 7647, Pages 52-53: *8,000* PSVs supplied 1948. To be *7,250* in 1949. *85,000* goods vehicles supplied in 1948. To be limited to *50,000* in 1949.

1950 Cmd 7915, Pages 28,42,43: 1949 saw an increase in road vehicles supplied to the home market. Manufacturers asked to restrict PSVs to *8,000* in 1950, compared to the *11,000* annual delivery rate in the second half of 1949. Goods vehicles delivered[14] in the second half of 1949 at an annual rate of *100,000*. To be cut to an annual rate of *65,000* in the second half of 1950.

1951 Cmd 8509, Page 30: There is to be a fall in home supplies of goods vehicles from 105,000 [in 1950] to 80,000. The actual was nearly 100,000. Much the biggest cuts will be in the home market for cars and commercial vehicles which are to be limited to 60,000 each. *New registrations actually reached 90,000.*

"Investment in road transport vehicles between 1948 & 1952 was consistently in excess of amounts considered appropriate for other investment by 25-100%". (BTC Review December 1954).

Government Economic Surveys: Rail transport.

1949 Cmd 7647, Page 51: "Arrears of track renewal to be overtaken only to the extent necessary for safety". *Consequential speed limits on unrenewed track would increase costs and traffic losses.*

1950 Cmd 7915, Page 30: "Restrictions on railways will be severe. Since the war, maintenance expenditure on BR has been severely limited. It has not been possible to carry out a programme for overtaking wartime arrears". *Expediency limited action, whilst the motor industry expanded.*

1951 Cmd 8509, Page 30: "Increased traffic placed severe strains on BR, due to a shortage of labour and materials. To ease the strain, coal and other traffic were diverted to road. BR will have substantial cuts in the programme for replacement of rolling stock and locos, work on stations, bridges, tunnels must be severely restricted & track renewal curtailed". *Government policies had restricted railway investment and supplies of materials, whilst competitors poached traffic with excess vehicles, having circumvented Government policy!*

In facing this daunting problem of railways - with their inherited rag-bag of assets - trying to compete with road transport with their new vehicles, the biggest errors made by BR managers were:
- Not closing lines on "safety grounds" after heavy wartime use, when materials were withheld.
- Paying Government for war assets instead of removing them at Government cost. (see page 12).
- Not publicising suppliers' failings and the consequential effect on performance and finance.
- Demonstrating a willingness to "make do and mend".

Management's biggest success was, probably, that of using relatively small amounts of its own capital - controlled as it was by Government Direction - to purchase machines to replace costly manpower engaged in track maintenance and renewal from 1948 onwards. (see page 85).

Post-war control of investment was not confined to BR, but BR was more severely restricted. This related to investing in-house resources - not Government cash. It was supposed to ensure that investment fitted a master Plan to put UK back on its feet. It failed. New diesel and electric locos, costing three times as much as a steam loco, would be treated as *capital*, replacement on a like-for-like basis was *maintenance*. Steam locos fell into the latter category. This principle was brought out by BR Chairman, Richard Marsh, in his autobiography - *"Off the Rails"*, in which he mentions that civil servants advocated replacing jointed track by jointed track instead of cheaper-to-maintain long welded rail, because the latter was investment! On nationalisation, BR had 20,211 steam locos, mostly in poor condition, and had no alternative but to replace some, and by 1955 had replaced about 10%. By 1955, the loco fleet was 11% less, to handle virtually the same traffic volume.

---

[14] Hauliers must have made huge wartime profits to afford nearly 0.5m new vehicles by 1950.

Chapter 6

BR was criticised for not embarking on piecemeal introduction of diesel or electric locos before 1955. They required heavier track and new maintenance facilities. BR was directed not to restore track to *pre-war* standards (see page 52). There was no prospect, as hindsight critics claim, that BR would have been allowed to buy American diesels - given UK's precarious currency balances, especially when, to protect industry they denied airlines American aircraft. (Barnett/2 Page 338). If Ministers would not admit that our infant aircraft industry, found seriously wanting in terms of cost, delivery and reliability, could not meet UK needs, the prospect of admitting that an older loco industry could not do so was nil. Riddles had grave doubts about diesel reliability. (Pearson/2, Page 112).

1955 Modernisation & Re-equipment Plan

"The BTC said they would like to come forward with a big programme for 10-25 years, and had set up a sub committee to prepare a plan". A DoT memo in October 1954 stated that the basis on which BTC seek to raise £600m is acceptable. Some argument will be put forward that some modernisation has an element of social service. The Chancellor opposed any subsidies. A letter from the Iron & Steel Federation in November, advocated modernisation and said that £67m of the £150m wartime Trust Fund was unspent[1], and devalued by inflation. (PRO: MT124/46). The Government authorised the BTC to submit a Modernisation Plan. A Planning Committee had been set up in April 1954 to prepare such a plan. "The Government will provide a **loan** of £500m". (BTC minutes, PRO: AN85/7). The BTC charged its Comptroller, Reginald Wilson, with the responsibility for setting out the traffic, economic forecasts and annual cash flow statements for the Plan.

Modernisation was overdue. Railways were in a poor state as a result of wartime control, government policies and inequitable post war control of materials that delayed replacement of war worn assets[2]. The Plan should have been funded by Government to redress its wartime neglect and repay railways for their war effort using vast sums the State seized. (see page 18). It was to cost £1,240m over 15 years, funded by the BTC, not Government. (DoT memo 31.5.56, PRO: MT132/32). £400m was to come from the Depreciation Fund[3] and the rest from Loans raised on the Market. Track and signalling would be improved to permit speeds of at least 100 mph[4] - well ahead of world standards. *"Experts" focused on a few pre-war trains, run at 100 mph over short distances*. The Plan was for a general service at 100 mph. Some lines would be electrified, others would have diesel traction. There would be closures. Freight services[5] and depots would be modernised. All freight wagons would be fitted with an automatic brake, and the size of coal and mineral wagons would be increased[6]. Office systems would be modernised. £85m return pa was forecast. A higher return required charges to be freed to permit increases justified by a modernised system, but statutory interference held charges down, whilst suppliers' prices continued to rise. BR prices, alone, were controlled. The slow closure procedure, with the MoT directing retention of loss making lines on social grounds, would hold down the return. There was need to reverse asset dereliction caused by Government, and the 1953 Act required the BTC, not to make a profit, but to break even.

---

[1] The Government had to sanction the level of investment, and the use of the Fund was closely controlled.

[2] White Paper, [Cmnd 813]: "It aimed to put right the accumulated effects of the starvation of capital investment".

[3] The Financial Times claimed (18.11.91), that in 1948, assets were written off, depreciation was met from taxes. In 1967, *"Railway Policy"* (Cmnd 3439, Appdx E): "Depreciation should continue to be assessed on a replacement cost basis". EEC Regulations in **1974** provided for a transfer of infrastructure renewals from capital to revenue account, representing nearly a third of BR capital spending, reducing *depreciation* provisions". (see also page 58).

[4] BBC radio on 27.2.03 credited Beeching - who joined BR six years later - with initiating 100 mph trains. In fact he opposed electrification (see also page 60) - the only form of traction then capable of 100 mph.

[5] See Chapter 11 for other examples of modernisation in freight operations.

[6] They were small due to tight clearances and curves in private sidings. Automatic brakes were damaged by tippling and moving equipment. Increases in size took years. Hauliers avoided clearance problems - by unloading in the street.

Main line electrification was planned of the east coast: Kings Cross-Leeds/York, and west coast: Euston-Birmingham/Manchester/Liverpool. In addition, the current Liverpool Street-Shenfield extension to Southend and Chelmsford would be extended to Ipswich, including three branches. Some 250 miles would be electrified on the Southern Region to embrace Ramsgate, Dover, Folkestone and Hastings. Commuter lines would also be electrified from Liverpool Street to Enfield, Chingford, Hertford and Bishops Stortford; also from Kings Cross/Moorgate to Hitchin and Letchworth. Other routes would have steam hauled services progressively replaced by diesel - either loco hauled or diesel multiple units [DMUs]. There were 19,000 steam locos on BR in 1955.

Way and Works included a major programme of bridge renewals to catch up on deferrals from the war and since[7]. These were forecast to cost £20m - £360m at today's prices. At least half was for overbridges carrying heavier road traffic weights than envisaged when they were built. There was to be no contribution from the Highways Budget - as there clearly should have been - and as was recommended by Government's own independent inquiry in 1930. (see page 8). Many sections of line had speed restrictions imposed as a consequence of Government's direction[7]. Faster trains and the heavier axle weights of electric and diesel locos required stronger track, maintained to high standards. There was to be extensive replacement of semaphore signals by colour light signals - many of which would be operated automatically by the passage of trains. Power operation of points and signals required fewer signal boxes - and hence, staff. Power signal boxes [PSBs], with centralised control would cover wide areas. £20m was allocated for the Automatic Warning System [AWS].

The Plan did not mention a consequence of a reduction in signal boxes. Lineside equipment had to be designed and installed to detect hot-boxes - axle boxes on rolling stock becoming overheated - a task hitherto dependent on the vigilance of staff in manual boxes. It did not plan modernisation of level crossings, which could not take place until Government abandoned laws on crossing protection, so that BR could adopt European practice that pre-dated the war. In the UK, it was assumed that our motorists and pedestrians were so stupid that they would be at risk, if BR adopted light controlled crossings that were no different to those on roads. The law changed in 1957.

In January, the MoT was satisfied the plan was sound. The DoT noted that the cost of steam locos was £20,25,000; compared to £80,000 for a diesel. The BTC was told that the Chancellor "made it clear in the House on February 3rd, that he expected to be consulted on the exact nature and timing of major items. The MoT notes that the BTC Chairman will brief him quarterly. In July, the MoT wrote personally to the Chancellor in reference to pressure to retard the modernisation plan, that he was unable to help. There was no record of the Chancellor's request in the file. (PRO: MT124/46).

On 21st January 1955, the Cabinet "was cautious, railway's future was doubtful, roads and aircraft would take over much traffic. On the other hand, it was pointed out that railways had been starved of capital for many years". (Cabinet Minutes). Despite these doubts, they were not slow to use it to prop up ailing private sector companies, (see page 59). The Plan contained elements that did not produce an adequate return, but this occurs in industry, as top executives from blue chip companies informed Government's Radcliffe Inquiry in 1960. (Lords Record Office: HMSO Pub - NP Reel 2641).

The Chancellor expressed admiration for the practical manner in which the plan has been worked out and set before us. We have no intention to subsidise the plan. (Modern Transport 12.2.55).

In February, the BTC informed the Federation of British Industry of the workload facing industry. The "Plan" was widely seen as beneficial to UK industry, in terms of regeneration of production and a shop window for exports; UK suppliers having long complained of a lack of opportunity to prove products in the UK market. (BTC Minutes). In July 1960, British Insulated Callenders Cables advertised: "The modernisation of BR has given manufacturers valuable experience in up to date forms of traction and is assisting them to secure export orders in the face of intensive competition". Regrettably, industry was not up to the task. (see pages 157-161). "Progress - and hence the delay - of the 1955 Modernisation Plan is largely in the hands of contractors". (BTC Minutes, December 1956).

---

[7] Work on track & bridges was deferred by Government direction (see pages 52,55). BR had to make-do-and-mend.

In December 1956, Sir Reginald Wilson[8], member of the Commission, who had already signed off to the Plan - having written the Introduction and parts dealing with traffic forecasts and finances - proposed that top priority be given to modernising freight, and bottom priority to suburban electric services. (BTC Minutes, 13.12.56). This would have gone down like a lead balloon in Whitehall, and its thousands of commuting civil servants. Ministers, who denationalised road haulage in 1953, and had secretly agreed that they be given every opportunity to abstract traffic from rail - facilitated by refusing concurrent freedom to BR (see page 28) - would not have accepted that tactic for one minute.

"The operation by more economic means or elimination of unremunerative passenger services is an essential feature of the Plan. The bus, requiring no special track is superior to rail in convenience and cheapness in thinly populated areas". (Cmd 9880: 1956 "Proposals for Railways", Para 50).

Hindsight critics have pointed to parts of the Plan that were of limited value, and for the return on the Plan. Government required the **BTC** to break even. To please the electorate, BTC's subsidiary, **BR** was not even required to do that, (see page 171). BR was criticised retrospectively for building marshalling yards. There were no prophecies from politicians[9], industry or media of industrial collapse or development of mega power stations. Indeed, in 1957, Ministry and industry had forecast increasing traffic. (see page 115). BR would have been damned had it said that they would not modernise freight wagons, handling, etc., on the grounds that industrial traffic would disappear.

The provision of a flyover at Bletchley has been retrospectively criticised - but BR was not warned that freight - the prime reason for the flyover - would decline as a consequence of industrial collapse. Its low use factor has caused much comment. What no one can assess is how many collisions may have been avoided, lives saved and delays avoided by this flyover. The cancellation of a flyover at Colwich near Stafford led to at least one collision and fatality in 1986. (see pages 62,188).

Contemporary opinion on the Plan was favourable:
"The Plan for the modernisation of railways is carefully thought out". (Economist 29.1.55). "Railways are not obsolete, and there is no possibility of a major part of traffic being transferred to roads. The forecast return of £85m on new investment looks adequate. The return is calculated on merely technical grounds, and allows nothing for the psychological effect on travellers, which should mean more traffic. For the most part, this is a list of things which should have been put in hand long ago. Government influence on railways and their capital programme has been so far reaching in many ways for years, that they can scarcely avoid the lion's share of responsibility. Government should guarantee the cost[10]. There is no question of the major part of the railways becoming superfluous. There is no possibility of the major part of traffic being transferred to roads within a few decades. The Plan will be funded by £800m from external *borrowing* and £400m from the Depreciation Fund". (Times 25.1.55).
"If BR management is given freedom, responsibility and tolerance, then the modernisation plan will be as wise as all the other stakes in the future voted by private business capital in Great Britain". (BTC Review, April 1955: Prof. L.L. Waters, Indiana University).

The MoT admitted that the BTC "inherited the position in which they find themselves. For 30 years railways have been unable to undertake modernisation, or keep up an adequate programme of replacement owing to the challenge of road transport[11]. During the war it was impossible[12] to provide resources for maintenance except to the very minimum extent .... increased strain of heavy

---

[8] An obituary said he was a lone outsider trying to put BR on an even keel, against massed opposition of career railway managers, and that he called for closures. *"The Railway Closure Controversy"* reveals that Blee - a career manager had initiated the programme. Wilson was one of 13 "outsiders" on the 15 strong Commission.

[9] The Treasury "do not pretend to be able to forecast the level of economy from year to year". (PRO: MT115/279)

[10] NB - "guarantee loans" - not pay for modernisation.

[11] BR could have fought that challenge, but Government policies prevented them from doing so.

[12] He should have said that it was politically expedient.

war traffic [and] emerged from the war with equipment out of date and all of it run down. It will take time to overtake decades of under-investment. Since the war, Governments were forced[13] seriously to restrict investment in railways". (White Paper "Proposals for Railways" 1956, Page 4).

"Progress of Modernisation is in contractors' hands". (BTC Minute December 1956). In 1957, the BTC stated: "Modern locos are heavier and have smaller wheels requiring improved track design. A contribution to containing inflation has been restriction on investment, which has damaged railways' commercial position. Here again, railway transport and roads, but not road vehicles, have since the war borne the brunt of Government restrictions imposed because of shortage of resources and materials, particularly steel". (BTC 1957 Report, Pages 3,50). *The cost of improved track was overlooked by critics who argued that dieselisation should have started in 1949, when steel supplies were inadequate, and Government blocked restoration of track even to pre-war standards.*

In 1957, it became apparent that industry was failing to produce locos and other assets required to meet the modernisation programme. "The programme of 782 locos is in excess of the total UK productive capacity". (PRO: AN85/11). The basis of allocation of new resources to different Regions was not equal, hence performance in some Regions would improve more quickly than others. The types of locos which were bought from the private sector were, in effect, what was available and were not as powerful as needed. The largest type was less powerful than a class 8 steam loco". (BTC minutes, 10.7.58). In July 1960, the Cabinet debated assisting the ailing North British Locomotive Company: "The Company employs 3,300, under not very effective management. It has lost a great deal of money in switching production from steam to diesel. Loans were made from Government Development Areas Committee: £1.75m; Clydesdale Bank: £1.5m, and General Electric Company: £0.5m to keep the company afloat". The Cabinet considered proposals to tell the company to reduce their tender by 8-10% to match lower tenders so they may get the contract! Referring to impending unemployment, the Scottish Secretary advocated BTC being given capital to buy more expensive North British locos[14]. (PRO: CAB). The Cabinet rejected all options, but it is revealing that they considered action that would have increased BR losses to support an ailing private sector company.

At a review meeting, the DoT thought BR coal forecasts were high, but the BTC said they were in the bottom range of Ministry statistics quoted in a recent debate, and that some unremunerative services had economic benefits to the community, not reflected in Accounts. (PRO: MT115/279).

"The Government debated a White Paper - the Reappraisal of the Modernisation Plan, (Cmnd 813), which stated that the shortfall was due to circumstances outside BTC control. The pace of the Plan was speeded up - *but not for long.* "The Reappraisal drew attention to the limitations caused by raising capital solely by means of Fixed Interest Loans". (BTC 1959 Report, Page 4). "Government slowed Modernisation down. The Select Committee said that the Plan is a whole and neither physical benefits nor financial results can be judged until all has been completed". (BTC 1960 Report, Pages 3,23). "Costs rose £400m due to higher costs. The BTC bid for capital was £243m in 1960, £247m in 1961, both cut to £220m, of which the BR share was to be pro rata". (PRO: MT115/279)

The MoT's Special Advisory Group [Stedeford Committee] reported to him in strict secrecy in 1960-61. Their Report and Papers were not released until 1991. The Report covered, inter alia, the Modernisation Plan, the forecast return of which had been approved by Government. They were impressed by the thorough and detailed technical investigation, but had doubts about the adequacy of the financial grounds. They concluded that much of the investment money being spent was "repairing obsolescence of the past 20-50 years", which in the view of Dr. Beeching [member of the Group, not then BR Chairman] had to be spent. Group members understood that the BTC was motivated by the statutory requirement with "*due regard to efficiency, economy and safety of operation and to the needs of the public, agriculture, commerce and industry*", i.e. of adequacy of service rather than what was profitable. In a letter to the MoT enclosing recommendations they said

---

[13] As Government did not act likewise on road transport (see pages 54,55), they could not claim it was forced.

[14] It would, almost certainly, have been an interest bearing loan.

that their Report "will not be given to the BTC". This was odd, if the BTC was, in any way, at fault. However, since the Tory Government had approved the Plan, any report critical of the Plan, was critical of them. The MoT told the Group that the Plan "was an assessment of the best kind of railway which could be provided, no account was taken of commercial outturn, but the Government had nevertheless approved the Plan and had confirmed in a White Paper that the proposals were commercially sound". He said "assessments were made 5-10 years ago, since when conditions and prospects for the future had changed considerably". (PRO: MT132/32).

The Group said: "It was the policy of former railway companies, continued by the BTC not to depreciate some assets, but to charge to revenue as and when it occurred. Many assets, following former railway practice, have never been depreciated". They listed "assets which should continue not to be subject to depreciation". They stated that the return on the Euston-Manchester-Liverpool electrification was less than could be gained from diesels. This took no account of delivery times, which would have delayed modernisation, nor the superior acceleration of electric locos with the same nominal hp rating. When the Plan was launched, available electric locos ran at 100mph, diesels were limited to 90mph. It took no account of the increased traffic - the "sparks" effect. BR needed to compare the benefits of alternative forms of traction - and that could not be done on a desk - it had to be done on the ground. The Group's recommendations reduced investment, delayed modernisation, causing retention of Victorian signal boxes, and cancellation of several projects, including a flyover at Colwich Junction, south of Stafford, which would have prevented at least one major collision - in 1986 - and reduced delays. The Group criticised the "value of electric traction for coal traffic, because its speed was of no benefit" - despite the fact that it had been in use on the most demanding gradients in the UK across the Pennines for six years. There, two electric locos - one front and one rear to prevent a runaway on a rising gradient - moved what had required four steam locos. Electric locos could do one thing that diesels could not do. They could control unbraked wagons down a 1 in 39 gradient by using rheostatic and regenerative braking, effectively pumping power *back* into the overhead line. When diesel locos began to haul freight, they soon lost control on falling gradients and BR had to introduce brake tenders - a wagon weighted with concrete. Ignoring this, and higher electric speeds, the Group calculated rates of return as diesel: 13.2%, electric: 10.8%. Electrification of the West Coast line produced a 65% increase in passengers, 50% in revenue. (BRB 1966 Report, Page 3). Ten years later, HSTs had up to 15-33% traffic increase on other routes, (see page 74).. Clearly, 1960s diesels, lacking the speed, would not have produced as much. *Subsequent experience showed that diesel locos were, initially, less reliable.*

Evidence to the Group reveals: "in 1951, BR gave six months notice to wagon repairers to cease placing wagons with them, all would be repaired by BR workshops to cut costs. Repairers described BR policy of building new bigger coal wagons "as over wagonning, leading to the scrapping of thousands of wooden bodied wagons". They appealed to Government and BR withdrew the notice. *"Powerful interests"* *at work again* - (see page 20). It is revealing that replacing 19th century design wagons by steel wagons of $33^{1}/_{3}$-100% higher capacity was seen in such a light. If this was the philosophy of UK industry, little wonder they lost a world lead in so many fields[15]. (see Table 10).

In May 1960, the MoT told the Group that he expected increased expenditure on an enlarged road programme which would affect rail traffic prospects and slow down investment. Despite this, BTC minutes in July state that the same MoT urged the BTC to "spend up to its allocation". Government approved resumption of Euston-Manchester-Liverpool electrification. (BRB 1961 Report, Page 6).

In March 1961, a Select Committee reported: "The BTC are asked to forecast investment for three years ahead - but budgets beyond the first year were not given approval, and the BTC has been unable to forward plan [on a basis] that future requirements will be met." It was a waste of money for Government to ask for plans, and neither approve nor reject them. (see page 72 re 20 year plans).

---

[15] "British wagon builders will not get foreign orders when all they show in their shop window, are their present wretched little trucks". (Reader's letter, *Modern Transport*, 22.6.46).

Financing Modernisation

Despite the evidence of the White Paper, Hansard, BTC Reports and legislation, it has been claimed that the 1955 Plan was financed by Government. One such[16] referred to an MoT file (PRO, MT124/177), said to mention a £250m Grant towards modernisation. Examination of the file - which relates to the closure of M&GN lines in East Anglia - reveals two references to this sum. One is in a memo from a Private Secretary to his Minister who was to open a fete in 1958 in his constituency and expected criticism of closure plans. The Secretary refers to a **loan** of £250m to tide BR over the years before the modernisation could pay off. The second reference was of an answer by Mr Tait, a senior BR executive at the closure hearings: "£250m is the amount Parliament has authorised BR to **borrow** in respect of subsequent [revenue] deficiencies". The Transport [Railway] Finances Act, 1957, authorised borrowing £250m to meet revenue deficits, that would arise due to the MoT uniquely freezing fares and charges that were well below inflation. (see pages 171-174,179).

Colin Boocock wrote in "*Spotlight on BR*": "The 1955 Modernisation Plan was supported by the Conservatives with hard cash: £1240m to be spent over 15 years". Christian Woolmar wrote in "*Broken Rails*": Professor Evans referred to the generous funding of the 1955 Modernisation Plan.

The Tory Government might have decided to finance modernisation, given a belated show of remorse for the financial mess to which they had almost single-handedly[17] reduced railways: by rejecting the "Square Deal", their inept wartime pricing, the £1 bn skimmed out of railways (see page 18) of which they should have refunded, at least, 20% as Excess Profits Tax, as applied to other industry. They might have done so to redress the consequences of leaving BR to operate for ten post-war years with a rag bag of assets, whilst competitors were given the most incredible licence to modernise with their excessive wartime profits. They might have done so to compensate for selling ex-military vehicles at knock down prices to road operators whilst overpricing BR for wagons and track which otherwise had only scrap value, (see page 12). BR managers had not acquiesced to the exorbitant cost of these "assets", and certainly did not wish to own the antiquated fleet of private owner wagons. (see page 50). Government might have funded modernisation to give industry a useful shot in the arm, as they were losing so much business to foreign industry. They didn't.

A minister stated: "Only £200m of modernisation is on track over 15 years, compared to £147m on roads over 4 years. BR money is a repayable loan. (Lords Hansard 2.3.55 vol. 191 cols. 655-720).

Modernisation was to be funded by the issue of British Transport Loan Stock. Government confirmed this in Parliament. Later, it inserted Sec 42 into the 1956 Finance Act which stipulated that, instead of issuing Loan Stock on the market, the MoT would make loans to the BTC for the purpose of BR investment. These loans were subject to interest and were to be repaid over 25 years. Finance Chapters of the BTC Annual Report & Accounts for 1956-62 clearly confirm this formula and set out the loans, interest paid and repayments. Government loaned £729m, and £219m came from depreciation funds and scrap sales. By 1963, when the Government muddied the waters by breaking up the BTC and reconstructing the capital, interest of £117m had been paid on the Government loan, and £131m of the advances had been repaid. These loans should not be confused with those advanced to the BTC by the MoT in pursuit of its ridiculous policy of holding fares below inflation. (see pages 171-174). The provisions of the [Finance] Act do not absolve the BTC of responsibility for the financial success of the Plan. (BTC 1956 Report, Page 10).

BR had to justify investment by economies, reduced assets or new revenue. Government missed an opportunity to use cost/benefit criteria, as for road improvements, to justify electrifying the North Wales Coast, which BR could not justify but local authorities desired to have. It would have cost less than the Conway estuary tunnel, which was a small part of the upgrading of the A55.

---

[16] In a letter to the author.

[17] Labour Party's 1947 Transport Act was the final straw in the ruin of rail finances by withholding the right to match costs to inflation and creating the circus of a dilatory Court of Law to decide fares & charges - delaying increases by over 12 years (see Appendix B), and a slow procedure to close rural lines facing motor, rather than horse transport.

Revision of the 1955 Plan

As a result of the secret Stedeford Committee Report (see page 59), the Plan was abridged by Ministerial restriction on what BR may borrow to finance it. Deletions included:-

- Electrification of lines from Birmingham to Lichfield and Rugeley, of the Nuneaton-Coventry-Leamington line and the Coventry Avoiding line - all parts of the West Coast scheme.
- The Colwich flyover. There were some costly consequences. (see page 58).
- Planned centralisation of signalling Nuneaton-Stafford-Crewe did not take place. Some twenty existing signal boxes had to be retained on the electrified and re-signalled West Coast route, albeit, signals controlled from them were replaced by modern colour lights.

Local authorities also blocked BR modernisation plans: -

- The City of London Court of Common Council refused permission for the erection of an office block over Fenchurch Street station on the grounds that "it was zoned for railway operations, and that offices in that zone would be contrary to policy to restrict office development in the central zone to sites already zoned for office development". (Modern Transport, 23.7.60, Page 10)
- An office block which would have made Euston station scheme self financing and reduced cross London travel was ruled out after months of argument by Camden Borough who sanctioned the huge Euston Centre office development scheme a stone's throw away". (BRB 1968 Report, Page 3).

The plan was further abridged by UK industry limitations:

- The plan to fit all wagons with automatic brakes was cancelled, when brake equipment was damaged by industrial wagon tipplers and capstans. As a result, freight train sizes were reduced and brake tenders were built as diesel locos had insufficient braking capabilities on unbraked wagons.
- Electrification of the east coast and GN suburban lines were cancelled due to the unacceptable time scale for delivery of materials and the shortage of specialised contractors.

There were two aspects crucially affecting the viability of modernisation to which the Stedeford Committee had drawn attention, which the MoT steadfastly ignored - and was able to ignore because only *he* knew of their unpublished recommendations: that closures should be expedited and that the control of fares which, they pointed out, were well below inflation, should be abandoned.

Both the MoT and local authorities blocked one aspect of the Plan - closures - which, by definition was accepted, because the Plan was approved by Government and warmly accepted in the country. His White Paper [Cmd 9880: 1956 "Proposals for Railways", Para 50]. mentioned it:

"The operation by more economic means or elimination of unremunerative passenger services is an essential feature of the Modernisation Plan. The bus, requiring no special track is clearly superior to rail in convenience and cheapness in thinly populated areas".

Politicians "have always been in favour of closing unremunerative lines ..... in other people's constituencies". (Hansard vol. 547, col. 711). Neither Government nor local authority was prepared to pay to keep a line open. In contrast, huge sums were paid to lawyers to represent local authorities objecting to closures. Not one of the many that claimed that branch lines could be made profitable, offered to take a line over and prove it! (see "*The Railway Closure Controversy*"). Worse, Ministers and MPs weakly collaborated with them to coerce BR into keeping loss making lines.

Whilst the Plan made no specific mention of the need to increase fares, not only to catch up on inflation, but to pay more for an improved service, it is likely that this was a deliberate ploy to avoid political objections to the Plan. It must have been obvious to any thinking mind that it was inevitable and just. Certainly Ministers and Chancellors who were weighing such matters on the wider scale, could have been in no doubt. Doubtless, to avoid raising expectations, the Plan made no mention of wage increases that would be inevitable against the background of non-stop leapfrogging in the industrial sector. However, whilst wage *rates* were bound to increase, modernisation would improve productivity, hence the *total* wages bill could be contained or even fall. The forecast Return on the investment did not cover this. Given an unwillingness of Government to pay for Modernisation from its ill-gotten wartime gains, there was only one other source - the one which applied in the private sector - that prices would rise to cover costs. Hence, the action of the MoT in

1956 to freeze *only* railway charges (see pages 171-174) - pace setting inflationary increases in the private sector were untouched - is both irresponsible and incomprehensible. This was probably the most important opportunity missed to enable railways to achieve viability.

The Plan's Achievements

Modernisation carried out under the Plan, scheduled to be completed in 15 years - by 1969 - included main line and commuter electrification, diesel traction for other areas, modern colour light signalling: automatic, semi-automatic and controlled, new power signal boxes [PSBs] covering extended areas, station reconstruction, track machines, continuous welded track, new rolling stock, rebuilt bridges - including hundreds to create clearance for overhead electric wires, flyovers, tunnels, modern telecomms and new marshalling yards. It also included rationalisation of assets, such as minor modernisation of some signal boxes to enable them to take over the role of adjoining boxes. BTC/BRB Annual Reports carried brief progress reports. The aspects which gained most public attention were traction, rolling stock and stations. The aspects that were really the most important, and upon which all other aspects were conditional were the remarkable steps forward in track and signalling modernisation. Without track improvements, the weight of electric and diesel locos was intolerable, and without advanced signalling, higher speeds were not possible.

Track

The BTC had stated in 1957, that "the operation at high speeds of diesel and electric locos with their greater weight and smaller wheel diameter gives rise to a new problem in track design". At the end of the 15 year Plan period, in 1969, a total of 4,300 track miles of CWR [continuous welded rail], had been laid. CWR was essential for improving the quality of ride. The Plan had included the expansion of the use of track maintenance machines. (see page 85). At this stage, track tamped mechanically had risen to 20,000 miles pa, with over 12,500 miles being mechanically lined. One of several outstanding bridge reconstructions was that, in 1963, of Grosvenor Road railway bridge - one of the busiest in the world - which carried all traffic from Victoria over nine electric tracks, which was replaced and strengthened to take ten tracks. Not less than seven tracks were in use during the work. Line speed was lifted to 100 mph on several routes from 1964 onwards. Experimental point heaters were first introduced at York, Darlington and Newcastle in 1961. They gave reliable service at further locations. In 1963; 2,084 had been installed and a further 1,904 were planned. Following the successful use of point heaters during the very severe weather in early 1963, the use of these appliances was extended and by the end of 1964, 4,010 sets had been installed.

Signalling

New multiple aspect [MAS] signals, which were essential for high speeds, were installed on 7,000 track miles, and the Automatic Warning System [AWS] on 3,157 miles. On other main line and commuter routes, hundreds of signalboxes, were modernised by the installation of power controlled signals. The application of electric power to control signals enabled many boxes to be closed and their role transferred to another box. The system of mechanical control limited the area which could be controlled because of the physical effort required to operate points. Many boxes existed to increase line capacity by reducing the length of a section - MAS overcame that problem. Many boxes were located at level crossings, which were protected by manually operated gates in accordance with Britain's outdated laws. Remote control was not feasible without a change in the law. That change eventually enabled BR to adopt modern systems and replace them with consequential economies. (see page 66). On nationalisation, there were 10,300 signalboxes. By 1955, there were 9,800. By the end of this stage of modernisation, the number was under 4,700, including PSBs. Some closed due to branch line closures. Some were closed by Operating Department schemes that replaced signal boxes by intermediate block signals to preserve the headway required for train running. Some were replaced by unmanned ground frames giving access to sidings. These were released remotely from a signal box, allowing a guard or other person to operate the frame's levers. Most were displaced by PSBs covering large areas. Among references to new PSBs, was one opened in Glasgow in 1961 which was the largest in the world; whilst those covering long routes included the 190 mile west coast route: Euston, Willesden, Watford, Bletchley, Rugby, Nuneaton, Birmingham, Walsall, Wolverhampton, Stoke-on-Trent; a 242 mile route: Gloucester, Birmingham, Walsall, Saltley, Trent and Derby; and the Paddington-Swindon route. By 1969, there were over 100 PSBs on BR. Some replaced as many as 30 signal boxes, with huge staff savings and marked improvement in train speeds.

Col. D. McMullen - Chief Railway Inspector [HMRI] to the MoT - told an Engineers conference: I note that the soundness of the signalling system from the early days has held up modernisation of signalling and I suppose that much of the responsibility for this lies with my predecessors in the Railway Inspectorate. The BR 3/4 aspect colour light system is, in my view, as good as, or better than any other system in the world. (Developments in Railway Traffic Engineering, Page 23).

Locos

By 1968, all steam operation - except BR's narrow gauge Vale of Rheidol Railway (see page 137) had ceased - 19,000 steam locos had been replaced by 328 electric, 4,183 diesel locos and by EMUs and DMUs. Regrettably, diesel locos, in particular, did not enjoy the reliability that was promised and was essential for punctuality and viability - and for the return on modernisation investment.

Electrification

The plan to electrify the west coast line from Euston was curtailed. (see page 62). The first stage: Crewe-Stafford, was implemented in 1960, then extended to Rugby-Manchester/Liverpool, and finally completed in March 1967. Approximately 200 electric locos and 95 EMUs were delivered for the project. Services were completely recast based on faster schedules, more reliable locos, and improved track layouts. Simultaneous changes to other services via Birmingham were made to improve connections. Passengers increased by 65%. These benefits, operational economies and increased income would have arisen a year earlier, had not the MoT directed a slow-down in 1960.

In the south, Kent Coast electrification had a full electric service from June 1962 - a total of 132 route miles. Authority was given in 1963 to replace the 39 existing six-car EMUs on London-Brighton-Eastbourne services with 54 new four-car units. In 1964, the MoT authorised extension of the Southern Region 3rd rail system by 90 miles to Bournemouth & Southampton. It was completed in 1967. Trains were lengthened from 8-10 cars to 12, composed of three units of four-cars.

In Scotland, electric services were in service on 27 route miles south of the Clyde from May 1962. The MoT authorised extension of Glasgow suburban electric service to Wemyss Bay in 1964: 37 miles. Nineteen three-car EMU were acquired for the new service. It was completed in 1967.

A full electric service was introduced on the LT&S in 1962. Units from this line had to be loaned earlier to other routes where EMU design defects required manufacturers' action. (see pages 158-159). Electrification of the LT&S was completed in June 1963. More modern high speed main line EMU began in 1963 on Liverpool Street-Clacton/Frinton/Walton, with a full accelerated service.

By the end of the 15 year period, over 2,000 route miles were equipped for electric traction, compared to 980 in 1955. Action was taken to improve and simplify existing electrification equipment. In 1968, BR reported that savings of £400 per track mile were likely from the development of a simple catenary system in place of a compound system hitherto used.

Diesel traction

The new Inter City Glasgow-Edinburgh diesel scheme, in 1957, was the first on BR. Modern inter-city DMUs were introduced on Cardiff-Birmingham-Derby, and Cardiff-Plymouth. services in 1961, and other inter-city services followed. By 1962, 1,673 diesel locos were in service of a total of 2,648 authorised. The fifth and last of the standard diesel loco types - Type 1, 650 hp - was delivered in 1964, 56 had been ordered.

By the end of the 15 year period, on non-electrified routes, all passenger services were either new DMUs or new diesel locos hauling mostly new coaches. (see page 65). From 1961, the East Coast route - on which electrification had been planned, but for which resources were not available, was provided instead with the most powerful diesel locos available in the UK - the English Electric

3,300 hp Deltic. Delivery took 3-4 years. Traffic increased and, although they experienced a series of failures, (see pages 159,160), on the whole, it proved successful until availability declined.

300 type 4 locos were equipped with air brakes and some with slow speed control which enabled a driver to set an MGR train to move at $^1/_2$ mph whilst loading or unloading - the design speed for use of bunker equipment. New diesel depots were commissioned at Burton, Cardiff, Derby, Margam, Millerhill, Paddington, Reading, Tinsley, Toton, Wellingborough. New under-floor wheel lathes at some depots eliminated the need to move locos to main works for tyre turning.

Rolling stock

At the start of 1955, there were 37,215 loco hauled coaches, 70 DMUs and 4,632 EMUs. After 15 years, the fleet had been reduced to 7,888 coaches, 3,649 DMUs and 7,332 EMUs - a 55% reduction. Passenger miles fell by only 7% in the same period. The DMUs had nearly all been built since 1955, as had 87% of the coaches and 57% of the EMUs. In 1962, BR reported that trials of its new B4 bogie for passenger coaches were satisfactory. It is lighter, gives a better ride than its predecessor, and is produced at a third of the cost. During the period, 206,000 wagons were built.

Stations

Many passenger stations were reconstructed. A scheme to combine Leeds City and Central stations was approved by the MoT in 1963. At 22 Inter City stations, manual ticket methods were replaced, in 1967, by new equipment which records transactions on audit rolls and magnetic tape for quicker management information. Work began on improvements to 102 stations in 1964.

Yards

In 1963, Tees [Newport] and Tyne yards opened, Healey Mills was partly open, Millerhill was fully open. Kingmoor [Carlisle] opened. Bescot Up was operational.

Telecomms

In 1963, a fully electronic teleprinter system - the first commercial system of its kind by any railway in the world was brought into use. Modern auto/manual telephone exchanges embracing extension trunk dialling [ETD] - equivalent to STD facilities being introduced about the same time for the UK public telephone system - opened in 1963, at ten locations. Automatic train reporting was provided on the LT&S to the Control Office - this gave Control instantaneous reports of the location of trains. More new telephone exchanges opened in 1967.

The scale of engineering involved cannot be comprehended by anyone outside BR[18]. Each Operating District on the west coast route, appointed a junior manager to a modernisation post, and I was selected for the Rugby District - 145 route miles, of which 123 were on the route being electrified. The task was to identify non-essential infrastructure and tracks for which electric traction was not essential (see page 146), and organise conflicting work on track, signalling, lifting or rebuilding bridges, building flyovers and erecting overhead equipment - all on an unprecedented scale. So much had to be done, that it could not be confined to weekends, but much took place on weekdays - with possessions and "between trains". The volume of weekday work eclipsed that normally carried out on weekends for normal track renewals. Weekend work was so complex, involving dozens of engineers' trains moving in and out of possessions, that careful planning and site supervision was needed to avoid admitting a train, out of sequence, and to arrange traincrew relief to avoid men working unduly long hours. This was exacerbated by crews having moved location - with the progress of work - to where limited road access and rural communication problems did not help. Engineers' trains were required both for taking materials onto site and for removal of debris - including waste ballast, masonry etc. from demolished buildings and rebuilt bridges - for disposal on BR waste tips. During the work, train services were maintained or re-routed. Close supervision of contract labour was vital, to avoid lines being wrongly declared safe to resume traffic and avoid

---

[18] The Chunnel & motorways are not in the same league, being built on virgin ground. The new boys have abandoned BR practice and close lines completely, with greater disruption to trains. It has not ended fatalities among track staff.

loss of life of those unused to working "between trains". The scale of work created heavy demands for traincrew, and required ingenuity to cover all engineers' trains. Solutions were found by those faced with the task. These included using freight trains to drop materials near to a site to avoid engineers' trains returning to depot, and using Inspectors, who were on site to maintain "safety of the line", to also take charge of trains without guards. (see page 146). In some cases we brought in men from lines not facing major works. Analogous situations in UK industry would have led to walkouts. Managers on other routes with major modernisation faced many problems.

"Too much BRB officers' time is taken up by the need to discuss in detail and justify individual projects with officers of the DoT. BRB feel strongly that whilst investment ceilings must conform to economic policy, the allocation of investment capital within the ceiling should be regarded as their own responsibility". (BRB 1969 Report, Page 12).

Level crossing modernisation

A change in legislation allowed BR to use level crossing systems prevalent in Europe from long before the war. Archaic laws blocked their use in the UK, until BR proposed that a joint BR/DoT team be sent to Europe and report on their suitability. The Report was favourable, but an Act of Parliament was required to enable them to be introduced, as an 1835 Act specified that gates must be provided. The ensuing 1957 Act did not prevent MPs from opposing modernisation.

It enabled replacement of manned by automatic half barrier crossings [AHBs], or later by other types, including remote control when UK industry began to develop new technology, such as CCTV. After some AHBs were installed, the MoT revised *his* requirements for their standards.

BR's first automatic half-barrier level crossings were brought into use at Uttoxeter and Millbrook. Lifting barriers replaced gates at five other crossings. (BTC 1961 Report, Page 29). At every location where a new system was planned, a site meeting took place, involving local authorities and others, at which the approval of the Ministry's Inspector of Railways was sought. In April 1964, MP George Brown supported objections by a council to the proposed installation of automatic half barriers. He called for full barriers, which required on site manpower to be retained. CCTV and remote control had not advanced sufficiently at the time. (PRO: MT114/413). This attitude was typical of politicians who claimed that BR costs - of which wages were 66% - should be reduced, but when the crunch came locally and affected local employment, the cry was to the barricades; not in my backyard; anywhere but here. Their claims that children would be at risk at a traffic light equipped level crossing with a half barrier, but not walking along or across roads with neither lights nor barriers was an analogy to which eyes and ears were firmly closed!

Due to undisciplined attitudes towards traffic signals[19], BR had to modify - at its own expense - many newly modernised crossings and install phones to provide for rare events. Some auto-barriers had to be converted to controlled crossings with CCTV, in case users, having disregarded lights, became trapped between barriers. A personally conducted test over an equivalent distance revealed that users could crawl and not be trapped, if lights began to flash *after* they began to cross. Similar safeguards were not imposed on road crossings, despite indiscipline towards road traffic lights being commonplace. Those claiming that crossing signals had failed, may have had difficulty convincing insurance companies. The changes destroyed the economic case for many locations.

By 1967 there were 202 AHBs, and nearly 200 gated crossings had been replaced by light controlled or open crossings. The MoT directed suspension of installation of AHBs in 1968. following an accident, which involved a police escorted large road transport load becoming stuck on Hixon level crossing in Staffordshire. It was struck by an express train with several fatalities. BR managers were surprised that no one with the load had taken action to warn trains. In 1969, he *again* revised standards - which his Department had specified at the outset in the 1950s, requiring

---

[19] Recently, the author saw a motorist try to overtake a car which had stopped at level crossing lights in Alsager [Cheshire]. The barrier came down on the roof of his car.

modifications to the 207 existing crossings - for which he paid not a penny. These add-on features would have cost less had the MoT decreed that they be installed at the start.

"Last year's Report referred to a Government Inquiry by Prof. Stott, on level crossing safety, which concluded they are safe, provided users observe correct procedures and found no evidence that equipment failure caused accidents. It suggested lower train speeds or converting some to half barriers. BR proposed the £24m cost be split between County Councils and BR". (CTCC 1987/8 Report, Page 10). Lower train speeds would not be needed if road users obeyed traffic signals.

Rural lines

BR inherited routes that would have closed in the 1920s or 1930s, but for Government policy, and the prospect of war, which was foreseen. BR had to face public hearings to justify the obvious - that many such lines were hopelessly uneconomic, and that no external funding was being offered.

The 1955 Modernisation Plan envisaged a reduction in slow and stopping services, elimination of some passenger services and the conversion of some stations into halts. By 1969, the BTC's Plan expected BR to "escape from the unsound and unjustifiable position of being obliged to retain un-remunerative services that have to be subsidised by fares receipts from express and other services".

Opponents of closures claimed that spending infinite amounts of capital would make loss making rural routes profitable. "Plans" claiming to prove the economics of their arguments and other anti-closure theories were demolished in "*The Railway Closure Controversy*". Some argued[20] that branch lines needed modernising first! No business would invest capital except where there was good demand and a good return. None would have invested in lines whose historic role was to block access to areas of near monopoly or poach traffic from other lines, but remained unprofitable in the heyday of railways. BR would have been savaged had it invested in the Somerset & Dorset line, M&GN or the like, rather than Euston-Manchester-Liverpool and main lines for which there was insufficient capital to replace scores of Victorian signal boxes on the West Coast line by a couple of PSBs, albeit they were converted to control multiple aspect signalling instead of oil lit signals.

"The Eastern Region said had all services been diesel operated, *direct* costs would have been covered by revenue, but there would have been no significant contribution to the cost of terminals, track, signalling and administration. It was a start". (Henshaw, Page 86). These were 45% of total costs. (BRB 1963 Report, Table 4A). It was a very *discouraging* start. Who would cover the rest until revenue did, should that ever occur? There were no reserves, as BR had not been allowed to create any. (BTC 1950 Report, Page 39). Any industry would have regarded it as a start - to bankruptcy!

"Much of the increase in passengers from dieselisation is in populous areas. To continue to operate services, the direct costs of which, even using diesels, exceeds receipts by a large margin, is to waste resources on a scale neither the BTC nor the country can afford". (BTC 1955 Report, Page 5). In 1956, the BTC pointed out that: "the CTCC and TUCCs accepted DMUs would not have turned loss into profit on lines already closed". (BTC 1956 Report, Page 9).

"There are services which however well modernised, will never pay in any circumstances. There is a tendency to think that all services can and should be dieselised or electrified forthwith, but the magnitude of capital cost is not generally realised". (CTCC[21] 1957 Report, Page 6). "Experience has shown that certain services cannot cover their direct costs even when operated by diesels". (BTC 1957 Report, Page 68). The response of the public to improved DMU services has not been sufficient to turn loss making services into profitable ones. (BTC 1961 Report, Page 77). This was insufficient proof for objectors who wanted *their* local under-utilised lines to be kept on standby for bad winters and car breakdowns, modernised and under-priced into the bargain. Where other industry would try new equipment once, and abandon it immediately when it did not improve profits - much less

---

[20] Branch Line Re-invigoration Society - see "*The Railway Closure Controversy*", Page 222
[21] Critics, who were joyous when CTCC support of a TUCC recommendation kept a loss making line open, claimed that they were acting under BR influence if they advocated closures! (e.g. Henshaw, Pages 84,88)

merely reduce losses which critics envisaged - BR had to be seen to be trying it out at 50 similar locations, and even then fireside experts would find fault. County Councils said an attempt should be made to make the Somerset & Dorset line profitable, by putting on diesels to see if it could be made economic. They offered no cash, and did not advise what should be done with the diesels if the line remained unprofitable. The manufacturers would not refund their cost. Is this how Councils make investment decisions? It is unnecessary to repeat the same experiment time after time after time in every rural area to gather data on the prospect of making a return on precious capital.

A favourite hobby horse was that loss making lines could be retained by using railbuses. An anonymous "expert" proposed a new type. An MP mentioned it in Parliament, but gave no details. His *one* page plan[22] contained no technical drawings and specified no weight. Another MP "had in mind an eight seater light diesel railcar". (Hansard, vol. 518, col. 1260). One driver to every eight passengers running on dedicated infrastructure could only be uneconomic. No road operator with such a vehicle could afford to pay for his own road.

In the Rural Transport debate (Hansard, vol. 547 cols. 699-779), another MP took a hypothetical ten mile line to prove the scope for railbuses. He claimed one would provide an hourly service. On that basis, the 1,535 miles - by then - closed, required 153 plus 27 for maintenance cover, *with all at one depot*, based on 85% availability forecast by manufacturers. The maintenance cover required would increase if they were spread over several depots. Critics proposed one at each branch terminus, which would require yet further units to cover short notice failure at such locations. A thirty year life was needed to get a return on rolling stock, giving a demand of six units pa. In the Debate, the MP claimed that they would cost less ordered in batches of six! There would be no mad rush from manufacturers, who would not regard six pa as a bulk order[23]. The advocates of railbuses did not back their theories by setting up companies to build and sell them on a sale or return basis.

In June 1960, the MoT said a railbus[24] cost £12,500. (Hansard vol. 590, col. 208). £2m was required for 180 units, plus interest on loans - money that would be at grave risk, as compared with spending it on main line stock. A typical scheme had revenue of £11,700, against movement costs of £14,470, but giving no contribution to cover infrastructure costs.

Provision would be needed on most routes for mail and parcels, as railbuses had no capacity for them. The theorists overlooked tail vans carrying mails, parcels, luggage in advance for independent schools and resorts, which could be hauled by standard diesel units, but not railbuses. They would have to be sent by road at extra cost and all rail infrastructure costs would fall on passengers.

Moving vehicles from branch lines to and from depots would create safety problems, as they could not be relied on to actuate track circuits. "The CTCC agreed light units as an alternative to closure were constrained by safety requirements". (BTC 1955 Report, Page 9). Experiments would be costly due to training men for a task that, if short lived, would increase losses. Contrary to popular belief, they could not be operated by one man, due to safety requirements imposed by MoT standards. A failed train on a running line, required simultaneous protection by two men. (PRO: AN85/47).

In 1958, the BTC - dominated by ex-civil servants - allowed themselves to be pressured into experimenting with railbuses, that proved financial failures. "All were withdrawn by 1968". (PRO: MT124/150). In 1954, the MoT wrote to an MP that [Sir Reginald] Wilson had suggested that light railways might be adopted as a solution to closure. In 1956, Wilson wrote to the MoT that "whilst there will still be pruning, it will not be fundamental in scale (PRO: MT113/5). MoT requirements do not permit one man operation. They experienced frequent withdrawal for works attention or local repairs. (Paper 19.5.60, PRO: AN85/52). "On three branches in 1959, it was found that lightweight units were too small for peak traffic. On another, there was so little traffic, it may have to be

---

[22] I found it in MT124/65 [PRO]. See "*The Railway Closure Controversy*", Appendix A7 for full details.

[23] Ford told the author that "mass production" of small diesel engines is a minimum of 300,000 pa. Mass production of lightweight railbuses was a childish flight of fancy. No company would have financed such a project, even in the hope of foreign sales. UK industry couldn't produce railcars cheaply enough to make them economic on branch lines.

[24] Railbuses cost three times as much as a road bus. (PRO: AN85/52 memo to BTC 19.5.60).

closed". (BTC 1959 Report, Page 28). Had Government been prepared to fund social experiments, it would have been a different matter. Clearly they were not, as they did nothing, until 1968, to contribute towards loss making lines, which the Minister directed must remain open.

In April 1978, a university lecturer submitted a plan to improve Cambrian line services that envisaged "doubling the service" - *his proposed train mileage was 50%, not 100%, more* - and "doubling passenger journeys" - *with no supporting evidence*. Nineteen trains were to be "re-timed beyond Shrewsbury or Wolverhampton". BR timed main *before* branch lines, for obvious reasons. There wasn't a single £ sign in his 24 page plan, hence, I had it costed. It required:

- £14m capital: £9.2m for signal boxes, rolling stock, locos and turntables for proposed steam locos; £4.8m to replace existing DMUs to improve reliability; requiring £3.5m to fund £14m capital.
- The plan required 85 extra staff - operating costs would rise by £0.95m pa.
- Revenue would have to rise by £4.45 pa [£3.5m + £0.95m] - *to hold losses at current levels* - nine times existing revenue! He envisaged 100% increase from *doubled passengers*, without fare rises, as he opposed "*continually increasing fares*" - trailing the RPI for 30 years! (see Appendix A)
- Track upgrading to allow bigger locos, coaching stock and higher speeds required even more cash.

He proposed a two year experiment - requiring £14m capital and £1.9m staff costs, to be recovered in **two years** - that could be implemented 'without much investment' in two months to '*demonstrate or disprove its' potential viability'*. Usually, unsolicited advisors were 100% confident, believing that BR refusals to fund their ideas denied their ultimate glory. He would use "*students at a low wage*" - a non runner. Students manning new signal boxes or driving extra trains was a risk BR would not take. Whom he would use outside vacations was not specified. He said that better stock and assets would not alone run trains punctually - it required 'benevolent heavenly protection' - *not least from tidal floods, road vehicles smashing crossing barriers or bridges and other external factors*. Unusually, he sent his plan to BR, not the media. After quoting the costs to him, we heard no more. These and other "plans" (see "*The Railway Closure Controversy*"), to which we had to reply, took eyes off the *real* ball: pursuing practical plans to improve services, revenue and productivity.

This line attracted another 'expert'. A teacher[25], in a letter in the Cambrian News in November 1983, urged BR to introduce radio signalling as if he had invented it. It was developed by BR at Derby, where I went with Eric Crosby, my Signalling Officer, two years before being aware of his existence, to examine its potential, which was evident to any BR Operating Manager. After considering several routes in the Region, I decided that, if it was approved by the MoT, it would be tried on the Cambrian line. He implied a lack of funds was holding it up, when we expected it to be self financing! It was mentioned in my letter to the Cambrian News, *two months prior to his letter.*

Dr. Joy, BR economist 1969-71, claimed in his book, (Page 17) that by 1968, branch line coaches were replaced twice. Before the 1955 Plan, they were allocated *fully depreciated* cast-off coaches from main lines to replace older coaches previously 'cascaded'. With the building of DMUs, some branches received new vehicles for the first time since before the War, some since they were opened! BR began in 1948 with 44,500 coaches, and by 1968, had built 24,600, scrapping 49,600 leaving a total of 19,500. (see BTC Annual Reports). His claim conveyed an impression that they were replaced twice with new coaches. These statistics prove that was not possible. Many lines closed without having had DMUs, e.g.: most of the 189 mile M&GN, closed 1959, had none; the 100 mile S&D, closed 1966, had none. His book was written from "an incomplete set of records". (Page 6).

Joy claimed that funds were squandered on branch lines in the 1950s.[26] (Joy, Page 44). He was confused by the purpose of newly built non corridor coaches, claiming firstly (Page 44), that they were for branch lines, and later (Page 52) that they were for commuters. They were for the latter, as they carried far more seated passengers than a similar length train of corridor stock.

---

[25] BR had *nothing* to learn from *his* profession, given the decline in educational standards, the decline in example to pupils & falling productivity of teachers compared to BR staff (see "*The Railway Closure Controversy*", Page 199).
[26] Up to 1959, the author worked on branches in eight counties - none had new assets. Dr. Joy joined BR in 1969

Modernisation, development and rationalisation[1] after 1955 attracted passengers, including ex-motorists, at main stations and through new Parkway stations[2] - the first was at Bristol in 1972.

The 1970s marked a second step in modernisation, with improved coach and wagon design, more electrification - notably on the West Coast, and further modernisation of signalling. However, the pace of modernisation was slower in this decade.

Among BR's significant achievements in modernising was the introduction of HSTs on the Great Western main line, East Coast main line, Midland main line and Cross Country. They were the fastest diesel powered trains in the world in the late 1970s and early 1980s, with average speeds better than the less intensively occupied Japanese Tokkaido line. BR also initiated extensive research by the world beating Derby Research Centre, non-existent since privatisation[3]. BR was more productive than any other major railway except Sweden, and operated with less public subsidy. Many world railways emulated BR innovations. (Alan Marshall in "Rail", December 1996).

The case for later electrification was not as strong as commonly believed. In 1964, a BRB Team remitted to check a scheme to extend electrification from Crewe to Scotland, found that economies from replacing steam by electric instead of by diesel would not fund fixed equipment. Comparing electric to steam in 1955 was justifiable as diesels were not then as reliable, but had improved by 1964. In comparison with diesel traction, a 30% increase in revenue was required - the prospect of which was subject to differing opinion, in view of external fares restraint. An improved service would justify higher fares, which were well below inflation, (see Appendix A). Hindsight critics do not acknowledge this, but are quick to point out that Plans ignored inflation driven wage increases. Experience shows that electric traction has many benefits and increases revenue. It also boosts private property values. Henry Johnson[4], General Manager of the London Midland Region put his weight behind the scheme, which was modified to increase the return, and went ahead. London-Glasgow electrified services came into operation in May 1974, and produced a 50% increase in business.

In 1970, BR launched a national real time computer - TOPS - to control wagons. It exposed industrial inefficiency in the detention and use of wagons, and resolved the problem of misleading despatch dates[5]. (see page 119). In 1979, Reg Owens, a computer expert on my staff, drew attention to a potential use for TOPS - in the control and allocation of locos. Some managers and staff were lukewarm about its benefits, but they were plain to see. By allocating locos in L.M. Regional Control instead of - as hitherto - at Divisional level, locos - especially those with special features such as air braked, slow speed control[6], electric train heating, etc. - could be deployed on trains that required these features, where hitherto they were sometimes deployed on trains that did not need these features. Locos would be allocated to departures, off depots or inbound trains. Maintenance - based on

---

[1] Closures of intermediate lightly used stations and junctions to branch lines facilitated higher average speeds, attracting new long distance passengers - a benefit not taken into account in justifying closures.

[2] They were subject to viability doubts - inside and outside BR. It was prudent, therefore, given other investment needs, to incur minimum investment to test the market. It proved a success. The attraction was minimum time between parking and boarding a train. Recently, new boys, who cannot bear to admit that they know less than BR managers, carp that they were built on the cheap, and need the razz-a-ma-taz of a city terminal, many of which have become obstacle courses of shops to passenger flow. Such a need can only arise from late trains that extend the time between parking and boarding trains. A former colleague tells of a Railtrack plan to shorten London Victoria platforms to accommodate shops. They seemed unaware that it would reduce train lengths, leading to serious overcrowding.

[3] Inadequate R&D has been a long standing shortcoming of UK industry - and a contributory cause of its decline.

[4] The HST project also went ahead, because Johnson - the first railwayman to be BR Chairman - took a bold decision. "He was held in high esteem by the commercial world and took on leadership of private sector companies after retiring". (Marsh, "*Off the Rails*", Page 184).

[5] Industrial managers invited to see TOPS in action were amazed at the speed & scale of its coverage. (see page 119)

[6] A loco with this facility could be set to move at 0.5 mph under a colliery bunker, loading coal on the move, and over a power station discharge point, unloading on the move. This was the design speed for the terminal equipment.

hours in traffic - became more economical because the record of computer generated hours was more precise than manually aggregated hours, so that a loco was not taken out of traffic for maintenance prematurely. Availability forecasts of locos coming off maintenance improved dramatically when I told the M&EE that Control would allocate on the basis of their forecast, and if that proved unreliable, ensuing delay would be debited to them. Hitherto, they told Control *after* a loco was placed for collection. This created a time lag in its use, because they could only then allocate a crew to move it. The new method changed the basis for determining loco availability, which had long been based on the number on maintenance depots at 06.00. Depots seemed adept at turning locos off depot at 05.59, and not accepting any on until 06.01. Timetable plans were based on the forecast availability of locos. If the M&EE said that there would be 85% availability, then that, largely dictated the number of trains in the timetable. If their 06.00 data corresponded to 85%, operators could not claim shortage of locos as a cause of delay or cancellation. It was not unknown for a driver to report that the loco that was reported as available off a depot - was not at the designated pick-up point. Using TOPS for locos produced a *real* percentage availability 24 hours per day, not at the historic - unreliable - 06.00. The new system was a success, and produced useful staff economies. As a measure of staff dedication, Controllers from other Regions came to Crewe Regional Control, in their own time, to see the system working at first hand. The other Regions introduced the system.

A further potential enhancement of TOPS was to control passenger vehicles. These were "owned" by Regions, and manually allocated. A BRB Paper had rejected the use of TOPS for coaches - seeing no benefit. I advocated that they be centrally owned and allocated, using TOPS, leading to better utilisation and more economical maintenance - as was achieved with locos - thereby reducing costs. The change was made, with ultimate benefit to InterCity and the other Passenger Businesses.

BR won Government approval to set up Railway Finance Ltd.[7], a rolling stock leasing company to be managed by bankers in which large companies will be shareholders. It will borrow money - a $50m Eurodollar loan was secured as a start - to buy locos and rolling stock worth £115m over five years and lease them to BR. Surplus tax allowances unused by BR can be exploited by the company to the tune of £40m most of which will be passed back to BR through leasing terms. BR will receive indirectly from the Inland Revenue an outright grant of £35m reducing rolling stock costs by a third.

1971: BR set up a leasing arrangement so that much needed rolling stock could be obtained over a five year period and paid for from revenue rather than capital. By this, rolling stock built by BR Workshops was sold to Leasing companies for BR use. (BRB 1971 Report, Page 21).

1972: £14m worth of rolling stock sold to leasing companies. (BRB 1972 Report, Page 19).

1973: £16.9m worth of stock sold to leasing companies. (BRB 1973 Report, Page 10).

1974: No further assets can be taken under these arrangements - the Government has terminated the practice. (BRB 1974 Report, Page 14).

Other companies leased wagons to use on BR. Privatisation revived the concept, when companies were created to own and lease stock to 25 train companies. In July 1956, the MoT said: "*By applying the ordinary principles of enlightened private enterprise, I am hopeful we are going to show how BR can make a profit*". (see page 171). This common private sector practice was denied to BR

Planned limits on investment have remained virtually unchanged for ten years. BRB is concerned at its inability regularly to renew its assets through the double constraint of the investment ceilings and finance limits, and the lost opportunity to improve results through relatively modest development investment. (BRB 1980 Report, Page 8).

In 1960 the MoT asked to see all schemes over £0.25m before authorisation, which meant that an Area Board, Works & Equipment Committee, the BTC itself and then the MoT were considering schemes. Hence, it is surprising that the DoT told the Select Committee: "We have no technical experts at all - and could not check what BR was proposing to do technically. Within three weeks of an announcement that BR investment for five years would total £891m, a 20% reduction was

---

[7] A similar scheme was worked out for property development at stations.

imposed as part of a cutback in the public sector". (BRB 1973 Report, Page 3). "In October 1975, the MoT confirmed a reduction in investment levels, which had been accepted by Government. This is an abandonment of the strategy propounded by the Board in the December 1972 Rail Policy Review to the MoT which formed the basis for the 1974 Act. No alternative strategy was agreed with Government. The Public Expenditure Paper (Cmnd 6393) stated: Investment is pegged in real terms 30% below the level accepted by Government as recently as 1973". (BRB 1975 Report, Pages 3,4).

In "*Transport Policy*", the MoT stated: Government have "decided to limit the growth of public expenditure in the interests of higher exports and investment generally, requiring a painful re-appraisal of the priority accorded to transport against competing claims of housing, education and the social services[8]. Investment options are: track and signalling, product improvement, electrifica-tion, slower introduction of HST, a less comfortable and slower service. Only the BRB has the knowledge to choose between relevant factors, but it will be open to Government to give broad guidance between, freight and Inter City; or between manpower saving investment and higher qual-ity rolling stock". (*Transport Policy*, 1976, Vol. 1, Pages 2,52). He was saying that BR has the expertise but Government will decide! They were focusing on railways, not *transport*.

A Select Committee reported in 1976-7: "Major projects, submitted by BR, are scrutinised and ap-praised by the DoT - normally schemes costing less than £2m are not scrutinised". *All were vetted at three levels on BR.* "Demand forecasting for freight is more difficult than passenger traffic[9]. New freight facilities applied for by private sector companies under the 1974 Act - to transfer freight from road to rail - are delayed or rejected by Local Authorities on environmental grounds, e.g. 18 schemes in the London Division of the Western Region. MoT investment criteria used in approving schemes was open to question. In 1976 the DoT approved a scheme to electrify Bedford - St.Pancras - Moorgate at a cost of £80m, but no rate of return was specified, whilst they had not approved the Picc-Vic scheme in Manchester[10] which claimed a 12% return and was above the minimum level required. The Bedford Scheme was with the DoT for over a year. BR and other witnesses com-plained of delays in approvals which prevented BR taking advantage of investment opportunities. This would appear to be the case in highly competitive areas such as roll-on, roll-off shipping and hovercraft. One reason for delay in entry into service of the HST on the Western Region was the time taken by the MoT to authorise the scheme - 15 months. BR placed an order for 60 Class 56 locos, 30 in Romania. The constraint in Britain appeared to be the difficulty of getting design facili-ties. Even allowing for the unsatisfactory state of the British engineering industry, it seems surpris-ing that even the task of adapting existing design work could not be completed here. The Committee recommended that the DoT should be strengthened by staff with expertise in transport planning". (Report, Pages 13,25,74,103, 108,120). *This confirms their lack of expertise.*

In February 1978, the Price Commission called for "a 20 year time scale of freight strategy to achieve sustained viability". (Report Page 8). As political horizons are the next election, long term strategies were academic - a five year plan was accepted for only three weeks in 1973. (see above).

Modernisation Progress 1970-79
Investment was cut in 1975, to 30% below the level accepted by Government in 1973. (BRB 1975 Report, Page 4). Investment needs to rise by 30% during the next ten years assuming a start in 1981/2. (BRB 1977 Report, Page 7). BR stated: "The results of under investment are showing through. We are replacing assets at a slower rate than any other European railway. Through Transmark - our Queen's Award-winning consultancy - we are hard at work in railway developments in 29 countries - at

---

[8] How reducing *transport* expenditure helps exports was not explained, all goods require *transport*.
[9] The MoT's 1963 Paper, "*Transport Needs of Great Britain in the next 20 years*", Para 33 stated: "Passenger forecasting is more difficult than freight"!
[10] Proposed Manchester Underground: Piccadilly to Victoria.

home we are running the railway very hard just to stand still. (BRB 1979 Report, Page 6). Unless investment lifts by 30% just to replace worn out assets, the consequences will be lower speeds, frequency, comfort and reliability. (BRB 1979 Report, Page 7). Fortunately, the Government began to listen to professional opinion, and accept their judgement on the financial return and the improved services that could be obtained from increased investment. Although, investment fell in this period, below that in the preceding 10-15 years, there was useful progress as BRB Annual Reports show:

Track

In 1972, construction of the Liverpool Loop and Link lines was authorised by the Merseyside PTE and brought into use in 1977. In the decade, engineers built a new tunnel in six weeks under schedule on the east coast main line at Penmanshiel after the older tunnel collapsed in a land-slip. They also rebuilt Britannia Bridge across the Menai Straits, linking Anglesey to the mainland, after it was destroyed by fire started by boys. Jointly with British Steel [BSC], BR developed new rail steels which will be less susceptible to brittle fracture and thermal cracking. It was expected that the higher cost would be counter balanced by longer life. Trials at three sites gave encouraging results. They offer longer life and greater protection against fractures. During the period, 4,800 miles of CWR were laid bringing the total, by the end of the decade. to 9,100. It would have been more, but for "a serious shortage of steel rails". (BRB 1973 Report). Novel forms of track construction, such as concrete slab were investigated, and tests began on trial lengths. Similar techniques were later used in the Channel Tunnel, saving the private company, Eurotunnel huge sums in R&D. There was a continued increase in the provision of new track machines. An important piece of modernisation, mentioned in Annual Reports, but unnoticed by the public involved breakdown and track renewal cranes. All 75 tonne steam powered cranes were converted to diesel power in 1978.

Signalling

Bristol PSB, commissioned in 1970, controlled 100 route miles. "Resignalling in connection with electrification of the West Coast main line is scheduled for completion in 1973". (BRB 1971 Report, Page 26). It opened on schedule: "Modernisation of signalling, including four PSBs, was completed at a cost of £30.4m, on the 401 miles from Euston to Glasgow. Major signalling modernisation took place at many other locations". (BRB 1973 Report, Page 8). The £23m London Bridge signalling scheme was completed in 1976. By the end of the decade, BR reported progress with five more major signalling schemes, and a sixth was authorised. Computer based train describers were installed at four signalling centres in 1975. The National Signalling Plan, prepared circa 1975, envisaged that most InterCity, commuter & important freight routes will be covered by 75 PSBs. In 1978, BR forecast that it would take 20 years to fulfil. Multiple Aspect Signalling [MAS], was further extended during the period. More routes were equipped with AWS. (BRB 1974 Report, Page 5).

230 signal boxes were closed arising from signalling modernisation. (BRB 1971 Report, Page 26). 463 signal boxes were closed. (BRB 1973 Report, Page 8). The number of signal boxes reduced to 2,084 - including 195 PSBs - a reduction of about 2,600 in the ten year period.

Some user operated barrier crossings were installed, beginning in 1970. CCTV for remotely controlled crossings was installed experimentally at three locations in 1971 and proved satisfactory. "More level crossings were modernised including 25 converted to CCTV". (BRB 1973 Report, Page 8). Preparations were in hand, beginning in 1979, to modernise about 1,000 level crossings at a rate of 100 pa compared to 40 at present saving £12.5m pa in operating costs.

Continuing progress was made with an internal extension dialling system, thereby reducing the use of the public network with corresponding savings. (BRB 1973 Report, Page 8). Work began on the installation of a coaxial cable London-York, the first phase of BR's national communications plan. Planning began for a national radio system, and should be in use, after trials, by 1980. (BRB 1974 Report, Page 5). It was in use by 1979.

Electrification

At the start of the decade, "electrification was limited to filling a gap in the network on the Lea Valley between London and Cambridge". London-Birmingham-Manchester-Liverpool services were strengthened and accelerated after 1969. Approval was given by Government in February 1970, for electrification of the west coast to be extended to Glasgow, at a cost of £25m. Electric services were extended to Preston in 1973, and the project was completed to Glasgow, on schedule, by May 1974.

In 1971, the MoT authorised the 71 mile GN suburban electrification[11] from Kings Cross & Moorgate to Royston. Work began in 1973, and was completed in 1978. Revenue quickly rose by 28%. Government approved a ten year rolling programme of electrification. Design work on the Bedford-St.Pancras line began in 1973, was submitted to the MoT for approval in 1975 and was complete by 1982. This service could have begun operating a year earlier than it did, but was held up by an industrial dispute over Driver Only Operation. Management refused to bring the trains - which had been designed with that objective in mind, and for which station improvements had been made to facilitate safe working - into service until there was an agreement on this issue. There was some criticism of BR by the Rail Watchdogs, but managers had the new trains placed alongside the main line, where they could be seen every day by staff, as a means of pressuring acceptance of them. Design work for electrification of the Bishops Stortford-Cambridge line also commenced in 1973.

The first batch of new electric trains was delivered to Southern Region suburban routes in 1979. Authority was given for a further 620 coaches to bring the total to 872 over the next four years. The electrified Argyle line under Glasgow city centre opened in 1979 - it was part of decade of expansion of partnership with PTEs.

Stations

In 1972, four major stations were being rebuilt, and two stations re-opened with local authority help. In 1972, stations opened at Alfreton & Mansfield Parkway, Bradford rail/bus interchange and Stevenage. Tenders were invited in 1972 for a new station to serve the National Exhibition Centre at Birmingham and Birmingham Airport. It opened in September 1976, at a cost of £6m. Named as Birmingham International, it was used in 1976 by 35% of visitors to the NEC [National Exhibition Centre]. Gatwick Airport station was also rebuilt in 1975.

Experimental multi ticket vending machines were installed from 1969 at some stations in commuter areas to ease queuing. Machines for selling InterCity tickets were extensively field tested in trials to be completed by April 1970. Also, in 1970, the first "stored-ride" automatic ticket machines were installed on the Glasgow-Weymss service. In 1973, 560 NCR ticket machines were ordered for use at InterCity ticket offices other than on the London Midland Region that had been supplied earlier with a different modern type.

Locos

A new class 87 electric loco was designed in 1971. An order was placed for thirty new electric locos of 5000 hp. Some diesel locos were converted to provide electric train heating to coaches instead of steam heating which was progressively being eliminated. During the decade, 36 new electric locos and 122 new diesel locos were added to the fleet. Regrettably, diesel locos in particular did not enjoy the performance reliability that was promised and was essential for punctuality.

HSTs (High Speed Train)

Work began on the first HST in 1971. The 125mph HST had to be able to stop within 2200 yards - the 100 mph braking distance, imposed by existing colour light signalling. It stopped in 1930 yards, with a new type disc brake. Approval was given for construction in 1973, of 27 HSTs for the Paddington-Bristol/South Wales routes. The MoT gave authority, in 1974, for 32 of the 42 HSTs, which BR had wished to order for the east coast main line. As HSTs were delivered, loco hauled stock was cascaded to other routes, replacing DMUs on some routes. The BRB reported: The annual mileage and frequency of HST in this country is unequalled. Services between London and the West Riding/North East/Scotland and London-West Country were strengthened and accelerated. HSTs produced increases in traffic of 15-33%. HSTs began to take over the east coast route from Deltic hauled trains in 1978, cutting an hour from the schedule. Deltics - claimed to be the most powerful

---

[11] Electrification of a large section of this line had been authorised in the 1955 Plan, but replaced by diesels.

in the world had taken over on the east coast in 1962 - but had had a chequered history with failures and breakdowns, leading to a series of modifications. The ensuing delays to trains had all been laid at the door of BR. Their availability had fallen from about 80% or so to 60%, which was below steam levels. By the end of the decade, the BR designed HST fleet comprised 136 power cars and 520 coaches.

APT (Advanced Passenger Train)

In the mid-1960s, BR's Research Department began to develop the APT to run at up to 150 mph on existing track. Railways in other countries expressed interest in the project. Government agreed to cover half of the £10m forecast cost - in the expectation that it would lead to exports, with benefit to employment and the economy. It was designed to tilt on curves - being negotiated at much higher speeds than conventional trains - in order to maintain passenger comfort. It was envisaged that the trains would be in service by 1974. Due to testing and other problems, they did not begin to run until 1979, between London and Glasgow. The train's formation was not ideal. Due to the refusal of HMRI to approve that a high voltage cable passed along the train to permit a power car at each end - as the French had already been doing with the TGV - the train had to be formed with two power cars in the middle of the train. Passengers were not allowed to pass through these cars except in emergency, and hence the train was effectively in two parts with duplicated catering and staff. The train began to run in 1979, at a maximum speed of 125 mph, as the full design speed of 150 mph was not permissible until the route had been equipped with a new signalling system which conveyed signal information into the cab: CAPT. Nevertheless, it seemed to be a project coming to fruition, but it began to suffer problems - and most significantly safety problems. (see page 192).

Rolling Stock

BR introduced air braked electrically heated coaches on inter city trains. Air conditioned coaches were introduced in 1971, on trains from London to Leeds, Hull, Newcastle and Edinburgh, and in 1972 to Birmingham, Wolverhampton, Manchester, Liverpool, Bristol and South Wales. By the end of 1972, 450 Mark IIe coaches were in service; and two Mark III prototype - intended as the coaches on the HSTs - were in service after testing. In 1973, BR ordered 300 Mark III coaches for the West Coast. The final batch of nearly 2,000 Mark IIe, was delivered in 1974. [Mark IIe and Mark III were air conditioned; the former had 62-64 seats, the latter was a longer vehicle with 70 seats].

Delivery of new electric rolling stock to the Southern Region in 1970 effected a notable improvement in service quality. Ten prototype EMUs were built to replace existing units. New stock on Southern Region outer suburban services and prototypes for inner suburban began trials at the end of 1971. By 1972, more new suburban trains were being tested on the Southern Region, and £70m was authorised for 111 four-car EMUs for the Region. The last of the pre-war Southern Railway passenger vehicles were replaced in 1972. In 1973, the building of 1,000 outer suburban vehicles for the Southern Region, neared completion. Authority was given in 1974, for 401 EMU vehicles to replace life expired vehicles on Liverpool Street-Southend and Liverpool-Southport/Ormskirk services. In 1975, work continued on nineteen 4-car EMU for Liverpool Street outer suburban services, the West Midlands PTE funded four 4-car EMUs for the Birmingham-Coventry service, and a programme began to refurbish some EMUs and DMUs. This was extensive refurbishment, not the mere re-painting of coaches undertaken after 1995 by private sector companies, some of whose trains still exhibited BR notices in 2003. Three new exterior carriage washing machines were provided. Stripping asbestos from locos and rolling stock was being undertaken at a cost of £6.7m of which £4.5m was already spent. (BRB 1979 Report, Page 27). During the decade, in addition to HST stock (see page 74), 943 coaches, 1136 EMU, 133 vehicles for conveyance of mails and parcels and 10,297 wagons were built to replace old stock. The total passenger carrying fleet had been reduced from 18,869 at the end of 1969 to 17,000, ten years later.

A design was completed for a new type steel carrying wagon, and for wagons to carry 8'6" containers, in 1970. In the same year, a new depot was built at Burton-on-Trent to carry out Planned Preventative Maintenance of MGR wagons.

Chapter 8

The BR 1982-86 Corporate Plan had to be revised in December following a Government decision to fix the External Financing Limit (see page 181), at the same level for the next three years. BR drew attention to the age of its assets: 66% of electric and diesel multiple trains are over 20 years old, with fleet average ages of 18.7 and 23.4 years respectively. Unless the External Finance Limit is raised, from its planned level - fixed at present levels for the next three years - to accommodate a more positive view of the future railway, the position will be critical. (BRB 1981 Report, Pages 7,9,10).

Re-organisation into business sectors, by Sir Robert Reid, the second railwayman to be Chairman, led to more modernisation. Annual Reports undermine claims that there was none for decades.

EEC Budget transport refunds were paid - in respect of railway investment in defined Development Areas - to UK Government. In 1980, it was £83m. (BRB 1980 Report). Railway investment in six defined development areas attracted EEC budget refunds amounting to £66m in 1982, 6% of the amount received in respect of UK public sector investment. These refunds were paid to the State and do not increase sums paid to BR. Investment on revenue account was £111m on signalling and track modernisation. In addition, £190m was spent on infrastructure renewals and rolling stock refurbishment. (BRB 1982 Report). In 1983, investment totalled £252m. In 1984/5, "Government authorised over £500m investment - this is more than authorised in the previous six years". In 1985/6 and 1986/7 investment was £412m, mainly on electrification and new trains. "The key result lies in reducing Government support while embarking on the biggest investment programme for 25 years. Investment doubled in real terms since 1983, and is planned to increase by 75% over the next three years". (BRB 1989/90 Report). Investment rose from £463m in 1987/8 to £715m in 1989/90, which BR stated was "the highest in real terms for 15 years", to £1384m in 1992/3 [+19% on last year], which was "mainly funded by borrowing". A billion was spent on the existing railway, and the rest in connection with Channel Tunnel services. (BRB 1992/3 Report).

The CTCC said that "Investment in non commercial sectors should be funded by Government rather than from BR resources". (CTCC 1987/88 Report, Page 8).

BRB Annual Reports reveal a gradually increasing tempo of investment from 1983 through to privatisation. The following pages present a summary, with the destination of the cash classified. The Reports show some investment as being applied to projects covering more than one type of asset:

- 1983: £123m on rolling stock, stations and facilities, £129m on signalling and track modernisation and £230m[1] on infrastructure renewals and rolling stock refurbishment.
- 1984/5: A £306m modernisation of the East Coast main line began. Local authorities and Development Funds contributed to a £4.7m modernisation of the Cambrian lines.
- 1985/6: Provincial Railways have started a massive investment in modern trains, stations, track and signalling aimed at reducing operating and maintenance costs and attracting more passengers. A three year plan for Cardiff Valley lines costing £2.5m was funded by local authorities. The next year, BR reported that overcrowding had occurred, and been relieved by extra coaches.
- 1987/8: Network SouthEast five year £1bn investment.
- 1989/90: Kent Link services will be improved by a £700m plan for 400 new trains, new depots, improved signalling and longer platforms to accommodate longer trains.
- 1990/1: Approval given for West Coast improvements: new trains, faster journeys, to be implemented in 1995. Strathclyde PTE increased its investment to £200m since 1983.
- 1993/4: Strathclyde PTE invested £51m including three new stations in and around Glasgow.

New routes opened and/or new services introduced
- 1982: Work carried out on the Selby diversionary line [enabling faster speeds] is being funded by the National Coal Board - to enable them to extract coal below the existing East Coast main line.
- 1986/7: Eleven mile Edinburgh-Bathgate line re-opened to passengers with local authority help.

---

[1] Charged direct to working expenses, and not therefore classified as investment.

- 1987/8: 18 miles of railway were re-opened to passenger services after being closed for 20 years.
- 1988/9: A link was constructed across Manchester for new south to north west train services.
- 1990/1: Rail link to Stansted Airport from London completed and service opened March 1991. New class 158 services Cleethorpes-Manchester and Leeds-Blackpool led to passenger increases. Many stations opened or re-opened. The Chiltern and North London lines introduced new services
- 1991/2: A 30 mile line being re-opened between Leicester and Burton-on-Trent, costing £16m, is mainly funded by local authorities. The Nottingham-Mansfield line is being re-opened, jointly funded by BR and local authorities. New trains and stations are part of a £4m re-opening plan for Bridgend-Maesteg, funded by local authorities and the European Development Fund.
- 1992/3: Work began on a £23m PTE project to re-open four miles from Birmingham Snow Hill. The objective was to cut delays by diverting trains from heavily congested New Street. Railtrack destroyed the plan, by selling vacated train paths to other train operating companies.
- 1993/4: a new Manchester Airport rail link opened, and carried 1m passengers in the first year

Track

1981-1991/2 Reports record 3,360 miles of continuous welded rail [CWR] laid, reducing track and rolling stock wear, giving faster speeds and more comfortable riding. By privatisation, CWR was in use on over 12,600 miles - 63% of the system. (see page 44). Reports record investment in bridges reconstructed: 58 in 1991/2 alone; and investment in track maintenance machinery. (see page 85)

Signalling

- 1980: Resignalling of 240 track miles from six projects was commissioned and 27 level crossings modernised. The Board's national teleprinter network was commissioned with 500 teleprinters. A new radio signalling system installed between Wick and Inverness has already saved £300,000.
- 1981: There has been a 4% saving in operating costs arising from new signalling and crossings. London Bridge and Victoria PSBs covering 414 track miles, will replace 52 signal boxes, cut staff by over 200, increase line capacity, and will improve safety, reliability and passenger information.
- 1982: Work continued on 178 miles of colour light signalling. 32 level crossings were modernised. Work continues on a £120m project to re-signal and improve track layouts on the Victoria-Hastings line. Simplified signalling systems for lightly used lines are being developed, to be tried initially on Dingwall-Kyle of Lochalsh in 1983.
- 1983: 160 miles colour light signalling commissioned and 48 level crossings modernised. Work began on BR's first solid state interlocking signal box.
- 1984/5: 181 miles of colour light signalling installed and 82 level crossings modernised. Brighton resignalling will be completed six months ahead of schedule. Work began on resignalling the Waterloo area. Radio signalling and modern level crossings being provided on the Cambrian lines
- 1985/6: 378 miles colour light signals installed; 108 crossings modernised. Brighton resignalling completed six months ahead of schedule. BR's first electronic solid state interlocking signalling commissioned at Leamington; radio signalling extended in Scotland and Essex. New automated crossings and modern signalling installed on routes where equipment was due to be replaced.
- 1986/7: The first of a new generation of solid state interlocking PSBs was completed at Inverness; with similar ones in hand at Oxted and Dorchester and others being planned. Colour light signalling installed on 369 miles and 67 level crossings modernised. TOPS was linked to power box train describers to produce up-to-date reports on punctuality on the West Coast main line
- 1987/8: Colour light signalling installed on 126 track miles, work in progress on a further 275 miles. 33 level crossings modernised.
- 1988/9: 245 miles new signalling being provided. New signalling centres being installed. 63 level crossings modernised and 14 modified. Prototype train operated crossing barriers at Beccles.
- 1989/90: Three electronic signalling centres installed at Liverpool Street, York and Glasgow, work continuing at Newcastle. 36 level crossings modernised and thirteen modified.
- 1990/1: World's biggest and most advanced electronic signalling centre at Newcastle controls 120 miles of the East Coast main line. 50 level crossings modernised, eleven modified.

- 1991/2: Maintained a world lead in integrated electronic signalling with completion of Newcastle, Glasgow and Marylebone signalling centres. Forty level crossings modernised and ten modified
- 1992/3 Major work included the Dartford line, Channel Tunnel routes and electronic signalling at Ashford. 35 crossings modernised. Contracts placed to resignal LT&S by 1995 at a cost of £50m.
- 1993/4: LT&S re-signalling work began. £3.8m provided by the Welsh Office to modernise signals between Radyr and Pontypridd.

By privatisation, there were some 900 signalboxes, including PSBs. Network Rail told the author they were unable to say how many they have now. Little modernisation seems to have taken place since 1994. In 1979, 546 level crossings had been modernised. By privatisation, it was 1102. Eight years later, Railtrack had modernised only 29 more. (see HMRI/H&SE Railway Annual Safety Reports).

Electrification

In 1981, BR/DoT stated in *Joint Review of Electrification*: "A substantial programme would be worthwhile - larger options show an 11% return. The best course is the largest option - 5,750 route miles". (Report Pages 1,4, & Table 1). The largest programme of electrification would bring electrified route up from 21% to 52%. (BRB 1980 Report, Page 10).

On non-electrified main lines, when ballast was deepened for high speed running and overbridges had to be lifted to maintain clearance, an opportunity was taken to provide sufficient headroom for later electrification. All new overbridges were built with such clearance. Hence, when a line such as the East Coast main line was electrified, costs were less than would have arisen had this work not taken place. BR Annual Reports record the following electrification projects:

- 1981: Government approved extending electrification from Colchester to Harwich & Norwich.
- 1982: Strathclyde PTE authorised electrification of the Glasgow-Ayr-Ardrossan route at a cost of £68m, of which they will fund £38m.
- 1983: Bishops Stortford-Cambridge authorised. Work in hand on 184 route miles will cost £170m
- 1984/5: The £24m Tonbridge-Hastings scheme will be completed May 1986. Government authorised East Coast electrification for £306m. Electrification to Norwich is on schedule. Development of 25kv equipment and installation has cut electrification costs by 25% in real terms compared to ten years ago. A new technique using steel piled foundations was proved on the Southminster line and will be adopted for two track sections of the east coast route, cutting costs.
- 1985/6: 42 route miles completed, with a further 103 miles due in 1986/7. East Coast scheme on schedule. Contracts let for 31 electric locos for East Coast, and 29 for the West Coast.
- 1986/7: Electric trains ran on part of the East Coast six months ahead of schedule. Electrification to Cambridge and on the Scottish Ayrline both completed four months early. By the end of the decade, BR will have electrified 60% of InterCity - 30% of total route mileage.
- 1987/8: The first new InterCity electric locos delivered. The first East Coast electric trains will run from London to Leeds in late 1988 - a year ahead of schedule. Services began on two newly electrified routes, traffic increased by 40%. North London line electrification enables freight to be hauled without a loco change from Stratford [London] to the Midlands and Scotland.
- 1989/90: First class 91 electric locos went into service seven months ahead of schedule. Electrification work began on Edinburgh-Carstairs, Cambridge-Kings Lynn and Lichfield-Redditch.
- 1990/1: The East Coast service opened on schedule and within budget. Helicopters were used to speed up installation of transformers. It was praised by foreign managements and the technical media. Current operators have decried the achievement, saying that every time the wind blows[2], the wire comes down. BR's Project Director says that the design took account of Met Office forecasts of wind speed. Hooton-Chester electric line opened with a 50% increase in passengers.

---

[2] "We are pleased with the electric service". (Eastern TUCC 1990/1 Report). Apart from "*freak weather in November 1993*" in Scotland, there is no reference to problems in TUCC 1990/1 to 1993/4 Reports, which TUCCs would not have ignored. After 1994, when Railtrack became responsible for all infrastructure, TUCC Reports mention problems, suggesting that changes were made in the maintenance or inspection of overhead equipment. Increased train mileages, of which franchisees boast, demanded increased maintenance and inspection of track and overhead equipment.

Work began on LT&S £84m electrification. New InterCity Midlands to Edinburgh service via newly electrified Carstairs route. Tender issued for new 155 mph trains[3] for new west coast services in 1995, involving signal and track improvements. Work progressed on Birmingham Cross-City electrified services [Lichfield-Redditch], funded by the PTE. West Yorkshire and Manchester PTEs plan to fund similar services. A £30m electric fleet began on North Clyde services.

- 1991/2: Work is in progress on four lines. NSE £700m modernisation continued as planned: the first Networker electric trains, of a fleet of 486 coaches were delivered, to enter service mid-1992. Slam door trains will be replaced by 1993[4]. Work began on Leeds-Bradford electrification. A line to Heathrow has been authorised. Approval is sought for a new north-south link across London
- 1992/3: Electrified route rose to 30% with completion of work on three projects. Two others are in hand. Following the success and increased income of the East Coast project, the top priority is a similar modernisation of the West Coast route with modern infrastructure and InterCity 225 trains
- 1993/4: 69 track miles electrified. Birmingham Cross-City electrification completed July 1993, The first new class 323 electric trains did not enter service until February owing to late delivery. Problems continued with these trains on commuter routes in West Midlands and Manchester. Modifications were made and reliability increased. Work began on the Heathrow Express rail link. New class 465 introduced on Kent Link services, and new Express units on two other routes.

Since privatisation, new electrification has been limited to completion of work in hand under BR.

Locos & Rolling Stock [5]

- 1980: The first new trains for 30 years, improved Liverpool Street-Shenfield services. InterCity 125 trains introduced on Paddington-West of England. New type brake blocks are saving £3m pa.
- 1981: Trials began with new lightweight diesels. New electric trains were delivered for the Liverpool Street-Shenfield service. Refurbishment continued of Kent coast & inner suburban trains
- 1982: £70m spent on new trains and £12m on refurbishment. A train maintenance depot opened at Norwich. Total investment was £140m spent mainly on freight and passenger rolling stock. Delivery of new trains completed for the Bedford-St.Pancras-Moorgate line, and 358 coaches were refurbished. 22 lightweight diesel trains ordered and tenders issued for other stock. Orders placed for 250 high capacity vans suitable for fork lift loading, the first being taken up by ICI and Ford.
- 1983: 60 new coaches are being built to provide more seats on InterCity services and improve quality on the west coast line to start late 1984. 54 new trains improved suburban services into Waterloo and 367 coaches were refurbished for London suburban services. Delivery began of 20 class 141 two-car lightweight diesel units for Yorkshire and 75 units of similar design have been authorised for delivery in 1985. More carriage washing machines installed.[6]
- 1984/5: A 25 year programme involves buying 1,500 locos. 614 coaches refurbished: 400 on the West Coast, 214 London & SouthEast. A new fleet of trains went into service with air suspension for a smoother ride. They will be cheaper to run and maintain than the 25 year old displaced trains. Some 340 others will be delivered by 1986. A further 75 units with wider bodies and 20% more seats were on order. Local authorities are helping to fund new trains on the Cambrian line.
- 1985/6: 377 coaches refurbished, work started on another 178. New trains delivered for London suburban services. New trains replace those built 25 years ago and are designed for minimum maintenance. InterCity 125 trains run two years between major overhauls. Authorisation given for 846 new coaches. The Provincial Sector plans to spend £100m to replace all 25 year old trains in the next five years, enabling it to reduce its maintenance bill by 25%.
- 1986/7: Introduced more new diesel trains. By the end of the decade, over 85% of diesel trains will be renewed. New carriage washing machines at four depots. New low bogie wagons increase payload and height, reduce maintenance costs, and are relevant to piggyback development

---

[3] It was recently announced that, even with track improvements, the new boys will run at only 125 mph in 2004/5
[4] Still in use in 2003, and operators wish to retain some. Former colleagues say they are more reliable than new stock.
[5] See also Chapter 11 for references to modernisation of freight wagons.
[6] Such machines had been in use for decades.

- 1987/8: Investment planned for next year includes a new generation of coaches. Ordered 45 four-car units and 24 two-car units able to run independently, off peak in commuter areas and lengthen trains in the peak. In 1988/9, 300 coaches will enter service. A new generation of diesel trains is being delivered. Orders placed for 204 coaches of a third generation class 156: 90 mph, air conditioning and trolley service for secondary routes. 100 freight locos ordered. Automatic identification system for locos and wagons on the move was developed for power station traffic.
- 1988/9: Around £4 billions investment over the next five years will be for commuter trains. 608 new coaches delivered and a further 1,009 refurbished. Revised maintenance schedules allowed diesel trains to run twice their forecast annual mileage. First of 100 new class 60 freight locos entered service. Ten new carriage washing machines were installed, and many refurbished. NSE acquired 500 new coaches in the last three years, and a further 290 ordered.
- 1989/90: 330 new coaches delivered, 700 others refurbished or modified. InterCity introduced the new Mark 4 coaches. New IC225 trains introduced on East Coast releasing HSTs for other routes. The IC225 [225 kph] was designed, developed and brought into service on time and within budget. 45 new low platform container wagons to convey exports through the Isle of Grain, where clearances are too restricted for conventional wagons. Delays in delivery of over 400 class 158s due to manufacturer's difficulties. (see Chapter 14). Orders placed for 400 Networker coaches for Kent, and further 442 agreed for delivery from summer 1991. 456 class 321 delivered on time and in budget.
- 1990/1: The first class 158s delivered to ScotRail moved Regional Railways closer to its aim of a fleet under seven years old by 1992, and helped maintain the higher volume achieved in recent years. Improved class 158 services increased traffic by 40%. Further deliveries would produce more passengers. New type trains introduced require less maintenance, facilitating an increase in train mileage. NSE switched from steel to aluminium trains. First of a fleet of 486 class 465 delivered to replace elderly Kent Link trains by 1993, with longer platforms to take 12 coach trains. Authorised purchase of 69 class 159 trains for Waterloo-Exeter route to start 1993/4. Air conditioned class 158 trains replaced the last loco hauled stock on Trans Pennine routes and Cardiff-Portsmouth, and will be introduced on other long distance secondary routes in 1991. Class 155 two-car trains being converted for single unit operation - all part of a £7m investment. "New type trains introduced on many routes require less maintenance, facilitating an increase in train mileage". Investment of £40m in 700 new container carrying wagons will boost rail/deepsea services.
- 1991/2: Class 158 trains introduced in 1990 had technical problems. Manufacturers carried out modifications. Late delivery of stock reported. Renewal of the Regional Railways fleet is complete. Authority to build 188 Networkers will complete renewal of the Kent Link fleet. 330 new passenger vehicles were delivered. By the end of 1992, Regional Railways rolling stock will average seven years old. Fifty new class 60 heavy-haul freight locos delivered. Modernisation of container services continued with delivery of the first of an order of 700 new container wagons.
- 1992/3: 400 new coaches delivered. Nearly a third of the new Networker fleet has been delivered
- 1993/4: 650 new passenger vehicles entered service - mainly electric units for NSE; 900 older vehicles were withdrawn. New fleet of class 92 electric locos for Channel Tunnel traffic.
- 1994/5: The first of 41 four-car Networker Express EMU was made available for testing. The provision of new rolling stock over recent years has enabled the withdrawal of more older coaches. New class 465 Networker trains introduced on Kent Link, replacing life expired 45 year old slam door stock. The last of 100 class 60 freight locos delivered. Strathclyde PTE spending £36m on new trains to service its new stations.

In this period 1980 to 1994, 339 locos, 61 power cars, 5,217 coaches & multiple units, 80 mail/parcels vehicles and 4,966 wagons were introduced. By 1994, the coaching fleet was only 24% of the 1948 fleet, compared to passenger miles which were 90% of the 1948 volume.

Stations

Annual Reports from 1981 to 1994/5 mention 168 stations being opened or re-opened, many with funding by local authorities and PTEs, all giving "improved disabled access as a standard feature".

Among new stations opened by BR was a new low level station at Kings Cross for Thameslink interchange and expansion. Hundreds of existing stations were modernised or refurbished and given improved disabled access, some with local authority help - notably 97 stations in Greater London in 1984/5. Some major station rebuilding took place, of which Liverpool Street, completed in 1991/2, was an outstanding example, providing improved passenger facilities and over one million square feet of office space and leisure amenities.

From 1987 to 1992, platforms were being extended to permit longer [12 coach] trains for new electric Networker trains. Carparks were being improved up to 1993/4, with CCTV provided at some carparks. Awards were given by the AA in commendation of the standards at some carparks. In 1987/8, BR opened a carpark at Reading holding 1,600 cars.

Improvements of station facilities included new automatic ticket issuing machines at stations on all major routes, beginning in 1983. A year later, trials of two new types of ticket machine having been completed, 150 were being installed on NSE stations. Two years later, after several years of development, computerised ticket machines were introduced, embracing seat reservations. By 1988, the changeover to computerised ticket machines - 4,600 in total - at stations and on trains was complete, replacing paperwork and improving management information. A further 2,300 portable machines, which accept credit cards, are on order for use on trains. In addition, 104 ticket vending machines were in use at busy NSE stations, with 290 more on order. Within a year, it was noted that "Queues have been cut by provision of 400 ticket issuing machines, 800 more have been ordered". More ticket issuing machines were installed in 1990/1.

More on-station information systems, with CCTV monitors for information and for security were being installed, especially in 1986/7, and up to 1993. In 1990, saw the first self service computer aided timetable - uses touch screen to give information - previously used only in Enquiry Bureaux .

Allied improvements included new telephone monitoring equipment in TEBx, which by 1984/5 covered 87 locations, to help reduce waiting time, and identify where 95% calls were not being answered within 30 seconds. (see page 105). Two years later, computer based systems in some Bureaux were enabling staff to answer more complex queries in a fraction of the time using normal methods.

These and many other projects (see below and Chapter 10), had been initiated even before privatisation was mooted, hence the credit was due to BR. The collective effect of these projects was to trigger increases in passengers, which would, without question, have escalated no less than they did over the years following privatisation - for which the newcomers have taken unwarranted credit. These facts demonstrate that the assets were *not* decrepit. In contrast, post-privatisation modernisation: electrification, signalling, rolling stock and track improvement has not matched forecasts.

The Channel Tunnel

For 100 years, railways sought authority for a Tunnel, which would have increased traffic. Had it been built 30-40 years ago, BR traffic would have expanded. It was blocked in 1881 by the military who could not defend a land frontier the width of a tunnel, in 1930 by Parliament, and since the war by the sea and road lobbies, and short sighted Governments.

The Government set up a Committee to consider the construction of a Channel Tunnel. It reported in 1930 that a tunnel was opposed because losses to shipping, agriculture and other industries would be greater than the estimated advantages. (Cmd 3515).

"In 7-8 years time, the Tunnel may handle much traffic now passing by sea and air, bringing additional freight and passengers to BR. The existing car-ferry services on the short sea routes will be affected, but the BRB shipbuilding policy has taken full account of this probability and ships now in service can be employed elsewhere after the Tunnel opens". (BRB 1969 Report, Page 11). British and French Channel Tunnel companies have been created to conduct the final studies and construct the Tunnel. (BRB 1971 Report, Page 14). It was kicked into touch by the road lobby. "Plans for a Channel Tunnel have been pronounced dead on several occasions, most recently in 1975. Government shelved the Channel Tunnel project". (BRB 1974 Report, Page 7). In 1978, British and French Railways revived the idea. A political announcement is awaited. (BRB 1981 Report, Page 13). We plan to invest £400m in trains, stations track and maintenance facilities in connection with the Channel Tunnel. (BRB 1985/6 Report, Page 6). We are investing heavily in international services to operate on the day the Tunnel opens. (BRB 1988/9 Report, Page 6). £370m is being invested in electric freight locos, electrifying track, and a new fleet of international wagons for services through the Channel Tunnel, with ten new terminals stretching from Scotland to Bristol. (BRB 1990/1 Report, Page 18)

The Waterloo terminal for the Chunnel was built by BR on time and within budget. In contrast, the private sector failed to do likewise with the Tunnel itself. It was horrendously over budget and over a year late. When the company thought it was ready, an inspection by HMRI[7] proved it wasn't.

Critics compared the speed of Eurostar trains on this side of the Channel with that in France. Had they conducted some very *basic* research, they would have learned that the TGV route in France was a brand new route, whereas in Kent attempts to create such a new route were blocked by NIMBYs. They would have learned that the lack of straight railway routes suitable for high speeds through Kent was directly attributable to 19th century NIMBYs and the machinations of politicians, lawyers and others who jointly pushed UK rail construction costs way above those of other countries. The blindness of those who blamed BR for delay in building a high speed link when faced with such opposition and Government indecision, is incomprehensible. "There were six years of appraisal of the alternative routes for the Channel Tunnel Link Line". (BRB 1994/5 Report, Page 25).

The delayed opening of a Tunnel - a year before privatisation - led to increases in passenger and freight traffic, for which the private sector is unjustifiably gaining credit. Many are from industries that objected to a rail tunnel! Originally, it would have been funded by private railways. After 1948, it should have been funded by money Government skimmed from wartime railways. Had it been built 30-40 years ago as BR sought to do, vast sums spent on airports would have been avoided.

No investment for decades?

It is claimed that there was no investment for decades. Preceding pages nullify the claim. *Investment levels in recent years mean that the railway has renewed much of its asset base.* (BRB 1989/90 Report, Page 3). If there had been "no investment", how could the private sector have been able to "sweat the assets"? That was only possible if assets were in prime condition, and being renewed more frequently by BR than necessary. Those who made this claim for not renewing infrastructure as frequently since 1994, have lost the plot. That even more investment would have created a better product is a truism, that applies to UK manufacturing, and may have avoided factory closures.

In March 1995, the MoT told the Select Committee on Transport, (4th Report. Pages 106,186):

> "*Since 1948, in today's prices, £54 bn had been invested in Railways - £15 bn of it since 1979*". i.e. under Conservative Party Administration. On the basis of DoT figures, the average since 1979 was £1 bn pa, compared to £1.2 bn pa for the preceding 32 years. BR Accounts paint a different picture - an average of £0.6 bn since 1979, and £ 0.78 bn before 1979. (see Table 3).

Inquiries of the DoT revealed that it was not "given by the State", as may have been inferred from radio reports but was "BR Investment: 1948 to 1994/5, at 1994/5 prices", i.e. invested by BR. It has not been possible to reconcile the difference. It may be due to the DoT including renewals.

Mrs. Dunwoody, Chair of the Transport Select Committee told the Minister: "BREL went into the private sector with large amounts of taxpayers' money having been used in previous two years[8] to update equipment". BRB 1985/6 & 1986/7 Accounts show a total of £30m. At 1994/5 prices, it averaged £22.8m pa over the two years. The average at 1994/5 prices of corresponding expenditure in the three preceding years, was £9.8m. BR Accounts should not have been debited with such an increase, with privatisation on the horizon.

---

[7] A former colleague told the author that BR offered to carry out a preliminary inspection to avoid possible embarrassment and delay, before HMRI attended, but the offer was rejected.

[8] A similar pattern appears prior to railway privatisation. BR Accounts show that the average investment, at 1994/5 prices, in BR in the two years prior to privatisation was £1.47 bn, compared to £0.43 bn in the preceding twelve years.

BR Capital Expenditure, £ billions : 1948-1994/5 at 1994/5 Prices							
	DoT	BTC/BRB			DoT	BTC/BRB	DoT pa	BTC/BRB pa
1948-62	22.3	14.4		1948-79	38.5	25.0	1.2	0.78
1963-94/5	31.6	19.0		1980-94/5	15.4	8.4	1.0	0.6
Totals	53.9	33.4			53.9	33.4		
Table 3: DoT letter & BTC/BRB Accounts adjusted by Central Statistical Office 1994 Deflator							

The total *BTC* investment in 1948-62 included in Annual Accounts, even including *non-BR* activities, was £18.7 billion, still less than the DoT figure of £22.3 billion for BR alone. According to the comprehensive and authoritative survey by Munby & Watson, which covered up to 1970 inclusive, Gross Investment on BR for 1948-70 inclusive, at 1994 prices was £21.5bn. BTC/BRB Accounts show £21 bn at 1994 prices for the same period; the DoT claims £30.6 bn.

Over BR's last ten years, track and signalling maintenance cost £832m pa at 1994 prices. (see BRB Accounts). This was not investment, but included like-for-like renewals.

The Special Advisory Group said that pre-1961 investment was "repairing the obsolescence of the past 20-50 years". Some 38% of the DoT total was pre-1961. Of 1948-62 investment, 79%. went on rolling stock[9], including replacement of inferior private owner wagons dumped on to BR, (see page 50), and Big Four rolling stock worn out in wartime. Investment on level crossings and bridges to meet heavier road traffic, should have been on the highways budget, leaving more for trains.

Inquiries of the DoT revealed that Grants to BR for 1969-1994/5 totalled £31,963m at 1994/5 prices. Of this £656m was, from 1975, for [*the burden of*] level crossings. Pro rata, BR's burden from 1948-74 had cost £886m, which was not paid by the MoT, nor the Treasury, nor the Highways Fund. No Grants are mentioned for bridges, which should also have been a highway debit from 1930. Surface maintenance of bridges was priced by Government in 1967 at £3.3-16.5m pa if transferred to Highway Authorities. (see page 130). On that basis, £10m pa being the midway point, from 1968, when it, at long last, became a Highways responsibility, it would have amounted, for 1948-68, at 1994 prices, to £1.8 billion, with no payment for the bridge structure, a burden which still fell on BR in 1994. Prior to 1975, Government contributed an underwhelming *total* of £5m - i.e. a total, not an annual payment - from "Road Funds" to bridge and level crossing costs. (see page 129).

The Grant for the 25 years included £2,708m to Passenger Transport Executives to hold down fares, as a subsidy to users, not BR. Rail assets were valued in 1947, at £1.5 billion [£28 billion at 1994 prices]. Governments overlook that this was a **State liability**, but required BR to buy itself from owners and donate BR to the State free of charge and debt! Debt arose from statutory underpricing, redemption of capital and interest thereon (see page 176), plus subsidies to buses, industry, passengers and the State via below RPI prices and rejected closures. Governments overlook a £1 bn wartime gain, (see page 18) that a stockbroker said would have increased 750 times over by 1991, if prudently invested. Government has not paid the *interest* on losses created by its laws and policies.

It is claimed that there was no investment on the west coast since the 1960s. Every weekend, *since 1960, except bank holidays* engineers had four line possessions south of Crewe, involving speed restrictions to replace track, sleepers, ballast etc. The line north of Crewe was modernised in the mid 1970s, (see pages 73-74), and was subject to a similar regime. £14.5m was invested in Crewe area infrastructure alone in 1985. New locos and rolling stock were introduced. BR renewals were about three times Railtrack levels. Had UK industry invested as much, it would still lead the world.

Had work begun on the next stage modernisation of west coast electric services in 1993/4 (see page 79), 140 mph trains would have been running for four years now, instead of being four years or so into the future. Unlike the new regime, BR carried out track renewals and comparable modernisation without prolonged route blockages and diversions, especially where there were parallel tracks.

---

[9] See Chapters 10 & 11 for more examples of investment in rolling stock during this period and subsequently.

References have been made to "*Victorian infrastructure*" and "*no investment for 40 years*". BR Annual Reports refute the latter. Victorian infrastructure is mainly on minor lines. There has been recent public criticism about the retention of oil lit signal lamps on routes through rural areas, where electric power would be costly to provide. It requires little imagination to picture the outrage of objectors to closures, had BR said that lines should close to avoid the cost of replacing oil lit signals by colour lights or even electric lit semaphore signals.

At privatisation, the average age of locos was 21 and passenger coaches 13 years[10], both within the 25 year depreciation period. The loco fleet was down to 42% of the 1970 fleet, and the coaches to 57% of the 1970 fleet. In contrast, passenger train miles were up 13% on the 1970 level. (BR Annual Reports). Any suggestion that rolling stock was decrepit is unwarranted. The average age of airliners is up to 41 years. ("*Airports, Airlines & Aircraft*"). On balance, one should feel safer in a 30 year old train, which should it breakdown has not so far to fall as a 40 year old airliner or ship.

Privatisation at work

Past investment in the BR era has been wasted in recent accidents, which destroy track, signal-ling, rolling stock, electric supplies, stations and bridges. Some may have been avoided if Railtrack had retained the tried and tested basis of track renewal frequencies, (see page 48), together with fre-quent visual track inspections and regular ultrasonic tests from cars (see page 44) attached to trains.

Rails in the Severn Tunnel - where very damp conditions caused corrosion - were replaced by BR every six years. Railtrack extended renewal to nine years. Following a series of track defects, the H&SE issued an Enforcement Order on Railtrack to impose a 20 mph restriction on trains using the tunnel. (H&SE 1999-2000 Report). No problems were experienced in the previous twenty years under BR. (see also page 196).

Saturday - not Sunday night, as a Minister said [Radio 4, 22.8.03] - was the base period for track re-newals. Some tasks could be encompassed between 22.00 Saturday and 06.00 Sunday, but 22.00 Saturday to 14.00 Sunday was common. At times, a major job such as a bridge reconstruction would require a line blocked from 22.00 Saturday to 06.00 Monday. Such occasions were kept to a mini-mum. Sunday afternoons and evenings were among the busiest for passengers. An eight hour Sun-day night closure had no merit, as the risk of over-run posed serious consequences for Monday morning travel. Bank Holiday weekends were avoided for infrastructure renewals, (see page 111), a principle usually only violated for emergency repairs, e.g. after a major derailment. Diverting pas-sengers onto road services, at a time when roads would be at their busiest, was a recipe for delays. Prolonged weekend blockages, and even months of weekday blockages, which are commonplace now, are to catch up on post-1994, not on BR, under-investment in track. (see pages 43-44,73,77).

The newcomers have painted themselves into a corner, having introduced differing types of trains that present serious problems when defects occur or lines are blocked. They have non-compatible couplings, often no buffers[11], heavy power needs, any of which impedes attempts to move a defective train. Jazzy ideas such as power controlled toilet doors are an invitation to problems. Some new types have been prevented from operating at all, even on the intended route because fragmentation led to oversights of structural limitations or power supply. Some new types face severe route limitations, which mean that, if a booked route is blocked or its electric supply fails, there will be less scope for the simple diversion, which was so easily applied under BR.

It an ill wind that blows no one any good. The beneficiary for this and other fragmentation problems is an Accrington coach company that spotted a niche market and now dominates the market for PSVs replacing trains throughout Britain in such circumstances. It is very busy!

---

[10] Based on an aggregation of new stock introduced each year. (see BR Accounts). In contrast, it was reported after eight years of privatisation that *new trains helped reduce fleet age by two months to 19.7 years*! (Times 13.12.02). Clearly the average age had been rising from the 13 year average age profile inherited from BR.
[11] Buffers are needed if a loco is used to push or pull a failed train

BR introduced modern techniques for managers, staff and unions, affecting all aspects of railways. Meanwhile, UK industry soldiered on with outdated methods, because they could not convince shareholders - much less labour - that more investment and new techniques were essential. (see Barnett/1 & Barnett/2). Unlike UK industry, after the new techniques were demonstrated to union and staff representatives at BR training schools, the value became obvious and acceptable. New techniques could have proved the essential lifeline to UK manufacturing industry, but became their death knell, as their managements failed to get the message across, and created industrial strife instead. Changes on BR led to staff operating modernised equipment - signalling, operations, track, maintenance and goods handling. Preceding chapters give an indication of the reduction in signal boxes, level crossings, locos, etc., which cut operating and maintenance staff. "All unions showed willingness to join with management in solving problems". (BRB 1969 Report, Page 40).

Track maintenance & renewal

Within BR, we were well aware of the scale of replacement of manpower by machines. However, a year ago - during an interview for BBC Radio "*You and Yours*", having criticised the reduction of visual track inspections in the new era, the interviewer said that surely this was compensated for by using machines instead of labour. I replied that BR had used track maintenance machines since the earliest days, and the ultrasonic equipment *now* boasted of, was used for decades - and more frequently. Clearly, outside BR it was assumed that BR depended on manpower not machines.

BTC/BRB Annual Reports reveal economies from the use of new machines - many imported. Some were developed by BR staff and BR scientists. They included machines for automatic tamping/levelling, automatic ballast profiling/regulating, automatic ballast consolidators, ballast cleaning, track lining and rail changing. There were machines to straighten rail welds and improve rail geometry; to remove rail head roughness - reducing maintenance and giving a smoother ride, twin jib track relaying cranes, relaying gantries, rail mounted inspection platforms to examine bridges above and below the railway, hand powered tools to consolidate ballast at switches and crossings. There were also automatic track recording trolleys, which checked track, with computer analysis.

The first reference to track machines will be found in the BTC Annual Report for 1948 (Page 120), their first year of existence! "*First Matisa tamping machines and ballast cleaner acquired, had difficulties in obtaining Swiss currency*" - due to Government restriction on foreign expenditure[1]. BTC minutes also record purchases *e.g.* "Purchase of five additional track laying units for £31,233". (PRO: AN85/5). Year after year, BTC/BRB Annual Reports carry more details, e.g.:

- 1949: Use of Matisa tampers extended; 15 more ordered. A Matisa ballast cleaner proved useful, consideration being given to the case for one designed for use on BR. Three more mechanical track relaying units are to be acquired. Trials of mechanised ballast scarifying units successful.
- 1950: The use of track machines is being further developed. Twelve Matisa tampers were delivered, extending mechanised maintenance, six relaying units, 27 ballast cleaners and fifteen mobile cranes for lifting concrete sleepers were ordered. At the year end, took delivery of fifteen tampers.
- 1951: Three Matisa ballast cleaners now in service, plus 15 made in UK, under licence].
- 1953: Orders placed for five of an improved ballast cleaner developed in conjunction with a manufacturer. Twelve tracklaying cranes are in use and five more had been ordered.
- 1956: Two additional Matisa ballast cleaners received - a total of 13 are in use.
- 1964: £2.1m authorised for track machines of the heavier type, including 27 automatic tamping and levelling machines, four twin jib track relaying cranes, ten sets of relaying gantries, nine ballast cleaners, 20 track lining machines, 12 rail changing machines.

---

[1] If BR had difficulty getting hard currency for *one* Matisa tamper, it clearly destroys criticism that BR could have replaced large numbers of steam locos by American diesels - their currency being indisputably hard.

- 1966: New equipment included nine ballast cleaners, which have four times the output of older machines, and seven automatic tampers, tamping as much in an hour as a gang did in a week,
- 1967: 35 older machines were scrapped. Acquired 24 new tampers which deal with two sleepers at once. Ordered 20 combined tamper/liner machines for delivery by the end of 1968.
- 1968: Over 100 automatic tamping machines are now in use together with 41 automatic track liners. Some machines combine tamping and lining, so that maintenance is carried out more quickly.
- 1969: Two automatic ballast profiling and regulating machines delivered. Four more ordered. Trials of two prototype 18 ton cranes began - specially developed by BR staff - have telescopic jibs to reach across three tracks, and are designed to speed up laying switch and crossing layouts in overhead electric areas. Automatic ballast consolidators ordered. Trial use of hand powered tools to consolidate ballast around switches and crossings. First machine to carry out four track operations: tamping, lining, consolidating, profiling expected in 1970.
- 1970: A new machine carries out three operations in one - tamping, lining, consolidation. It improves stability of track and requires shorter possessions.
- 1971: 22 combined tamping/lining/consolidating machines were commissioned and produced good results, working faster than the separate machines. A new type rail mounted hydraulic inspection platform is used to examine bridges below and above the railway, avoiding erection of scaffolding.
- 1972: A track lining machine and two ballast consolidators suitable for third rail were introduced. Acquired four additional ballast regulators. These new machines enable more work to be done quicker, and help increase resistance to rail distortion.
- 1978: The building of 12-tonne cranes and twin-jib tracklayers has now begun as part of a £13m investment in a new fleet of cranes over a ten year period.
- 1980: Evaluating a machine to change rails on lines where sleepers have a longer life than rails. Machines are being developed to prepare more recovered rails to use on secondary lines
- 1984/5: A prototype pneumatic ballast injection machine from Plasser offers a four-fold improvement in the durability of track maintenance and reduces traffic disruption. An experimental laser controlled bulldozer improves ballast levelling in relaying and allows higher speeds after lines are reopened to traffic. A structure gauging train was introduced to streamline trackside clearance measurement, improve capability for moving non-standard loads, and assist studies into new traffic opportunities and vehicle design. (It should have prevented gauge problems - see page 84).
- 1985/6: Development in machinery and techniques mean that disruption to traffic is much less than it used to be while the railway is renewed, and takes place without passengers being aware.
- 1986/7: Trials with two track machines, developed by BR Research were completed: RASTIC which strengthens rail welds and improves rail top; SUPERLEV which removes railhead roughness - both reduced the amount of track maintenance needed and give a more comfortable ride.
- 1987/8: New techniques for track relaying are eliminating the need for many speed restrictions previously needed while track was consolidated. Trials with new dynamic track stabilisers previously only used to consolidate track after maintenance are effective after track renewal - twelve have been ordered. Trains will be able to run at line speeds of up to 125 mph immediately a line is re-opened for traffic, shortening journey times and reducing costs. This will reduce the time taken in maintenance. Savings in engineering costs and those on fuel and brake wear together with a general improvement in Sunday travel for customers will save £20m for InterCity.
- 1989/90: Use of dynamic track stabilisers and automatic track alignment systems continued to lower operating costs and improve quality.

The use of such machines was so commonplace as to not warrant mention in subsequent Reports.

Extent of progress
- 1965: At the beginning of the year, mechanised tamping was 1,000 miles pa, and by the end of the year was up to 12,000 miles pa. Permanent-way staff were cut by 12.5% to 20,000.
- 1966: By the end of the year, modern machine track maintenance had spread to over 72% of BR.

- 1966-7: Mechanised track tamping on 10,300 track miles in 1966, rose to 13,300 in 1967; track lined mechanically rose from 3,800 to 8,500 track miles.
- 1967: Mr. A. Paterson, BR Chief Civil Engineer said the life of a rail in continuous welded form will extend life by a third - to an average 24 instead of 18 year intervals, saving £340 per mile in maintenance, plus savings on train fuel costs, rolling stock and track renewals". Mr. A. Butland[2] stated "when the changeover to mechanisation is complete - we are 70% there - an investment of £5.6m will give an annual return of £6m". (Developments in Railway Traffic Engineering, Pages 7 & 21).
- 1968: Track tamped in 1968 totalled 15,000 miles and lined mechanically 10,500 miles. Mechanised maintenance covers 80% of BR. Extension to the rest should be completed in 1969.
- 1969: Mechanisation of track work extended over practically the whole of the system. 20,000 miles of track were mechanically tamped and 12,500 miles mechanically lined.
- 1971: 20,000 miles of track were mechanically tamped and 14,500 miles mechanically lined.
- 1973: There were fewer incidents of broken rails, because of early detection of cracks by the ultrasonic flaw detection train and portable detectors.
- 1976: New track inspection equipment delivered that will ensure that engineers have up-to-date information on the state of the track.
- 1980: Improved techniques and mechanised maintenance will bring further savings in staff costs in a labour force already reduced in the last two decades from 52,000 to 22,000.
- 1990/1: New technology and sophisticated project control enable engineers to reballast up to $1^1/_2$ miles in a 52 hour possession.

Ultrasonic testing of tracks
- 1954: A new design of track recording car [TRC] is being studied.
- 1956-8: A track recording car ordered in March 1956 for £50,300 had risen by October 1958 to £72,975. (PRO: AN85/9 & AN85/12).
- 1964: A computer is used to process TRC data.
- 1962: Development of a 30 mph TRC was reported in 1962.
- 1966: Small static length gangs have been replaced by mobile gangs. To compensate for reduced visual checks, TRCs are now used. They unerringly pick out faults that cannot be detected by the eye. All cars are fitted with "Neptune" - electronic data evaluating equipment devised by BR. They print out data on faults, so that they can be corrected at once. At the same time it provides a permanent record of every inch of track.
- 1968: Sixty new portable [ultrasonic] machines, giving a visible and audible indication of hidden defects were introduced in 1968. Staff trained to operate 60 new pulse echo flaw detectors - portable electronic machines which find hidden defects. Start made on development of rail flaw detecting car, and on automatic data processing for use with the detector vehicle.
- 1970: Classification of track condition and preparation of a track maintenance programme was facilitated by a computer to process data provided by track recording trolleys. A new ultrasonic rail flaw detecting car is able to cover 40,000 miles pa.
- 1971: The new ultrasonic rail flaw detecting car introduced in 1970 came up to expectations in its accuracy and sensitivity. A year's experience indicates that 16,000 miles a year of rail examination by the car will meet the stipulated frequency for all lines, and this the car can maintain.
- 1972: The ultrasonic rail flaw detector has carried out its second year of testing, and many thousands of miles have been examined. A significant number of cracked rails were detected in good time. Tests made on fracture-tough and wear-resistant rails.
- 1973: Fewer broken rails due to early detection by ultrasonic detector trains and portable detectors
- 1976: A high speed TRC measuring track geometry developed at BR's Railway Technical Centre was tested satisfactorily at 125 mph and computer analysis of rail ultrasonic records to detect possible flaws was introduced

---

[2] As BRB Chief Civil Engineer, he initiated mechanisation of track maintenance, CWR & concrete sleepers.

- 1977: A high speed TRC, developed by BR's civil engineer to measure quality of track during journeys at speeds up to 125 mph, was handed over this year. It has already proved its usefulness in regular operation.
- 1987/8: New track recording units analyse track geometry at speed.

New techniques associated with mechanised maintenance led to the opening of a new training school for track staff at Watford to further improve their skills. (BRB 1968 Report, Page 40).

Management techniques

In 1969, BR created a Management Services Department to bring together Data Processing, Organisation & Methods, Operational Research and Work Study, which had been functioning independently of each other from the 1950s. (BRB 1969 Report, Page 43).

Work & Method Study

A Work Study Training School was set up at Watford. (BTC 1956 Report, Page 15). The principle adopted by BR was to bring in a few experts to train recruits from within BR, who would then train other BR staff to go out in the field to conduct work studies - involving Timing & Methods - and who would also conduct Appreciation Courses that were attended by managers, unions and staff.

"Many of the work study schemes in operation ...... increased output and substantial improvements in performance. The use of work study in the initial planning of new works schemes was developed to great advantage, particularly in connection with Modernisation. Work study methods were also considered and applied to a number of operations normally regarded as non-technical: including terminals, cartage and seat reservation. The greatest progress was made in the Civil Engineering Dept - there are now 6,000 staff working under work studied schemes in that Dept. Other Divisions are using work study ... and the majority now have a nucleus staff trained in the technique. The Work Study Training Centre at Watford has continued to perform a valuable service in instructing senior and middle management in the elements of work study technique. In addition, each of the six Regions of BR set up a Work Study Training School"[3]. (BTC 1957 Report, Pages 10-11).

"Work study was supported by the unions. 40,000 staff are working under work study schemes. Half of civil engineering staff are on work study. Work study is gaining ground in other Departments". The Joint Productivity Council in October 1960 issued a Joint Declaration of the advantages of work study. (BTC 1960 Report, Pages 3,11).

The Commission was told that "on the previous day, a meeting of the BR Joint Productivity Council had issued a Joint [Management/Union] Report of the need to accelerate the application of work study. Due to poor press coverage, given by the national media, a Statement had been placed in the advertising columns of the Press. (BTC minutes 20.10.60).

Clearly, media disinterest in anything demonstrating that poor old nationalised BR was progressing faster then UK industry, is not a new phenomenon. It would be unthinkable that BR - whose managers and unions were regularly criticised as being inefficient - be given free publicity that proved that they were more forward looking than industry. In April 1993, a Sunday Times article criticised BR and the unions and likened BR practice to a Peter Sellers' film, *overlooking that the film involved a factory strike precipitated by a stop watch. BR had used stop watches for work study for over 30 years without causing disputes*[4].

The greater part of the work of the Civil Engineering Department has been covered by work study. Total BR staff covered was 45,000. Reference was made in earlier Reports to the application of work study to passenger and goods stations. The number of schemes is being increased as rapidly as

---

[3] Beeching has been credited with introducing Work & Method Study to BR. He didn't. It was well advanced before he took over in 1962. The Author's "Staff History" records that he attended a course in August 1958. BTC Reports mention progress on Work Study and other techniques long before Beeching. (see above).
[4] Work study men were [first] brought into shipbuilders Cammell Laird in 1966. Evidently, they didn't understand the work, and hence seemed to make errors. Shop stewards were sent on work study course in 1966. (Anthony Burton, *"The Rise and Fall of British Shipbuilding"*, Pages 229, 230). They were ten years behind BR.

possible. Almost all of the station investigations have resulted in improved methods. The application of work study to some of the larger and older marshalling yards and carriage cleaning is making good progress. Some of the most satisfactory applications during 1961 have been in the field of motive power maintenance. Work study is assisting in minimising costs of maintenance of the rapidly growing fleet of diesel trains. Where maintenance staff requirements were initially assessed on the basis of continental railways with similar units, it has now been established, by the use of work study that less staff and fewer maintenance depots will be required than originally contemplated. (BTC 1961 Report, Pages 11-13).

Some 68,000 [up 19%] staff are under work study schemes, including 35,000 civil engineer's staff - 66% of his labour force. (BRB 1963 Report, Page 39). Over 75,000 staff are covered by work study investigations. The number of staff to whom the technique is applied are increasing at the rate of 10-15% pa. There are 1,870 work study practitioners and instructors. 75% of civil engineers staff are now working under work study schemes. Work study has also extended to traffic staff. An increase in 50% of traffic staff brought the total to 31,500. (BRB 1964 Report, Page 40).

An experimental freight train incentive bonus scheme involved development of work measurement data by work study staff. Clerical work data was also developed for administrative procedures. Training for managers and practitioners is given at BR's school at Watford on work study. (BTC 1967 Report, Page 34).

Organisation & Method

The Commission decided that Organisation & Method should be applied throughout the undertaking. This technique bears a similar relationship to administrative matters as work study does to manufacturing and associated manual work. (BTC 1957 Report, Page 20). O&M units were set up in six railway Regions. Appreciation courses were established at the BTC Staff College. (BTC 1960 Report, Page 12). A start was made on drawing up a programme of job evaluation for clerical and supervisory staff. (BRB 1969 Report, Page 40). The newly developed system of clerical work data continued to arouse interest within and outside the industry. BR trained their own staff and also instructors for other industries. BR developed models for business planning. A wide range of management and specialist courses continued to be provided at Watford, and attracted interest outside BR. (BRB 1969 Report, Page 43).

Operational Research

Operational research began in 1953 (BTC Review April 1953). The Operational Research Unit has placed research contracts with the University of Leeds to seek a mathematical technique for the optimum scheduling of locos. (BTC 1961 Report, Page 23). Computers were successfully employed in the application of linear programming in distributing empty wagons. (BTC 1961 Report, Page 23).

A wide range of techniques are used including statistical methods, multiple regression analysis and linear programming. (BTC 1965 Report, Page 44). The Operational Research unit is looking into mathematical techniques for the optimum scheduling of locos. (BTC 1967 Report, Page 27).

Computers

A computer was ordered for R&D. Two computers installed as part of office mechanisation, are the first on European railways. Before this, 90% of paybills were mechanically produced. (BTC 1957 Report, Pages 22,30). By the end of 1960, fifteen electronic computers were installed, six ordered and a further nine were envisaged. (BTC 1960 Report, Page 36). BR was among first users of conventional punched card equipment, and it was a logical step to move into the computer field at an early stage in the development of these machines. By the end of 1960, BR had 60 data processing centres equipped with computers and electronic calculators. (BTC Review Jan. 1964). Exploitation of computers is taking place where practicable and economical. Computers are also used to improve distribution of empty wagons. (BRB 1961 Report, Page 23). New computer centres were opened at Crewe and Peterborough. (BTC 1967 Report, Page 27). BR has a very powerful and sophisticated data handling system. (BRB 1968 Report, Page 35). Increasing use was made of computers to deal with renewals. (BRB 1969 Report). 1973 saw computing move into design of train services, pathing and resource scheduling, and many other aspects of operations.

Research

The computer used at the research establishment at Derby is believed to be the only railway-owned computer in the world engaged solely on scientific and engineering work. (BTC 1961 Report). It is comparatively unusual to find, in the world, a railway system supporting its own major programme of R&D. (1979 Report). It contrasted with UK industry that abhorred the use of scientists, preferring to depend on methods handed down since the industrial revolution, (see Barnett[1], Pages 94-97), the BTC inherited them from the Big Four, and continued to make full use of them. When the BTC was abolished, they were placed under the BRB. In 1986, a House of Lords Select Committee on Science & Technology was impressed by the range of work undertaken. BTC/BRB Annual Reports included regular summaries of their research embracing:-

adhesion, axlebox design, ballast, batteries, brakes, bogies, bridges, carbon-fibre, computer-aided design, corrosion, diesel exhaust fumes, electric traction, engine life, fastenings, locos, metal fatigue, oils - including "laundering" for further use, paints, plastics, rails, sleepers, springs, track circuits, track machines, track-to-train control, vehicles, waterproofing bridges,

Most of these led to improved designs and lower costs. BR research provides an important support role for the private sector of the British railway manufacturing industry. Many projects initiated at Derby are offered to industry e.g. a high speed pantograph, new type motors for trains and a new freight bogie. (1979 Report). They were acknowledged as world leaders - "There is overseas interest in this project. BR is eighteen months ahead of the world" (1962 Report) - and their advice was regularly sought. Various developments they had initiated were sold under licence to foreign railways and to UK manufacturers. "Laboratories at Derby are provided with equipment which are among the most advanced in the world". (1963 Report).

A special grease developed by the Department is used instead of oil for lubricating points. Frequency of attention is reduced, and a saving made of £0.2m on one Region. Studies into track led to a breakthrough in knowledge of compaction of ballast. Work on rail failure and fatigue included experiments with tougher steels. Ultrasonic track recording was developed and improved. A "walking-stick" type of ultrasonic rail flaw detector was developed to speed manual inspection. Trials to prevent rail cracks and fractures were successful. A dry slide base plate for track switches won an invention award and will save £3m pa. An experimental length of concrete slab track was laid, which was registered as PACT - a BR trademark. (This was used in the Channel Tunnel, saving the company huge development costs). Royal Albert Bridge at Saltash was subject to model stress analysis, leading to a strengthening procedure that avoided more costly solutions. A structure gauging train was developed. Laser control of ballast cleaners has reduced the new ballast needed when track work is carried out. Computers on tampers ensure that aligning of tracks gives a better ride. A new powerful computer simulation package, VISION, was created, to model rail operations on complex networks and enables infrastructure or timetable improvements to be planned efficiently and quickly. Two products for improving track alignment and flaw testing are now in use.

They developed a computerised technique of overhead system design to bring all-round cost savings, reducing the time taken to install overhead equipment - cutting costs and interference with services. Electrification costs were cut by over £10,000 per mile using these techniques. Costs of a scheme in Scotland were cut by £0.5m from a projected £1.25m.

Rolling stock development reduced energy consumption, improved brake performance and will be incorporated in commuter trains. A new multi-grade lubricating oil was developed following joint research with major oil companies, saving £3m pa. Work was undertaken on a method of predicting deterioration of vehicles or equipment. A prototype advanced bogie is 30% lighter, has less drag, makes less noise, uses less energy and is cheaper to operate and maintain. A computer for scheduling traction and rolling stock maintenance has been installed in Sheffield; other depots will follow. Techniques have been developed for improving the crash-worthiness of rail vehicles.

New systems developed for use in major signal centres and branch lines: interfacing colour TV monitors with two earlier developments - solid state interlocking [SSI] and automatic route setting provide more efficient control at large PSBs at lower cost; and radio signalling for lightly used lines.

Quicker response to phone enquiries owes much to a computer aided timetable system installed at thirty sites in 1988/9.

Critical Path Analysis

Critical Path Analysis was introduced on BR for the control and progress of its Modernisation Plan beginning in the late 1950s. Sometimes referred to as Network Analysis, it comprised a network of lines, each representing an individual task or process within the complete scheme of a major project (see below). Lines in the diagram would be endorsed to show the title of the task concerned. Each had a forecast period of time (usually expressed in weeks) needed to complete that task. The circles in the diagram would contain the aggregate duration of the preceding tasks by the shortest and longest routes. Where those figures were the same, would identify the Critical Path. The total time estimated to complete the whole project was the sum of the periods of the longest path - the Critical Path. To ensure that a project was completed on schedule, no task on that path must be allowed to exceed its forecast span, and if one did, action needed to be taken to recover an equivalent period of time in a succeeding phase on the critical path. Tasks on a non-critical path that over-ran, would not be a problem, unless the revised sum of periods on that path exceeded that on the original critical path. Otherwise, such tasks, if over-running, need not be expedited, if that would incur additional cost. To reduce the overall length of a project, tasks on the critical path were reviewed to determine which could be shortened. Such changes may then have created a different critical path.

Network analysis is used for management decision and control purposes on work ranging from bridge repairs and loco maintenance to large capital projects. (BTC 1965 Report, Page 45).

On BR, we assumed that this technique was in general use by the private sector. Hence, when attending the Senior Executive Course at Manchester Business School in 1982 - as one of only three from the public sector - it was a surprise to discover that it was new to most of those from the private sector[5]. The technique had other potential non-constructional uses - back in 1968, the system had been introduced by career railwayman Gerry Papworth to plan and control the complex task of preparing and publishing the annual timetable, and all associated documentation including train-crew rosters, loco and carriage workings, etc.

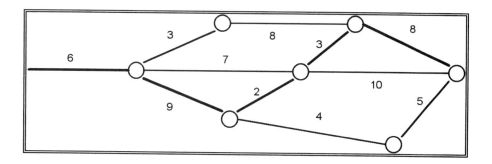

---

[5] In 1971, a shop steward said that "shipbuilding managers didn't understand the problems, we were talking to them about Critical Path Analysis, and they thought that we were talking about a Greek tanker owner". (Anthony Burton, *"The Rise and Fall of British Shipbuilding"*, Page 236).

Chapter 10   Passenger business

It is astonishing that anyone can claim that BR was *always* raising fares, implying that private sector prices were stuck in a time warp, when rail fares, *alone*, were below the RPI from 1948 to 1990 due to external direction and interference, (see Appendix A), a fact unnoticed by those who claim to be able to add two and two. The major beneficiary was Government. Lower fares held down the Government payroll for 2.55m people: armed forces: 0.85m, civil servants: 1.01m, post office: 0.25m, health service: 0.45m. (CSO Annual Abstracts 1952/3). The next major group were London commuters, especially the LT&S line, who enjoyed cheaper travel than the rest of the UK[1]. In 1950, the BTC said they had long enjoyed a privileged position and were still the cheapest at 0.55d per mile. (see "*Blueprints for Bankruptcy*", Page 98). Despite this they called for the line to be improved above levels enjoyed by those paying higher fares. The line was electrified at the expense of those with less modern services. Their claim to be the "Misery Line" was self inflicted by avarice

In March 1951, the Chancellor proposed to Cabinet that BR be relieved of £3m pa armed forces concessions for Duty travel: 3.4% of revenue. The Minister of Defence blocked the proposal. (PRO: CAB). No change was made. Significant gains for the Defence budget continued until 1962, when conscription ended. Under the 1883 Act, BR also had to subsidise half-rate off duty travel by armed forces personnel and their families. Had their fares kept pace with the RPI, Government would have had to increase pay or fail to increase regular strength so as to end conscription by 1962.

In December 1990, a Daily Telegraph article quoted £3,225 for a Diss to London annual season[2]. £3,225 reveals nothing. Expressed as 4.6p per mile, one seventh the cost by an average car, would have impressed readers less. By car, the 69,350 miles pa would cost £20,000 pa, and after a year, the car's value expressed in pence. Life expectancy is reduced by tension and carbon monoxide and every minute of the journeys wasted - equal to 60 days pa to a conscientious businessman, of which there must be too few, hence the balance of payments problem.

Audited accounts prove that fares were held below inflation from 1948. Incredibly, the MoT ignored this, when, in 1956, he uniquely froze rail fares for the sixth year since the start of the war.

year	index of		passenger revenue £m		revenue lost £m	
	average fares	retail prices	actual	inflation linked	in year	1956 prices
1949	93	105	114	129	15	21
1950	91	108	107	127	20	27
1951	89	113	107	136	29	38
1952	93	127	112	153	41	47
1953	96	133	115	159	44	49
1954	96	135	117	165	48	52
1955	100	140	118	165	47	50
1956	104	147	128	181	53	53
Total						336

Table 4 - Source: BTC Annual Reports & Retail Price Index, 1948 = 100

BR fares decided externally

The 1947 Act required the BTC, of which BR was a part, "*to pay its way, taking one year with another*". Hence, a Financial Times article (18.11.91) was wrong in stating that, "from 1948, the purpose of BR was to provide a social service, the cost of assets was written off, interest and deprecia-

---

[1] The London, Tilbury & Southend Railway Act 1852 limited fares to 0.5d compared with the usual 1d per mile.
[2] In 2002, a standard season costs £4476 - a 39% increase, compared to a rise of 31% in the inflation rate (source: ONS). No letters of complaint appear to have been published in the paper regarding this huge increase.

tion charges being met from taxation". Successive Acts retained the objective, although Government made it impossible by interfering with BR prices, but not those of their suppliers. The Act created a law court - the Transport Tribunal to rule on rail charges. Objections could be lodged by "any body representative of persons using services to which the scheme relates". This included local authorities, and associations created for the purpose. At the 1951 Hearing, BTC executives were in the witness box for 15 days and answered 4,858 questions. The Act stated that the Tribunal should not do anything to prevent the BTC from discharging its duty to pay its way. It did not provide for the situation when the BTC said it needed increases and the Tribunal disagreed. The Act required the BTC to submit Schemes relating to BR passenger, BR freight, London Transport rail & road, road haulage, canals and ports, within two years of passing the Act on 6th August 1947, six months before the BTC came into being, leaving an inadequate 18 months for these tasks. No reason was given for "Charges Schemes". No supplier, competitor nor industry had them. The Tribunal's role continued to 1968. (see pages 32,177). Thousands of objections to fare increases at Hearings included:

- "BR had not cut costs in 1950". In fact, they had shed 19,000 jobs - unlike the rest of UK industry.
- "A fare of one penny per mile should be reintroduced" - the fare charged in 1830 !
- Things would improve next year - or the year after - to justify no increases - soon proved false.
- "When people move home from London, the fare should be unaltered for the longer journey".
- Barristers said: there is no point in a fare increase that led to no increase in passengers carried[3].
- Some County Councils pleaded for restraint on Seasons because of student travel[4].
- "Old coaches should not be replaced by new coaches as it would increase fares".
- When the BTC submitted its third fares application in six years, the LCC challenged the Tribunal's jurisdiction based on a clause in the Act requiring 12 months[5] to elapse after authorising a Scheme before considering an alteration. When the Tribunal ruled that it had jurisdiction, the LCC took it to the Court of Appeal, which rejected the case, referring it back to the Tribunal.

Objectors to rail fare increases admitted that bus fares were higher[6]. BTC said that municipal and privately owned bus companies had withdrawn workers fares, but BR was compelled to keep them.

As if it was not incredibly Quixotic to have a solitary UK industry applying to a Court of Law for permission to increase prices, bureaucrats managed to make it more farcical. In 1967, after BR had been given legal permission by the Tribunal to increase fares, the decision was then referred to the NBPI, which approved the judicially authorised increases, but referred them back to the Tribunal, which then reduced some of the increases that it had previously authorised! The Tribunal's role[7] on rail charges was terminated in 1969, but political control continued. (see pages 177-178).

Annual Reports of the BTC and its successor, BRB, continually drew attention to the fact that fares were trailing inflation. Typical extracts from these Reports were:

- Fares in comparison with pre-war are up 90%, prices are up 160%. LT costs were 130% above pre-war whilst fares had risen by only 63%. It was not generally appreciated that BR fares outside London were generally higher than those in the London Area. (BTC 1952 Report, Pages 24,56).
- "London fares went up in December 1955 by 4% but were still only double pre-war, whereas the RPI was up $2^1/_2$ times". (BTC 1955 Report, Page 5).
- The public pay three times as much as pre-war for many goods and services, but complain that fares are too high. In real terms, fares have fallen since 1938 and real wages have risen by about a half. (BTC 1956 Report, Page 65).
- Average real fares per mile were lower in 1957 than in 1938. (BTC 1957 Report Page 48).

---

[3] The objective was more net revenue, not more passengers. These are not synonymous.
[4] Their Rates rose six times as much as fares. See "*The Railway Closure Controversy*" Appx C. Councils should subsidise student travel not BR. Accounts showed that fares were below 1938 levels; how much restraint did they want?
[5] It is doubtful that it was anticipated that 17 months could elapse between Application and Authorisation!
[6] "No sooner is a line closed than bus fares rose to heights which made it difficult for constituents to travel at reasonable prices". (Hansard 23.6.58, vol. 590, col. 202). see also "*The Railway Closure Controversy*".
[7] See "*Blueprints for Bankruptcy*" for a record of the Tribunal's disastrous effect on BR finances.

• The majority of passengers in the peak are season ticket holders. On BR they pay half of the standard 2nd class fare of 2d per mile. (BTC 1957 Report, Page 58, Para 184).

• Most fares are below pre-war in real terms. The discount of quarterly Season tickets against Ordinary fares was 75% at 70 miles, 55% at 20 miles. (BTC 1959 Report, Pages 62, 64-65)

• "Years of statutory control and the publicity arising from the processes of Public Inquiry have given the belief that higher fares are an inflationary factor. In fact, during the first 15 years of inflation which began with the Second World War, fares rose much less than necessary to compensate for the fall in the value of money. Even with the rise in the past 10 years, the average fare level remains at or below prewar - though it is widely accepted that prices of services in a modern economy must be expected to rise faster than the prices of manufactured goods[8]. Discounts in Seasons on the basis of five return journeys per week at the end of 1961 - was 40% at 10 miles, 55% at 20 miles and 75% at 70 miles. A growth in the peak to which these travellers contribute justifies reducing that discount[9]. Transport charges have been falling in comparison with delivered prices of commodities[10]. Over half of the increase in expenses was due to increased prices and cessation in 1961 of Government's contribution towards the cost of road bridges over railways and level crossings". (BTC 1961 Report Pages 59,62,68,75).

No application was submitted to the Tribunal to increase fares in 1948, 1949, 1952, 1959, 1961, 1965 and 1967. In addition, the application made in 1956 was withdrawn after Ministerial pressure. Such a record, even without the staggering 12 year delay imparted into raising charges in an unsuccessful attempt to match inflation was unmatched by any industry, business or enterprise in the UK

"Passenger fares appear to have been well shielded from the effects of inflation". (*"Paying for Railways"*, 1958, Pages 281,294, by Political & Economic Planning - an independent research group).

In a 1977 *"Fares Fair"* Report, the CTCC stated: "Information supplied by BR indicates, that over the past 40 years, average fare levels have lagged behind the cost of living. This may surprise many; if borne out by closer investigation, it deserves wider prominence". (Page 31). There is no record of any investigation by them. Average fares are in BTC/BRB Reports - which were supplied to them. The RPI is published by the CSO. (see Appendix A). Later Reports reveal they retained their blinkers:

• "The fare structure needs simplifying. BR was urged to increase the spread of InterCity savers so that passengers who do not qualify for a railcard will benefit from reduced fares". They criticised BR because the South East sector offered £2 anywhere in November to Senior Citizens, other areas did not. (CTCC 1983 Report Pages 4,12). *The remit was to cut the subsidy, not provide equality.*

• The CTCC criticised the unevenness of 1986 increases that varied from 5% to 14%. BR said they were charging what the market would bear. The CTCC said: It was their role to guard against erosion of opportunity for off peak travel[11]". (CTCC 1985/6 Report, Page 13).

• "Fare rises should be in line with inflation". (CTCC 1990/1 Report, Page 16). *That is **not** a private sector policy. They did not advocate that policy from 1948.*

Their *Fares Fair* Report also stated BR should divorce itself from the notion that market pricing exists to help some social groupings at the expense of others[12]. BR should be invited to state what proportion of journeys it ultimately seeks to sell at a reduced fare[13]. There is a risk of undermining the fairness of the standard fare[14]. BR should eliminate attempts to fiddle with the South East rush hour problem by half-hearted repricing[15]. (Pages 28,29,30). In view of their perennial criticism, it is

---

[8] This was not from a BR manager but from Dr. Beeching imported from that icon of the private sector - ICI.

[9] It was to be many years before there was a meaningful narrowing of this gap.

[10] Included transport charges, which traders unjustifiably said had caused their increases - see Tables 8 & 11.

[11] This role was not specified in the Acts that set out their remit.

[12] Of hundreds of managers known to me, not one held that view.

[13] Other transport, travel agents and hoteliers do not. The new boys are far more secretive.

[14] Market forces are not based on fairness as passengers are now learning in the shiny new privatised era.

[15] *"Blueprints for Bankruptcy"* accurately forecast that "privatised operators' repricing will be not be half hearted"

interesting to note that the Chairmen of the CTCC, and Scottish and Welsh TUCCs told the top secret 1961 Special Advisory Group, that BR should be free to decide its fares! (PRO: MT132/85).

"Past experience of resistance to price increases is usually temporary. Over the past decade[16], fares have been market oriented. BR estimate that it produces 6-10% more revenue". (1978 Price Commission Report, Page 3). Despite this view - shared by Select Committees - that general fare reductions as distinct from BR's selective reductions would not increase revenue, many claim that slashed fares would solve BR problems[17]. A 25% cut needs 33% more volume for the same *gross* revenue. Where trains are loaded over 75%, more coaches would be needed and some platforms would have to be longer, requiring more volume to cover these costs, **to hold losses at existing levels**. Still more would be needed to cut losses, which theorists expect to follow fare cuts. Logical minds, seeing that 40-50% more volume is essential on a 25% fare reduction, must address the down side scenario - who picks up the tab if net revenue falls? Some would not travel more, but pay less; some would travel more, but pay the same; few would spend *more* on rail travel. Savings, would be deployed elsewhere[18]. A perspective of fares can be gleaned by comparing newspaper prices. Rail fares in 1991 were seventeen times 1948 levels, (see Appendix A), newspapers were up to 80 times higher.

BR introduced senior citizen railcards in 1975[19], using pension books - issued to women at 60, men at 65 - as a basis for sale. MPs criticised BR for discriminating against 60 year old men. Cards were not introduced as a social service, nor to cut fares to those in gainful employment, but to increase net revenue. One MP, told that it was due to BR having to use a state pension book as proof of eligibility, and would continue to do so if the pensionable age for men was reduced, said that it was impertinent to link Government's policy on pensionable age to their issue. He was clearly unwilling to listen to the opinions of a BR manager. Despite his opinion, and without a change in the age limit, I increased Divisional sales of the cards, by selling them in bulk to local authorities, having persuaded their chief executives to offer them as an alternative to bus passes. Sales to them went up 600% - it brought in an estimated £1.4m revenue pa. Later, BR gave way to political pressure and conceded cards to 60 year old men. Government continued to discriminate against them! Businessmen could be heard boasting of savings from using these cards, thereby cutting BR revenue. Bus passes for men remained available only to those over 65 until recently. MPs should have been pursuing the entire private sector to offer one third off prices to over-60s!

Critics claimed higher fares cut passengers. Higher prices did not have that effect with other expenditure. People grumbled, but wages were rising, so they paid up. The problem was that Government policies and intervention held fares so far behind costs, that huge increases were eventually needed to catch up on the RPI. Nevertheless, critics focus on increases in the late 1980s that were above *prevailing* inflation, ignoring that they were caused by past under-pricing. A 1993 Sunday Times article selected 1982 as a start point to compare fares to inflation. It is unclear why 1982 was selected as fares of nationalised railways were still below inflation, (see Appendix A). Had losses caused by Government policies been repaid to BR, and Ministers ceased to interfere in management decisions, that would have been the time for a new start point.

In his book (Page 145), Dr. Joy - ex civil servant, one time Economist with BR - argued that fares control was irrelevant to viability. He was wrong: without control, sub standard fares and captive business would have been priced up, that subject to competition priced selectively, and that seeping away due to car mania, unaffected. Without control, BR would not have waited $9^1/_4$ years between need and implementation. (see Appendix B). Effective competition with cars over long distances was achieved by accelerations facilitated by closure of minor stations, removal of branch line junctions, and conversion of disused goods yards into carparks. This could have been achieved earlier but for

---

[16] After the end of the Tribunal's statutory control.

[17] A view held by the Wrexham-Birkenhead Rail Users Association, who, in 1982, urged BR to cut fares. Fares were *trailing* the RPI. I said: "Fare increases will stand comparison with anything you can name". They didn't reply.

[18] Reduced fares increased volume but *gross* revenue fell. (evidence to the Tribunal, see "*Blueprints for Bankruptcy*")

[19] Brochures issued by the new boys give an impression that reduced fares for senior citizens are a new innovation.

the slow procedures which BR had to pursue, to close lines, some of which had struggled to be profitable when competing with the horse. A private sector company would have swept them out of the way before modernising. Net revenue would have increased, given pricing freedom and new assets purchased by extra revenue would have generated new business. Had BR been permitted to match fares to the RPI, from 1948, they would have gained over £11 bn. (see Appendix A). It is significant that after 1985, with fares outpacing prevailing inflation, many trains were full[20].

Passenger Traffic Groups

There were three passenger traffic groups: fast & semi-fast; stopping-trains; suburban. These categories were in general use for many years.

Fast & semi-fast

After modernisation, this group was best placed to compete with road transport. Often, their reliability was affected by stopping services using the same route or passing to or from branch lines

Stopping

These called at all or most stations on a line. Hence, average speeds were low and uncompetitive when motor vehicles replaced the horse. Many routes - not all designated as branch lines - had struggled to compete with the horse. There were attempts to prove that they could have been made to pay given infinite amounts of capital. These have been disproved by fact and figure[21].

"Receipts from steam hauled stopping trains do not cover direct costs by tens of millions. Where there is prospect of traffic to be developed, all means of making services earn enough to cover direct costs will be examined before withdrawal is proposed: recasting services to improve rolling stock use, diesel or electric traction. If diesels doubled receipts and halved costs, a substantial percentage of stopping services would still not cover direct costs". (BR Memo March 1956, PRO: AN103/3).

Stopping services tended to create delays or reduce the speed of fast services, at junctions and elsewhere. Withdrawal led to faster schedules for long distance services.

Commuter

Seasons, used by peak commuters, were held further below inflation than other fares from 1940, when Government directed lower increases than other fares and prices. No increases took place until 1946, when Seasons were again favoured. The gap continued to widen, until by the end of 1961, a Season for 10 miles had a discount against other fares of 40%, and 70% at 70 miles. Revenue was lowest when costs were highest. Commuters' earnings had increased substantially.

Government policy held down fares for London commuters, the biggest group of whom were Government employees. Government ignored the recommendation of the secret Special Advisory Group to end the fares role of the Transport Tribunal in 1961, even, for commuters. This and other aspects of the Report that criticised Government, were concealed, and in the 1962 Act that was supposed to set BR free to act like a commercial business retained the Tribunal to control London area fares - peak and off peak. It was not done on the grounds that BR had a monopoly - in 1955-6, two Tory Ministers stated that there was no monopoly - one said "BR had never had a monopoly".

Travel at peak times is often very expensive in resources which has little or no use at other times. Fares in the 1970s were artificially held down[22]. Government believes that commuters should have a period of years to adjust to fares that are bound to rise to cover higher costs of assets. The more successful BR is in other parts of its business, the less the burden on commuters will be! (Transport Policy, 1977, Cmnd 6836, Pages 28-29). Commuters had been subsidised for 30 years. Why should it continue? There was no justification for them to be subsidised by other passengers or low railway wages. Off peak fares have little effect on the peak and have been available since the earliest days. Such fares should be calculated after peak fares have been increased to cover all costs.

---

[20] "The highest number of passengers for 20 years". (CTCC 1988/9 Report, Page 5). "Trains were overpriced and overcrowded". (Henshaw, Page 224). Fares cannot be too high if trains are overcrowded.

[21] See "The Railway Closure Controversy".

[22] They were held down by Government Directive, not managerial decision - since the 1940s.

	Thousands of Southern Region passengers per quarter hour, starting at							
	07.45	0.800	08.15	08.30	08.45	09.00	09.15	09.30
1951	22	17.5	26.25	42	42.65	39	26.5	18
1968	11	28.75	43.75	55.25	52.25	40.5	25	13.75
% change	-50	+64	+66	+31.5	+13	+4	-6	-24
Table 5 - Source : NBPI 1969 Report, Appendix G [ii]								

In 1976, the DoT published a Consultation Document "*Transport Policy*" packed with mundane statements that proved that they were out of touch with reality, e.g. "The peak has been a *factor* in keeping unit costs high". (Vol. 1, Page 6). This was *the* definitive understatement:

Improvements & Developments - An industry in decline?

Nominated managers had responsibility for developing ways of increasing revenue and cutting costs on specified routes. Some ideas were opposed by local authorities unable to see the wood for the trees. In 1982, councils opposed a plan linking North Wales-Manchester and Manchester-Scarborough trains, creating coast-to-coast trains, requiring fewer coaches, but with as many trains. The object was to make more productive use of assets - but locally it was promoted as an improved service, soon confirmed by increased loadings. Some complained of losing an interval service, which the line had never had. The new service was closer to an interval. A typical rural route with no prospect of viability without subsidy was the Cambrian Coast line: Shrewsbury to Aberystwyth/ Pwhelli. (see page 69). Over the years, the attraction of this coast had plummeted. A Barmouth hotelier said that he had seen the peak fall from 12 to 7 weeks, and feared a further fall. This was due to Britons opting for cheap foreign holidays, not as train spotters believed due to BR refusing to carry passengers for next to nothing. Some holidaymakers used rail for day trips, on trains that were full in the summer. Critics suggested that BR should carry *them* at lower fares. As the service provided was the maximum possible in the limited holiday season, no more passengers could be carried. Critics could not see that providing more stock to stand idle for most of the year, whilst revenue fell resulting from their naive pricing theories meant bigger losses. The school term overlapped the start of the summer service by 2-3 weeks. BR managers approached the issue logically, and proposed that local authorities alter school terms to avoid this, releasing trains otherwise occupied by pupils travelling to school. The plan included closure of the small Pwhelli train crew depot.

Stations opened and others re-opened when local authorities provided cash on the same basis as for buses. Had they subsidised rail services when closure threatened, closure would have been avoided. Other improvements that attracted passengers are mentioned in Chapters 6,7,8. "In four years, the Chairman had opened or re-opened 26 stations". (BRB 1980 Report, Page 9). In 1981, the new Gatwick Airport station opened after being reconstructed to handle a forecast traffic growth.

The increase in traffic 1965-69, on LMR electrification was 92%; and on Glasgow-Wemyss Bay was 59%. (Scottish electrification book quoting Hansard 4.2.72, col. 216).

BRB Reports reveal achievements and projects developed by BR, which increased passengers, and would bring even more in the years ahead[23]. They include:
- 1966: Euston-Manchester/Liverpool electrification accompanied by a dramatic increase in train speeds up to 100 mph and upsurge of 50% in receipts; 65% in journeys. Journey times cut by up to a third. Motorail terminal opened at Olympia - the first of its kind in the world.
- 1967: Faster journey times by eliminating stops and exploiting 100 mph line speeds. Additional services to Yorkshire and the North East. TV advertising used for the first time by BR.
- 1968: Increased revenue from west coast electrics and new Southern Region electric services on the Bournemouth line. Accelerated Inter City services have shown that very satisfactory increases

---

[23] No one can judge to what extent these led to the current level of business. Developments that will reverse the trend are ill judged manpower cuts and fragmentation which gave unions negotiating leverage that did not exist before

in traffic can be achieved by higher speeds, especially if associated with electrification. Departed from the traditional policy of charging fares by mileage. Re-pricing of traffic yielding £70m pa.

- 1969: Continuing growth of Inter City journeys. Journey times cut on north east/south west axis. A standard pattern of services was introduced from Birmingham. Improved traffic levels on Midland mainline, West Country, South Coast, East Anglia and east coast services. West coast revenue was 11% higher than 1968, even though the services were introduced $3^1/_2$ years ago.
- 1970: Ticket vending machines installed at commuter stations. A strong market research programme provided customer preference data. Faster services London-Yorkshire, London-Scotland and to other cities. Journey times cut. A standard pattern of service was introduced from Birmingham. Increases in journeys on LMR electrified lines: 13%, St.Pancras-Sheffield: 10%.
- 1971: Substantial improvement in Edinburgh-Glasgow services using modern push-pull coaches 35 trains each way, with a half-hour interval. Volume up 10%, revenue up 24%.
- 1972: Half-hourly service Euston-Birmingham, hourly Paddington-Bristol. Bristol Parkway opened with parking for 600 cars. New services North England-South Wales/West Country/Hampshire are faster and more frequent than ever before and give facility for day return visits
- 1973: With electrification completed to Preston, first results suggest an appreciable growth in traffic. Motorail increased by 3%. A five year rail-drive contract was signed with Godfrey Davis.
- 1974: Approval sought for ten HSTs to complete replacement of east coast loco hauled trains. Student Railcard introduced - sold 128,000. West coast electric services began to Glasgow.
- 1975: West Yorks PTE doubled Leeds-Bradford trains using refurbished DMUs. Senior Citizen railcards introduced for mid-week travel at half fare, sales of 20,600. Student Cards sold 149,400
- 1976: IC125 [125mph] - the world's fastest regular diesel service - began with HSTs London-Bristol/South Wales. 480,000 Senior Citizen & 190,000 Student Railcards sold. Business up 15%
- 1977: 82 IC125 run daily London-Bristol/South Wales. Senior Citizen cards up 51%. Student Cards are available to student nurses and mature students. Offer to cyclists to take cycles free. Moorgate-Welwyn Garden City/Hertford revenue up 28%. Liverpool Loop & Link services began.
- 1978: The PTE's new Longbridge-Four Oaks service was an immediate success, with a threefold increase in journeys. On Saturday 10th June 0.5m Senior Citizens travelled free on Railcards - 900,000 cards were sold. Student card sales now at 300,000. IC125 services started Kings Cross-Edinburgh. Over ten days, some 1,400 extra services were run to the NEC motor show[24], eliciting praise from the organisers. BR has the most extensive high speed network in the world developed from historic routes rather than purpose built. The full GN electric service went into operation.
- 1979: Passenger miles were the highest since 1961, when the network was 30% bigger. Under five's were freed from paying fares. Over 20% of those using Family Railcards are converts from the family car. Senior Citizen card sales are now 970,000 pa; Student card sales are now 490,000 pa. East coast traffic increased - with the use of HSTs on the London-West Riding route - by 13%.
- 1980: Passenger journeys increased 2%, and were the highest for nine years. Two million Railcards were sold, adding an estimated £100m to revenue. The regiment of Railcard holders was swollen by 75,000 extra Railcard sales to senior citizens, who in six weeks in the winter, made midweek trips anywhere at a cost of £1. Sold a million tickets. Other Railcards include those for Students, Families and Disabled. InterCity 125 brought in extra 7% traffic on the East Coast".
- 1981: Sales of 2.6m Railcards produced £140m revenue. A new card gave annual season holders and spouses reduced rate travel. IC125 trains on new routes, pave the way to a speed-up from 1982. New trains delivered to the London commuter area. Refurbishment continued elsewhere.
- !982: Passenger train loads rose 5%. 1982 will prove a turning point in modernising railways. BR came out of 1982, stronger than it went in. We are running the same network but since mid-1981 have cut costs by £250m, needing fewer locos, wagons, yards, staff. Railcard sales again passed the two million mark, producing £140m revenue. InterCity revenue was increasing. Sheffield-

---

[24] Over the ensuing years, BR continued to provide a comprehensive service for events at the NEC.

London InterCity 125 mph services began with minimum investment by redeployment of the HST fleet. Passengers increased immediately. These modern trains covered 45% of InterCity mileage.

- 1983: Automatic ticket machines and computer seat reservation extended to all main routes. By the end of 1984, improvements at 55 core stations will make them fully accessible to disabled travellers. Passenger receipts were up 25% on 1982.
- 1984/5: Increased passengers. Revenue improved on budget and in real terms. Better information systems at stations. Train maintenance costs are 8% below 1980 levels. Three million railcards sold. An extension of Saver fares is attracting more passengers to off-peak trains. Train lengths increased on East Coast, Midland main lines and West Coast, where the line speed was raised to 110 mph. Gatwick Express - frequent air conditioned trains linked Victoria with Gatwick - journeys have increased by one third - nearly three million passengers using it up to March 1985. Falling traffic on the Cardiff Valley lines has been reversed with passenger journeys up 25%.
- 1985/6: Passenger volume is the highest since 1979 - the year before de-regulation of coach travel. Twelve Travel Centres opened. More passengers attracted to off-peak services. The decline in peak hour commuters into London has been reversed with a 4% increase. A major factor in the increase has been the runaway success of the Capitalcard zonal season, with 160,000 sold in the first year. Development of North West-East Anglia axis by new long distance services.
- 1986/7: Cross London services linking North West and South East launched. New one-day Capitalcard, for use on Underground, buses and Network trains. Complements the Capitalcard carried by 0.25m commuters. The Network Card costing £10 gives one third reduction for off peak travel.
- 1987/8: Our success in attracting more passengers through provision of new trains and discounted fares led to overcrowding on some trains. The Monopolies Commission recognised improvements since their last report. Renewals of the diesel fleet brought dramatic improvements in journey times. Weekend First facility, allowing passengers access to 1st Class on payment of £3 supplement, proved popular. 75% of NSE commuters travel on a Capitalcard season; 1m travel each month on the Day Capitalcard, launched in 1986 - 20% is newly attracted to rail. Rapid renewal of the fleet brought more passengers and lower maintenance costs. New trains give new journey opportunities, e.g. a half hourly Trans Pennine service increased traffic by 18%.
- 1988/9: Unprecedented increase in London commuters. The volume lost through 14 years of continuous decline has been restored in four years - 21% of investment will be for commuter services, providing extra seats. Converting surplus first class coaches to standard and more trains provided more InterCity seats. Significant growth in leisure travel. InterCity income rose 10% and volume 4%. NSE earnings up 11%. New cross-London Thameslink service opened May 1988 - 20,000 passengers daily in the first year; the original 60 train fleet was increased by 24 to meet demand. Overcrowding has been reduced by timetable changes. Off peak traffic is up: One Day Travelcard was sold to 1.5m customers monthly - up 31%. Provincial Sector passenger mileage is up 9%, earning 6% more in real terms; now marketing services in what was once regarded as a no-growth area. A favourable report by the Monopolies Commission on the Sector. Frequent direct express services with new trains have increased travel by 22%. Further growth expected from 226 new air conditioned trains, with another 196 on order, leading to an extension of the express network, releasing Sprinter and Super Sprinter trains to replace 30 year old trains on Midlands local services. The majority of Provincial Sector passengers use trains that are under four years old
- 1989/90: More trains to principal destinations, and faster journey times. Strong growth in leisure travel. A successful marketing campaign contributed to significant revenue growth. Peak NSE traffic continued to grow, a record 42% of all commuters into central London were carried on NSE routes. Provincial income from express services up 9%, rural 1%, PTEs 4% and other urban 8%.
- 1990/1: New direct Midlands-Edinburgh electric services. Simplified fares with free reservation during holiday peaks eliminated overcrowding. Regional Railways had a 10% increase in revenue. InterCity plan to improve west coast services. A new route to Stansted airport, [then a minor airport], will open giving a direct London service. Train miles have been rising for the past ten years

- 1991/2: BR runs more trains at over 100 mph than any country in Europe. A comprehensive network of long distance trains enabled InterCity to capture market share and bring in new income. Improved journey times increased revenue in Scotland and North England by 40%. Hiring of privately owned self-discharging ballast trains reduced time needed for major track renewals. East Coast electrification, completed on schedule and within budget, drew praise from abroad, and released HSTs to other main lines, producing substantial savings in journey times. Improvements followed completion of signalling and infrastructure on the Chiltern line. Despite recession, income continued to rise. NSE £700m project on schedule. Class 465 Networker electric trains were delivered. Class 158 services increased traffic by 40%. Further deliveries will increase passengers
- 1992/3: In the last ten years, journey times on main routes have been dramatically reduced[25]. The new IC225 trains have cut the Kings Cross-Edinburgh journey to 4 hours. Inter City standard class journeys are up 5%. A marketing campaign achieved its target of a £10m boost to revenue. Customer satisfaction surveys rated InterCity between 87-97%* for various criteria. Penalty fares are proving an effective deterrent to fraudulent travel and were extended to nine more routes. Being extended to the two remaining routes on NSE. The number of commuters using Chiltern lines rose 25% - many were new customers attracted from road following modernisation. Continual expansion by Regional Railways into new services and stations and maximum use of a modern fleet of trains has brought further growth. Passenger miles rose by 7% overall: journeys on inter-urban by 4%, and urban routes by 6%. Partnerships between BR, local authorities and PTEs led to improved services. Bridgend-Maesteg re-opened to passengers and is already carrying 5,000 per week. The majority of passengers - some 93%* - rated Regional Railways staff as very helpful.
- 1993/4: Manchester Airport rail link opened and carried 1m passengers in the first year, with new services across the Pennines and to Barrow-in-Furness. The first section of the Robin Hood line opened and is used by 6,000 passengers weekly. Hooton-Chester electric line opened - funded by the county council and the European Development Fund - passengers increased by 50%. More frequent trains were introduced between Cleethorpes and Manchester, and an hourly service Leeds-Blackpool. New services on Chiltern and North London lines. LT&S electrification started. New type trains on many routes. Penalty fares scheme extended[26] to all NSE routes. New lines opened in the Birmingham area, and existing lines improved with PTE help. Strathclyde PTE funded improvements. Car parking was upgraded at 'gateway' stations on the outskirts of London - some gained AA Awards. A £2m national Tele-sales office opened in Newcastle in 1993 with freephone access for bookings by credit card, and using the new Tribute ticketing system - a £17m development jointly with European Passenger Services - accessing databases covering timetables, fares, reservations. New or improved services included London to Stratford-on-Avon, Worcester and Hereford. Plans finalised for other new services. NSE had a continuing rise in customer satisfaction measured by independent research. Independent research rated Regional Railways highly.*
- 1994/5: Passenger business rose by 8% over 1993/4. Growth stopped in June 1994 when a dispute began between Railtrack and signal workers. As a result, passenger miles declined to 17.8bn[27] from 18.9bn in the previous year. £153m passenger business was lost, which returned slowly. Many new enhanced services were introduced on the network.

"The efforts of Regional Railways deserve recognition. The introduction of express services linking Liverpool with Ely on an hourly basis with trains diverging thence to Stansted and Norwich alternatively was a major and welcome innovation. Services beyond Cambridge to Stansted proved to be before its time". (John Glover: "Privatised Railways". Page 8). He was praising the pre-privatised Regional Railways, broken up in 1994 to be formed into Train Operating companies for franchising.

---

[25] Some services have worsened since privatisation.
* In contrast, passenger satisfaction now is 74%. (Rail N^O 464, July, 2003).
[26] Recorded journeys would increase reflecting those who had hitherto travelled free.
[27] If 8% growth is added to 18.9bn, there would have been 20.4bn - which reduces subsequent increase claims.

Punctuality

There are many causes of delay. They include: staff shortage, bad weather, dilatory passengers, defective private sector equipment and trains, vandals, terrorists, staff errors, planning errors, road vehicles, aircraft[28], fires and escapes of gases on lineside industrial premises - and very rarely - disputes. A late running train can also cause ensuing delay to an advertised connection.

Most think that BR alone should have no problem with snow, assuming a supernatural power shields tracks. A common criticism is that "everyone knows of the inability to run trains when it snows". The most vociferous are motorists who switch to rail. It was especially noticeable on rural lines, which were blessed with the carriage of bread at such times! In February 1969, at Leicester, within an hour of the first flurries, there was a blizzard. Later, despite worsening conditions, a passenger berated the supervisor for delay and *demanded* to know when his train would depart as he had a flight to catch. It had not occurred to him that the airport may be snowbound and he did not take up an offer to phone them at BR expense, foreseeing embarrassment. BR was moving, unlike road vehicles that had hardly moved in the road fronting the station for over an hour. He declined a refund, admitting he *"had not realised how bad things were"*. Naturally - unlike railway staff, he stayed under cover! Why did people criticise BR for *delay* when other transport was *immobile*?

Not one paused to consider that BR staff had to get to work on snowbound roads congested with immobile traffic. If those in industry had been as dedicated as BR staff in such conditions, there would be no balance of payments problem. In bad weather, fewer trains run, as staff are delayed en route to work, but BR was besieged by bad weather travellers. They have *no* idea of the difficulty signalmen face on minor roads to get to a main line signalbox. Instead of a word of thanks to staff who *had* taken the strain, passengers made silly gestures with a wrist watch because - in appalling conditions BR had not kept to schedule - a word without meaning to motorists *even in good weather*

It is accepted that snow closes roads and airports, but BR was criticised for being unable to run like model railways. Motorists leave cars at home and trudge, past several bus stops to a station, where they grumble about the inability of BR to cope with the problem that brought them there. They are blissfully unaware that the private sector has failed to invent anything to prevent snow blocking open tracks. Since most have not tackled wind blown snow, perspiring inside thick clothing, and done nothing more arduous than switch on an extra heater in the office that is hardly surprising. It will not occur to them that the private sector railways "coped better with snow" before the war, because the labour force was much greater and staff lived in low standard railway company housing close to the line on which they worked, but now have moved to more desirable areas.

It is ridiculous to compare problems with countries where winter lasts from September to April. Their expensive snow clearing equipment will be in use for 50% a year instead of BR's 1%. When the Met Office can predict the onset of bad weather by the clock instead of the calendar, and without codicils that it may be 50 miles east or west of a line on the map, then problems will evaporate. In BR days, the moment a warning was received of the possibility of adverse weather, Operating managers had thousands of men called out to help station and yard staff and others on duty, and ran extra locos to try to keep main lines clear of snow[29]. Point heaters keep points free of ice, but are no help with windblown snow. No industry can afford to operate emergency measures wastefully. If they did, the customer would pay more, effectively throughout the year. Few realise that the cost of snow machines for use on five days pa, would be added to the cost of *all* passengers and would fall disproportionately on regular, rather than bad weather, passengers.

European railways, often hailed as paragons of efficiency, fared little better in coping with snow. (Eastern TUCC 1990/1 Report). A reader wrote to the Daily Telegraph in February 2003, to dispute claims that Norway coped better with snow.

---

[28] Lines that run across the flight path of a runway - laid 100 years after railways - are fitted with signals controlled from airport control towers for use when a pilot is likely to land on the railway rather than the runway.

[29] Praise for the "dedication of ScotRail staff in keeping trains moving in appalling conditions", (Hansard 2.2.93 vol. 218, col. 155), overlooked that it happened - throughout BR - in *every* such winter of my 40 years with railways!

Leaves on the line delayed trains and attracted sarcastic comment. Broadcasters who cannot get the time right, lose track of guests' names and play the wrong tape, could be relied on to trawl this up. *"Blueprints for Bankruptcy"* carried a forecast that privatised rail would have the same problem and would tackle it by contentious spraying - they have. That it was created by "green phobia" is shown by photos at the same location showing a treeless lineside in 1969 and a forest like one in 2001. (The Hunts Post 14.11.01). Such growth is outside the railway boundary. (see page 43).

The incidence of vehicle drivers who crashed through level crossings or walls or off bridges and ended on the tracks did not begin with the tragedy near Selby in 2001. Serious delays arose, and lives were put at risk, when lorry and bus drivers who did not know their vehicle height, collided with bridges. Some ignored bridge weight restriction notices putting many lives at risk. Pending a BR bridge engineer's examination, trains were diverted, cancelled or delayed. Repairs required diversions or severe speed restrictions, reactionary delay was often widespread. The scale of it led to a special investigation by the Health & Safety Executive. Damage to level crossings, bridges, walls, track, signals had to be repaired before punctual operation could resume. Restoration was noticeably quicker under BR than it is now. Then, there was no need for lawyers, insurers or committees to meet to decide who would pay the bill before work began.

In 1975, farmers protesting against the import of Irish cattle[30] blocked an Anglesey level crossing and its approaches with some 200 - mostly new - vehicles, which the County Police had unsuccessfully tried to move, starting at one end of the double line of vehicles. Their action spread delay to London, Birmingham, Manchester and the Midlands. Being responsible for operating the train service, and, hence, clearing up accidents and obstructions, I ordered the Chester breakdown crane to clear the line. When it arrived, owners moved vehicles at once, as predicted - none would risk them being lifted by a rusty crane sling, to be placed on the bankside or in wagons taken along for the purpose. It was a solution not foreseen by the police. They weren't told it was coming for fear that they would raise objections.

To give access between fields, farms have "Accommodation" level crossings, at which accidents occur when users do not carry out simple instructions. At "Occupation" - crossings giving access to a few houses - residents fail to close gates or lower barriers, in accordance with displayed notices, leading to others crossing without stopping and looking both ways, thereby risking accidents.

Rubbish thrown onto tracks by the public - included mattresses, perambulators - that caused damage, delays and cancellations. This is a problem to be found in most urban areas. The reactionary effect spread beyond the immediate locality. Suicide by standing on the line causes appalling delays. Police demanded that trains be stopped and that the one that hit the lately departed be held for examination. Whom they would call with the expertise to examine it and test its' brakes was not disclosed. In most cases the train concerned was long gone. Each case delayed scores of trains.

Passengers delayed trains that were about to depart. Typically, staff trying to stop them were abused. The worst offenders were commuters, a practice only curtailed by closing barrier gates, which some BR managers wished to remove as part of a new "Open" image. Some pushed through, with a curse, saving minutes by not waiting for the next train. In 1979, one of 40 recommendations in my Report for improving punctuality was to close terminal station barrier gates 45-60 seconds before departure of trains. When it was implemented, it was greeted with criticism. No aircraft, ships nor buses are held up for dilatory passengers!

Despite reminders by train staff - prompting sarcastic comments - passengers left articles behind, and rushed back, causing delay. In a typical case, at Watford, a train was delayed five minutes by a passenger who could not remember in which coach he had been! On my advice, the conductor, in making his announcement as the train approached Euston, laid the delay at that passenger's door.

---

[30] BR ended the cattle service in November 1975 when it became unprofitable, earning more criticism.

Disputes caused problems, but management action minimised the effect:

- In the 1960s, signalmen's disputes at Crewe were overcome by managers taking over for several days. This practice was repeated in other areas at different times, but was conditional on staff in adjoining boxes continuing to work. There could never be enough managers to cover all boxes.
- Overtime bans in 1968 and 1974 left jobs uncovered, but some managers exploited Rules and Regulations - the basis of safe train working - not red tape as critics think. These were safe measures, despite consecutive signal boxes, not equipped with "switching-out" facilities being unmanned[31] for the first time since 1926. HQ said "rosters of signalmen must not be changed", but, daily, I re-rostered *relief* signalmen to unusual shifts to keep routes open. When a train was held at Brightside, Sheffield, which was without a signalman, the station master went to operate the box, as he was qualified to do in an emergency[32], but the box ahead refused to accept the train. Signalmen were reminded that "when the dispute is over, we will want our passengers back". Controllers who overheard, thought it a forlorn hope - due to my record on staff economies, but the train proceeded. BR staff co-operate, where in analogous situations, private sector staff do not.
- In 1979, Warrington PSB staff demanded their re-grading claim be dealt with immediately. Their union would not take the case out of turn. The staff banned overtime, including Sunday duty. I had Special Instructions drawn up and issued to permit trains to run through the area, when the PSB was unmanned. Signalling Regulations for mechanical boxes included such provision, but those for PSBs didn't - the need had seemed remote. It had never been tried. Had the instructions caused a mishap, my head would have been on the block. Had there been any risk, the instructions would not have been issued. The strategy worked. After a few days, staff resumed normal duties.

They did not see these arrangements as proof of running the railway for *their* benefit! (see page 140).

In my time, performance statistics were compiled without adjusting for external causes. Purchases from the private sector including unreliable locos, rolling stock and other equipment caused delays, that were attributed - along with delays arising from late delivery by suppliers - to Engineering Departments! (see Chapter 14). Delays and cancellations caused by vandalism, terrorism, suicides, and also fires, explosions and the emission of gases on lineside industrial premises, were attributed to the Operating Department! Any recompense - of which there was little - did not compensate for delays and cancellation of trains. Unwisely, BR did not publicise these external causes of delay.

No claim led to more nodding heads than "*Mussolini got trains to run on time by threatening to shoot drivers*". No journalist nor critic quoted a source. Contact with the Italian Embassy and Cultural Library failed to confirm the claim. Neither Mussolini's autobiography nor six biographies/ histories of Fascism mention such a threat, but say that he got rid of critical editors and politicians. The books reveal that poor Italian railways delayed cross-border imports and that tourists did *not* agree that trains ran on time. Mussolini imposed an eight hour day on *all* workers. Similar action here would have prevented traffic loss to road, as the eight hour day imposed on railways by Government in 1919 has never been matched by similar legislation on road transport.

In October, 1995, the "*Today*" newspaper quoted an MP, who rejected criticisms of connections broken in the new era, saying that trains held for connections multiply delay. It showed how little politicians knew about railways. BR managers had known of the potential for delay since "*Adam was a lad*", which they addressed by specifying "*Connectional margins*" - the maximum - say five minutes - which selected trains can be held for a delayed arrival, but *only if it is known* an incoming train will arrive, connection be made and the train leave within the margin. If it is forecast that connection cannot be made within that margin, the forward train must depart without waiting. Some

---

[31] At Sheffield, the author kept trains running with six such consecutive signal boxes closed. Signalmen taking duty after the boxes had been unmanned on the first night shift, were astonished that services had been maintained.

[32] They were examined annually in signalling knowledge to confirm their ability to work signal boxes in event of short notice absence, implement "single line working" when one line of a double track route was blocked or examine a line if potential defects arose. They carried out these duties day or night, weekday or weekend. (see pages 119,140,191).

trains were held, but for good reasons, some had no margin and had to depart without waiting for delayed arrivals. Margins were determined so as to ensure that a delayed connection would not cause delay to other trains into which it was required to make connection en route. This avoided the snowball effect which the MP appeared to assume was overlooked by experienced BR managers.

From 1948, BR had punctuality targets for passenger services, and for fast freight services. They were progressively lifted. Originally, they were for internal use only. District Officers had to explain delays on daily telephone conferences, and were required to take action to avoid repetition. Targets and achievements were set out in Annual Reports that were supplied to Watchdogs and the media. Watchdogs and politicians thought it would be useful for BR to set an example to other businesses and industry that did not publish *any* performance *nor* complaints data. It led to the Citizens Charter, which focused on rail travel - the micro area of public expenditure - instead of the macro areas - such as mortgages, cars, etc. These far more important areas - not to mention, BR's competitors: air, sea, and road - have still to respond to political vision by following BR's example.

When targets were not achieved, it was the responsibility of the Operating Department to examine the causes, study trends and develop ways of reducing delays. Judging from criticism, outsiders must have assumed that no action was taken to resolve a problem that was deemed to be as easy as turning up the controller of a model railway, or telling drivers to drive faster. What these table-top experts did not comprehend was that trains were timed to run at maximum permitted speed subject to track safety speed limits on the one hand, and safe speed limits for locos and rolling stock on the other. Timetables had an element built in for *planned* speed restrictions arising from *planned* track work, but none for unplanned problems - such as bridge bashing lorries, etc. Any manager telling a driver to exceed such speed limits would be in deep trouble for inciting an unsafe practice, unlike road transport, where exceeding limits seems to be endemic. Retired BR managers were not surprised to hear some, who sought to take over trains after 1993, say that getting drivers to drive faster was their solution to unpunctuality! BR could have improved punctuality by ceasing to hold connections, extending journey times, cancelling trains, missing scheduled stops, or ending the practice of special stops by trains at stations where passengers are waiting for a badly delayed or cancelled service.[33] It would have brought down the wrath of the Ministers, MPs and Watchdogs. BR managers looked for, and found, better ways.

"Passengers are entitled to expect trains to be on time. A target of five minutes late is inadequate for the discipline of the service". (CTCC 1983 Report, Page 3). "Punctuality targets should be 100% in all cases. We dispute the value of any other target". (CTCC 1984/85 Report, Page 8). They were out of touch with reality[34]. Seven years later, they published "*New Opportunities for Rail Passengers*?", in which they stated (Page 41): "Privatisation will not eliminate problems such as train failures, mishaps or other failures". *This concedes that 100% is unachievable. Users accept other transport is not 100% reliable. No industry achieves 100%. Manufacturers work to tolerances that are less than perfect, and recall potentially harmful products. Anyone experienced in motivation sets targets above present achievement, but not so high as to demotivate, and raises them as targets are achieved. A 100% target is not realistic in **any** walk of life.* (see Chapter 14). Watchdogs now accept standards of less than 100% from privatised rail companies, although they were forecast to achieve 100%, despite punctuality of their parent companies not being 100%. (see MP's view - page 164)

An investigation of performance in 1979, (see page 157), revealed that reliability needed investment on rolling stock, track and signalling which was not transmitted into moving goal posts by increased speeds. Manpower adequate for 100% reliability faces problems when the unforeseen arises: vandals, bad weather, public or industry initiated delays and equipment that is not 100% reliable.

---

[33] All of these practices are widely adopted now.

[34] Sir Bob Reid, BR Chairman, and former oil industry executive, stated: We all need targets to aim at, and they must be targets that we have a realistic hope of achieving through our own efforts. (BRB 1991/2 Report, Page 4).

Telephone Enquiries

Unlike the rest of industry, BR published its performance targets and achievements in respect of telephone enquiries: "Not more than 5% calls should get an engaged signal". *This didn't come from the private sector who do not have standards approaching these. Computers purchased by BR to monitor standards, could not produce this data, as the private sector had not got around to it. BT used to monitor lines, on request, free of charge, but later required payment.* "The privatised system is required to answer 90%, not 95%". (CRUCC 1997/8 Report). "Not more than 10% of calls to Telephone Enquiries should ring out for over 30 seconds". *Private sector businesses prefer "entertaining" callers with unsolicited music. Under the privatised regime, two phone calls or more are often necessary to obtain what could be obtained with one from BR.* (see page 163).

In 1981, the CTCC had received "a considerable number of complaints about the difficulty in contacting Telephone Enquiries". There were no statistics. Such generalities are useless in tackling problems. My investigation in 1985, revealed that two of 22 Telephone Enquiry Bureaux [TEBx] on the London Midland Region were answering 60-70% - well below BR's target. They were open for sixteen hours daily. BT was asked to conduct checks, which showed that some calls were made when these offices were closed during the night. Few businesses provided 24 hour cover. Directories were amended to show the opening hours. Standards at remaining offices ranged up to 94%. Changes recommended to reduce unanswered calls included better private sector equipment for routing calls within a TEB, and generating data on unanswered calls which existing equipment did not provide. The private sector had yet to turn their minds to producing equipment that would do so. Breakdowns and a degree of inaccuracy were revealed in existing equipment. Even if staff could have "doctored" figures there was no inducement for them to make figures look good - poor figures could infer the need for more staff. The Region was dealing with about 200,000 calls per week that is 10.4m calls pa. On that basis, BR as a whole was dealing with around 45m. "No centralised monitoring of performance is provided [by BR]". (CTCC 1989/90 Report, Page 28)

The CTCC[35] published the only independent surveys of unanswered calls for all TEBx in the BR era. Data in their 1992/3 Report did not enable a national average to be calculated, but showed that 74.5% of the Bureaux met the target. Their 1993/4 Report set out percentages, total calls made and unanswered. From these, simple calculations reveal that, overall, BR answered 88.5% of calls.

Some Area Committee [TUCC] Reports recorded criticisms, but some also recorded praise. "Response rates remain generally satisfactory". "The number of complaints on TEBx is low". (Eastern TUCC 1991/2, 1992/4). For many years before privatisation there was no reference to TEBx in the Reports of the Scottish Area, nor for the Southern Area, whilst the Western Area mostly had no references to TEBx. Standards for Wales showed that over 90% responses were commonplace, but some locations fell to 80% on rare occasion. The Yorkshire Area reported "*Difficulty in contacting TEBx frequently causes complaints*" but had no statistics to put this into perspective. In the three years before privatisation, the North West Area recorded that calls answered ranged from a low of 80% to 94%.

Complaints

In 1983, BR complaints totalled 63,000 - a staggering figure - until related to total passengers, when it became apparent, that 99.991% were *not* complaining[36]. As it seemed likely that some of the 0.009% who complained had been given redress, I decided to examine complaints files to ascertain to what extent BR had redressed complaints, and found that staff were categorising as complaints, letters that were not complaints about BR services, representing 33% of total "complaints". (see Table 6). Files revealed that 55% of the balance were given refunds; and others an apology or

---

[35] They were renamed Central Rail Users Committee - CRUCC - then the Rail Passengers Council

[36] Watchdogs never made this calculation - *until* privatised railways were praised for having 99.885% passengers not complaining. (North East RUCC 1997/8). This is worse than BR. Since 1997/8, complaints increased to 1% or more.

explanation - all deemed to redress a private sector complaint. Some 9% of letters of complaint to BR also included praise or thanks for some particular act. TUCC files revealed that, in 1983, only 1,800 [2.8%] were dissatisfied with BR's reply, and took up their complaint with TUCCs, which had been publicising their complaints role. The following Table gives examples for each category.

Comments, suggestions, etc. Suggestions on fares reductions. Passengers suspected of fraud. Information requested regarding conveyance of cycles on trains. Unfounded rumours of station closures.	5%
Unreasonable complaints Unable to hear tannoy in privately owned station shops. A man travelling 89 miles allowed *nine minutes* from arrival at Birmingham to start of a speech he was to give - the train was delayed by an accident. *By road, an extra hour is prudent.* Passengers asked for train to Castleton and complained on arrival at Castleton, Lancs - staff had not realised they referred to a Derbyshire village with no station. A man had "no time to get a ticket" from an open station, and was charged £2 on train supplement. *No one runs from a shop promising to pay later, but passengers believe that, alone among all other buyers, they should be allowed to take the "goods" now and pay later.*	6%
Passenger's errors and misconduct . Alleged reservations not available, passenger had looked at return instead of outward reservation ticket. Claim for sleeper berth refund after alighting for refreshments en route and missing train that departed on time - his fare was paid for by a sponsor "because BR refused to sponsor the journey in aid of charity" - BR offered to refund the sponsor or charity if given their name and address - there was no reply. Reserved seats were taken by others, but no complaint made to the guard who collected fares.	3%
Unsubstantiated errors Wrong information two months earlier: complainant could give no details of train or date but claimed for a taxi. Dirty train four months earlier - again no details. *No company refunds on that basis.* Train late, missed concert, demanded refund, "rail tickets handed in" - BR asked to see unused concert tickets as proof, but no reply received.	3%
Complaints from non travellers or those not planning to travel Repositioned signals "enabled drivers to look into the windows of houses". Two complaints of a potato thrown at a conservatory from a train by a passenger. No BT phones at small stations. Cars vandalised in BR car-park 200 yards away. No car-park authority accepts responsibility for damage or loss in car-parks, but those who accept that situation, take a different - usually sarcastic - stance where BR is concerned.	11%
Fares Fare levels are not an element of quality of service - there is an option not to buy. Most buyers would like to pay less for cars or anything else. Pricing is a matter of commercial judgement. Overcrowded trains are symptomatic of *under-pricing*.	5%

Table 6: Passenger Complaints - Source: L.M. Region investigation in 1985

Had any industry published statistics, it would have excluded non-quality of service matters and redressed complaints. Such action by BR, although analogous to private sector definitions of complaints, would have been seen as "doctoring the books". Instead, my Report recommended that BR cease to supply statistics to the CTCC/TUCCs, as complaints to them of "dissatisfaction with BR's reply" was the true scale of complaint, and comparable with Trading Standards statistics. These should have formed the basis for their statistics. It was illogical that BR alone should treat resolved complaints as dissatisfied - unlike the private sector. BRB acted on the Report, and ceased to supply statistics to the CTCC/TUCCs. The last year in which the CTCC records BR complaints was 1984. Annual Reports by the CTCC included generalisations about staff attitudes, that were unhelpful in pursuing improvement. Questioned regarding these subjective comments, the CTCC replied that the TUCCs would have details. None could produce any objective data to back up the CTCC generalisations. Consultants, MVA reported that passengers said that "staff were usually courteous and helpful, barrier staff are usually helpful, travel centre staff are very helpful".

The role of TUCCs on complaints was defined by the CTCC, viz. - to take up a complaint, in respect of which, a passenger received an unsatisfactory reply from BR. They did not publish the number of *these* net complaints, preferring to publish the gross number of complaints made to BR, which included non-Quality of service matters and *suggestions* and before any were given redress. Only 2.8% complainants took their case to TUCCs. Statistics published pre-1985 by TUCCs did not reflect CTCC criteria, as being dissatisfied with a BR reply. When they began to publish statistics based on their proper role - after BR ceased to supply data - inquiries revealed that some TUCCs included in statistics, non-BR complaints and first time complaints - those coming directly to them *before* BR had given a reply that could be deemed unsatisfactory. This boosted their statistics[37], enabling them to say that "complaints was a growth business". (CTCC Report 1991/92).

A comparison with pre-1985 requires exclusion of complaints against organisations other then BR, suggestions and "Representations" that are not complaints, and "First time" complaints, on which BR had not had an opportunity to reply. Inquiries revealed that some complaints concerned private sector Travel Agents, which TUCCs were unable to quantify due to pressure of work! Others related to London Transport, Docklands Light Railway, Victoria bus station and Caledonian MacBrayne Shipping - none were part of BR, but inclusion inflated complaints attributed to BR[38]. One TUCC included complaints about privatisation, which was against Government, not BR; one "reserves the right to progress a complaint even if the person is satisfied with the BR reply!" "First Time" complaints included in TUCC statistics varied from nil to 90% of the total - the Eastern could not quantify the number of First Time complaints due to "pressure of work", but conceded there were some. The number of complaints recorded by the CTCC and TUCCs was as follows:

TUCC	Total	First Time	Statutory
Eastern	801	?	801
LRPC	1,400	1,027	373
Midlands	523	474	49
North East	1,077	901	176
North West	1,443	866	577
Scotland	469	0	469
Southern	811	0	811
Wales	621	488	133
Western	1,108	886	222
Totals	8,253	4,642	3,611
CTCC Total	8,371		
Table 7 - Source : CTCC & TUCC Reports 1990/91			

One TUCC expressed concern "about BR practice of giving vouchers instead of cash refunds. The system has now changed". (Midlands TUCC 1987-9 Report, Page 11). The practice has reverted since privatisation, but the use of vouchers does not appear to have been subject to Watchdog criticism[39].

---

[37] See "*Blueprints for Bankruptcy*", Pages 127-128.

[38] For more detail - see "*Blueprints for Bankruptcy*", Chapter 5.

[39] See page 161 for complaints in the privatised era. See also Annual Reports of the RUCCs from 1996/7.

The CTCC proposed that "Overcrowding should be included in compensation terms". (CTCC 1991/2 Report, Page 4). If overcrowding was a cause for compensation, services could be drastically reduced as more people crammed into fewer trains to secure refunds!

In some years, passengers complained of a lack of information in the period preceding a timetable change, when timetables or brochures were not available. Sometimes, this was due to planning overruns due to pressure to make short notice changes to cut costs or improve services. Some overruns were due to awaiting MoT decisions on line closures and service withdrawals. At other times, delay was due to printers. On occasions, BR staff went to the printers to collect some publications or proofs to save a day in transit. Staff even had to resort to amending old station departure sheets in ink to display these rather than nothing. Among post sale date errors were timetables with pages missing and others with loose pages. All complaints were levelled at BR. The printing strike from the end of June to mid August had an adverse influence on revenue as it seriously affected the advertising of excursions. (BTC 1959 Report, Page 58). Other failures affecting rail revenue were not exposed as they should have been as BTC/BRB minutes reveal. (see pages 157-161).

BR had an arrangement whereby managers from one Region made incognito visits to another Region, posing as passengers, paying for tickets, checking on punctuality, information, the condition of trains and stations and reporting on unsatisfactory aspects of service.

Competition

A Daily Telegraph article [June 1993], said that a rail lobby campaign led to an Act requiring a man to walk ahead of road vehicles, with a red flag and held back road transport until repealed in 1878. The 1865 Locomotives on Highways Act was aimed at the *only* form of mechanical road transport - steam powered - and was passed 20 years before the car was invented - 55 years before lorries were capable of competing with rail. Had the internal combustion engine not been invented, steam powered vehicles would have made no inroads into rail traffic. Railways had no cause to fear slow traction engines, nor the puny motor car when it appeared. The most ardent advocate of the early car did not foresee its future. The Act was aimed at protecting horses, as the man with the red flag was required to stop the locomotive when horses approached and assist in conducting them past the locomotive. If a lobby was responsible for the red flag, it must have been the vast horse lobby. The belief in a powerful rail lobby was not new. "In 1938, there were 24 railway directors in the Lords and 11 in the Commons - in total constituting a strong railway lobby".[40] That was 2.5% of members - Commons: 615, Lords: 775. Members with industrial connections were anti-rail and most, as car users or owners, were in the powerful road lobby. The rail lobby was so weak, it could not persuade Government to concede equality with road haulage, (see pages 8-11), nor to publish strategically insensitive correspondence on the war Rental terms. (see "*Square Deal Denied*" Page 138).

Whilst road transport businesses were able to obtain vehicles in higher numbers than were built pre-war, and in excess of Government's own post-war policy limits, railways were not allowed to match pre-war replacement levels, (see pages 52,54,55). Little wonder, BR passengers became dissatisfied with overcrowded trains.

Most bus and coach operators did not provide facilities which BR was expected to provide. Bus shelters, lay-bys or lanes are a cost to the community, whether or not they use buses. Some road operators live off the backs of BR, as revealed by a letter from a coach driver to the Liverpool Echo, in 1984. He complained about the condition of Lime Street station *men's* toilets, into which he had taken it upon himself to conduct his *female* passengers, when the station was under reconstruction. There was little wonder coach companies charge low fares if they did not provide such facilities. In July 1994, a speaker from Centro [West Midlands Transport] told retired BR managers that bus lanes and bus priority measures are provided for 40 bus companies. A new Coventry bus station cost £5m. Companies pay towards bus station running costs but not for capital costs nor for bus lanes.

---

[40] Bonavia "*Railway Policy Between the Wars*", Page 7.

Cabinet discussed a Licensing Authority decision to refuse a licence to a bus company following objections by bus operators and the BTC. Prime Minister Churchill said: "Steps to be taken to facilitate new bus services to compete with BR before BR gets its freedom[41]". (Cabinet minutes, 7.4.52). They were not competing only with BR, but also with bus operators, who had also objected to the application for a licence. He was, once again, interfering with a statutory body!

Bus conditions of service typically reserve "*the right to alter, cancel or withdraw services without notice, and not be liable for loss, as a result of delay to services. Running times are approximate and the company does not undertake that services will start or arrive at the time specified in the timetable*". Many of those now running railways are bus companies.

Holiday travel by rail declined with increased car ownership and coaches picking up in residential areas, built away from railways. "Experts" compared the static level of rail travel to motoring[42]. (MoT "*Transport Policy*", 1976, Page 93). Critics claimed that closures precipitated a growth in car ownership. The reverse is the case. A few bought cars due to closures, but far more did so to be "like the Joneses". Many bought cars for their greater flexibility. Some enjoyed a lift for a share of petrol costs. Councils saw closures as the thin end of a wedge that would drain people away. None foresaw that cars would *benefit* rural areas. Travelling by car from or to a rural area would always be quicker than by rail. Councils saw only the local issue - "their" branch line - "this one is a special case", fearing that those without a car, may be disadvantaged by closure, if only for an annual journey. They wanted to will the end but not the means. Reports indicate that many buy a car as soon as they can afford it. It is a social symbol. The availability and cost of public transport rarely enters the equation. "Cars were desirable commodities which enhanced the image of their owners. Every young man should have one". [Transport & Road Research Laboratory Report N° 808].

"Not enough parking at Inter City stations". ("*Which*?" June 1986). Most towns have insufficient, few bus stations have *any*, airport parking is horrendously expensive. There would have been riots if BR charged similar rates. Privatised rail has made up for lost time, by *massive* increases in charges.

In May 1991, a Sunday Times article said "mass transit systems have to be able to compete for every journey mile undertaken". That is impractical as many begin from isolated houses, farms and villages with no railway. In 1989/91, 73% of car journeys were less than five miles, 47% less than two miles. (Transport Research Laboratory Report, N° 104). Transfer of these is inconceivable.

The rate of growth of car ownership was much faster than the rate of line and station closures:

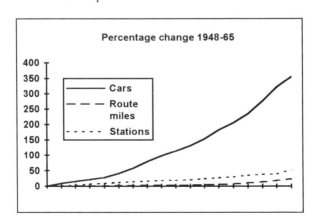

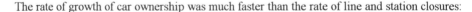

---

[41] BR had not get real freedom by the time railways were privatised over 40 years later!
[42] Had the car not existed, travel would not have expanded as much. Journeys to the country or shopping centres are made because people have a car. Most of the current market is unsuited to rail and would not exist without the car.

In comparing motoring costs and rail fares, motorists think only of the cost of the petrol, which is but a fraction of the costs. A car left in a garage for twelve months, not having driven a mile, will fall in value. A car used for above average mileage, has a lower resale value. The CTCC Memorandum - Appendix "H" in the 1969 NBPI Report - compared costs by train and car:-

- "BR Season fares per mile: 1.8p, 1.45p, 1.25p, 1.08p respectively for 10, 20, 30 and 40 miles".
- "Motoring costs per mile; Full Costs: under 1000 cc: 7.47p; 1-1.5 litre: 8.56p; Costs excluding depreciation: 3.12p and 3.79p respectively". *When motorists claim mileage for the use of a private car on business, they do not claim petrol costs, but full costs!*

That comparisons should be made with "Full Costs" is borne out by a "*Which*" survey in 2002, that revealed the unsurprising news that *buying a new car from the cheap end of the market may be a false economy as it is likely to lose its value faster than a more expensive model.*

BR introduced Saver tickets from major cities to compete with coaches but were pressured by MPs to introduced them nationally. It did not attract more traffic in rural areas and hit revenue where there was no competition. Crewe had no competition. Staff, who hitherto believed that lower fares would cut losses, attributed revenue falls at Crewe to the enforced introduction of Savers

BR commissioned more market research than is realised, covering users of all transport - employing external companies or BR staff. Annual Reports bear witness to this, as did Management Briefs.

Intensive sales campaign aimed at business travellers, industrialists and leading executives of prominent firms. Market research being expanded. (BRB 1963 Report, Pages 10,14). An analysis of passenger reaction to new coaching stock based on a report by a firm of consultants will be used as a guide to any modification needed before new features are introduced into design for new construction. (BRB 1964 Report, Page 46). To aid market research, a travel panel was set up - a cross section of passengers reporting on a weekly basis of journeys by all means of transport. (BRB 1968 Report, Page 19). A strong market research programme provided better information on customer preference. Surveys made of individual traffic flows. (BRB 1969 Report, Page 17).

"A strong market research programme provided customer preference data. More than 6m different point-to-point journeys are possible on BR. Computers are used to analyse sales to determine changes in passenger flows. A new system - National Passenger Accounting & Analysis System - will be operative by 1971. It is designed to analyse sales and group them by services and groups of services". (BRB 1970 Report, Page 13). Market research on price elasticity. (BRB 1971 Report, Page 9).

Catering - and that BR Sandwich

The most enduring criticism is of BR sandwiches. It became the foundation of the repertoire of lazy comedians. Personal experience, on trains and stations across the country - and being difficult to please - is of *never* having had unsatisfactory food on BR, but of suffering food poisoning at private sector hands that exclude roadside, burger and "greasy" cafes. An *endemic* feature of private sector catering is ostensibly hot food on cold plates. The excuses advanced in reply to complaints are admissions of incompetence. Some station refreshment rooms were used by private sector office workers from nearby businesses - that at Rugby enjoyed a high reputation. Critics are blissfully unaware - having not troubled to peruse BRB Annual Reports, especially from 1986 onwards - that private sector businesses were providing on-train catering:

- pre-wrapped sandwiches bought in from the private sector, increased sales from 2.5m to 6m.
- private sector companies supplying meals prepared in shore based kitchens, for main line trains, led to increased sales of 70%.
- Eight different companies supplying on-train services.
- InterCity is one of the biggest purchasers of pre-packed sandwiches, some 8m packs pa.
- Privately operated trolley services now operate on many services.
- Catering by private contractors on over twenty longer routes.
- Regional Railways relies exclusively on the private sector for on-train catering.

"*There should be train catering at all times of the day*". ("*Which?*" June 1986). Far too many private sector caterers have a *fixation* for closing at 2.0 pm. As only 9% use rail, a campaign is needed for motorists using non-motorway routes. Critics of BR may be unaware that recycled sandwiches are put back on sale by *high street shops* after re-dating them. (Daily Telegraph, 24.1.03).

Privatisation Pays?

Some BR practices have diminished. A cancelled train is not replaced by one making extra calls if another company is involved, nor by a bus from the parent company's fleet! BR had to hire buses at *full* cost. On "*Any Questions*" [1.6.02], another MP said that a train arriving 15" late was satisfactory. In many contacts with MPs, not *one* conceded even one minute late as acceptable. Watchdogs told BR that five minutes late was unacceptable. (see page 104).

Missing out scheduled stops to improve punctuality is a new practice. Trains were re-routed to by-pass Leeds, passengers had to change at Sheffield. (BBC Radio 4, 4.10.02). These practices were not pursued by BR - the phone would have been hot from Whitehall to the Chairman. Such practices will be found with bus companies, who cancel buses without warning, never seem to run to time and display no timetables at many bus stops. Some keep old vehicles in service using Northern Ireland registration numbers which do not include a letter denoting the year. The SRA announced a £2m fine on *one* company for 1,000 cancelled trains per week during Summer 2001 on the Trans Pennine route. It is doubtful that there were 1,000 cancelled on this route per year, under BR.

"Traditional engineering work on bank holidays, overran at Paddington". (BBC Radio 4 Report, Easter 2003). The practice of carrying out engineering work at bank holidays, only became *traditional* under Railtrack. Under BR, engineers were not allowed bank holiday possessions. Over a bank holiday in May 2000, Railtrack reduced access to/from Euston from *seven* routes to *two* - one in and one out. A track circuit failure on the outward route was caused by contractors damaging signalling cables. Railtrack compounded the problem by allowing inbound trains into the station until every platform was occupied. Departing passengers were allowed onto these trains with assurances that departures would not be long delayed. Three hours later, thousands of passengers were told to find their own way home! Had BR been left with one line in and none out, Control would have terminated inbound trains at convenient stations, for passengers to be sent on by Underground or bus, whilst the trains would have been turned round to form northbound departures. Passengers from Euston would have been sent to join these trains by Underground or bus. Moreover, under BR, drivers were instructed to pass a signal at danger, proceed cautiously to a signal beyond the defect, and report by phone to the signalbox. Asked if they could do this, they said that can't do that now. In 35 years experience of the practice, I never encountered a situation in which safety was jeopardised. To my personal knowledge, Railtrack was twice faced with this problem at Euston, and made no arrangements for passengers. It is probable that this incompetence has been repeated.

Presumably these new practices were not envisaged by Government when they forecast: "improvements in efficiency and quality of service". ("*Britain's Railways: A New Age*", Page 3).

Government moved the goal posts. BR was required to cut the subsidy. Now the objective is more passengers, so the subsidy rises. (see pages 47,182-184). It should facilitate lower fares. ATOC compared passenger km in 1999/2000, with BR in 1995/6, to claim it was 27% up (letter 19.2.00). As a base year, it was irrelevant. Prior to the 1990/2 recession, it had risen to 34 bn. However, preparation for privatisation, with massive fragmentation was bound to take eyes off the ball. Despite that, BR post-recession traffic had risen 8% in 1994, when Railtrack precipitated a strike, cutting traffic, (see pages 45,100). A fair comparison is with pre-recession traffic. That was not matched until 1997/8. No one can say what would have been attained by BR, had it been left to continue its programme of improvements. (see pages 76-81, 97-100). The SRA says that passengers in 2002/3 are 20% up on 1995/6. That is a reversal from 27% - doubtless, due to huge fare increases, delays and poor service.

According to ATOC a journey over two companies' services counts as two journeys. Under BR, it was one journey. Comparisons of passenger journey numbers need to take account of this change.

BR freight decline stemmed from policies that predated nationalisation, (see Chapter 1). Government rejection of the *"Square Deal"* cost railways 40% of their merchandise traffic. The pre-war rates system, enforced to 1957, was based on a 1921 traffic analysis and cross subsidies.

Pre-war Tory Government justified anti-rail policies by claiming that their objective was coordination[1], (see page 9). It was a phantom policy. When they resumed office in 1951, they threw that out, restored competition, but withheld the *"Square Deal"*. Rail charges uniquely frozen in wartime, created an unstable post-war base. A post-war policy of legally controlled charges reopened the inequitable rail-road issue, so that by 1957 - when partial rates freedom was granted - BR merchandise traffic was down 25% - worth £30m at average rates. Other traffic had increased 8% by 1957. An 8% increase in merchandise would have been worth £11m, giving a Government created loss of £41m pa. Politicians had a phobia that matching inflation would cause losses to BR, although it did not do so in other industries, which *exceeded* the RPI. The media saw the danger of Government's inequitable policies. (see pages 167,173,174). Had railways not been nationalised, Government would have had to concede the *"Square Deal"*, or face big increases in charges being approved by the Railway Rates Tribunal to attain the profit of £51m pa enshrined in the 1921 Act, which could not have been legally denied under the Act. They would have had a better financial base than nationalised railways, which began life in 1948, with charges at 1941 levels. There can be no doubt, from the evidence of Government papers (see pages 8,14,15,19), that railways would have been nationalised by a Tory Government to protect the electorate from facing the reality of charges being allowed to catch up on inflation, as had had to be allowed after the 1914-18 war. (see *"Square Deal Denied"*).

In May 1950, the Tory Opposition criticised the prospect of waiting to 1954, for a Freight Charges Scheme, (Keesings 10697A). When they became the Government in 1951, it was delayed until 1957!

"A & B licence holders are not exposed to free competition. They compete with each other and with BR, but applications for licences are opposed by existing carriers". (BTC 1951 Report, Page 31). An impression had been created by the road lobby that opposition to expansion of road haulage was only from BR. The 1933 Act was actively used by hauliers to restrict entry to the transport industry. BR was not given freight rates freedom until nine years after road haulage was denationalised.

BR freight charges controlled externally[2]

The 1947 Act created the Court of the Transport Tribunal to consider BR Charges Schemes, for which no reason was given. No supplier, competitor, nor industry had them. Objections could be lodged by "any body representative of any class of persons using the services or facilities to which the scheme relates". Industrial or trade organisations could object. "If Draft Schemes provide for charges which are unduly low, any body representative of persons providing services[3] similar to those to which Schemes relate could object. If the BTC wish to increase a rate which was unduly low by reason of the competition of road, canal or shipping, any trader aggrieved by raising the rate may appeal to the Tribunal". *A competitor could increase rates to narrow the margin of undercutting below rail rates, but BR could be prevented from doing likewise, forcing BR to hang on to unprofitable traffic! Traders using own vehicles for most traffic could block increases on the rest.*

"An industrial transport 'expert' deplored inflated transport charges which industry had no alternative but to pass on to the public, after cushioning their impact by economies and improved methods. Many trades lost *no* time in advancing prices by a proportion estimated to represent the

---

[1] *"Transport Policy in Great Britain"* (Page 23), states "Brunner argues the demand for co-ordination came from railways". Brunner quotes no source for his claim. Railways sought equality - not co-ordination - by hauliers having equal regulation, and when Government failed to act, for railways being equally free of regulation, also rejected by Government. During the Second World War, road hauliers called for co-ordination. (see *"Square Deal Denied"*).

[2] For a fuller account of the Tribunal's role and that of the MoT - see *"Blueprints for Bankruptcy"*.

[3] Road transport, canal carriers and coastal shipping! In no other case did competitors have such powers.

higher cost of freight. Some put up prices within hours. Nationalised transport provided the cushion. After economies of millions of pounds annually, the BTC have been forced to carry higher costs of their materials for periods of months and up to a year at a time, before the Tribunal's sanction could be obtained to higher charges. The present level of railway freight charges, 120% over pre-war compares with a level of wholesale prices which is 225% higher. (BTC Review, April 1952, Page 20).

Joy claimed that "by 1951, the BTC had all the powers pre-war railways sought". (Page 145). They didn't. They sought equality with hauliers: commercial freedom - abolition of legally controlled maximum charges and an end to publication of charges which hauliers exploited until 1957 to cream -off traffic. Unlike hauliers, BR was compelled to accept uneconomic traffic. (see pages 112,118).

Until a Scheme was approved by the Court of the Transport Tribunal, the BTC - not BR - had to submit applications to the MoT, to increase charges to meet roaring inflation. In some instances, he asked the Tribunal "acting as a Consultative Council" for advice. Sometimes, he accepted their advice, but on occasion, he rejected it. The effect was to reduce and delay increases, so that revenue fell further behind costs as inflation pushed up the cost of materials and supplies. (see Tables 8 & 11). An example of this procedure occurred in 1956:

> The MoT stated that he was limiting to 5% - half of what was requested although the Tribunal had said 10% was "urgently necessary" and had postponed an increase for a period of at least six months. An MP pointed out that "freight charges including this 5% will have gone up by 185% compared to pre-war, the Wholesale Price Index was up by 244%. The MoT is preventing the BTC from meeting its objectives". (17.5.56 Hansard vol. 552, cols. 2340-3).

Had BR been given equal pricing freedom as its competitors, there would have been no financial losses. Even without increased freight traffic, and had freight charges been pegged to inflation rates - unlike completely free suppliers and competitors - BR would have been £212m better off by 1956:

year	rates index	price index	freight receipts £m		revenue lost £m	
			actual	inflation linked	in year	1955 prices
1949	97	105	216	234	18	26
1950	107	120	239	268	29	38
1951	119	146	272	334	62	65
1952	134	149	345	384	39	40
1953	138	150	364	396	32	33
1954	148	151	379	387	8	8
1955	154	155	383	385	2	2
Total						212

Table 8 - Source: BTC Annual Reports & Wholesale Price Index; 1948 = 100

It was alleged that BR took six years to prepare a Freight Charges Scheme. (Joy, Page 40). In 1951, a Draft Scheme, based on integration, was about to be submitted to the Tribunal, when Government told them to consult coastal shipping who feared losing protection against rail rates. BR was then told to shelve the Scheme, due to a change in policy later embodied in the 1953 Act. (BTC 1951 Report, Page 76). By this, "Schemes must provide, not for fixed or standard charges previously envisaged by Government, but for maximum charges below which BR could vary actual charges being made to individual consignors. BTC had to start work on a new Scheme which was completed by December. It is imperative to have a free system of charging and to adjust rates to attract traffic to rail which is suitable". (BTC 1954 Report, Page 56). As they had to submit a new Freight Scheme, the "freedom" envisaged in the 1953 Act was illusory and delayed viability. A revised Scheme was submitted to the Tribunal in 1955, and took a further two years before it could be implemented.

Consideration by the Transport Tribunal was so slow that the Draft **1955 Freight Charges Scheme** became the **1957 Scheme**. The promised 'freedom' was *less* than a pale image of long enjoyed road transport freedom. It imposed lower maxima than BTC sought and said it was undesirable to fix maximum rates for consignments over 100 tons in owners' wagons. (see page 172). BTC said "authorised maximum rates were lower than charges currently levied for an appreciable quantity of good loading traffic passing over medium distances". The Tribunal retained jurisdiction over a third of traffic. Neither road nor sea transport had maxima imposed nor charges reduced. Until 1st July 1957, rate books remained open to inspection, by traders and competitors - four years after road haulage was denationalised. Chargeable distances by the shortest route had to be calculated, there being 7,000 stations it required 50m distances to be calculated, even with a new computer, the task took a year. The BTC Chief Commercial Officer said that unfavourable consequences would arise following from some of the Tribunal's decisions on the New Freight Charges Scheme. He said that the new Freight Charges Scheme had been severely mauled by the Tribunal and had cut BR revenue for *existing* traffic by £6-8m pa! (BTC minutes Oct. 1957). Say **£7m pa**. (see Table 12).

The Charges Scheme was "appreciably restricted by the Tribunal". (MoT Paper: "*Proposals for Railways*", Page 24). *It was supposed to give BR freedom enjoyed by hauliers*. Hauliers - by law - could examine all rail rates until 1957, and some until 1962. There was no justification for requiring BR to produce a Charges Scheme nor have it debated in a Court of Law, with an ensuing four year delay after the passing of the 1953 Act, before partial freedom was conceded in 1957, and a further five year delay before total freedom from judicial control. Political control remained thereafter.

Government benefited from low rail freight rates and delayed increases, (see Appendix B) and by subsiding inefficient industry via uneconomic rail charges instead of from the Exchequer. The BTC told the Tribunal in its 1950 Freight Charges submission that receipts for Government freight were 1947: *£47m*, 1948: *£40m*, 1949: *£35m*. Over these years, its self imposed discounts were overtly worth £60m, (see page 14). The covert gain was £100m, since, to match inflation, rates should have been 145% above pre-war, not 55%, (see pages 19 & 18 respectively).

When all industry was supposed to be subject to pricing control by the NBPI, their effectiveness with road haulage was at variance with that with BR, who dare not fail to give all the data required. In contrast, the NBPI Report [Cmd 2968], in April 1966, reported that it had sought from hauliers "information on costs and charges, but the poor response made firm conclusions impossible".

Dr. Joy said (Page 24), that statutory freight rates imposed on BR were not damaging, claiming that for this to be so, BR would have had to show that it would have been better off without low rated traffic. On the contrary, they needed to show that they would be better off if all traffic was conveyed at rates determined by BR, not by courts of law, and not open to inspection by competitors, as their predecessors had called for in the thirties. (see "*Square Deal Denied*"). He said that the pricing of unprofitable traffic off rail had always been available and that the 1953 Act "implied the freedom of railways to accept traffic only at rates that ensured its profitability". Acts do not **imply**. This one **directed** that a new Charges Scheme be prepared, to provide for *maximum* rates. By definition, controlled maximum rates block charging freedom. Until 1962, maximum rates were controlled by the Tribunal. BR proposals to increase rates on unprofitable smalls and returned empties were reduced by the Tribunal and the MoT. The 1953 Act did not, as he claimed, (Page 116), remove the "*common carrier obligation*". An Economist article (see page 28), and an independent 1958 Report confirms it did not: "Maximum freight rates must still be authorised by the Tribunal. BR does not have the power to price out of the market, traffic carried at very high cost. As common carriers they cannot refuse such traffic or marginal traffic of firms sending the bulk by their own vehicles". ("*Paying for Railways*", 1958, Pages 281,294, Political & Economic Planning - an independent research group). It was still there in 1977. (see page 126). Nor was it simply a matter of closing branch lines on the premise that unprofitable traffic was confined to them. Rates control ensured that all lines had some unprofitable traffic. The 1854 Act "Reasonable facilities" clause was not repealed until 1962. He said that commercial freedom under the 1953 Act was "*subject only to a maximum rate*", (Page 116), or "prescribed limits" (see page 26). This unique freedom did not apply to other industry. It was akin to telling a prisoner that he was free, provided he did not leave the jail! A maximum rate precluded *"pricing unprofitable traffic off"*, which he advocated could have been done. (see page 114). The Tribunal reduced proposed maximum rates in the 1957 Scheme, heralded by Government five years earlier as the **shortly** forthcoming freedom for BR! Some new maxima were below rates which BR already charged. (see page 114). He stated that "Commercial Managers could ignore[4] pressures from the Transport Tribunal". (Page 58), They exercised, not **"pressures"**, but **legal** control of freight and passenger charges, until 1962 and 1968 respectively. The MoT would have stepped in had they done so. Only he ignored this Court of Law. (see pages 170-1). Joy claimed that a 1939-56 fall in rates proved that control was irrelevant to the attraction or retention of traffic, (Page 145). This ignores the disparity of rates in lower and higher classes, (see page 7), the latter being above average, were undercut by hauliers - who had legal access to BR rate books - and that extra unprofitable traffic would not balance the books, as it would require increased staff. Creaming-off forced average rates down. Rates below average were mainly for bulk traffics, which were not susceptible to competition - a lower rate could not attract bulk traffic when BR was carrying virtually all of it, hence speedier price rises would improve finances. Replacing the archaic rates structure by a freedom to price near the average would have attracted or retained higher value goods without losing lower valued traffic.

Audited BTC Reports & Accounts prove that freight charges were held below Price Indices from 1948, after seven years of similar policies during extended "wartime" control, until judicial control ended in 1962, to be replaced by occasional political direction. Year after year these Reports revealed that charges were below pre-war levels, and drew attention to ever rising materials costs

It took $3^1/_2$ years to close the Heysham-Belfast service. Plans to abandon the conveyance of stray pigeons led to 270 MP's letters. (Richard Marsh, BR Chairman 1969-71, *"Off the Rails"*, Pages 191,199)

Traffic Loss

The MoT admitted that 2,000 railway owned coal wagons had been sold to Belgium[5], and 710 locos exported despite serious UK shortages between June and September. (Modern Transport 9.11.46)

BR management failed to outguess Government, industry and other experts who had not forecast changes that decimated BR revenue and left them with £millions of assets reduced to scrap value:
- Engineering, shipbuilding and machine tools would almost vanish.
- The decline in the UK motor car industry, and demise of the UK motor cycle industry.
- The collapse of cotton, textile and other industries.
- The recession in steel[6] and coal around 1958, 1961 and 1963.
- The reduction in use of coal in the generation of electricity, and building of mega power stations.
- The replacement of coal gas by natural gas.

The Ministry of Power estimated that the coal equivalent demand for power and energy will rise from the 1954 level of 254m tons to 284m tons in 1960, to 314m tons in 1965 and to 374m tons in 1975. The analysis suggests that by 1960, 230m tons will be drawn direct from coal, in 1970 it will rise to 240m tons and then remain static. The plan assumes no imports. The steel industry plans for the future are well defined. The 1956 production of crude steel was 20.6m tons. In 1958, the industry expects it to rise to 23.5m tons, requiring 20m tons of pig-iron. We must anticipate more iron ore, more coke. Home iron ore output is expected to rise from present level of 14-15m tons pa to 23-24m tons in the early sixties. (BTC Officers Conference April 1957, Page 43). An article by the National Coal Board Director of Research, J. Bronowski, forecast a promising future for coal, despite atomic energy, with declining USA oil production after 1960. (BTC Review, August 1956)

Although rare, disputes had adverse effects. The 1955 two-week ASLEF strike had longer term effects than other disputes. The effects could have been reduced, and reversed, had BR been free of

---

[4] To ignore them was to flout a Court of Law - in 40 years, I met no one who contemplated doing so.

[5] These would be of higher capacity than the wretched wooden boxes on wheels owned by non-railway companies, at which the Belgians would certainly have turned up their noses. BR had to buy them under the 1947 Act.

[6] Steel was nationalised in 1949, denationalised in 1953, renationalised in 1967, and denationalised - in 1988. Hence, when production fell, it was in the private sector. "It caused the fall in coal traffic". (BTC 1961 Report, Page 66).

rigid statutory control of charges and able to quote flexibly, rates and conditions to attract traffic to rail, especially during the 1956 Suez Crisis. But BR was engaged in pursuing Government's ill conceived policy of preparing a Freight Charges Scheme to present to a Court of Law and scores of objecting trade and industrial associations, who had total freedom, and proved it by uninhibited increases. Government action had delayed that Scheme for six years. No doubt, unions and staff became exasperated by Government's rail policies, but industrial action was not the way to respond.

Industrial action to support other unions by "blacking" traffic was not reciprocated - no traffic was forced on to rail after a dispute ended, when it was in the power of those who load lorries to refuse to do so. There were reports that Sheffield steel industry employees would do so - but they backed off. Had railway support been rewarded or reciprocated, motorists would have applauded rail unions

In 1994, an MP said on radio, that rail freight loss stemmed from a Freightliner dispute. Freightliner was never forecast to recover 25m tons pa lost to road pre-war, and 23m tons pa lost 1946-61, due to Government refusal to give railways legal equality with road transport. Their policies cut BR capacity to carry traffic, but gave road hauliers extra to cream-off more. (see page 55). Freightliner forecast 3% growth over 10 years, *if* the economy grew by 3% pa, (1963 Reshaping Report Appendix 4). The potential of Freightliner could not be realised given the legal disparities between rail and road, and hidden subsidies enjoyed by road haulage, which *still* exist. (see pages 130,187). The economy grew, on average, 2%. The MP overlooked that "crane failure and delay by contractors at Freightliner terminals affected traffic expansion". (BRB 1969 Report, Page 15).

Traffic switched to road, because "the driver was *always* with the load". Now it is clear that it is phoney. As they cannot prevent refugees getting in, they cannot prevent someone taking goods out.

An opportunity to regain traffic was lost due to external control of charges. The MoT told Parliament in December 1956, that BR was offering competitive terms to attract traffic in the Suez Crisis: "It was BR policy to quote terms which will encourage movement of traffic by rail". How they could do so as rates were still held in the paralytic grip of pre-war legislation pending implementation of the Freight Charges Scheme, which was to apply from *July 1957*, was not explained. The only rates which BR could legally offer were those which road haulage had been undercutting for 30 years. Had BR been given pricing freedom in 1953 when road haulage was denationalised, BR could have been selective in securing good paying traffic on medium or long term contracts, during the Suez Crisis. BR was denied that opportunity and could not adjust prices at will, as hauliers did to reflect costs and maximise profit. BR was still bound to offer 'reasonable facilities' to all, which meant they could not pick and choose. Road hauliers were totally free, and during the Suez Crisis, used BR to carry traffic for part of a journey, to eke out fuel rations, whilst they remained as the carrier to individual companies keeping BR at arm's length from senders[7]. Some companies transferred "C" licence traffic at short notice to BR in the Crisis, and had it moved currently, but after the Crisis, reverted to past arrangements[7]. As common carriers BR could not refuse any traffic, however uneconomic, from competitors or traders. It was no coincidence that Government blocked increases in rail charges during this, as in other wars. (see Chapter 1). "Some manufacturers and distributors, without perhaps fully weighing up the true economies, withdrew during 1957, traffic which the railways had not failed to handle efficiently during the Suez crisis". (BTC 1957 Report, Page 70).

Inadequate checks on maintenance, overloading, over-speeding and excessive hours, hold road costs down. Union opposition to "open terminals" delayed transfer of road traffic to Freightliner. This *delay* contrasts with the *permanent loss* of freight due to *Government inertia* on the rates and equality issues from 1921 to 1962. By the time Freightliner arrived, road transport was well entrenched. Millions of tons of private siding traffic was lost, and those sidings removed, because Government's archaic rates system made much of that traffic unprofitable and had encouraged the

---

[7] As Assistant to the Goods Agent at Doncaster, the Author experienced this at first hand. Traffic was offered at very short notice which required quick action to re-deploy staff and obtain wagons - including some to move Ford cars. This was achieved and traffic moved smoothly. For a time BR became part of the Ford despatch process for new cars.

use of private sidings for uneconomic lower class traffic, whilst higher class profitable traffic was sent by road. Once the base load of overnight express freight trains began to fall, their viability was undermined, precipitating a downward spiral, and a worsening of transits. Pre-war railways had warned that Government's 19th century monopoly inspired rates system was bleeding traffic away. DoT and Cabinet papers confirm that they knew this to be true. (see "*Square Deal Denied*").

Restrictions affecting competition with road transport were not repealed until 1962, and for shipping until 1980. In October 1964, the MoT reminded BR that they were still subject to shipping objections to "unfair rates", when he directed BR - under the 1962 Act, Sec. 53 - to **raise** rates for china clay from Cornwall to Kent following an objection by shipping interests. (BRB minutes, Oct 1964). Customers paid higher rail rates rather than divert to sea. It proved that rail rates were not too high - contrary to popular belief, especially that of politicians. That was *not* in the national interest. Hauliers were not compelled to raise rates when railways objected to unfair competition.

In its 1993 Report, "*Taming the Truck*", Transport 2000 stated: Since the introduction of the 38 tonne limit for lorries, mileage of the heaviest lorries has increased by 82%, much with part loads. It has meant a less efficient industry, more pollution, road damage and accidents". New research shows that "HGVs pay 59-69% of costs they impose on society. If HGVs travelling over 150km were replaced by rail, lorry mileage would be cut by half. Per tonne carried, rail produces 80% less carbon dioxide than road. 30% of lorries are running empty. (Transport 2000: "*Goods without the Bads*")

Amateurs labour under an illusion that attracting business was easy for BR, but impossible in their industries! A **Birkenhead** rail users association newsletter[8] stated that a paper mill, planned in Shotton, would draw timber from northern forests, and asked "What is BR doing to compete for the traffic?" What was *UK industry* doing to compete for orders? Vast tracts of UK industry vanished. **Birkenhead** shipbuilders Cammell Laird closed[9], having lost orders from *existing* customers - easier than from *new* customers to BR. They said that "dangerous lorry movements would be kept off roads" by moving timber [by road] from widespread forests to unspecified railheads! In stating that the mill was to be built *on the site of a closed steelworks*, the penny hadn't dropped that another industry had failed to compete for orders. They claimed that fatalities caused when a broken down mini-bus was struck by a lorry, would have been avoided had the lorry's traffic been on rail. They ignore that an accident could happen between forest and railhead, and that fatalities would not have occurred had the mini-bus been 100% reliable - the standard BR is told to achieve. Not once does the £ sign appear in the article. They do not comprehend that BR freight was decimated by:-
- the archaic rates system forced on railways by Government from 1921 to 1957,
- BR having to appear in a court of law to alter freight rates - by which time the traffic had gone
- the appalling misuse and unwarranted detention of BR wagons on industrial premises
- disappearance of heavy freight due to industrial complacency and abysmal industrial relations.
"As far as I can tell" - writes the ex-teacher editor on page 17 in their newsletter - "no approach for business has been made by BR". BR's reporting system did not provide for sending marketing reports to amateurs for evaluation. Had they sent copies of confidential school or industrial reports, BR might have reciprocated. Page 19 of their bulletin notes: "BR is carrying millions of bricks; and is conveying city waste to landfill sites". The latter is a major growth business. In the event, the paper mill *was* built and makes substantial use of rail transport.

Amateurs believed that a will to find traffic plus diesel locos would make branch lines profitable where there was no industry! What they did not comprehend was that locos operating a single shift on branch lines stand idle for 16 hours per day, destroying the economy of modern locos that had to be near 24 hour operation. To assume, that "work could be found for them" was their naive belief.

---

[8] This same "Rail-Users" organisation had convened a meeting in 1983 at a hotel which was miles from the nearest station so that all had to travel by road! They called on BR to cut fares and electrify the line. (see footnote page 95).
[9] See footnotes on pages 88 & 91.

Unprofitable traffic

Firms exploited BR's legal obligation to carry any traffic, at charges controlled by a court of law.

"The obligation to carry includes:

[a] Operating regular services that are unprofitable;

[b] Equal treatment to users;

[c] A uniform tariff that does not reflect costs in areas with low or high volume.

Where BRS charge less than the [statutory] rail rate, traffic goes by road; where the BR rate is less than road and perhaps below cost, it may go by rail. Remunerative is lost to rail, only the unremunerative remains"[10]. (BTC 1950 Report, Pages 29,57).

"Due to further steep cost increases[11], the BTC asked on 17th November for increased rail rates: 10% on freight, 20% on smalls, 50% on returned empties[12]. The MoT authorised 10% on all traffic from 31st December. (BTC 1951 Report, Page 78).

Exploitation included using BR to deliver to the far reaches of Scotland, Cornwall and other rural areas, whilst reserving main routes for road haulage and their own vehicles. When BR tried to increase rates to reflect that profitable flows - which cross subsidised unprofitable flows - had been creamed off leaving BR with unprofitable flows, manufacturers and traders objected!

Sir Brian Robertson told the Royal United Services Institution in 1956: "BR are not working at full efficiency, because they have been prevented from keeping equipment up to date. With this they are expected to accept the skimmed milk, while others walk off with the cream, BR are expected to carry awkward consignments for remote destinations at standard charges, while those for easily accessible destinations are carried by firm's own road transport". (BTC Chairman's Paper, Page 11).

Another ploy was to despatch by rail, empty boxes as "*returned empties*" when the outward journey was by road. (see page 9). A consignment note certified that these were "*returned* empties", charged a cheap rate to reflect a principle that BR benefited from a loaded journey. As road traffic grew, and BR realised the scale of this practice, staff were reminded that empty boxes or crates not carried outward by rail, were to be charged at Company's Risk - the top parcels rate - unless the consignee signed for Owner's Risk conditions. It was impossible to check every "returned empty" against a previous delivery, but we were helped by the laziness of industrial and retail employees who failed to remove inward labels on rail transits, which included a parcels stamp to the value paid for a transit, or, if from major companies, a "ledger label" instead of stamps[13]. Parcels stamps and ledger labels were over-stamped with the date of despatch. A "returned empty" not bearing this evidence of an inward journey was immediately suspect, and checks could be made on inward records. Regular offenders were identified. By signing a consignment note *before despatch certifying inward transit by rail,* an empty could be sent at the cheaper Owner's Risk rates.

Transits

Critics pointed to wagon *turn-round* statistics, which some confused with "*transits*". A former railway engineer[14] said that "transits were commonly two weeks from loading to unloading". Personal experience during four years as Assistant Goods Agent at Doncaster and Sunderland, was that inward transits were *commonly* overnight, and mainly next day delivery[15] - although some firms delayed acceptance due to their internal problems, often exacerbated by their out of date premises.

---

[10] Due to Government's statutory rates system which was based on cross subsidies between high & low value traffics. Hauliers altered rates at will. The BTC could do so for BRS - its road haulage subsidiary, but not BR. BRS rates were increased without external approval: in 1950 & 1955 by 7.5% and 1951 & 1952 by 12.5%. (BTC Reports 1950-5).

[11] Including wages increased by Government (see pages 131-132)

[12] Neither smalls nor returned empties were of interest to hauliers.

[13] BR staff had to remove or deface inward address labels, parcel stamps and ledger labels to avoid misdirection.

[14] C. Boocock "*Spotlight on BR*", Page 12.

[15] Some wagons were detained under load by the practices of senders and consignees. (see pages 119,121,122).

At Doncaster, BR had the first overnight service forming part of a production line, carrying parts from Dagenham for Ford Motors' subsidiary, Briggs Motors. All were delivered next day in a sequence specified by them. Complaints of very badly delayed transits were unusual. A wagon stopped en route by a defect may take two weeks, but it was unusual[16]. Each goods depot and some marshalling yards were organised to tranship loads from defective wagons or adjust displaced loads.

Nineteen years' operating experience at Rugby, Sheffield, Leicester, Stoke and Crewe revealed that many delays were caused by slow acceptance of wagons into firms' sidings that extended *perceived* transits and avoided detention charges. Transits were also extended by firms and collieries that held wagons for days before despatch to form train loads to benefit from special trainload charges. This worsened instead of improving wagon utilisation, which was expected to arise by the bypassing of marshalling yards by 'block loads'. Worse, senders tended to label wagons - with dates - as loaded. In both freight handling and movements' roles, personal drives initiated improvements in wagon utilisation, and often involved analysis of transits. (see pages 146,147).

In 1966, BR introduced Advanced Traffic Information [ATI] to enable staff to plan local services before trunk trains arrived. Hitherto, there was no record of wagons on trains. The only record was on arrival or departure from depots or private sidings. Under ATI, wagon details were telexed to the next yard - destination, contents, origin and despatch date. Seeing unplanned benefits in the form of management information, I arranged for Tinsley Yard, Sheffield, records to be analysed for misrouting, delays, wagon utilisation and unsafe train loads, and was surprised by some discoveries: e.g.

- A wagon from Parkgate Iron & Steel Co. had a label date three days prior to departure from Tinsley, ten miles away. Inquiries revealed wagons were labelled at the point of loading and many were not placed in BR sidings by their locos on the same day. BR records showed that it was handed to BR three days after the label date, and moved to Tinsley on the same day.
- A wagon from Hadfield's, a mile from Tinsley, with a label date a week before despatch from Tinsley. Inquiries revealed that it was handed to BR on the label date and recalled by the firm to load an item which had been overlooked. It returned to BR a week later.

Follow-up investigations revealed that, in large industrial siding complexes, wagons routinely took a day or two, sometimes more, to move from the loading point to the exchange sidings to hand over to BR. There were small locations, where ante-dating was due to loading being spread over 2-3 days. Some Engineering Departments had similar practices. All gave a false impression of transits. Staff were told to endorse labels with the date handed to BR and to inform senders.

Transits were less predictable where BR was landed with the residue without notice, whether or not rail capacity was immediately available, after hauliers had taken that for which they had immediate resources. Use of computers to control freight, for which I argued ("*Modern Transport*", Nov. 1968), would have created a more level playing field. TOPS began to fill that role after 1975.

In 1969, Leicester coal merchants asked for a reduction in detention charges because of "*bunching*" - wagons arriving together, presumed delayed by BR. Inquiries revealed that there was no delay - the cause was simultaneous despatch from different collieries! They were advised to complain to the Coal Board. Merchants were *notorious* for the time they took to unload wagons - a week or more was common. Collieries also prolonged "transits" by holding loaded wagons waiting orders.

In 1975, BR implemented TOPS - a real time computer to control the wagon fleet[17] displacing ATI. During the wagon census prior to loading the computer, many "lost" wagons were found inside industrial premises. To publicise it, industrial managers were invited on 25th October, when the full

---

[16] As an example: when a wagon of vegetables was detached due to a defect, the author, as Station Master was called out in the night, and having roused a porter, together they transhipped the traffic and sent it forward. Mostly, goods traffic would be transhipped during the next day; whereas wagons of mineral traffic would be repaired.

[17] In 1979, the author introduced operational and maintenance control of locos on TOPS in the London Midland Region, (see page 70), leading to improved utilisation of locos, fewer train delays and staff economies.

system was officially "on-line", to see what it could provide. Hitherto if a customer asked BR to trace a wagon, staff took details and phoned back. With TOPS, they would say hang on, give an answer in seconds. BRB knew that customers may be sceptical, hence the demonstration. Among them, was the Transport Manager of Shelton Steel Works, who was asked for details of overdue wagons. He phoned his office and gave six, which the computer revealed had been consigned by the sender to *Shotton* Steel Works, many miles away, and had arrived there. The sender had not told Shelton that the wagons had been re-consigned after initially advising them of despatch to Shelton.

Some companies that had specified train schedules for despatches of freight traffic in train loads from private sidings, failed, from time to time, to assemble a train to meet those departure times. Newspaper publishers in Manchester frequently failed to get papers to the station by the scheduled time, and declined a suggestion that trains be re-timed to depart later. Their trains caused knock-on delay to other trains, including some carrying overnight postal traffic. All delays were attributed to BR incompetence.

Alleged "Transit Delays"
Industry made false claims of delay and loss. BR was used as a useful whipping boy to excuse industrial and commercial failings. The practice of claiming that goods were delayed on rail - when they had not even been despatched - probably not even manufactured - was endemic. From personal experience in the late 1940s and early 1950s, it was clear that BR was falsely blamed for some "delays". Asked by a sender to trace a package, we contacted the destination and often received proof of delivery. Asked by a trader to trace a package despatched to them but not received, we contacted the forwarding point to be often told: "*not forwarded from here*". After passing these replies on, no more was heard. A loss would lead to a claim, requiring both stations to certify on a claims form that a package was lost in transit - not a chore for the customer as it was compiled by BR staff. When no claim was made there was no cause for complaint. Eventually, it became evident that these were common practices. A supplier promising delivery dates they could not maintain, said a package was despatched to keep a customer quiet. Receipt was denied to delay payment. On the post-war seller's market, supply did not keep pace with demand. These practices led to a rundown of UK industry, but first, BR lost business as gullible traders directed suppliers to use other transport.

The practice of blaming railways for imaginary delays occurred on the domestic scene:
- A Sheffield retailer was asked in 1965 to guarantee carpets would be laid within three weeks. He could "*but the unforeseen may arise*". Asked "*Like what?*", he said "*They come from Kilmarnock and may be delayed on rail*". Outlining my freight movements job, he was assured: "*The transit will be monitored door to door*". "*There may be other problems*", was his next line, as we were leaving.
- In 1967, a Sheffield coal merchant was *unable to make a delivery because of delays on BR*. Being responsible for freight in the Sheffield Division, I asked for details of the wagon numbers, sending point and reported date of despatch, promising to ensure that the wagons were expedited. He promised to get back. Instead, the overdue order was delivered within hours.

In 1969, a business friend admitted that he blamed Liverpool Docks for delay to goods which had not left the USA, justifying this to avoid losing the order! Those using BR after 1975 found that transits were monitored by computer, so any looking for a "whipping boy" had to look elsewhere.

There have been many petty criticisms of BR over the years, but none to match: "*Someone proved it was quicker to walk across London with a parcel than send by rail*"[18]. If anyone offered such a

---

[18] "*The Great Railway Conspiracy*", Henshaw, Page 147. The facility to cross London was blocked by Parliament that decreed no railways between New Road and the Thames. He refers to an unnamed "town in Nottinghamshire", to which he claimed that passenger services could have been re-instated, without paying infrastructure costs as these were fully covered by coal. Neither the Coal Board nor its customers would have continued to fund all infrastructure costs in such circumstances. This and other theories have been demolished in "*The Railway Closure Controversy*".

consignment, no one would have been more surprised than the parcel clerk, who may not have realised that someone, with nothing better to do, was trying to score a silly point to confirm that London passengers had priority over parcels. The critic fails to mention the stations between which it was offered for carriage, nor the year, much less, the date and time of day: i.e. whether peak or off-peak. One would get very short shrift making such a vague complaint about any other business!

Wagon Utilisation

Restricted acceptance of wagons into private sidings, lengthened transits and worsened wagon utilisation. It caused traffic loss elsewhere - due to non availability of wagons - and congested marshalling yards which delayed transits of other traffic. Senders gained a false impression of delay in transit. If a firm restricted acceptance, they should be debited with wagons en route to them because they were avoiding charges that would arise if all wagons were placed in their sidings. BR staff were not always sharp enough on this issue, fearing loss of traffic. Most did not see that the poor utilisation arising from restricted acceptance increased costs and lost revenue elsewhere.

Due to outdated handling methods, ports held thousands of wagons to await the arrival of ships. Imported timber was loaded loose in wagons at the docks. In 1957, at Doncaster, it was being manually unloaded, plank by plank, and stacked on BR road trailers for delivery. A small company - T. Jenkinson - unloaded by hand, a bigger company - South Yorkshire Woodwork Co., - by fork lift. BR staff placed it on trailers with cross laths every few courses to facilitate unloading by fork lift, from which only one company benefited. We received for this company, from Hull, trainloads of fifty wagons, each holding only about five tons in a 13 ton capacity wagon, diagonally loaded loosely across the rear rave, in a way that precluded unloading by fork lift. As trains passed over a branch line close to the rear of their premises, BR tried to persuade them have to have a private siding, but they knew when they were well off. Unloading four wagons by hand took two men a day. All wagons were free of demurrage because traffic was invoiced delivery paid. Had wagons been placed in a siding, demurrage would have been charged. The company was not too expeditious in unloading BR lorries and it took about two weeks to clear a train. Due to excessive detention at both ends, utilisation was appalling. As the traffic was intermittent, it did not justify taking on more men, and casuals may have hurt themselves. To improve productivity, staff were instructed to unload by crane onto trailers equipped with bolsters and stanchions that I had had made in BR wagon shops from scrap materials. Resulting loads were untidy, but not more so than those loaded at ports. Jenkinson accepted them - they unloaded by hand. The South Yorkshire Co. objected: they had been "*in the trade for 30 years, timber had never been packaged, and never will be*". BR offered to resume loading trailers by hand, provided the company paid the difference in labour charges. The offer was declined - they wanted something for nothing. It was left on rail because there was no cheaper alternative. Years later, the importation of pre-packaged loads, made timber viable for road transport, so the 100 year service by rail was forgotten.

The principal reasons for poor wagon utilisation were, (BTC Review, Dec 1954 & Dec 1956):
- bad weather, accidents, excessive discharge times, town or works holidays.
- fluctuations in forwardings at different periods of the year, e.g. peak demand for coal in December and January, with traincrew requirements at a high level, often leading to costly weekend working
- fluctuations in coal consumption - the lowest month is 2.4m tons, the highest: 4.6m tons
- the time wagons spend at collieries waiting to be loaded and standing unlabelled with coal for which orders are not immediately available. On most days there are upwards of 80,000 wagons in colliery sidings, although the daily output requires an average of 45,000
- loading & despatching traffic in advance, in excess of a consignee's ability to discharge currently
- delays at terminals waiting discharge - some coal shipment ports are among the worst offenders
- Extended journey times result from refusals to accept.
"Unloading methods of coal wagons by industry are antediluvian". (Times 26.5.55, Page 7).

wagon type	N° of wagons	turnround time available stock	terminal time	movement time loaded	empty	remainder days	remainder % of movement & terminal time
		days	days	days	days	days	
open goods	232,416	13.4	4.5	1.9	0.6	6.4	91.5
covered goods	140,043	5.8	2.9	1.4	0.4	1.1	23.4
mineral	508,816	10.6	3.7	1.7	1.2	4.0	60.6
steel carrying	55,279	11.7	4.7	1.9	1.5	3.6	44.4
others (cattle)	4,989	20.2	2.0	2.0	3.0	13.2	188.6

Table 9 - Source: The Reshaping of British Railways, 1963, Page 47

In the pre-TOPS era, ascertaining the *number* of wagons en route was difficult, obtaining full *details* was virtually impossible. The real time TOPS computer made it a piece of cake. If the pipeline was congested and the consignee unable or unwilling to reduce it, in addition to levying detention charges, options were to stop the loading of specific commodities or wagons for that consignee from all, or selected points of origin. Some senders diverted traffic to road, worsening the pipeline delay, because consignees unloaded lorries in preference to wagons[19]. That was not an argument against placing stops on traffic, but for industry to get its act together and regulate materials flow. If BR had not been in the freight business, haulier "A" with hundreds of lorries in a pipeline would not have sat quietly while the consignee accepted traffic via haulier "B". No haulier would tolerate what industry expected of BR. Industry was production led which may explain why so many UK industries lost a world lead. (see Table 10). Consequently, the works with this failing, have closed or drastically reduced in size, and hence, hauliers were not put to the pipeline test.

An example of severe and continuous terminal congestion was that at Steel, Peech & Tozer, in Sheffield. Restricted acceptances congested BR Ickles sidings adjoining their works. BR staff had to put the "block" on acceptances from Tinsley marshalling yard to ease congestion. On one occasion in 1966, when charges were raised on all their wagons held back at Tinsley, the firm disputed BR figures. To prove our figures, Ickles was cleared of every wagon not consigned to them, and filled with their wagons. Until the backlog was cleared, they were debited with detention charges. This did not reduce traffic, indeed they approached BR to set up new movements from other steelworks. I met their management and explained my plan to close Ickles as a BR facility. The sidings could be sold to them as an extension to their sidings, to function as exchange sidings between BR and them. They were pleased with the idea and the sale went ahead within a year. This reduced BR asset and staff costs, gained capital, reduced pipeline delays and raised detention charges more quickly.

A common industrial practice was to over order wagons, "in case they were needed" worsening utilisation of wagons. A major factor in utilisation was the wide variation in seasonal demand - especially for coal wagons, and the practice of using them for storage. The practice of over-ordering began in the war, when traffic increased by 50%, with virtually the same wagon fleet. Industry did not speed up wagon turnround, since wagon detention charges reduced by the Railway Rates Tribunal, (see page 8), exerted no financial pressure for them to do so and Government took no action during the war to enforce payment of detention charges nor expedite turnround (see page 22). Over-ordering continued after the war whilst BR operated an old fleet, depleted by excessive war use and not replaced by modern wagons, because Government limited the use of railway funds and industry failed to ensure enough materials. It persisted even after wagon supplies improved, creating false shortages. The pre-TOPS system for wagon ordering looked good on paper, but was easy to manipulate. Some companies complained that BR did not return their privately owned empty wagons promptly from destinations, but were often contradicted, when TOPS revealed that the wagons were still under load and had not been released by the consignee.

---

[19] Metal Box Co. told the Author it was because hauliers' *hourly* detention charge exceeded BR's *daily* charge.

"Experts" criticise poor wagon utilisation unaware that seasonal demands by collieries and others led to huge numbers being stored for months. In the 1960s, in the Sheffield Division, upwards of 7,000 coal wagons were stabled during the summer and were not needed until November or December. A dozen other Divisions had to store varying numbers of seasonally surplus wagons.

In 1967, the National Coal Board, which was noted for poor wagon turnround - Beeching said they underpaid BR by £9m pa for detention - proposed a joint investigation into *"Maldistribution and Misuse of BR High Capacity Wagons"*. Eastern Region HQ agreed and contacted one of my staff to represent BR instead of requesting a nomination. Their Joint Report showed that BR did not supply the number of high capacity wagons ordered by some collieries, albeit, they were supplied with sufficient other types to compensate. There was no data on Misuse. Whilst "Maldistribution" was a BR failing, "Misuse" was a Coal Board failing. Guided by colliery records and criticisms, the investigation focused on BR failings. We knew that they loaded high capacity wagons - intended for industrial coal - to domestic coal merchants. That was misuse, not least because merchants took up to two weeks to unload a standard 16 ton wagon. Industries unloaded high capacity wagons in days.

At the next coal/electricity/railway liaison meeting, I opposed discussion "until the 'misuse' aspect had been investigated". Arthur Cutts, the Coal Board representative was quick: *"misuse is due to geological problems"*. This was an example of the belief in other industry, that only they, not BR, had *"circumstances beyond their control"*. My reply was: "Maldistribution is due to geographical problems, and the remit should be completed". The revised report pinpointed misuse: wagons irregularly loaded with domestic coal from collieries that had been correctly supplied with high capacity wagons for industrial consumers; and similar consignments from collieries incorrectly supplied, which should have turned those wagons out empty for transfer to collieries needing them. We accepted respective failings at the next meeting and undertook to improve arrangements. Had the original report been accepted, responsibility for not meeting wagon orders would have been laid solely on BR, by electricity board managers whose complaint about the use of standard 16 ton wagons had led to the investigation. Due to the phraseology of the remit, that did not happen. The "geographical" reason for incorrect supply of wagons to collieries was that trains of mixed type wagons ran direct from collieries to industrial sidings and returned in trains of mixed empty wagons. If trains from power stations and steel works ran via marshalling yards to sort wagons of varying capacities, urgent supplies to collieries would have been delayed. BR asked industry to separate wagon types after unloading, where it was possible without delay or cost to themselves, to break the vicious circle and the Coal Board was asked to cease loading domestic coal in high capacity wagons. Within a few years, trains composed entirely of 32 ton capacity Merry-Go-Round [MGR] wagons reduced the problem, whilst TOPS improved the distribution and use of all wagon types.

Each year, the Coal Board reported the tonnage of coal grounded due to wagon shortages. In 1978, my Report on the subject, pointed out that they were counting tonnages over and over again, and, in the process, probably concealing the scale of unsaleable coal. If coal was grounded, the wagon order was adjusted in the following week to move it, in addition to current tonnage, hence the annual grounded tonnage was that in week 52, not the total of weeks 1-52. Regional managers were unaware that BRB minuted in January 1969, that the Coal Board was claiming coal grounded due to wagon shortage, when "undistributed stocks had fallen by 0.34m tons". (PRO: AN167/3, released 1999).

In 1970/1, British Steel sent BR a weekly analysis of wagon types received at Shotton, requesting that all coal be in high capacity wagons. BR staff had been accepting the implied criticism. Research revealed that collieries did not order enough high capacity wagons for the planned tonnage. Hence, when BR met the order, there were not enough. As short notice provision was likely to be 16 ton wagons, collieries would load them. High capacity wagons loaded to domestic customers against agreed policy would not have been a surprise, but under ordering was. The Coal Board explanation was that it was due to "geological problems". They were under ordering in case they did not mine as much coal as *they* had forecast! This policy followed the tougher line on wagon detention charges.

Mined tonnages were regularly meeting or exceeding forecasts. Under ordering supplemented by short notice supply reduced detention charges. Shotton was informed of the cause of the problem.

Steelworks over-ordered wagons to be "on the safe side". They did not keep the longest wagons for the longest steel, and ran short, having used many for short lengths. They had "production" problems. Steel was "*cut by computer*" and placed on the nearest wagon. They used BR wagons to move steel within the works, for which a hire charge was due, if there was no rail journey to follow, but it was not known unless they declared it. Using BR wagons for internal use in private sidings was commonplace. Some used BR wagons to hold goods awaiting orders or shipment release or to send later by road creating artificial shortages which lost BR more traffic and created more complaints.

Turnround by railway departments was poor. The first to come to notice during my 1960 campaign to improve utilisation in the Rugby District was the M&EE. Motive power depots kept a wagon or two to load rubbish. The Rugby shedmaster was told that he had a £1000[20] waste bin, when the local authority would supply one and empty it free - as BR was a ratepayer. He claimed that he didn't keep *one* wagon continually as it was despatched to be unloaded at a railway tip - *creating further costs*. He was told, as it was immediately replaced by another wagon, one wagon was being kept in perpetuity. The change was made, and other engineering departments asked to follow suit.

Railway Workshops had a very poor record for wagon turnround. They were similar to industrial firms in labelling at the loading point, thereby creating a false impression of prolonged transits.

Increased wagon capacity

The pre-war private sector coal trade refused to replace *their* 19th century 10-12 ton wagons, which conveyed most coal traffic, with high capacity wagons. This was typical of the reluctance of UK industry to modernise. The 1925 Coal Commission recommended a Standing Committee to review and improve methods to reduce costs of coal and improve wagon utilisation. They advocated 20 ton wagons be progressively introduced and that private wagon owners should form their wagons into district pools. The Standing Committee was set up in 1927, but was unable to persuade the trade to accept larger wagons or district pools. Before 1948, railways were legally unable to prevent the use of these slow, small capacity wagons. The Government had legal powers to acquire and replace them, and considered doing so, but lacked the will. They feared "*powerful interests*". (see page 20). The pre-1948 standard was 12 tons, BR new standard was 16 tons, with 24.5 ton wagons on selected flows - but by the late 1950's only 9% of collieries could load the larger wagons.

Due to the "Reasonable facilities" clause, (see page 5), BR had to keep small wagons to serve sidings with tight curves and buildings suited to the horse drawn era. "BR concluded that a 24.5 ton wagon was the ideal size, but colliery screens will have to be raised, and that gradients and curves in many private sidings were unsafe or unsuitable". (BTC minutes, May 1952). It was not to be. "The 24.5 ton wagon can no longer be regarded as the standard for coal and mineral traffics due to the restrictions imposed on wagon size by colliery screens and industrial private sidings. (BTC minutes 16.2.56). Britain's railway companies had long been criticised for the small size of railway wagons in comparison with those in Europe and the USA. The "cottage industry" scale of industries in this country was the root cause. UK industry was reluctant to bring itself into the 20th century. Examples of their backwardness abound in books by historians such as Correlli Barnett.

"BR is trying to move to a 35 ton mineral wagon if the Coal Board and coal trade[21] would improve their terminals". (BTC minutes, Feb. 1956). BR was unsuccessful, no progress being made until 32 ton Merry-Go-Round [MGR] wagons were introduced in 1965. Even then expansion was slow. "BR is pressing the coal trade to co-operate to establish more coal concentration depots to follow the one which was opened in that year, but progress was very slow". (BTC minutes, Nov. 1958).

---

[20] Then the approximate cost of such a wagon. "Concern was recorded of the uncontrolled growth of wagons allocated to service departments". (BRB minutes 11.6.64). The Operating Dept set up the Central Wagon Authority which improved the control, utilisation and turnround of wagons, and reduced wasteful Departmental use.

[21] Joy said (Page 52) that no action was taken before Beeching to improve the handling of coal traffic. He was wrong.

Career railwayman, Gerry Fiennes developed the concept of "Merry-Go-Round" [MGR] wagons - new high capacity wagons, running as permanently coupled trains, loading and unloading on the move, which the Coal and Electricity Boards agreed to use. They had the best load/tare ratio possible on a two axled automatic discharge hopper wagon with a net load of 32 tons. BR built 5,000 wagons to start the concept in 1965. The Electricity Board began building new power stations, incorporating terminals to unload them. Implementation was delayed by constructional delays including the collapse of six cooling towers at the new Ferrybridge power station and faults in new generators. Whilst there had been investment in new underground equipment, surface installations at collieries had changed little since opening. The Coal Board took years to modernise loading. BR had to pay half the cost of the bunkers. (BRB minutes 28.4.66). Only 27 collieries had loading bunkers by 1977, leaving a similar number to be converted. They said that many would not be modernised. It may have made coal less competitive. It had an adverse effect on BR finances. BR had to begin using the wagons because new power stations had no facilities to unload any other types. BR had to retain staff at locations where they would not have been required had the Coal Board used the MGR wagons as planned. Colliery staff would not uncouple automatic brakes on wagons to enable them to be loaded singly, in the traditional way at collieries which did not have new loading bunkers. BR staff had to uncouple the brake pipes on wagons before placing them in such collieries and then re-couple them after they were loaded, undermining the whole concept of keeping them permanently coupled. Wagons should have achieved three loads per day, but due to the lack of colliery bunkers, were achieving two loads per week. There was a strong case for a Minister issuing a Direction to the Coal Board - instead of to BR on fares (see page 171) - to provide modern facilities in the national interest, since it would have lowered the cost of electricity.

The Electricity Board was not helpful in maximising the utilisation of the new wagons. New power stations were equipped with dual discharge tracks for unloading trains, but it was the usual practice to use only one track, when alternate use of both tracks would have expedited turnround and improved the productivity of men, locos and wagons. "A lack of progress by the Electricity Generating Board to accept 32 ton MGR wagons was noted". (BRB minutes 10.10.68).

The concept envisaged wagons remaining coupled from colliery to power station and back - hence the name - Merry-Go-Round. The London Midland Region M&EE called for wagons to remain in "Sets", each Set to have Planned Preventative Maintenance at four-monthly intervals. The theory was that no wagon would have maintenance too soon or too late. I was responsible for Regional operations and would not agree, but would ensure wagons were sent for maintenance when due.
- Most of the Region's collieries did not have bunkers, Sets were split and rarely re-formed.
- Train sizes varied due to colliery facilities and en route gradients. On the London Midland Region, 27 collieries despatched coal to six power stations, in 18 different train loads in a range of 20-45 wagons Adoption of his plan would cut trains to the lowest, thereby increasing costs.
- A wagon could drop out of a "Set" at any time due to a defect or a derailment.

In consultation with the British Steel Corporation [BSC], a new design of two axled air braked wagon was developed and 300 were introduced for inter works movements for trainloads Scotland - South Wales. A new 100 ton gross laden weight 40ft long wagon was introduced to carry semi-finished steel between Works. Services are being developed to move lime in BSC wagons. Modern two-tier Cartic wagons were built for home produced and imported cars; and more privately owned 100 ton wagons for aggregates, cement and oil were introduced. (BRB 1971 Report, Page 5). Rotary tippler wagons of 100 ton capacity were developed for BSC traffic. (BRB 1973 Report, Page 5).

An industry in decline?
Achievements in the freight field were not as good as those in the passenger field - due to Government failing to create a level playing field. Had they imposed on road transport the same eight hour day in 1919, road transport would have been stifled at birth. Had it been imposed after the war, and

coupled with like directions to improve safety, BR would not have lost so much freight. Even now, a blind eye is turned towards dangerous practices - tailgating, excessive speeds, pulling out to overtake equally slow vehicles with inadequate warning, etc. Mobile CCTV provided to tackle these problems - to the exclusion of cars - would reduce accidents and transfer freight to rail.

Protection for industry and competitors was ended reluctantly. "The last vestiges of the common carrier obligation will have to be abandoned". (*Transport Policy* 1977, Cmnd 6836, Para. 188). The 1980 Act ended protection for the shipping industry, eighteen years after Stedeford recommended it.

Government belatedly tried to wean industry back to rail. The 1974 Railways Act provided Grants to companies to encourage transfer of freight to rail for environmental or other reasons. [Sec. 8]. "Councils delayed or rejected schemes to transfer freight from road". (Select Committee Report 1977).

Despite Government inertia on unsafe road transport, and local authority apathy, there were successes as the BRB Annual Reports reveal:

- 1963: Daily company trains are operated e.g. Dagenham-Halewood for Ford Motors. Ten year agreement with the Central Electricity Generating Board [CEGB] on MGR.
- 1964: Construction of MGR wagons began.
- 1966: Gratifying to observe the world wide growth in containerisation alongside the pioneering development by BR, which has attracted the attention of 24 foreign railways.
- 1967: First MGR trains began to run in March from Monktonhall colliery to a Scottish power station at Cockenzie. These were followed by others from Bevercotes to West Burton. Oil carrying doubled in 1967 [12m tons] over 1963, and was 20% up on 1966. Market research of freight included the demand and supply of sand & aggregate; car transport and exports.
- 1968: Nine new power stations equipped for MGR. Ten rapid loading bunkers commissioned at collieries in 1968. Substantial contracts to move cars and components within UK and abroad.
- 1969: Rationalisation in the car industry provided an opportunity for rail transport. The start of a successful company high capacity container service to Europe, is now followed by a similar service within the UK. Trainload movement of car bodies has increased.
- 1970: Growth in oil and car business.
- 1971: Decline in coal and steel was the main cause of reduction in profits. New Cartic wagon had a role in the upsurge in demand for home & imported cars. Ford Motors strike depressed traffic.
- 1972: Fifty customer owned freight terminals opened. Oil, aggregates, cars, car components, increased, much carried in privately owned wagons.
- 1973: Secured contract for 60m tonnes of imported ore, and 50,000 tons pa from the British Aluminium smelter at Invergordon. 1m tons pa of pulverised fly ash from CEGB. GLC despatch 0.3m tons pa of domestic refuse. 47 railheads opened for roadstone, 144 more are under negotiation.
- 1974: 23 collieries have rapid loading facilities for MGR, 19 more collieries are in hand.
- 1976: Trains with gross 3,000 tonnes load on a 10 year contract with British Steel Corporation, carrying imported ore, are the heaviest ever in Britain.
- 1979: Reduction of 43% in the wagon fleet over the past 5 years whilst carrying the same volume.
- 1981: A year of recovery after the disastrous three month steel strike hit Railfreight. Results were up 53%. More grants were made to companies to provide facilities to transfer traffic from road to rail. Since this principle was launched under the 1974 Act, over a hundred schemes have been implemented. This year's schemes involved 2m tonnes pa.
- 1982: Railfreight achieved an operating surplus, despite the recession. Fourteen new projects approved for transfer of freight from road to rail. New contracts signed for food, oil and domestic refuse disposal. Freight train loads rose by 1%.
- 1983: Seventeen projects were approved by Government for transfer of traffic from road to rail, bringing the total to 134 since the scheme began nine years ago.
- 1984/5: Railfreight receives no subsidy. Freight customers have access to BR's transit and monitoring computer. Freight train loads continued to increase. New developments included a modernised operation for scrap metal transport, based on a fleet of privately owned wagons, increased

movement of car components, bulk chemicals, new flows of limestone, and stone in new privately owned wagons with the highest ever payload of 82 tonnes.

- 1985/6: Railfreight built up new traffics, including household waste disposal from Avon County Council. More new customers transferred traffic from road to rail.
- 1986/7: Contracts signed, some for 10-15 years, embracing oil, food, aggregates, china clay.
- 1987/8: New techniques in the use of men and machines enable Railfreight to move the same volume as five years ago - before the coal strike - with greatly reduced resources and greater customer satisfaction. Despite strong road competition, new contracts signed for coal, oil, aggregates, with some flows up by 10%. Freight customers investing in rail loading facilities.
- 1988/9: Customers are investing in freight wagons - 50% are privately owned. Railfreight increased its operating surplus by 50% to £69.4m. Traffic up by 5m tons. New traffic includes opencast coal for shipment to Ireland. New contracts for up to 15 years, signed for coal, oil, aggregates and disposal of household waste. 35% share in deepsea container traffic via Tilbury & Felixstowe.
- 1989/90: Despite recession, Railfreight produced £59.4m profit. A major exhibition was attended by 1,700 customers and potential customers. Contracts signed for 1m tons of spoil from London, other traffic transferred from road. Export coal through a new terminal. Materials moved for constructing the Channel Tunnel. New container services from Bedford and North Wales to Ireland
- 1990/1: Railfreight holds 21% of Charterail a joint venture with the private sector launched 1990 using new technology to attack UK distribution markets currently using road-only systems.
- 1991/2: Trainload freight had a surplus of £67.5m from £505m turnover. Contracts secured for materials for the Channel Tunnel. Services began to the new Thamesport deepsea terminal on the Isle of Grain using special small wheeled wagons to overcome height restrictions on the route.
- 1992/3: Significant new contracts won: coal - both domestic and imported, a ten year contract for 0.5m tonnes limestone pa, 0.5m tonnes pa of household waste from Manchester, building materials and oil. A fifteen mile line in Wales re-opened to carry 2.5m tonnes of coal pa.
- 1993/4: Railfreight began via the Channel Tunnel, including major contracts for cars and car parts between UK and Europe. Ten year contract with British Gypsum and other long term contracts signed. Contract for irradiated fuel extended; record tonnages of steel from Port Talbot; bigger trains run with steel and scrap, five year oil contract; new facilities for imported coal at Bristol.
- 1994/5: New trainload business from Allied Steel, Blue Circle and others. 150 trains were running through the Tunnel, with new traffic on contract. Introduced new class 92 - UK's most powerful freight loco. Jointly with British Steel, wagons were modified to carry hot rolled steel coil.

Future Prospects

Developments over the past twenty years are a good foundation for expansion of rail freight over the ensuing years. "The freight facilities scheme will be broadened. A new grant will be introduced to contribute towards access charges. The provisional allocation for the next three years is £43m". ("*Britain's Railways: A New Age*", 1994, Page 17). Railtrack claimed to have "helped freight back to rail, after years of decline" (1997-8 Report), but doesn't explain how. In its last full year, BR freight had the highest turnover for five years. A large proportion of new traffic is imported coal that would have gone by rail. New operators said that there was not a level playing field between road and rail. (Chartered Institute of Transport Newsletter, Feb 1997). This confirms long held BR views. Government is financing the training of 1,000 LGV drivers to resolve a driver shortage, which is the hauliers' duty. It mirrors attitudes in UK industry that ceased to train apprentices, long ago. Overdue action by Government to address unsafe road transport practices will open a floodgate for freight transfer. The admitted insecurity of loads, arising from the ease of access into lorries by refugees will boost rail. Introduction of safer road transport drivers' hours under European Directive - which should have been addressed by UK Government decades ago - will have a major impact on costs and will influence traffic to rail. Some alert businesses will have realised that, and begun to switch flows to create close links with rail operators. Being an established customer secures benefits.

Chapter 12   More costly political policies

"When State corporations were set up, Parliament denied itself the right to exercise [direct] administrative control. Yet MP's seek information; query the conduct of an undertaking even down to local matters" (BTC Chairman's Paper to the Royal United Services Institution, February 1956, Page 9).

"Unfortunately Government cannot keep its hands off the BTC, because it burns them every time. If it had been able to resist the temptation to interfere, much trouble would have been avoided". (Railway Gazette, 22.11.57). This interference did not begin as a consequence of Government "handouts" - since it began from Day One, twelve years before the Government had given a penny piece to railways, and only then because its insane policies had driven BR into insolvency, and they belatedly realised that no industry could survive with prices forcibly held below inflation, "supported" by interest bearing loans. Government propelled BR into deficit by:

- legal and political interference in fares & charges, that were held below inflation, (see Chapter 15)
- forcing BR to pay higher wages than they could afford, (see pages 131-132),
- permitting inflationary materials prices so that BR's funds were worth less, (see Tables 2,8,11),
- allowing road transport, but not BR, to modernise, (see pages 52-55),
- allowing road operators pricing freedom, ability to reject unprofitable traffic, unsafe practices and excessive driver hours; which enabled them to poach profitable rail traffic. (see pages 186-187).

Ministerial re-organisations distracted managers from managing the few aspects in which they had freedom. "The inherent capabilities of rail are not achieved due to the frequently changing statutory position and different Government views on integration or competition". (BRB 1968 Report, Page 2).

Political interference was not justified by linking it to the "subsidy", which was to passengers, not BR. "Grant aid is not a charity, but a method of providing the community with services which appropriate authorities has ascertained are required". (BRB 1970 Report, Page 2). Governments should have funded the consequences of their interference and decisions, twenty years before they did so. The biggest errors of BTC/BRB Chairmen were:-

- Not rejecting pricing interference without equivalent control of suppliers' prices.
- Believing Government promises of "commercial freedom" - *tomorrow*.
- Not demanding that closures be made free of TUCCs second guessing their losses.

Despite creating organisations, making key appointments, taking key decisions, ignoring solicited advice, overturning legal decisions, forcing up costs and holding down prices, Ministers blamed BR for losses! No business would have survived such policies. No businessman would have tolerated them. There were other aspects that represented an unfair burden on railways.

The unwarranted burden of bridges & crossings

Government failed to respond to pleas to relieve railways of rapidly increasing costs for resurfacing and strengthening bridges and level crossings to cope with heavier road traffic, which arose from the inequitable rail/road rates policy. Increased road traffic on level crossings, hitherto manned by resident keepers, required more staff working shifts to meet MoT safety standards. When railways were built, there was very little road traffic during night hours. These were totally unwarranted burdens on railways, and a direct subsidy from rail to road transport.

Footpaths across railways were regularly inspected and maintained to avoid users tripping or slipping and then be at risk of being hit by a train. No comparable cost applies with roads. They are an unnecessary hazard. Some trains are delayed by vandals using these paths. When a motorway is built, no problem arises in closing or diverting footpaths. In the interests of pedestrian safety, the State should fund the diversion of footpaths.

In December 1949, the DoT view was "that responsibility for bridges should be transferred to highway authorities". The Treasury opposed a change. (PRO: MT39/671). The BTC "urged a review of bridge costs, which the 1932 Salter Conference - with equal road and rail representation - agreed should be a road authority responsibility". (BTC 1951 Report, Page 11). The MoT's attention was drawn to costs of bridges and level crossings. If occupation and accommodation crossings user had increased, highway authorities should take them over, or if changed by development, the user should pay to make them safe or provide alternative access. (BTC 1951 Report, Page 17). *These non-public crossings served farms and a few private houses.*

The Cabinet decided on 12th March 1951 that "BR should be relieved of the cost of overbridges and burdens which dated from when they had a monopoly[1]". (PRO: CAB). This euphoria was short lived: "The MoT is unable to relieve the BTC of bridge costs, but proposed a fact finding meeting between BTC & highway authorities. (BTC 1952 Report Page 13). *A meeting was unnecessary - traffic had increased since 1932. The DoT was unable to trace a Report or any record of such a meeting[2].*

In Swain v. Southern Railway, in 1938, relating to a cyclist who was thrown from his cycle by a rut in a road bridge over the railway, it was ruled that the company had neglected its duty to maintain the road over the bridge, and they were held liable. If the accident had happened a few yards further on, the cyclist would have asked the courts in vain for redress. Maintenance of roads over bridges and fences cost BR £1.7m in 1955. (BTC Review December 1956).

In his 1956 Paper "*Proposals for Railways*" the MoT stated: "BR reported that level crossing staff costs had increased by £0.2m pa to £1m pa, due to increased road traffic". "BR could not try modern methods for level crossing design and operation to reduce mounting costs - due to heavier road traffic - without a change in the law". (Cmd 9880 Page 25). "British practice *favoured* staffed level crossings". (Henshaw Page 92). On the contrary, the law *required* it!

The 1957 Railways Bill sought to end some provisions of the Highways [Railway Crossings] Act 1839 and the 1854 Act, and introduce new methods of control. Parliament was told: crossing operating costs were over £1m pa. (Hansard, vol. 566, col. 1247). The ensuing Act permitted new methods.

"The Prime Minister is considering affording relief on bridges & crossings" - (BTC Minutes, August 1958) - *26 years after the Salter recommendation.* In 1958, after repeated protests regarding maintenance costs of surfaces on bridges and crossings, subjected to ever increasing wear by road transport, Government conceded an underwhelming £2m pa. Deducting crossing staff costs left £1m to cover surface maintenance costs at 33,000 overbridges and 4,600 public crossings. £1m spent wholly on surface maintenance equated to £27 pa per location or 5p pa per square metre of surface. The contribution was withdrawn in 1961 (see below), re-inflating BR losses.

"With increasing road traffic, the cost of manning and maintaining crossings and maintaining road bridges over railways has grown in recent decades. In 1958, the MoT paid £2m pa towards these BR costs, but this ceased by 1961. BRB continue to bear costs of £2.5m". (BRB 1964 Report, Page 79)

In 1967, the MoT stated: "BR costs in 1965 of road bridges were £1.5m and level crossings: £1m[3]. For $2^1/_2$ years up to 1960, the DoT paid BR £2m towards the cost of bridges and crossings[4]. It was stopped because it was thought administratively more convenient to deal with this through the revenue deficit. If bridges were transferred to Local Authorities, compensation would be £100 to £500 per bridge pa". *This would total £3.3-£16.5m pa.* (see page 83). The Paper "recommended that the BR payment of £40,000 pa to the MoT [which began in 1946], for trunk road bridges be discontinued and responsibility for surfaces of overbridges be borne by Local Authorities. Recommended that costs of bridges and crossings be taken into account in re-capitalisation[5]. The present statutory framework for bridges and level crossings is complicated and unsatisfactory. Main disadvantages are a lack of clearly defined obligations and [*external*] administrative difficulties which often prevent the removal of bridges which are no longer necessary". (*Railway Policy*, Cmnd 3439, Pages 19,51)

---

[1] Note this clear inference that there was no BR monopoly in 1951.

[2] Letter to the author 22.11.94.

[3] £1.5m is mentioned for crossings on Page 51 of the Ministry Paper.

[4] Their total contribution, between 1948 and 1968, when they began to pay for bridge surfaces, but not structures, was an underwhelming £5m (£2m pa for $2^1/_2$ years). Funding of crossings was delayed until 1975. (see page 83).

[5] Including these costs in re-capitalisation inflated "losses" and obscured the scale of the problem.

It will cost £6m to strengthen overbridges. Government will pay half (BRB minutes 22.7.67). Government - or road users - should have paid the whole amount. This was scandalous. It was a hidden subsidy by BR to its competitors - counted as "losses" - which had been paid for decades.

Under the 1968 Act, BR was relieved of liability for *surfacing* public roads carried by bridges over the railway, but was still responsible for keeping bridges strong enough to carry road traffic. Of 10,000 bridges examined, 650 required strengthening. A further 400 will be permanently protected by weight restriction signs. (BRB 1968 Report, Page 41). Bridge *surfaces* became a highway authority responsibility 36 years after a Government appointed body recommended it (see page 8), but the more costly sub structure remained as an unwarranted cost to BR. When railways were built, overbridges were adequate for the prevailing loads of horse drawn vehicles, and that should have been the extent of their liability in perpetuity. There was no justification for railways to be burdened with the higher and continually increasing costs arising from heavier axle loads of an expanding road fleet. (see "*Square Deal Denied*", Chapter 6).

A Select Committee reported in 1976/7: "BR is entitled under European Economic Community regulations to half the cost of providing and maintaining level crossings". (Select Committee Report, Page 12). These grants were made under Regulation 1192/69, the first payment to BR being in 1975. From 1975 to 1993/4 inclusive, they averaged £18.6m pa. In effect, they reduced the amount of the PSO, hence the Government benefited, not BR. It highlights the real cost burden of level crossings, which BR had been bearing since 1948 - a burden that should have been met from the highways budget, as 20th century level crossing user was way above anything envisaged in the early 19th century when railways were built. It reveals the scale of the burden in years before any Government support was forthcoming. From April 1994, the Grant was paid to Railtrack, not Government. (BRB 1994/5 Report, Page 54). This was, effectively, a further increase on the subsidy to the new boys.

Railtrack is likely to spend £400m to strengthen road bridges as Government has refused to pay the costs. (Independent 30.8.95). BR had this burden for 50 years, plus surface costs for 20 years.

Fences

Railways were obliged to erect and maintain fences to identify a boundary and prevent trespass from railways onto adjoining property, not to prevent the converse. Parliament would be hard pressed to justify fences to protect children from railways, but not, from roads, rivers and canals. The Regulation of Railways Act 1842 required railways to provide and maintain lineside fencing. In 1948, there were 40,000 miles, and are now about 20,000 miles.

Comparable costs are not borne by road users. Fences adjoining roads are a landowner's responsibility to prevent trespass or prevent livestock from straying onto roads. When new roads are built which involve compulsory purchase of land, highway authorities erect new boundary fences or hedges, but after a year they become the responsibility of the adjoining landowner. A farmer is compensated for an animal killed on the line after breaking through a BR fence and damaging a train, whereas, on the road, he is sued if a vehicle is damaged.

In Walker Bros. & Lancashire County Council v BRB, 1984, it was ruled that BR had to fence *closed* routes. The case related to the closed Colne-Skipton line. The Council later bought the line and inherited responsibility. If a closed route is widened by a factor of 4-5 by compulsory purchase of adjoining property, and "converted" to a road, fencing costs fall on landowners after a year.

No criticism is levelled at highway, rivers nor canal authorities that adequate fencing of roads and waterways would have prevented the deaths of children, whereas, BR was savagely criticised if "*children wander onto lines because of inadequate fencing*". In 1969, I met a Radio Leicester reporter following such a complaint. The site was on a steep embankment, up which children *wandering* was difficult to conceive. The nearest houses were a quarter of a mile away, beyond a field and across a road. He asked *Will BR improve its fencing if a child is killed?*, and was asked: *Why are unaccompanied children crossing a road and a field to get to the railway? Parents' fear should be the road fronting their houses, not a distant railway.* The interview was not broadcast.

Historic legacy

BR had to cover railway museum losses of £93,000 pa. These are part of the national heritage and the cost should be borne by the nation. This was not accepted by the MoT. BRB should receive assistance for this cost. (BRB 1963 Report, Pages 27,42). Losses fell to £60,000 pa in 1964. The cost should fall on those responsible for museums. (BRB 1964 Report, Page 79). The 1968 Act will relieve BR of the cost of museums and pass them to the Department of Education. (BRB 1969 Report, Page 57). Given average losses of £75,000 pa, losses would have totalled £1.6m unadjusted for inflation.

BR had to maintain disused historic buildings. No like burden fell on competitors. The hysteria that follows failure to maintain them in original condition, regardles of costs or availability of matching materials, defies belief. "1256 buildings were listed. On average, BR spent £1.26m pa to preserve them". ("*Conserving the Railway Heritage*", Page 143). Under privatisation, they will become a direct charge on the Exchequer. Buildings damaged by HGVs are not, of course, charged to them.

The CTCC deplore the excessive amounts that BR has had to spend on historically listed buildings, when the need to raise basic standards at stations is so great. (CTCC 1982 Report, Page 10).

Government interfered to push up wages!

"BR offered 5% increase, unions sought up to 15%, but would accept 7.5% A strike would dislocate the whole country and BR should bear this in mind when considering the problem of adding £2.75m to costs". The Minister of Labour intervened and set up a Court of Inquiry before the railway industrial machinery - which provided for independent arbitration - was exhausted. "The Court - including two Trade Union officials - unanimously agreed that BR could not be expected to offer more than 5% and increases should be linked to greater efficiency. The MoT said that staff not affected by this claim would require similar treatment. The Minister of Labour is to continue with his efforts. BR had offered increases costing £6.75m, the Court sat for six days and lifted it to £7m - which it said was all BR could afford - but which the unions rejected. The Minister of Labour informed the Cabinet that he had told BR that it was a mistake to link pay to productivity. He met BR and unions after which a further £2.25m was offered and rejected. *At Government request*, BR resumed negotiations and a settlement reached at a cost of £12m. Claims by staff, not involved in the original claim lifted the total to £18.5m". (PRO: CAB, Feb 1951; BTC 1950 & 1951 Reports).

Following a strike call in December 1953, after unions had rejected the decision by the independent Railway Staff National Tribunal, the Tory Minister of Labour intervened, to avert a strike, after which a new offer was made and the strike called off. (PRO: CAB Dec 1953).

In December 1954, unions rejected the final BTC offer. The Tory Cabinet (PRO: CAB Dec 1954) agreed it would "be helpful if the BTC could indicate some possibility of improving its offer". The MoT told the Cabinet he had asked the Chairman "if he could make such an offer if assured that the BTC need not be concerned about the size of its deficit, which could be justified on three grounds":

- "The Government would favourably consider the [1955] Modernisation Plan".
- "The Freight Charges Scheme would *shortly* come into operation". *Government had told BR to scrap the 1951 Scheme, a new scheme had not been submitted to the Transport Tribunal who had said, in 1951, that it would take three years, from submission to implementation.*
- "The Government believed that staff would co-operate in efficiency".

The Cabinet "agreed it was unlikely the BTC would offer more unless Government shared responsibility for the higher deficit; and agreed a statement: "If the Tribunal conclude the claim should be met, in whole or in part, the BTC will consult the MoT as to means by which the additional cost should be met". The next day it changed: consultation would relate to "any consequences which acceptance of such a recommendation might entail in relation to their statutory duty under the 1947 Act". The Minister set up a Court of Inquiry, under Sir John Cameron QC. He stated: "Having willed the end, the Nation must will the means" and "the statutory requirement that the BTC must pay its way, taking one year with another, should not be allowed to stand in the way of legitimate wage claims. BR wages should be no worse than those in comparable industries". The Tory Government accepted his report. BTC Chairman, Sir Brian Robertson said: "Where the money was to come from was none of my business". (Hansard vol 536, col 154). An MP asked if Government would - as its acceptance implied - fund its decision to avoid inflating BR losses. There was no answer.

In April 1958, a meeting took place involving the Prime Minister, Ministers, BTC and unions. Unions were given 3% and promised a Pay Inquiry. In August, they agreed to invite Mr. Guillebaud to conduct an Inquiry. (BTC 1958 Report, Page 11). It was March 1960, when he reported and awarded increases of 8-10% plus differentials based on comparability with other industries, which the Prime Minister told Parliament was accepted by Government. (10.3.60 Hansard vol. 619, col. 643).

The Cabinet noted that the BR working week was longer than any industry. They agreed that "The BTC should be authorised to offer a reduction of not more than two hours [in the working week] provided that the effective date was 1st January 1962, if possible. (PRO: CAB 128/35, 14.3.61).

At the end of 1961, the unions were offered $2^1/_2$%. They asked to meet the Prime Minister who met them on 14th February and urged them to accept 3%, which they did. (BRB 1962 Report, Page 17)

In 1965, a Labour Government appointed Jack Scamp to inquire into the Single Manning Agreement. Staff costs were increased in March "by the PM's settlement". (BRB 1966 Report, Page 1).

Government set up another Court of Inquiry in 1967, under Prof. Robertson. "*Beer & Sandwiches*" in Downing Street had become a catch-phrase in industrial relations.

In 1972, the Tory Government, having given way on miners' wages decided to use a new law to compel rail unions to ballot members on the dispute. BR management forecast this measure would be counter productive. As predicted, staff voted overwhelmingly to support union leadership.

Without interference, which encouraged brinkmanship, BR would have rejected increases it could not afford and unlike industry was not allowed to pass on to customers. Ministers acted precipitously to avert strikes. It was obvious that failure to face threats would lead to escalating demands. The 1955 strike lasted only two weeks, when managers refused to concede demands, and much rail traffic continued to move during the strike, by rail, BR cartage, BRS and other road transport.

Legal and quasi-legal costs

Delay caused by Applications to the Tribunal from 1948 to 1968, to seek increases in charges, aggregated to a staggering $12^3/_4$ years. (see Appendix B). "During 1953, BTC made several thousand appearances on fares and charges or licensing of goods and passenger services - not all brief, one was 16th February to 24th April, all required a great deal of preparation". (BTC 1953 Report, Page 12).

At Tribunal Hearings, the BTC - later BRB - were represented by QCs and junior barristers. Their substantial fees plus the costs of staff who had to prepare data for inclusion in the massive volumes of documents required by the Court, and the fees of solicitors who had to review the papers before they were seen by barristers was an unquantified, but clearly substantial and unjustified burden. More costs were involved arising from the many months spent in court by BR executives. No other industry has ever been faced with such a nonsense. BR also had to fund the Tribunal itself, and the venues in which Hearings were conducted. (see page 177). This, plus time to prepare cases, represented a huge and costly delay in adjusting prices to match inflation and suppliers' increases.

Sometimes, lawyers represented local authorities objecting to closures, appearing before TUCCs, which were not law courts, but resembled a Roman amphitheatre. Some cases went to a Law Court. Huge legal fees were paid by ratepayers - not all of whom used railways. In some cases, BR was obliged to brief counsel. When it did, objectors' cases disappeared in smoke. (see "*The Railway Closure Controversy*"). Costs incurred in preparing cases to publicly justify closures are impossible to calculate, but must have been staggering. BR also had to fund the CTCC and TUCCs.

Closures

If railways had not been nationalised, the Big Four would have wasted no time in closing unprofitable lines. They would have been obliged to do so, because of a responsibility to shareholders. There would have been no circus of hearings. Government may have subsidised these lines, had they considered them as vital as objectors and their MPs have claimed. As Government was happily subsidising agriculture, airlines, shipbuilding, fishing and industry - often, in areas where rail closures were opposed - subsidising socially necessary branch lines would have been just.

The 1947 Act [Sec.2-7], placed no restriction on closures: The BTC "*may dispose of any part of the undertaking which in their opinion is not required for the discharge of their duties*". Road/Rail integration required by the Act and an inevitable growth in cars was *bound* to cause closures. The 1953 Act, made no change[6]. In June 1962, Parliament was told that no passenger closure would be effected without the consent of the Minister, who would have powers to attach conditions to the consent, or give directions to the Railways Board. These powers would be used to ensure the provision and continuance of alternative bus services, where justified. (Hansard, vol. 657, col. 465).

In 1955, an MP said: "When a businessman finds he is losing business, he does not put up the shutters[7], he looks for ways of increasing business". (Hansard, vol. 536 col. 1801). The evidence is that they *do* cease to provide a product. "It is not made now, no one wants it" - when you have asked for it! In 1954-5, 7,227 private sector businesses were wound-up, i.e. "put up the shutters". It is certain that none were prevented from increasing prices, nor directed by Government to pay wages they couldn't afford, nor prevented from closing branches. Companies shut down production and transfer it to the Far East, then import products under the original well-known brand names! A transport example of putting-up the shutters arose at a Transport Tribunal hearing in 1956, when a witness said his family gave up operating buses, because receipts couldn't be made to match increasing costs.

The 1955 Plan stated that closures - begun in 1949 by Blee - would continue. Robertson drew attention to uneconomic lines and traffic, and that Government did *not* subsidise railways. The first subsidies were paid in 1969. Until then losses had to be made good from "elsewhere". Government dreamed up a winner in 1956 - providing interest bearing loans, whilst uniquely freezing fares - then trailing inflation by 34 points! No industry, however skilled its managers would have survived such insane policies. No critic offered to put money where their mouth was. Local authorities did not take over a line to prove their claim that running at a profit was easy. Amateurs said they could - if staff worked for nothing. Such a policy applied in industry would have seen household names still produced in the UK instead of the Far East. "The unavoidable counterpart to modernisation is that services on which traffic decline cannot be reversed and losses recovered by normal business methods must be closed down in favour of more suitable means of transport". (BTC 1957 Report, Page 5).

From September 1962 to June 1963, action on closures was suspended. (BRB 1963 Report, Page 2). The 1962 Act required BR to give six weeks notice[8] of a proposed closure. and was the first Act to give the TUCCs a role on closures, but reduced it from that which they had taken upon themselves - making decisions - to simply reporting on the scale of hardship. Hitherto, a TUCC considered a proposed closure, often at a "Public Inquiry", made recommendations to the CTCC, which either:-
 • Supported the TUCC recommendation and forwarded it to the MoT,
 • Overruled the TUCC recommendation - a rare occurrence,
 • Referred the case back to the TUCC for re-consideration - an even rarer occurrence.
It seemed the most convoluted a bureaucrat could devise - but they made it worse: In its 1965 Report, the BRB noted that two new procedural steps, added to the time proposals await a decision:
 • The MoT scrutinises all proposals before statutory announcement to the public is begun.
 • All proposals are referred to the new Regional Economic Planning Councils and Boards.
Others await the MoT's conurbation studies. For closures recently announced, the procedure took three years. Preparation and progressing submissions absorbs considerable management effort which could be directed at improving efficiency and reducing costs of main services. BR must defer

---

[6] "The BTC is required under the 1854 Railway & Canal Traffic Act to afford reasonable facilities to the public. It is a pity that the Conservative Government did not repeal this so that closure would be at BTC discretion, as an essential part of its programme for competition". (A. Walters, University of Birmingham; British Transport Review Dec 1954).
[7] The private sector railway companies have closed lines and plan to close more despite higher subsidies!
[8] The private sector gives five minutes notice to staff and public of closure or transfer to the Far East.

lifting track and other assets, until the MoT consents. Under the Sifting procedure, the MoT looks at proposals before publication, leading to delays of over two months. (BRB 1965 Report, Pages 4,30).

The problem

Paradoxically, there were critics who said that BR was closing too many lines, whilst others said they were closing too few! "The BTC are criticised for not closing a large number of branch and secondary lines, yet, when, after careful study a decision is reached that a line should be closed, opposition is well organised and strong protests are made. Those who protest are never able to offer a solution to securing enough traffic". (BTC 1950 Report, Page 24). "In many rural areas the traffic needed to make a reasonable service pay is non existent". (CTCC 1951 Report, Page 9). "Losses on lightly used lines had to be made good by other users of nationalised transport. We are satisfied that savings are compiled by the BTC on a very conservative basis". (CTCC 1954 Report, Pages 3,4). "We are running trains whose costs are more than five times receipts, so that if we halved costs and doubled receipts, they would still lose money". (BTC Review, April 1956, Page 58).

The public is "prone to use private and public road transport in their daily life and only remember railways when closure is threatened. The causes of unprofitability of branch lines lie in history - many were built to keep a rival out of the area or in a burst of enthusiasm engendered by specula- tors, which took no account of traffic potential. Many were placed badly in relation to villages they were meant to serve. Nobody wants to walk a few hundred yards to a station". (Railway Gazette, 13.4.56, Pages 183-184). *Many lines were remote due to the 19th Century NIMBY factor.*

There is rarely sufficient traffic to provide both road and rail with an economic return where branch traffic is light and stations happen, for historical reasons, to be inconveniently situated". (CTCC 1954 Report Page 7). "Early development led to a dense network to minimise horse transport; even then there was excessive construction and many services did not pay. Stopping passenger services produce almost 50% of the loss for 10% of the revenue. If they were discontinued and freight loading ceased at small stations it would save £25m pa". (BTC 1961 Report, Pages 3,4,5).

BR can never be viable without action to relieve them of a social burden which should be financed from sources other than railway revenue. (Beeching, BRB 1965 Report, Page 2).

The procedure

To cut dead wood, BR had to face public hearings. BR did not have a monopoly, as Tory Minis- ters had confirmed. No other business delays action, nor gives proof that it needs to do so. No pro- test is heard. David Blee, a member of the Railway Executive, set up a committee in 1949 to review unremunerative routes: service development, light units, cutting costs or closure. (PRO: AN4/2, 31.3.49)[9]. This undermines an obituary of BTC member, ex-civil servant Sir Reginald Wilson, which claimed that *he* initiated closures: "*as the lone outsider, Wilson pressured career railway managers to effect closures*". He was one of 13 of the 15 BTC members with no rail background. At a meeting on 11th October 1951, Wilson stated that he had no time to get down to the railway problem. (PRO: AN6/10). BTC minutes prior to Blee's initiative contain no reference to pressure on the Executive. The BTC, dominated by ex-civil servants delayed closures, by requiring the Executive to obtain prior approval. (PRO: AN85/17). Submissions to the BTC had to include all financial data, including long term renewals. Blee pointed out that the case for closure was often clear before all data was gathered, and proposed a "shortened procedure". The BTC agreed, but civil service minds insisted full details be supplied within six months. This thwarted the objective, as no less time would be spent on each case. (PRO: AN97/20). The BTC told the Executive to consult TUCCs before submis- sion. (PRO: AN85/4). If they opposed closure, the MoT invariably supported them. The MoT told Parliament: "Since 1951, there has been a procedure under which BR advise TUCCs of proposals and no service has been withdrawn without their approval". (Hansard, 22.2.53, vol. 566, col. 103).

---

[9] Predating claims that the Railway Development Association - formed in *November 1951* - initiated such ideas.

At a meeting on 19th April 1955, BTC representatives told Treasury and DoT officials that closures to date had saved £1m pa, and that the BTC wished for faster progress. (PRO: MT47/405).

In February 1958, Blee told Robertson that he objected to new BTC proposals for advertising closures which would cause delay: "I am brought back to the conclusion that so long as Parliament lays an obligation on us to balance our accounts, it is wrong for another authority to question the basis of our judgement to the proper management of the industry. The Acts do not require alternative facilities to be made available". (PRO: AN6/57). The same point was made by Sir Leonard Sinclair, member of the BTC and former Chairman of Esso: "The BTC ought to be able to say it had sufficient justification to close. Delays, even of three months, were quite wrong". (PRO: AN85/16, 21.1.61).

A 1966 White Paper "*Transport Policy*" stated: "There are services which have little or no prospect of becoming remunerative, on the basis of revenue from users, yet their value to the community outweighs their accounting cost to BR. These socially necessary services include commuter services whose closure would add to road congestion and some services in remote areas where reasonable alternatives are impracticable or excessively costly. Each closure proposal will go through the normal procedures *and* consultation with Regional Economic Planning Councils". (Cmd 3057, Pages 4,5)

Objections to closures

We are concerned that a TUCC could not consider objections by a non user. (CTCC 1991/2 Report, Page 10). A non-user of a shop, cinema or theatre has no right to object to its closure. There was no reason to treat railways differently. Objectors enjoyed the support of MPs - who were happy to see closures in *other* constituencies[10]. Much local authority opposition was inspired by the effect on the local economy of railway job losses. Principal objections and claims made by critics, included:-

- Reduce fares - that were already trailing inflation by up to 40 points!
- Local authorities claimed that BR could cut costs *and* reduce fares[11].
- Branch lines feed main lines - main lines generated 99% of traffic from towns on the main line.
- Modernise - the source of funds was shrouded in mystery. (see "*The Railway Closure Controversy*").
- Carry more freight - noticeably, councils did not direct their purchases be sent by rail. Objectors did not comprehend that to be competitive, freight could not subsidise passengers, as they sought.
- Adopting plans of amateurs[12] - *some were anonymous* - some were based on healthy staff working 365 days pa; others envisaged unpaid labour. All ignored the need for maintenance spares.
- By unstaffed stations. BR said they lack many facilities. The CTCC dismissed this, called for de-staffing, and then afterwards made a "U" turn: "CTCC endorsed a TUCC view that destaffing has lowered standards[13] and left passengers with few facilities". (CTCC 1988/9 Report, Page 18)
- The line is needed in a bad winter[14] - which come every seven years - or the next war[15] .
- "Borrow a DMU from another line for an experiment". As a consequence the "donor line" would revert to steam - which would go down like a lead balloon.
- Resulting increased travel by road may cause increased deaths on the road. No cash was offered to BR to reflect this, and no financial line of entry was allowed in BR accounts for deaths avoided.

---

[10] See page 62, and see the Rural Transport Debate (Hansard vol. 547, col. 711).

[11] *Their* record between 1948 & 1962, when *they* were objecting to closures and to fares being increased, was uninspiring. Council rates rose much faster than fares. (see "*The Railway Closure Controversy*", Appendix C).

[12] Henshaw praised amateurs' plans, but gave no details. I traced them. They were impractical and uneconomic. He referred to an MP backing an expert's plan for light railways. I found it - the author was a coach station manager - and demolished it, along with the aforementioned and several other plans. (see "*The Railway Closure Controversy*")

[13] They had earlier suggested: If trains only use unstaffed halts in daytime, lighting difficulties envisaged by BR can be disregarded. (CTCC 1962 Report, Para. 30). *Darkness comes early in the winter, so services would be restricted.*

[14] In a typical case, an MP called for reinstatement of services "as in the 1947 winter - **nine years earlier** - a village was cut off for eight weeks". (Hansard, vol. 547, col. 1576). *It was needed one week in 58!* In another case "bread was taken daily to snowbound villages". Spring and bad memories ended support, until closure was threatened.

[15] Railways did not gain, in wartime, but lost - unlike other industry that tucked away huge profits, (e.g. see Barnett/1, Page 360), failed to meet post-war demands for steel and other goods, and failed to manufacture *reliable* products.

- Losses - which objectors accepted did exist - could be cut, but not eliminated.
- Passengers will not use buses to main line stations, but will travel by road throughout[16].
- Other countries modernised rural lines - "in France and Holland, whose railways were revived after the war, services were withdrawn from a larger proportion of their system than UK". (BTC 1955 Report,Page 9). "In Holland, 691 stations out of 1,000 have closed". (Hansard vol 551,col 1675)
- "Railcars should stop anywhere to pick up - not just at stations". (Hansard, vol. 536, col. 1802). Boarding from cess level is difficult. The repeated emphasis of luggage, prams, cycles was not mentioned in *this* debate. It required special trains for a few lines. No company would consider it.
- The Railway Development Association said a railbus was cheaper to run than a road bus, as rail paid no fuel tax nor road fund licence. (PRO: MT124/65). They *contributed* to road costs. BR pay all infrastructure costs. A railbus cost much more. (see page 68). An MP briefed by the Association suggested a railbus, (Hansard, vol 551, col 1648), converted from a road bus as in Ireland. (see below)
- Isle of Wight Council argued that losses would - after unspecified economies - be less than the cost of upgrading roads to take rail traffic. They did not pursue the *logical* course of paying rail losses to avoid road costs, but expected mainland passengers to subsidise this wealthy backwater.

"The CTCC had visited Ulster and Eire and noted that diesels had not prevented losses which now threaten remaining services, and that for sparse traffic of rural areas, railway units are handicapped in comparison with road, by higher capital and running costs and being tied to track, on which halts and stations are often some distance from places they serve. On railway lines from which services have already been withdrawn, no change in the type of rail unit could have converted loss into profit". (BTC 1956 Report, Page 9). The CTCC visited Ireland to view railbuses. "ingeniously adapted from *obsolescent* road buses. In the North of Ireland, they have not succeeded in preventing losses which now threaten the continued operation of many of the remaining rail services". (Times, 4.4.57, Page 7). Had BR publicised an intention to use vehicles like these pre-war vintage buses, criticism would have reverberated around the country and Parliament. Great Northern of Ireland Railways can fix flanged wheels on a standard bus, as their gauge is wider than BR's. They have four which have not prevented losses. They can only be driven from one end, requiring a turntable at each end of a branch. BR locos and DMUs returned without turning. Irish Railways are not to continue with experiments. It is not clear why those in rural areas would prefer to walk to a station, to use a bus which runs on rails, rather than one that runs on roads. (PRO: MT124/65).

The most ingenuous closure objection was to the former Great Central - unprofitable in the horse era - with claims of passengers driven away by poor service, when most places were served by better routes and post-war GC speeds were cut by colliery subsidence. Freight was cut by recessions and industrial decline and then decimated by "re-routing" coal via the Super-Grid from mega power stations in the coalfields. A claim that it could be the Chunnel link lacks realism, implying a terminus 30 miles south of Sheffield - as only the extension of the MSLR to London had the more generous structural gauge. Moreover, the south end of the extension was over routes built by other companies to UK gauge standards. The Metropolitan line through London, envisaged as part of the route, was not to the European gauge. Most traffic would have to tranship to road or rail for most of its journey! The prospect of TGVs thundering down that subsidence ridden line at 45 mph, to a field in Derbyshire - not Sheffield, as claimed (BBC Radio 27.2.03 - "*Back to Beeching*") is laughable.

Henshaw claimed in the programme that the Buxton line, which was proposed for closure was viable: "a very successful line". When the penny pinching Treasury finally agreed to pay for MoT decisions to keep open socially necessary lines - 21 years after BR was formed - it paid £362,000 pa for that line! In his book, Henshaw praised a plan to keep open the Somerset & Dorset line, but gave no details. Fortunately, there was a copy in the British Library and using data from the same sources as the authors of the plan, plus public sources that they had studiously ignored, I proved with fact

---

[16] Objectors claimed passengers would use new buses linking villages to branch line stations with infrequent services, so as to enjoy the opportunity to change again at the very same main line stations, that had more frequent services.

and figure that they were hopelessly wrong[17]. Although other "plans" have been traced and demolished (see "*The Railway Closure Controversy*"), that on Buxton has proved elusive. It is nonsense to claim that closures were to justify motorway construction. If all traffic displaced from branch lines had been brought together on a special motorway - it would have looked like the M1 on opening day. His "conspiracy" theory was aimed at the wrong target. The *real* conspirators were those who opposed fares matching inflation, limited their use of branches to every seventh winter, and advanced uncommercial and impractical plans, the funding of which was to come from "elsewhere".

BR was criticised for preparing "false" accounts for closures. (see page 141). Critics did not mean **the Accounts**, prepared as directed by the MoT and audited by independent accountants. That may have brought legal action by the Auditors. They meant financial appraisals prepared to assess alternative courses of action. Sir Peter MacDonald, the Isle of Wight MP, told Parliament: "*We hear from commercial industries that if they rendered accounts in the same manner as Nationalised Industries they would find themselves in gaol*". Asked by an MP to substantiate that, he said: "*objectors challenged railways to substantiate accounts* [on closures]. *If commercial enterprises were to render accounts without substantiating them, in the same manner they would be up against the Board of Trade and the Companies Act and find themselves in gaol, that is opinion of many people*". (Hansard, vol. 523, cols. 874-7). He was comparing chalk and cheese - brief Annual Accounts of private sector companies that *never* produce a piece of paper to justify closure, with financial appraisals made by BR in respect of closures for which masses of paper are demanded by occasional or non-users, for debate in a modern version of the Coliseum. Following one such criticism by an MP, Parliament was told that "Sir Harold Barton, a public auditor who audits BR accounts, asked if he would supply as much in annual reports of a company, said he would not be thanked by shareholders if he burdened them with half the information, the BTC supplies". (Hansard, vol 547, col 733)

It is claimed (BBC Radio 27.2.03), that of £30m planned by closing 5,000 miles and 1,900 stations, Beeching saved only £7m "proving the fallacy of savings from closures". There are reasons for not achieving £30m. Training costs for operating and maintenance staff on new locos, signalling, track machines, etc., and bus subsidies would consume part of the savings from closures. He left in May 1965. By the end of 1964, 1,080 miles and 773 stations had closed. Adding half of those closed in 1965, brings totals to 1,580 miles and 973 stations. Given that and the aforementioned costs, £7m looks about right. The rest were delayed by objectors or the MoT. BR had to keep a route after withdrawal of services before he consented to ending maintenance of formation, bridges, tunnels, viaducts, drainage and fences. Many on his list never closed. Savings were checked. (see page 142).

Perhaps the most absurd display of the role of TUCCs occurred in 1988, when BR implemented my 1983 recommendation to sell the narrow gauge summer only Vale of Rheidol line[18] to a private company. It was not being closed, but the TUCC invited objections and held a Public Hearing. If a comparable railway decides to close or sell out to another owner, there will be *no* TUCC inquiry.

"Arguments for retaining seaside branches [during the summer at least] were overwhelming". (Henshaw, Page 204). Where the staff would go for 8-9 months each year was not explained.

Delays

TUCCs met only on a few occasions annually to consider closures. In March 1956, the BTC requested the MoT to direct them to expedite proposals and curtail requests for extra data where the case was clear. They minuted in April, that he had done so. (PRO: AN85/9). The DoT believed that there is a "tendency of local authorities and others to prolong hearings". (DoT Memo, PRO: MT115/9). "In December 1958, again seeking alleviation of closure procedures from the MoT". (PRO: AN85/12).

---

[17] See "*The Railway Closure Controversy*". It required all to travel an average 86 miles, at 2d per mile, with an average train load of 105, compared to prevailing national averages of 20 miles, 1.97d and 90 respectively. Other assumptions were equally naive.

[18] I was Divisional Manager, Stoke on Trent. It was in my Division. (see "*Blueprints for Bankruptcy*", Pages 142-4)

"Beeching's Report held up closure of uneconomic lines that would have gone through before but were held up for inclusion in the Report[19]. Proposals were dramatised in the Report when BR could have gone on closing them. Marples claimed that the Reshaping Report was the first clear report on railways. That was not true - they just hadn't been reading the others. The Report caused traders to withdraw freight before a line was put forward for closure and even on some which would not close - just to be on the safe side. With the Railway Executive practice, revenue held to the last. (Pearson/2 Pages 26,103,104). Beeching's plans included 435 stations "*already under consideration, of which 235 have already been closed*" and some proposed by the BTC and rejected by the TUCC and MoT[20].

Government should have covered losses from the day they were submitted. BTC/BRB Minutes and Annual Reports, media reports etc., referred to delays in closures. A selection includes:-
- TUCCs averaged 9-10 months to progress a closure before passing to the MoT for a decision, despite BTC calls in 1956 and 1958 to speed the process. (BTC Minutes, Mch 1956 & Dec 1958)
- Sir Brian Robertson said that retention of loss making lines was wrong, but no one seemed to care - he could only mean the Government. (Address to Royal United Services Institution, 1956).
- The "Bluebell line" which closed in 1955 after a TUCC Inquiry, was re-opened in 1957, when someone who *always* travelled by road, objected that closure contravened an 1878 Act*.
- The MoT, having refused permission to close on twelve cases, "means that the deficit will not be reduced. The nation should see how much deficit is due to political decision". (Times, 5.11.64).
- "Withdrawal of services delayed by difficulty in establishing bus services, required by the MoT as a condition of closure, sometimes resulted in indefinite postponement". (BRB 1965 Report).
- £3m pa is incurred on services that the MoT refused authority to close. "Five services, approved for closure before July, at the year end, were waiting granting of licences to road operators. In some cases, a licence depended on road improvements! Until June, we required authority before disposing of assets. MoT assent is needed before disposing of track beds". (BRB 1966 Report).
- Delay by the MoT to closures cost £4m pa from 1963 to the end of 1967. Other closures at some stage in the procedure are costing another £4m pa. (BRB 1967 Report).
- Closure of Irish Sea services involved $3^1/_2$ years consultation and negotiation. (BRB 1975 Report).
- Many lines, that had never run at a profit, took years to close. Two lines took ten years to close, including one re-opened after it was severed by sea storms.*

Even unopposed closures incurred delay, as they had to be publicised, and time given for objections

Subsidies as an alternative to closure

In 1959-60, a Select Committee said: Government should decide whether unprofitable services are provided and bear the cost. The MoT said this affects other nationalised industries. *He was wrong. They avoided the problem by pricing up, BR could not.* (see page 24). He said: "For the time being, such losses will be covered by contributions from public funds". This was a reference to the 1962 Act provision to cover losses for five years. Social costs arising from blocked or delayed closures were still counted as BR *losses*. The MoT's 1960 Paper (Cmnd 1248, Page 4) stated: "The practical test is how far users are prepared to pay economic prices for services provided. This will settle the size and pattern of the railway system". *External control of fares prevented such tests.*

After 1960, Grants were paid to cover losses arising *directly* from the 1956 direction to BR to freeze fares and charges which trailed inflation. They were not subsidies for services, but were paid so as to emphasise that BR needed handouts due to incompetence in not finding ways to make lines

---

[19] "Action was suspended on closures from 1.9.62 to 1.6.63" (BRB 1963 Report, Page 2).

[20] A BBC radio programme (27.2.03) suggested that Beeching was "brought from outside", to replace BR managers, but he replaced a retired general who had replaced a retired civil servant. Only two chairmen were railwaymen, the fifth and the eighth: Sir Henry Johnson - two years after Beeching, and Sir Robert Reid, 12 years after Johnson. Long before becoming Chairman, Beeching said in a secret Report to the MoT, that BR should be run by railwaymen - when he took over he replaced Area Boards composed of outsiders - by insiders - and praised their achievements.

* See "*The Railway Closures Controversy*".

profitable on the crumbs objecting businesses put on rail - often only in the winter[21] - in areas where subsidies were paid to fishing, agriculture and industry, whose own prices were not, of course, subject to any external control at all. Some admitted to only using rail when roads were snowbound!

"BR cannot break even, if burdened with losses on socially necessary lines which they are refused permission to close. The time has come to face this: services requiring assistance will be identified and costed so that a decision can be made whether the social benefit from maintenance of a service is sufficient to justify the cost of continuing; the MoT not the BRB will decide. Where the MoT decides against a grant, BR may submit an application to close". ("*Railway Policy*" 1967 Cmnd 3439, Pages 1,2). Of 34 cases waiting a decision, the Minister withheld Grant on ten. (BRB 1968 Report Page 20). *Having introduced, at long last, Grants for loss making lines which BR was not allowed to close, he was refusing such Grants. Managers believed that the purpose of Grants was to relieve BR of an unjust burden, and "be quick about it"*.

Until 1969 - when the 1968 Act became effective - BR received no subsidy for loss making lines. The Act did not provide for losses between submission and the MoT's decision - usually a year or so. The change to treating such lines as a Government social cost - not a BR loss - was overdue. Uneconomic lines or replacement buses should have been overtly subsidised from 1948, instead of via BR Accounts which inflated "losses" - it may have sharpened DoT action. "It is not Government intention that BR should embark on a programme of major route closure". (BRB 1983 Report, Page 4).

Re-opening of stations

The Transport Act 1962 [Amendment] Act 1981 - called the "Speller" Act, after the sponsoring MP - permitted reopened stations to be again closed, without a formal TUCC inquiry, if they still prove uneconomic. In 1994, a Minister said: "We have opened or re-opened 220 stations". None of them was opened by *Ministerial* initiative. A local authority source stated that apart from a few opened on BR initiative, the rest were due to initiative and funding by local authorities or Passenger Transport Authorities. Had they underwritten original losses, stations would not have closed.

Few councils funded rural services in the 1970s & 1980s. BR was criticised for closing stations that have now reopened. Losses that fell for twenty years on BR, could not have continued in the faint hope that the tide may change, with councils finding cash. Self proclaimed experts claimed that uneconomic lines could be run profitably - given unlimited investment, but none offered to fund their ideas[21]. Hopes of Lottery funds have spawned new groups - e.g. Wensleydale, Weardale and Alnwick - whose plans lack realism; one "*only needed to move one factory and build two bridges*".

It was said in a Sunday Telegraph article in June 2000, that a project to re-open the Wensleydale line, closed in 1954, would be "user friendly". What "user-friendly" service would they have run in 1954, for 5,310 people from 12 stations on a 22 mile line, but without £0.5m from sponsors, and only interest bearing loans? The line *never* paid a dividend. The North Eastern Railway financed it in 1863, to block competitors reaching rich pickings in the north east. To run it *commercially*, it cannot be dependent on unpaid labour - two-thirds of operating costs - **all** staff must be paid minimum wages and interest paid on capital - as applied to BR in 1954. Any fool could make a business "profitable" given free labour. They will be in for a rude awakening when the forecast millions of tourists do *not* materialise. Given a bad winter, villagers and farmers will use the line - until roads are clear! This was the reality of rural branch lines. They envisaged a train *every two hours* - which would go down like a lead balloon with motorists. They got further publicity for their uncommercial project from Tyne-Tees TV. The presenter asked whether mistakes made 40-50-60 years ago with railways could be put right. A reply to a request to identify the mistakes envisaged, focused on closures, and overmanning[22]. If mistakes made 40-50-60 years ago by UK industry could be put right, their output would improve the UK economy and generate rail traffic.

---

[21] See "*The Railway Closure Controversy*".

[22] On manning see page 141. On closures, the reality and their losses - see "*The Railway Closure Controversy*".

Chapter 13   Rationalisation & economy

Continual reviews by BR managers cut costs. There was no year, since 1948, in which economies were not made. BR never claimed that there was no room to improve productivity. That stage will *never* be achieved in *any* industry. Any industry believing that it has exhausted the scope to improve productivity is not one for the wise investor. Unlike economies made by the newcomers, BR kept enough staff to run advertised services! "BR applied relentless downward pressure on costs". (*Railway World*, October 2002).

The most fatuous allegation is that "BR was run for the benefit of unions/staff". It is out of touch with reality. Staff who lost jobs when lines closed, did not believe that[1]. For 30 years, my jobs had 24 hour "On Call" duty - required to turn out to resolve problems: suicides, obstructed crossings, fires on industrial premises, vandals, defective private sector equipment, bad weather, train failures, etc. - for the benefit of passengers and freight customers[2]. The only member of staff that I - then a station master - turned out for was a signalman whose father died suddenly, and whose mother was ill, and in accordance with common practice, worked the box - which had manually operated level crossing gates - on the London-Edinburgh main line - in a snowstorm - having had to cycle over two miles to get there. The beneficiaries in mind were passengers and freight that would have been delayed until a relief signalman could take over his signalbox[3].

Scores of economy schemes - to improve productivity by reducing jobs of supervisors, clerical staff and other grades, and economising on assets - which were personally initiated, devised and implemented over 25 years, in two Regions, were not regarded by staff as being for *their* benefit, despite explaining that they were essential for BR's long term future. Anyone trying to run the railway for the benefit of staff, would not have worked over 12 hours on three consecutive days at a weekend, unpaid, to get a route open after an accident, but would have taken three weeks - as now applies. It would have enhanced the pay of breakdown, track and other staff. Neither would I have devised methods of operation to counteract official and unofficial disputes, so that trains could run with fewer signal boxes open. These measures required more ingenuity and in-depth knowledge of the rules governing safe working, and eclipse those of putting a few managers in key modern boxes - a method that would have been ineffective in areas signalled by older systems.

Dr Joy (Page 78), claimed that BR staff reductions did not arise from improved productivity because staff "were not working harder". Improved productivity in any industry mainly arises from:
- More capital investment and Research & Development expenditure. (see Chapters 6-9).
- Elimination of unproductive time, including "tea breaks" - not given to signalmen, traincrews, station staff, controllers, clerical staff, technicians, etc. - which UK industry tried vainly to end.
- Improved product design - to reduce the labour element in production and maintenance - an area in which UK industry consistently lost ground to foreign competition.
- Ending demarcation. BR took action long before UK industry which was notoriously ineffective.
- Work study, which was accepted on BR. In UK industry, a stop watch was a signal to stop work.
- Method study and other management techniques. (see Chapter 9 for techniques used on BR).
- Training and improved Health and Safety conditions.

The incidence of staff "working **harder**", in any industry, is rarely significant in improving productivity, being immeasurable. Some may "work faster" or longer hours, but with risks to safety if operating machines or driving - both of concern on railways. BR managers were active in exploiting productive and measurable avenues, were improving productivity and training their successors to do likewise, long before Beeching. It was - probably still is - unknown outside BR, that from time

---

[1] Industries run for the benefit of staff were engineering, shipbuilding, motor manufacturing and civil service.

[2] In May 1991, a Sunday Times article said that BR "hates its customers", If BR hated their customers, no managers would have responded to night hours' calls, without pay, to resolve problems, many due to external misdemeanours.

[3] Until the District Office opened and arranged relief, I took over at Barnby Moor at 6.0am on Monday morning from a man on a 12 hour night shift. He was due back at 2.0pm. This enabled men to rotate shifts over the weekend.

immemorial, key staff: controllers, supervisors, signalmen, ticket office staff and others, arrived *early* for duty, by 10-20 minutes, *for which they were not paid*, to ensure a smooth, safe hand-over. Dr. Joy was probably unaware of this dedication to duty, as he did not mention it in his book.

Joy claimed that BR had 50,000 more staff than needed from 1948 to 1962, (Page 52), but advanced no evidence. Economies were made from Day One: roster changes, closures and productivity reviews. Some savings were temporarily counter balanced by extra staff needed for modernisation works. He claimed (Page 137), that motor vans had drivers' mates, "to hold the reins of long deposed horses".[4] Motors towing trailers were required by law to have a second man; those delivering vulnerable goods: wine, spirits, tobacco, carpets had a guard to stop thefts. Rationing and shortages created a black market until about 1951, which fed from stolen goods. Some items needed two people to unload. In the 1951 wage negotiations, BR reviewed the "*unnecessary use of vanguards in London*" - but did not mention a problem elsewhere. Few industries could claim to have rid themselves of unproductive staff twenty years later, or there would still be a UK manufacturing base.

A Tyne-Tees TV producer referred, in a programme in December 2000, to "mistakes made by BR over the past 40-50-60 years". He later stated, that he had in mind, claims that false figures were produced to justify closures of lines now being re-opened; and overmanning of office staff. The number of office staff was dictated by requirements on timetabling, scheduling rolling stock & locos, train-crew rosters, other staff rosters, accountancy, sales, calculation & payment of wages, publicity, development of plans & designs, plans for changes in services, safety programmes, accident inquiries, records of maintenance of assets, ordering/issuing - and chasing up late delivery of - stores including uniforms, control of train movements, holiday arrangements, travel concessions, welfare, recruitment, ticket and goods offices, phone and oral inquiries, planning applications, liaison with local authorities & organisations, replying to customers, analysis of market research, staff & public suggestions and many other activities, including typing letters and reports required by the above - not least to Government and politicians. Office staff also produced the mass of statistics demanded by the MoT, which had increased even from the horrendous volume demanded pre-war. This was reduced by the MoT when Beeching arrived. Office staff had to produce data on complaints and performance, the equal of which is *not* seen from other industries. No other industry supplied such data to an independent body. Despite these factors, BR cut office staff by the use of O&M economy schemes (see Chapter 9), by merging Districts to form Divisions, and later merging some Divisions together, and by replacing ground level station masters etc. by fewer Area Managers. Later with advances in technology and communications, Regions and Divisions were eliminated. BR appears to have neglected to publicise these changes and all other economies.

On the allegation of 'false figures', he was referred to "*The Railway Closure Controversy*", which disproves his claim, and told that lines being re-opened are funded by local authorities - which refused funds to prevent closure. The Special Advisory Group, composed of top private sector executives - set up in the expectation that it would find nothing but criticism of BR - noted that BR "had cautiously forecast a 5.5% *fall* in passenger miles - from closures - between 1957 & 1963, but passenger miles had *increased* by 10%". *This counters criticisms that BR underestimated the effects of closures.* Increases arose from faster main line services consequent upon junction closures - a financial effect not embraced in closure proposals. It is ignored that cinemas and theatres had closed in thousands, but are now re-opening. They had faced the same problem - lack of patronage at a price that would cover costs, and severe competition. No one was prepared to provide funds to keep *them* open until the tide turned. Now some are re-opening, but no one carps about *their* mistakes in closing *them* down. Shipyards should, by the same token, have also been kept going by their management, without Government funding, in the faint hope that Government would eventually

---

[4] Depots at which the author worked in the early 1950s had horse drawn vehicles - common in UK towns - *all* without mates. At depots, at which he later worked, the only motor vehicles with mates were either towing trailers or delivering vulnerable goods.

pick up the tab. "Independent accountants check BR closure figures". (Hansard 12.12.68, vol. 775, col. 212). Lines opened by amateurs are dependent on handouts and unpaid labour!

External Advice
The Monopolies & Mergers Commission reported in 1980, on south east commuter services:
- BR should consider what economies could be made through a reduced use of rolling stock where this could be done without unreasonably affecting the quality of service. (Report Page 183). *Reductions that do not affect quality of service can be assessed. To do so where the service is worsened "but not unreasonably" begs the question as to who will judge whether it is unreasonable - BR, MoT, Select Committee, a TUCC or* **one** *of its millions of passengers.*
- BR should be continuously employing a variety of measures ranging from shortening trains, taking out trains and altering stopping patterns. (Report Page 183). *BR did so* **continually**, *and was invariably criticised for so doing by politicians and others.*

BRB responded in 1982 to the Serpell Committee's "Review of Railway Finances":
"There were two Reports - which are in some ways contrary - and this means there is a danger of increasing confusion. But the results of the one investigated indicated that a combination of certain network options with increased investment could prove beneficial. BRB regrets the Committee did not have time to pursue this line of enquiry. The results - of mathematical modelling - seem inherently implausible in many instances". The Committee said: "There are no significant arrears of track renewal", but BR had reported a six month backlog. "They criticised BR Plans for being over optimistic, yet they count £220m, of largely unsubstantiated savings, in their own calculations. They outlined three options without estimating costs or benefits. They chose, without reason, to double financial savings which BR believe would result from reduced maintenance. They made no estimates of revenue effects when recommending reductions in service quality". (Pages 3,9,10.11,12). On network size, BRB said: "The mathematical model on which the options are based is, in the Board's view, inadequate to form a basis for policy decisions. The Committee were too unsure of it themselves to discuss it with BR". (BRB Management Brief, January 1983).

Serpell was a civil servant on the Special Advisory Group. (see page 29). The civil service's record in economy is inauspicious.[5] He forecast that Inter City would never pay. It did. (see page 36).

Economies & productivity arising from developments at the centre
In the summer of 1948, the 48 hour working week was cut to 44 hours - UK industry already had a 40 hour week. It required extra posts to cover 24 hour operations. Despite this, "the manpower establishment is now below pre-war levels". (BTC 1950 Report, Page 40). Traffic was higher.

Management at the centre initiated many schemes, plans and projects to cut costs: P&E [Pay & Efficiency Deals], computers and other new technology, work & method study[6], modern equipment[7], line or station closures. Economy began in 1948 on Day One of nationalisation - with the "Razor Gangs", followed by branch line reviews, unremunerative facilities, modernisation. "Work Study was supported by the unions". (BTC 1960, Pages 3,11).

BR staff fell from 649,000 in 1948 to 476,500 in 1962: 27% - before Beeching, and a further 14% during his era. By privatisation, manpower was down 84.5% on 1948. The ratio of passenger miles/freight ton miles per man in 1962 - with modernisation incomplete and creating extra manpower demands for modernisation works - had improved over 1948 by 14%, and by 1994 by 303%. Changes in operating methods, reduced route mileage and new productivity agreements led to reduction in staff numbers by over 50% between 1963 and 1970. (BRB 1970 Report, Page 4).

---

[5] See "*Your Disobedient Servant*" by former senior civil servant, Leslie Chapman, published 1978. After reading his book, I was convinced BR managers had nothing to learn from politicians or civil servants on economies.
[6] Beeching was credited with introducing Work & Method Study to BR. He didn't. (see pages 88-89).
[7] Notably, but not exclusively track maintenance machines.

Another source states that "there was a reduction in railway manpower from 526,862 at the beginning of 1960 to just over 260,000 at the end of 1969. That includes a very small figure of 27,000 transferred to the NFC". (BR-LMR Lecture & Debating Society, March 1970, Page 6).

Through two P&E deals in preceding years, BR had linked pay successfully to productivity and a third stage was in hand. Unlike many private sector pay deals, these were subject to monitored savings. "BRB had planned P&E, Stage III, but it was upset by a wages explosion caused by the local authorities settlement in October 1969 of 20-25%. Other industries made substantial offers. BR staff could not be expected to settle for increases linked to productivity when others had got pay without strings. BR staff settled for 8% in May and 3% in August". (BRB 1970 Report, Page 31).

A 1980 Agreement on shorter hours specified that it must not increase costs. No formula was proposed by unions. Management proposed flexible rostering. The ensuing poor media image was due to bad presentation by BRB. A Scottish depot claimed on TV to have it already because some drivers signed on at progressively earlier times during the week. This created a long weekend, but was of no value to management, as it could lead to a driver being too late back from a day's work to take minimum rest before the next turn of duty, thus increasing relief complements. On "Any Questions" someone spoke of creating unsocial shifts by altering *signing on times*. The concept reduced overtime and cut unproductive time at the *end* of shifts, by altering *signing off times*, and avoiding a 3% increase in staff that would otherwise arise from shorter hours. The scale of unsocial signing on times remained largely unaltered. Only those with no rail experience could be surprised by the scale of unsocial shifts which are an unavoidable factor of 24 hour operation. "It was expected to save £9m pa". (Times 19.1.82). Flexible rostering replaced the eight hour day forced on railways by Government (see page 5), not to road transport levels which are unsafe, but within the range 7-9 hours, with a 39 hour week. When private sector managers[8] were told that it would cut overtime they said they would not risk such a change. Failing to eliminate demarcation and waste was at the *root* of industrial decline. BR Annual Reports regularly identified productivity improvements, e.g.:

1970: During the past decade, changes in operating methods and productivity agreements for increased versatility led to massive reductions in staff.

1979: Productivity agreement with track renewals staff provides for a 40 hour week spread over four days including Sunday as part of the week, as the heaviest load is at weekends. BR is among industries with the lowest number days lost through strikes.

1981: BR reduced locos by 7%, coaches 10% and wagons 26%, contrasting with a drop of 3% in passenger miles and 0.8% in freight tonne miles. Staff numbers were cut by 4% and average hours by 4.5%. Overtime hours fell by 8% equivalent to saving 1,500 staff. Train miles per man continued to increase by 1% pa. Since 1977, asset reduction has been significant, while route mileage remained virtually the same. Admin staff were reduced by 1,400 - 18% of the total staff reduction. Total staff reduction this year was 33% of the reduction sought for the years 1981-5. Pending agreement on further productivity, a 3% wage award was withheld.

1982: Train miles per crew improved 2%, and the overall index of labour productivity 8%. Track and signalling costs have fallen since 1979, by an average 2% pa; admin costs by 5% and operating costs by 4%. 20,500 jobs were taken out in two years. Total railway staff fell by 10% in the last two years. BR forecast a manpower reduction by 1986 of 16,000. A pay increase of 6%, awarded in September 1982, was held over until 1983, pending satisfactory progress on the productivity items outstanding from the 1981 ACAS agreement. New agreements resulted in economies from variable rosters.

1983: Staff cuts of 39,000 in three years. Admin costs cut by £6m equal to 1.7%.

1984/5: The Divisional tier of management has been removed saving 6,000 staff. Staff has fallen 17% in five years. BR staff productivity is higher than most of the eight major European

---

[8] During the Senior Executive Course N° 29 at Manchester Business School in early 1982, (see also page 91).

railways - equal to Switzerland and only bettered by the Netherlands. Increased staff and asset productivity cut train operating and maintenance costs by 7% in real terms compared to 1982.

1985/6: Staff productivity rose by 3%. BR identified ways of reducing the cost of maintenance and improving the availability of expensive new equipment. BR staff are expected to fall to 159,000 by 1990/1[9]. Train km per member of staff was BR: 2752, Europe: 2060; PSO as a percentage of GDP - BR: 0.3%, Europe: 0.76%.

1986/7: The railway staff reduction since 1983 was 13%.

1988/9: Productivity increased 8% in terms of train miles per member of staff. Admin staff were cut 20% in three years. Costs were cut by more efficient rolling stock and track maintenance.

1993/4: Staff reduced by 6.9% and operating costs by 10.6%.

1994/5: After allowing for staff transferred to Railtrack, staff had fallen 9.1% during the year.

In 1983, BR decided to withdraw some sleeper services, but would retain car-sleeper services and Anglo-Scottish. Councillors opposed withdrawal of the uneconomic Holyhead-London sleeping cars. The CTCC "endeavoured to maintain some kind of sleeper service between Newcastle and London, with the backing of users. Withdrawal would affect the economic viability of the North East". (CTCC 1987/8 Report, Page 16). They did not say that the backing included guarantees to cover losses. It is difficult to visualise how viability could be affected. A three hour sleeper journey with five hours occupying expensive platform space - since eight hours sleep is the norm - shouts out loss maker. Investors would rank sleepers between English cities as yesterday's business. It focuses attention on BR's dilemma. If they adopted advice against their better judgement and it failed, they are blamed; if they rejected it, they are not prepared to listen. Private sector companies have not reinstated them.

Clwyd County Council opposed the 1984 plan prepared by the London Midland Region to partially single the Wrexham-Bidston line. The fear was refuted that "Nissan's possible new factory at Shotton would be at risk because BR would be unable to move car trains on the single line". The *only* practical location for a factory siding was alongside the unaffected double track. So far as potential passenger growth was concerned, they were told that volume could increase by **1600%** on the existing trains. Above that the service could then be doubled - to take a **3200%** increase - and still run on a single line. The proposed single line could be re-doubled should traffic ever require it.

Many councils opposed economies intended to secure a line's future: modern level crossings, signals controlled from main centres, singling, all incurring investment; and unstaffed halts. Their Luddite attitude could only hasten closure. They called for fare cuts or more trains that would widen the gap, or for more staff, prompted by a desire for a "nice station garden". When lines were about to close, they supported modern crossings and economies previously opposed.

The Operating Department was at the centre of most productivity. Whilst, commercial managers specified timetable requirements to meet researched needs, train planners in the Regional Operating Department were charged with meeting those specifications, so as to maximise productivity of track, traincrews, locos and coaching stock. It was the task of their current-operations colleagues to operate the plan, identifying weaknesses for correction. Hence, most reductions in track, locos and rolling stock were not initiated, as some believed, by engineers. In the era of the Motive Power Superintendent [MPS], when footplate staff were under him, virtually all economies in those staff resulted from train planning or operating reviews and line closures. Train planners produced detailed individual rosters to cover trains[10], MPS roster staff simply booked men for each of those rosters. This was not appreciated by some within BR. An accountancy colleague who mentioned recent reductions in footplate staff in the Sheffield Division, was surprised to learn that they arose - in their entirety - from a re-organisation of local freight train workings initiated by me to overcome a shortage of guards, reduce traffic delay and cut overtime costs. It was based on an analysis of

---

[9] In fact, they fell to 136,277.

[10] Some local freight services - usually called "trips" were planned by Divisional level Operating staff.

traffic[11]. It recast services, reduced footplate staff and guards, and, as traincrew rosters for local trains was an Operating function, my staff prepared the new rosters, setting out the savings. It went through without a hitch. A few years later, footplate staff were transferred to the Operating function, leaving the MPS to concentrate on maintaining locos and multiple units. The historical logic of locating footplate staff and steam engines together under the same manager, ended with new forms of traction that returned to depot less frequently.

In the early 1970s, train planners took on the task of preparing point-to-point timings, hitherto done by the M&EE, and produced faster schedules, by timing trains between junctions at full line speed, inserting allowances at certain locations en route to allow for temporary speed restrictions for engineering work. This replaced the M&EE. practice of providing point-to-point times that were less than the maximum possible, to allow for speed restrictions.

When the Chester branch of the British Institute of Management visited the London Midland Region, Crewe office in March 1979, they were told that my job as Regional Operations Officer was similar to a works production manager. My roofless "factory" was 2,500 miles long, with customers constantly on the "factory floor" wanting our "product" the instant that it was produced. BR had no margin from their gaze for quality inspections to put things right before the customer uses it, as the private sector has, but despite which, they still sell defective goods. They grasped the analogy and admitted that the unique nature of our task had not occurred to them. They were not alone.

In August 1993, the Sunday Times claimed: "Privatisation would sweep away inefficient practices and ingrained demarcation that BR executives never managed to break". They did not identify *one*. BR pursued such issues more vigorously than the private sector, or they would not have lost a world lead in *every* field. (see Table 10). BR Pay & Efficiency Deals in the late 1960s included tackling demarcation by merging duties of many staff including mechanical and electrical fitters - unheard of in UK's demarcation ridden industry. Redundancy arising from modernisation or rationalisation was not resisted with violence or strikes as it was in UK industry.

If staff were slow to accept change, it hit the headlines, but there were countless cases of rational-isation, new methods and staff economy, which progressed unknown outside BR. Had industry been as effective, UK would not be a major importer. Staff accepted change when managers demonstrated plans would work, setting out in writing, under Joint Consultation - a good system introduced in 1956 - proposed changes to working arrangements and manpower levels, facilitating a smooth intro-duction of change. Thereby BR secured substantial economies without disruption. Mostly, staff and unions co-operated with change which reduced jobs, on a scale not seen in UK industry. Changes did not cause battles - such as Wapping, nor walkouts so commonly seen at Longbridge and Dagen-ham. The negative tended to get public attention: "good news" is not news. Hence, BR disputes got more coverage than warranted, especially as BR had under 10% of the market. "The majority of BR staff have the interests of passengers at heart". (CTCC 1983 Report, Page 11). A 1986 Report by MVA, independent consultants praised BR staff for being helpful and courteous.

There were three key years in BR history: 1969: marking the end of the first modernisation plan; 1981: which marked the start of the Business Sector re-organisation and 1994: before fragmentation.

By 1969, taking 1948 as an index of 100, total rail staff compared to route miles had fallen by 37%; traffic handled per member of staff had risen by 58%; passenger miles per coach had risen by 33% and freight ton miles per wagon had risen by 81%. By 1981, compared to 1948, staff to route miles had halved; traffic handled per member of staff had doubled; passenger miles per coach was up $2^1/_2$ times; freight ton-miles per wagon quadrupled. By 1994, compared to 1948, total rail staff compared to route miles had fallen by 81%; traffic handled per member of staff was $2^1/_2$ times more; passenger miles per coach more than tripled and freight ton miles per wagon was 20 times greater.

---

[11] Analyses had hitherto required deployment of special staff to take records in a yard. I had this one made from "cut cards" - the cut list prepared by a shunter to enable wagons to be shunted into the relevant sidings.

Individual projects to improve productivity

On their own initiative, managers and engineers throughout BR developed and implemented thousands of schemes of varying size and complexity[12]. In addition, staff put forward many economies under the BR Suggestions Scheme. It is unfortunate that BR did not publicise details to change subjective opinions of politicians and journalists who had not set foot inside the industry. It would have warned the bidders for rail franchises that there was less flesh on the bone than they were led to believe. A selection of my personal initiatives for economy schemes, may serve - when multiplied many times over, to reflect similar initiatives throughout BR - to indicate the scale of such activity:

Staff economies
- Leaving trains of unbraked wagons on running lines within engineering possessions in the Rugby District without guards, (see page 66). It raised eyebrows! They couldn't be left without footplate staff because BR was still using steam. Similar action in industry would have precipitated a strike
- Single manning passenger shunt locos at Leicester, attaching or detaching vehicles to/from passenger trains. This was permissible under P&E II, which left the initiative to area managers who had to convince staff that it was safe in a station area. It could not be implemented in some Areas.
- Reducing weekend station costs at Leicester.
- Switching shunting loco maintenance from Sundays to weekday nights, where there was capacity.
- Reduction in staff and in overtime and rest day working costs of Tinsley traincrew. (see page 144).
- Merging duties of traffic and loading inspectors involved in cross main line movements of hot ingots between steel works at Sheffield, cut them by 50% - which some claimed was impossible.
- Reducing Operating Department office staff in the Stoke Division, based on workload reviews.
- Closing the Control Office at Chester and transferring its role to Stoke Control.
- Whilst TOPS was an HQ scheme, local savings not in their plan were feasible. These included cutting out wagon distribution staff - on Day One of my Division being 'cutover' to TOPS.
- Later, as Regional Operations Officer, used TOPS to allocate locos to trains, thereby reducing controllers - "office staff" - and improving loco utilisation. (see pages 70-71).

Asset economies
Initial wagon economies: Doncaster 1956-7, Sunderland 1958-9 and Rugby 1960-1, predated Phillip Shirley, who joined BR in 1962, and was said to have *inspired rolling stock reductions*.[13]
- Doncaster: expedited wagon discharge using a capstan to draw wagons into the goods shed - quicker and cheaper than by shunt engine; centralising full load traffic at one location, which also improved utilisation of staff and cranes; and a new method of unloading timber. (see page 121).
- Sunderland: at the cost of some overtime, quicker unloading of goods for storage in warehouses contrary to a policy that focused on staff costs[14] but ignored the cost of wagon detention; a change in the sequence of moving wagons from goods depot to marshalling yard led to more wagons making overnight transits; pressing shipyards to accept steel quicker, by weekend delivery cut detention of special wagons. Their cramped 19th century layouts did little to facilitate acceptance.
- Rugby: introduced as a regular item at Station Masters' meetings, in the Rugby District, freight rolling stock utilisation, to pressure them to expedite wagon discharge and movement. It was introduced later onto the agenda of Area Managers meetings in the Stoke Division.
- Economies in track and signalling in the Rugby District: eliminating sidings and facilities and avoiding electrification of sidings that had been included in the 1955 Modernisation Plan.

---

[12] Some 1,500 individual productivity schemes were implemented. (BRB 1981 Report, Page 20).

[13] Bonavia "*BR - the First 25 years*", Page 134. The first that I heard of his involvement, was an edict to paint wagons all the same colour. It made it difficult to spot costly brake fitted wagons which had been painted a different colour to unbraked wagons. Brake fitted wagons were needed to provide front end brake power for diesel locos.

[14] Depot performance was judged and compared with other Depots at District level by a "Tonnage & Wages Return", which calculated the cost per ton of goods handled. When our cost increased due to overtime payments on warehouse traffic, I argued that Returns should include the cost of wagon time. No change was made in it, during my time there.

Staff & asset economies

- Yard closures[15] at Hawkesbury Lane, Penistone, Warsop, Langwith, by diversion of traffic to other yards. (see also other yard closures and economies below).
- Signalboxes in the Leicester Area & Stoke Division replaced by ground frames operated by guards
- Trains conveyed thousands of tons of chalk daily from Leighton Buzzard to Blisworth, to form into trains for Rugby and Southam cement works. The flow used several hundred 24.5 ton capacity tippler wagons, augmented by 16 ton coal wagons. There was pressure to release the latter for coal each winter, but it had not been possible with the existing train plan. My plan formed trains at Leighton Buzzard in two sections, with trains running direct to Rugby, detaching there, then on to Southam via Marton Jc, where the loco ran round the train. (see below). This released the coal wagons, saved a few locos, closed three signalboxes, Blisworth yard and traincrew depot; closed a steeply graded 20 mile long single-line branch and removed the junction at Weedon, thereby cutting costs that would have been incurred when the main line was electrified and re-signalled.

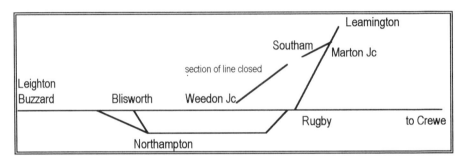

- Closed Ickles yard by transferring work to other yards, enabling BR to sell the yard. (see page 122).
- Closed Rotherham [Masborough] yard which HQ planners of the new Tinsley yard intended to retain to shunt empty wagons. It became clear that Tinsley could handle them. A bonus from this closure was that the Terminals Manager used the site to create a Freightliner terminal at low cost.
- Wath had two yards - A & B - to handle westbound and eastbound traffic respectively. My scheme concentrated all into B yard, saving staff and shunting engines. Consultation was limited to Wath staff only - there was no transfer of work elsewhere, hence Sectional Council was not involved[16].
- Crewe [Basford Hall] had two main yards. My traffic analysis revealed that with some re-routing of traffic, closure of both yards was feasible. They closed with substantial savings.
- Bigger train loads resulted from my idea to re-locate the proposed bunker of a new opencast site at Kidsgrove, Staffs. The original plan was for trains of 24 MGR wagons, but the bunker could be re-located to take 26. To extend more, required costly earthworks. The proposed bunker at Hem Heath colliery, intended to cater for 26 wagon trains, could I found, be re-located to increase loads to 34. This proved useful when the Coal Board secured orders to power stations on routes with easier gradients. Neither created extra costs, but cut movement costs and improved loco utilisation Whereas HQ initiated national agreements, such as P&E, Flexible Rostering etc., achievement of the bulk of the savings would only result from the actions of Area Managers or Divisional Officers who identified to which jobs, changes could be applied, and progressed those economies through Joint Consultation. Likewise with all personal initiatives, Area Managers or Divisional Officers were required to conduct joint consultation meetings[17] with affected staff.

---

[15] Yard closures cut staff costs, saved shunting locos, improved wagon transits and led to economies in track.

[16] Contrary to a railway magazine report, it was not a consequence of the Eastern/NE Region merger. HQ had no prior knowledge of it until it was a fait accompli. Only Yard Master, George Rimmington and I consulted with the staff.

[17] I also chaired meetings on my operational plan for the opening of Tinsley, which was achieved smoothly over one weekend, & schemes initiated at Regional level, e.g.: freight train incentive schemes, National Freight Train Plan.

Chapter 14   Which perfect industry?

The title for this chapter arises from a spur of the moment question in an off-duty period to a sarcastic critic: *"Which perfect industry do you work for?"*, followed by: *"I have been looking for a one for thirty years and haven't found one yet"* - a question posed many times since. It is a great conversation stopper, because it has never produced a reply and always leads to a change of subject.

A proposal by the CTCC that BR should not price up unless quality is improved should have been applied to all industry and commerce. Most have increased prices on goods whose quality did not change. Inflation would then be solved at a stroke. In 1991, industry criticised BR for not quoting Chunnel rates to apply when the Chunnel was - wrongly - forecast to open in 18 months time. Contemporary traders' quotations had a six months time limit.

BR was often told that it was inefficient[1]. Norman Fowler stated in his political biography that "everyone knew that the [railway] business was overstaffed". There was no comparison with other industry, other than to point out: "BR had 230,000 staff in 1976 whilst the National Bus Company [NBC] had 20,000 buses and 68,000 staff". No conclusion can be drawn from that. Excluding locos, BR staff operated twelve times as many passenger *and freight* vehicles as NBC! Moreover, the effective size of the NBC fleet is reduced as vehicles were cannibalised to keep others in service, (see NBC Annual Accounts). Fleet size related to manpower is meaningless in productivity terms.

For an effective comparison, statistics must be put into context. The first step is to note that - by law - PSV drivers were permitted to work eleven hours daily - it was fourteen until 1968. The law imposed no limit on other bus company staff. In contrast, Government forced railways to adopt the eight hour day for *all* staff in 1919, without concern for cost - the sole reason for bus drivers being allowed to work such long hours - which a Government White Paper (Cmnd 3481) stated were being "substantially exceeded". That increases 68,000 staff to an equivalent of, at least, 93,500.

Total BR staff included shipping, hovercraft, workshops, hotels and property; excluding these, leaves 182,695. (BRB 1976 Report). Unlike BR, NBC do not maintain *their* highway, whereas BR maintained theirs *and* thousands of bridges over which NBC vehicles travel. BR Annual Reports had to provide far more data than NBC - not to mention other industry - but did not separate staff employed on BR's 'highway' in 1976. When infrastructure maintenance transferred to Railtrack, BRB Reports show a 17% fall. Applying 17% to 1976 manpower reduces 182,695 to 151,600. One must then deduct staff devoted to freight, which is not one of hundreds of statistics demanded by the MoT - even when Accounts & Statistics ran to 300 pages! There are only two options for estimating the freight element: train miles or traction hours. Non-passenger train miles were 28% of all train miles. (BRB 1976 Report). Deducting 28% from 151,600 leaves 109,150. With this - 16.7% more than the *realistic* NBC figure of 93,500 - BR earned 41% *more* passenger revenue! Non-passenger traction hours were 38.6% of the total. (BRB 1976 Report). Deducting that from 151,600 leaves 93,080 passenger staff - 0.5% below the comparable NBC staffing. As passenger speeds are higher than freight and terminal turnrounds quicker, traction hours are a more reliable basis.

Reflecting, in the 1970s, on personal misfortunes at the hands of every branch of the private sector, and a mounting catalogue of complaints, it became apparent that no business was perfect. Whereas, BR published data - others published nothing with which BR could be compared. This led me to challenge the doctrinaire belief that BR performance was worse than the rest of industry. The crucial question is against which benchmarks were BR compared? BR was - wisely - not compared with the field of activity under Government's nose, judging from an exposé of gross inefficiency by a

---

[1] There were exceptions: Wm. Vane Tory MP: "It is greatly to the credit of railways that they operated as well as they did. Criticism of dirty trains is criticism of ourselves - very soon we will have the strongest claim to be considered the dirtiest people in Europe". (Hansard vol. 566, col. 1216). Minister John McGregor: "Privatisation is no criticism of BR or its achievements, which have been considerable. BR's record on productivity, service, safety and punctuality is impressive; it is known to run one of the most efficient railway systems in Europe". (*Britain's Railways: A New Age*")

former senior civil servant[2]. The Treasury issued a Glossary of Management Techniques[3] in 1967. It included critical path analysis[4], costing, operational research, budgetary control, management accounting, management by objectives, management development, work & method study. Ministers always claim that growth is due to Government policy, and recession to international problems!

Sir Peter Parker, Chairman of BR - previously *and* subsequently in the private sector - stated: "This country's railways are second to none in giving value for money". (BRB 1982 Report, Page 12).

Foreign railways

Critics compare BR with *selected* foreign railways. (see also page 70). Unlike, BR lines which have mixed traffic, mixed speeds and closer headways, "Japan's Shinhansen line has 130 mph passenger trains every twelve minutes. It was financed with special low interest rate loans". (Rail Policy, 1981).

The most popular comparison was with French railways, which was properly funded by *their* Government to shoulder the burden of rural transport long before ours. Critics overlook that European railways were restored after the war, with Marshall Aid and UK help at the expense of BR, (see pages 19,49). Our Government blew Marshall Aid on the Empire - keeping good livings for diplomats and the Foreign Office - bolstering up Sterling and supporting the aircraft industry[5]. (see Barnett/2, Pages 229,368). It did not recompense railways for war work and losses on a comparable basis with UK industry, nor refund any of the £1 billion screwed out of railways, (see page 18). UK industry was given post-war assistance and repaid Government by losing a world lead. It became clear that BR was criticised on a *subjective* - often anecdotal - rather than an objective basis, because no statistics were *ever* advanced that compared BR with other UK transport, industry or commerce. To compare BR to French high speed railways is *complete* nonsense. With Government money, they built a brand new straighter, passenger only route with all trains at the same speed, no level crossings and no intermediate junctions. All permit higher speeds and less scope for delay, simple operational factors that few seem to comprehend. To create the Chunnel-London link, BR had to produce *five* costly alternative plans to pacify voters, and none was accepted. Had the French been told to tunnel the TGV route, it would probably never have got off the drawing board.

A reader wrote to the Daily Telegraph (10.6.01), that German trains don't run on time. My experience of travel in Europe is of lengthy stops at stations for connections and splitting of train sections. These margins are of considerable value in regaining time, and should make punctual running easy.

UK transport

BR was not competing with foreign railways but with UK based car, lorry, bus and air - *none* of which publishes performance figures. BR was encumbered with a unique "Watchdog": the Transport Users Committees - whose costs BR had to bear for 20 years! They were never really "*Transport*" focused, since they never covered air services, nor private railways and only covered buses and ships hitherto owned by the Big Four railways. The biased interpretation by these watchdogs of BR statistics, supplied to them on a regular basis, led them to erroneous conclusions. It never occurred to them to compare BR with competitors, nor to relate complaints as a percentage of total travel. There was an illusion, fostered by those who had spent too long on the playroom floor with their model trains, that trains could always run on time. It never dawned on them that railways were subject to the same external factors that impeded bus, car, sea and air travel. BR suffered delays caused by other transport: cars, buses, lorries and aircraft descending onto the track. The reverse was extremely rare. Equipment problems in the private sector are due to 'teething

---

[2] See "*Your Disobedient Servant*" by Leslie Chapman. Files in the PRO contain draft after draft of letters and memos, each amended by a higher level bureaucrat. Obviously they are not perfect or they would get them right at the first attempt - and these are people with better education standards than base level BR staff, whom they chose to criticise.

[3] All of which had been used on BR for many years - see Chapter 9.

[4] See reference on page 91 to ignorance in the shipbuilding industry to this technique in 1971, but long used by BR.

[5] They spent £13.4m on the eight engined Brabazon & ten engined SR45 flying-boat, neither of which entered service

troubles' or 'gremlins', in the public sector, failures of similar - private sector - equipment are attributed to incompetence. BR was also criticised for overcrowded trains, some of which resulted directly from the closure of airports in fog, when airlines dumped their passengers at the nearest station. The volume of criticism, even in the most *appalling* weather, never ceased. (see page 101).

Government was ill advised on the need for a Citizens Charter. Rail passengers already had many watchdogs. There were none for the 90% using other transport. Neither is there effective protection for customers of other businesses - "*guarantees*" being overrated, (see page 153). The private sector had the good sense not to publish self critical data. Other transport might set an example by giving *unqualified* guarantees, instead of advising passengers to insure against delay or cancellation.

In 1989, BBC TV Railwatch criticised BR facilities for disabled. Changes in the preceding 20 years had given disabled people more mobility, but BR had made provision, unlike road transport. BR vehicles have a 30 year life span - motor coach and bus lives are much shorter. "A Minister said that disabled should have the same access as others to public transport, and that all new BR design has to meet standards for disabled access, but buses are more difficult[6]." (CTCC 1990/91 Report, Page 19). In April 1995, replying to comments on the lack of access on PSVs, a Minister told BBC listeners that "disabled access would be provided as PSVs are replaced". Had road transport begun, at the same time as BR, to provide access, every PSV would, long ago, have had unrestricted access. Logically, they should have been converted *before* trains, to provide transport to a station.

In April 1996, an airline spokesman on Radio 4 said that they would have to increase fares if "bumping" ceased. The interviewer said they could reduce profits. The spokesman said: "Bumping is a voluntary off-loading scheme for flights which are full or slightly overfull". Victims have booked in advance. What if there are no volunteers? Had BR tried to apply a similar policy, it would have been vetoed by the MoT. An MP called for airline standards for trains. The last thing rail passengers want is cramped seats, bumping off and lost luggage.

A pre-privatisation idea from some in other forms of transport, was that they would improve rail punctuality by getting drivers to drive faster. They did not realise that trains are timed at their maximum safe speed. Some operators have reduced train delays, at the expense of delaying passengers. (see page 110). It must have irked them that in the rail arena, they have to compensate passengers for delay, in contrast to the standard exclusion clause for that inconvenience in bus, air and sea company conditions.

Other UK industry

BR should have been compared with UK industry as BR faced UK inflation, UK suppliers' failures, UK working attitudes and wage expectations, UK Nimbys[7], UK vandals and litter louts, UK's lower technical and education standards and UK Government policies - that unlike the rest of Europe - were anti-rail. BR suffered the effects of worse industrial decline than the rest of Europe[8].

In contrast to railways, which handled a much increased volume of traffic with reduced assets during and at the end of the war, the privately owned steel industry was a story of decline. Government subsidies were paid to industry, post-war, despite the fact that they, unlike BR, could determine their own prices. In 1948, £22m was paid to the privately owned steel industry. (Hansard vol. 454, col. 33). Agriculture became more "profitable" backed by Government. The Agriculture Act 1947 guaranteed food prices and generous subsidies for farmers. All this was paid for by the taxpayer, providing accusations of feather bedding. (Channel 4 Books, "*Green & Pleasant Land*", Pages 171-172). BR was criticised for failing to make rural branch lines profitable - when fares were well below inflation and Government refused to pay subsidies - by industry and agriculture that were subsidised in the very same areas in which they objected to unsubsidised BR closing lines that

---

[6] Not with "Enlightened private enterprise". (see page 171).
[7] Who blocked high speed lines from the Chunnel, and closures of lines which had failed to compete with the horse.
[8] See "*Mrs Thatcher's Revolution*" by Peter Jenkins.

objectors were rarely using! (see "*The Railway Closure Controversy*"). There is an illusion that a profitable company is efficient, whereas it could, by more effort have been more profitable and/or have reduced prices. Some closed when demand for their type of product was not falling.

Some BR managers were Luddites, some not innovative, some made errors - all faults in the private sector, or there would be a thriving industry and no balance of payments deficit. BR managers failed - as the private sector did - to ensure a 100% staff turnout. Illnesses that keep commuters at home were not expected to affect BR, where the consequences were apparent at once, but private sector failings, affecting far more, rarely become public knowledge. Recalls of tens of thousands of motor vehicle and goods do not reveal how many are inconvenienced. The term "operational glitches" is used in the private sector when new products or services experience introductional problems. It is a euphemism for a cock-up - the term used if analogous problems arose with BR. Noticeably, private sector euphemisms (see page 161), have been adopted with alacrity by the the *private sector* rail industry! That regarded as good private sector practice was condemned if adopted by BR: avoiding excess capacity, pricing to maximise income, dropping unprofitable lines.

In 1951, David Blee, of the Railway Executive was Guest of Honour at the luncheon of the Transport Committee of the Association of British Chambers of Commerce. Later he wrote: "The words of welcome by the Chairman turned out to be wholly critical". His revised address, developed on the spot - on a menu card - began by saying that he "had resigned from one of their Councils because they did not support measures he took to increase membership, reduce its costs and make it more effective". He said that: "The BTC was not a monopoly[9], and was not in the same street as many trades and industries where price rings[10] were abundantly apparent whenever we went out to tender. What BR bought from industry in 1939 per £100 now cost £259, whilst our charges at 90% of 1939 levels represented the efficiency and economy of the past three years. Everything I buy has gone up". Answering criticisms of delays, he said that with expanding demand for transport, BR had difficulty in expanding resources fast enough. He drew attention to the national manpower shortage by the example of the Birmingham area where 33,000 vacancies were chased by 6,000 unemployed.[11] Demonstrating that the private sector had not been able to meet expanding demand without delays, he added that "if I wanted to buy a car[12], I would put my name on a waiting list and hope to get it in two years, whilst the wait for a refrigerator was only one year". (PRO: AN6/10).

Some companies make obscene salary increases and set up share options enabling executives to buy shares below market price and resell, making huge profits, without the risk faced by share holders. A company, whose share price had plunged to the floor said its share option scheme was to motivate managers! Yet, it is a common theory that they are motivated by fear of losing a job if they are ineffective, but many leave with golden handshakes. They claim that without obscene severance protection, they would take their talents elsewhere. But that presupposes, that there are high paid vacancies - that there are more top jobs than fat cats! Cutting top salaries and perks would send an encouraging message to the shop floor. A BBC programme: "Bosses bonanza", killed the myth that share prices rise due to brilliant management, but are mainly due to the way the market moves. Some trying to justify pay-offs for incompetence claim that a share price fall may be due to external factors, overlooking that Directors had tried to justify bigger salaries by share rises!

Industry created a bad image by unsightly tips, rusting cars and scrap on their side of the fence. The Dickensian appearance of lineside industry emitting filthy, malodorous smoke, made rail travel unattractive, particularly as it made coaches very dirty. When industry lost markets to foreign competition and closed down, dereliction created greater eyesores. Leakage of poisonous gases and fires on lineside premises caused fire brigades to block lines, delaying and cancelling trains.

---

[9] The MoT said in 1956 that the BTC (which included BR) "have never had a complete monopoly" (Cmd 9880).
[10] The BTC drew attention to "price fixing by trade organisations". (BTC minutes 15.12.55).
[11] To which industry responded by improving wages instead of productivity. (see footnote page 175).
[12] For a BR manager to admit to buying a car risked the sarcasm of those, who did not criticise bus managers for doing likewise - even though buses ran near their houses, unlike trains, which 19th century NIMBYs had opposed.

The recall of defective goods - some life threatening - confirms that the private sector is *not* perfect, and cannot claim to set an example for the public sector. The message of advertisements recalling products - many with life-threatening defects - seems not to have registered on the news pages. Many are couched in similar terms: "*A small number of items have been found to have a fault during our ongoing rigorous testing and quality control*" - not explaining why quality control did not discover faults **before** sale. Some retailers do not advertise, but merely display a notice on the premises, on the arrogant assumption that past customers will re-visit. The message is that the private sector does not, contrary to popular opinion, equate with 100% reliability. Recalls include aerosols, alcoholic and non-alcoholic drinks, caravan equipment, cars and accessories [including baby seats], clothing, confectionery, domestic appliances [including boilers, electric showers, microwaves and TVs], food, instruction leaflets, kitchenware, ladders, office equipment, tools and accessories, toys, and even items of safety protection such as RCDs and fire extinguishers!

UK industry declined, the Engineering Council said "*because our competitors learned too well*"[13]

Steel making	Post war : 3rd in the world	1984: 10th
Shipbuilding	1900: 60% built in UK	1984: 3%
Motor cycles	Exported to 100 countries	1984: All imported
Cars in UK[14]	Pre-war almost all British	1984: Over 50% foreign
Machine tools	Pioneered in Britain	1984: 3.1% of world production
Radio	Discovered in Britain	1984: Import 96%
Computers	Britain made the first one[15]	1984: 5% of the market
Textile machines	Once made all world supplies	1984: 8% of the market

Table 10 - Source : Engineering Council advertisement, November 1984

None were subject to statutory controls faced by BR; some were subsidised by Government pre-war and post-war: shipbuilding[16], aircraft, motors, textiles, (see Hansard); others by low rail rates enforced by Government, (see Chapter 1). A failure to modernise methods and products or end demarcation caused industrial decline. It caused unforecast BR revenue losses, exacerbating financial problems created by Government, leaving BR with surplus assets reduced to scrap value: track, signalling, bridges, marshalling yards, locos, wagons - hitherto needed to serve heavy industry. Private sector industries were rescued from bankruptcy by taxpayers' money. Others went bankrupt by the thousand, leaving shareholders and suppliers unpaid. (see "*The Railway Closure Controversy*", Page 49).

Between 1950-77, UK's share of world trade fell by almost two thirds, whilst Germany's rose by over 50% and Japan's by 350%. (Jenkins, "*Mrs. Thatcher's Revolution*", Page 32). Instead of blaming Government, cheap foreign labour, the rate of exchange or the public sector, companies should make a *real* effort to sell UK manufactured goods. More employment would enable retailers to sell more UK goods and deter them from asking, as Longton [Staffs] retailers did, for BR to bail them out by offering ultra cheap fares to bring to them, shoppers whom, otherwise, they were unable to attract by car, bus or on foot! On 13th December, 1993, the Bank of England warned of the consequences of "retail stores continuing to raise prices to widen profit margins, and urged price restraint".

The balance of payments is not helped by imports bearing historic UK manufacturing names. Presumably, this commonplace practice of transferring production to the Far East was not what the MoT had in mind, in 1956, when he spoke of introducing BR to "*some enlightened principles of private enterprise to enable them to make a profit*". (Hansard, vol. 555, col. 1320). BR could not follow this practice and were constrained from buying cheaper materials and reliable equipment abroad by

---

[13] A claim that is incredibly arrogant, but typical of UK industry. (see Barnett/1, Page 6).

[14] The industry had a notorious record - see page 153.

[15] This claim has been dismissed by Correlli Barnett (see Barnett/2, Page 308)

[16] Between 1948-62, shipbuilding tonnage per man fell by 12.5%, whilst the BR passenger/staff ratio rose by 30%.

Government trying to help the private sector by enforcing a "Buy British" policy on BR, as it tried - unsuccessfully - to do with airlines. The excess of "experts", who could run BR more cheaply, whilst being unable to produce goods cheaper in the UK is legendary. Paradoxically, foreign companies who set up in the UK have revived industries that our native born industrialists had abandoned as unprofitable! Transfer of production abroad has now been followed by transfer of Call Centres - a practice that could be emulated by shiny new privatised railways, but not State owned railways. None of those who moved abroad or went bankrupt had ever faced the stringent legal controls of prices to which BR was subject. Had they been they would most certainly have disagreed with Dr. Joy that external control of prices was not damaging to viability. (Joy, Page 145).

As passengers criticise BR peak service, whilst not giving instant service in their own peak, so it is with companies. A printer in Leicester phoned, before Christmas 1969 to complain that a parcel to Newcastle-upon-Tyne had not been delivered. The pre-Christmas period was our heaviest peak, with heavy flows from manufacturers, traders, mail order companies and Post Office. Congestion in towns delayed deliveries and most consignees would not extend hours for deliveries, preferring to use BR depots to hold surplus stock, hence, some delay was unavoidable. He considered it nothing short of incompetence to fail to deliver currently even at Christmas. When the analogy of seasonal peak demand for *his* products was mentioned, to which his business like all others could not respond as quickly as at other times, one could almost hear the penny drop. He became quite affable and said that no one had ever put BR problems into that perspective, and asked that we do our best.

What excuse does UK industry have for failing to match German or Japanese car production - even when using the same tools and machines? UK industry was complacent and unwilling to modernise. Industrialists, politicians, military leaders and scientists were confident that pre-war Germany could not have achieved higher standards than the UK, despite warnings. (see Tom Bower[17] and other historians). This attitude continued long after the war allowing other countries to leave the UK far behind. After the war, Government threw money at the *private sector*: cotton, aircraft, motor and other industries - and much good did it do. Complacent industrialists did not believe that other countries could outsell UK exports, much less threaten the domestic market! Having lost a world lead in every field, that small rump of industry, which BR was told to emulate, had to adopt foreign methods - but too late to rejoin the first division. (see loco design on page 160).

"The story of the motor industry was of long years of mismanagement and notoriously bad industrial relations[18]. By 1986, Austin Rover had only 17% of the domestic market[19], and 4% of the European. In Germany, Ford could turn out an Escort in the half the time as the UK. Bill Hayden testified to a Select Committee it takes an hour to get started in the morning[20], they walk off the job before lunch and don't come back on time". (Peter Jenkins "*Mrs Thatcher's Revolution*", Pages 205,257)

The DoT was instructed to prepare a plan for measuring and publishing [BR] standards of performance". (John Major: "*The Autobiography*", Page 252). Regrettably, similar action has not been initiated for industry or the UK might still be a major supplier to the world, instead of a minor supplier in its own backyard, and towns would have no empty shops. BR data had been published for decades in the Reports of the Consultative Committees created in the 1947 Act, and picked up by the media. Conveniently, figures for BR's competitors and industry were shrouded in mystery.

Most "guarantees" are for 10% of the expected product life. If BR had given similar guarantees on punctuality, they would have guaranteed the first 10% of a journey. A money back guarantee was

---

[17] "*The Paperclip Conspiracy*", by Tom Bower.
[18] When the author attended a Management Course in 1973, one of the speakers was the "Grievance Manager" at Fords. It was evident that, not only were industrial relations poor, but they made concessions to meet staff demands that we would not tolerate. In contrast, when Cambrian line guards said that they would not collect fares unless a bonus was paid, I directed that they would not be allowed to sign on, and made it plain that we were not going to run trains - which didn't cover their costs anyway - for nothing. The guards changed their mind and collected fares.
[19] As the British Motor Corporation, it had enjoyed 44% ("*British Leyland - the truth about the cars*" - Jeff Daniels).
[20] In sharp contrast to BR staff arriving before time - (see page 141).

proposed for BR. That should have started in the private sector, which the public sector is supposed to emulate. They may then improve products enough to end the balance of payments deficit. BR managers were often asked if they would guarantee not to inconvenience customers in future. They should have asked to be pointed in the direction of a company prepared to make such a guarantee. A company that promises to replace a defective item, does not qualify. In the 1980s, trains from Manchester were often delayed up to 30 minutes, because some publishers did not get newspapers to the station to meet scheduled departures, which they did not wish to be changed! These delayed other trains, including those carrying Post Office mails. All delay was blamed on BR.

In contrast to action taken by BR for disabled provision, a conference in 1983 with business managers, including one in a wheelchair, had to be re-arranged when it transpired that a *new* four star hotel in Chester had no lifts. In 1992, at a Wigan hotel, the lift "had been out of order for months, and they did not know a guest was in a wheelchair". We pointed out that they did not need to know in advance, as their brochure boasted of facilities for disabled visitors. They should have amended the brochure, as they admitted, that due to legal argument it may be months before it was repaired.

In December 1990, a CBI spokesman said on TV that what was needed was for the public sector to treat customers as the private sector does. BR customers must always be believed to be right, even with no "proof of purchase", due to the belief that no BR complainant could be dishonest. In contrast, the private sector says: "No one else complained" - *why that invalidates mine is unclear*; "You have misused it"; "It has not been properly maintained" - *without evidence*; and, at best, apologies instead of refunds or compensation, as they try to wriggle out of responsibility. Consumers must be cynical of the professed *sincerity* of apologies. Those who replace defective goods expect customers to make an extra journey. Attention should be focused on excuses: "not made now, it's not viable" - an excuse not accepted from the public sector, or "there is no demand" - when someone has just asked for it! The frequency of apologies for being "out of stock" undermines the belief voiced on TV by the MoT in 1993 that road transport was providing a just-in-time delivery service - even after 40 years' domination of High Street deliveries. That facility is a distant dream.

BR was criticised if telephone enquiries had more than 5% of engaged signals, or had no answer within 30 seconds. (see page 105). Repeated experience with business call centres, retailers and others, is one of wading through keypad options[21], before being told that "all agents are busy, but will be with you shortly", repeated - with endless jingles - for as long as you continue paying for a call. You "may hang on - *your call is important to us*" - and we will get to it in 30 minutes - or ring back and face the same obstacle course. BR Enquiries was not compared to this. Most people would rather have 20 *free* engaged signals. It is arrogant to claim that the time of their staff is more precious than that of the caller. When will they wake up and use an answerphone to take a message and promise to ring back? Two typical responses were: "It is a very busy period" - it was a Thursday not a Bank Holiday; and: "You are in a high priority queue" - which begs the question of who is in the low priority queue as the line was devoted solely to quotations for car insurance.

One hears on radio & TV - those bastions of "slip-of-the-tongue" and "sorry for the breakdown" - "Government should concentrate on getting trains to run on time". They should first get industry to make 100% reliable products, benefiting *everyone*. Attention should next be given to getting other transport 100% reliable, benefiting over 90% of the population. Trains should be third in the queue.

Labour

In April 1993, a Sunday Times article stated that: "Staff complain representatives give themselves the best shifts", "Union officials are given time off", "Drivers and signalmen get extra pay for walking time", "Staff queued up to an hour to collect pay", and likened BR practice to the Peter Sellers' film -"*I'm alright, Jack*". Representatives were elected by *secret* ballot and easily ousted. "Union officials" are not paid by BR, so *cannot* be given time off - *staff representatives* have time

---

[21] In one case, the author progressed through eight levels of options, before speaking to someone.

off for meetings with managers, some only once per year. It was so unrewarding, as economies were pushed through, that at some depots, few wanted the unpaid job. In the 1950s, at Sunderland, where W.W. Wright was Goods Agent, only one man took it, instead of four as set out in Agreements. Proposed roster changes were discussed and their ideas adopted if they were *less* costly! Walking time applied to *relief* signalmen working away from home station. Payments to private sector staff working away, including tax-free mileage "expenses", made BR look like Scrooge. Walking time for a driver occurs, for example, when he walks from a station to a depot for a loco. It is part of a roster and cannot attract *extra* pay! It is unlikely that those walking to another part of a factory or to a meeting, or journalists en route to a story, travel in their own time. In 40 years, from the Thames to the Tyne, that included paying wages, I *never* encountered nor heard of staff queuing for an hour. Some could not spared from duty for five minutes and had pay taken to them. That film involved a *factory* strike caused by a stop watch. BR used stop watches without disputes! (see page 88).

In January 1988, customers of Forte at an M1 service area, who had to queue in a doorway when there were empty tables out of use, were told it was because "*it was difficult to ensure a 100% staff turnout*" - a response not accepted by BR's critics.

Unlike BR managers and supervisors who take over the job of someone who was temporarily absent from the "shop floor", including when absent due to an industrial dispute, (see pages 103,140), the practice was not emulated in private sector industry. If managers in industry had got on the production line in such circumstances, to try to avoid loss of orders - they would have had a walkout!

In contrast to BR labour relations, demarcation in UK industry was a national disgrace - especially in key export industries: motor manufacturing and shipbuilding, which lost a world lead in every field. Manpower and productivity of shipbuilding - one of few where figures are clearly identifiable, showed a steady worsenment, in contrast to BR's improvement. (see "*The Railway Closure Controversy*" Page 199). In contrast to industry, BR suffered no walkouts with its modernisation.

In contrast to BR building to schedule and within budget, UK industry fails to do either. Hence, retrospective allegations that BR modernised the East Coast line "on the cheap" seem like sour grapes. Ferry companies could be accused of buying ships on the cheap by not adopting recommendations on safety that would have given them a huge marketing advantage against competing ferries.

In October 1972, a Stockport careers teacher visiting North Staffs employers was surprised that juniors in non-clerical BR jobs had to be able to read and write. He was taken to Stoke PSB, where a boy was recording details of train movements, taking phone messages, etc. He had thought juniors would be "making tea and sweeping up". Obviously, this is what he had experienced in industry.

Complaints

Personal experience of private sector failures, led me to conduct an investigation into complaints received by BR. It revealed that 33% of what were recorded as complaints were not complaints about service, (see Table 6). Of the balance, 55% were given a voucher or cheque, and the rest an apology, which is accepted as adequate from the private sector, but sneered at if from the public sector. Only 2% - 0.0002% of passengers - wrote again expressing dissatisfaction with BR's reply.

Published BR statistics unbalanced by any from other industry created an impression that the private sector was perfect, and BR alone was not. Some boast of 1% complaints. *Gross* complaints to BR, before any refund or apology - which the private sector regards as full resolvement - was 0.009%, (see page 105). It is argued that not all dissatisfied passengers complain. That is true of private sector customers. Many grumble at supermarket, bank and other queues, but few are likely to put pen to paper. Some companies claim no complaints because they replace goods or gave a refund - but that follows a complaint. BR gave refunds, (see page 105), without intervention by TUCCs.

The private sector seems to shy away from the word "complaint", when replying to an unambiguous letter of complaint:

- "thank you for your comments" = you cannot seriously be complaining about *our* product;
- "We are sorry you *may* have been inconvenienced", your letter spells out that you *have* been;

- "thank you for taking the time to write" = your complaint, no matter how serious to you, is trivial in their eyes, and not worth the postage.
- "Our computer made an error" - oblivious of the adage: "*rubbish in, rubbish out*".

On BBC, in March 1992, the CTCC criticised BR for compensation targets being too high. They are low compared to the private sector who do not pay *any* compensation for late delivery. Indeed, you will be considered unreasonable if you have the temerity to complain that a delivery does not arrive on the promised day, much less the promised time of day. Regrettably, apologies for defective products, unfulfilled promises of delivery, unpunctual visits to make quotations or commencement of work by tradesmen are not exchangeable for coin of the realm at banks.

Pricing

Ministers continue to ignore statements by Tory MoTs in 1955 that "railways are not a monopoly", and in 1956 that the BTC "have not had and never have had a complete monopoly", (see pages 28,129,172), and a Cabinet minute (PRO: CAB, 12.3.51), to the same effect. With BR, there are many avenues for complaints. Where effective monopoly exists there are none. One supplier put up prices in stages by 38% during 1988, without apology, warning or explanation when the RPI rose 7% - there was no other supplier. When inflation was in single figures, my car insurance leapt 23%, Leisure Club fee rose 280% over two years and a domestic appliance part from the sole national supplier increased by 1119% over $4^{1}/_{2}$ years. These put the public sector firmly in the shade.

In June 1991, a report that "*car insurance is set to rise by 25%*", was not greeted with the hysteria greeting BR increases. Two years earlier, the media reported that the MoT had vetoed more modest BR increases. As ten times as many travel by car as train, Government should veto car insurance rises above the RPI. In 1989, my car insurance premium, with maximum No Claims Bonus increased *three times the rate of inflation*. The company did not reply to three complaints which, it later admitted, had been received. The Chief Executive refused to divulge statistics on "*an increase in claims in the area*", which was at variance with local police-to-Homewatch and media information regarding car thefts and accidents, but offered the empty solace that the level of increase of other companies was an "across the board 50%". For the insurance industry to top that with 25% gave BR formidable latitude for decades. A year later, an eight col. cms report said that car insurance was to rise 30% more! Reports in 1994 of a 15% reduction in premiums were greeted warmly. They had forgotten inflation busting increases in past years which facilitated a decrease!

A perspective of BR fares can be gleaned from a comparison with newspaper prices: In 1991, fares were seventeen times 1948 levels, newspapers were up to eighty times higher. (see also Appendix A). BR was constrained from applying common private sector practices, e.g.:
- Do not advertise price increases, publicise only bargain offers, which may be to a limited number of customers. Unlucky customers never know how few have benefited from the "Bargain Offer".
- Charge more in peaks, or for items in short supply, like hotels, which increased prices during a rail strike on 28th June 1989 due to "*a shortage of accommodation*", not due to increased costs.
- Increase car-park fees to match those of airport and private sector parks. *Private sector* railways have increased parking fees by over 500%! BR was told by critics that parking should be free.
- Charge for telephone enquiries, like BT or Gatwick Airport.
- Charge outrageously higher prices on Mother's - and similar - Days.
- Demonstrate "seasonal goodwill" in December - by higher prices!

These - and many more - are the real "*Principles of Enlightened Private Enterprise*" (see page 171), which if adopted by BR would have produced cries of outrage. BR fares trailed the RPI for nearly 40 years. (see Appendix A). A perspective of freight rates, up to the year when BR was given partial rates freedom (see page 114), can be gleaned from Table 11.

Price index	1938	1955	1957	Corresponding BR index
Manufactured goods	100	102	101	
	100	84	81	Merchandise rates
Building materials	100	118	116	
	100	98	99	Mineral rates
Coal	100	162	184	
	100#	108*	108*	Coal rates
# Excludes hire cost of private owner wagons			* Includes cost of BR wagons	
Table 11- Source: BTC 1955 Report, Diagram 7a; BTC 1957 Report, Diagrams 3a,3b,3c				

BR suppliers

Government's plan to help industry by enforcing low freight rates, plus Freight Rebates designed to subsidise them (see pages 7,11), failed. When war came, industry could not meet UK needs. The 'cradle of the Industrial Revolution' had fallen so far behind foreign competitors that for most of the war, steel was the biggest single commodity shipped from the USA, which also supplied ships and aircraft. UK industry could not meet post-war demand for steel and materials required by BR to repair war damaged infrastructure and replace ageing rolling stock, (see pages 52-54), but pushed up prices (see Table 2). Government expected BR to 'contain those price increases', which industry could not contain, (see pages 173,174). Industry failed to improve productivity and tackle demarcation. The BTC repeatedly protested about unrestrained price increases, which, with Government's unique restraint on BR prices, created the deficits which politicians and others criticised!

Few knew how much BR spent in the private sector, and hence, did not realise that many reliability problems stemmed therefrom. Breakdown of private sector supplied equipment in the public sector is attributed to incompetence - but in the private sector is attributed to 'gremlins'. A 1982 BR press release stated that purchases cost £1254m, of which 80% was from the private sector. Three years later, it was 95% - £1606m from British firms. (BRB 1985/6 Report, Page 6). In 1979, my investigation into punctuality and reliability revealed that, contrary to prevailing opinion, far more delays and cancellations were caused by equipment and material defects, than by staff. Clearly, a significant proportion of complaints should be laid at the door of suppliers, not attributed to BR - an injured party. Resolvement required more reliable equipment, which may need to be sought abroad.

Delayed deliveries of rolling stock caused recasting of services, unpunctuality and cancellation, increased costs and lost revenue. Cannibalisation of EMUs to keep others in service was costly, but necessary. Some units were borrowed from other routes to provide a minimal service, causing cancellations elsewhere. New electric services were postponed on some routes. Due to the '30 year rule' being exercised on even the most *mundane* public records, it is not possible to ascertain what problems arose with equipment supplied by the private sector, after 1972.

BTC Minutes (PRO: AN85/1 to AN85/16):

- April 1956: Poor availability of diesel locos with 55% availability for traffic, compared to 80% for steam. Waiting spare parts was identified as the major cause, followed by manufacturing faults.
- November 1956: Late deliveries by contractors are causing under-spending on new coaches, thereby delaying replacement of old coaches.
- March 1958: Time out of service of main line diesels noted; some unreliable, may be scrapped
- October 1958: The price of a track recording car had risen 57% over the March 1956 quoted price.
- July 1959: Unsatisfactory performance of some main line diesel locos, particularly North British.
- November 1959: Certain diesel loco types whose performance was unsatisfactory and is unlikely to improve - which were causing poor time-keeping, incurring excessive maintenance, and required excessive stocks of spares to keep them in service - will have to be prematurely scrapped.
- December 1960: Suspended Glasgow suburban electric services. Had taken up with suppliers AEI

[Associated Electrical Industries] regarding technical difficulties which they would resolve[22].

- January 1961: Problems with the reliability of Glasgow electric trains.
- April 1961: Traction motor failures were due to faults in manufacturing for which the firm accepted responsibility. Their replacement programme was inadequate to prevent prolonged risk of serious operating difficulties. AEI were falling behind in their programme for modifying trains. Transformers of General Electric manufacture must be rewound if essential reliability was to be obtained - cost £100,000. Under the contract, BR could insist on the firm paying for most, if not all, of the work. Consultants advise a strong line should be taken with English Electric to ensure most rapid replacement of motors. BR had to rely on the expertise of manufacturers in detailed design of transformers and rectifiers. Delay in provision of reliable stock postponed the opening of LT&S and Chelmsford-Colchester electric services causing increased costs and loss of revenue.
- May 1961: Failure of General Electric Co. [GEC] transformers on Eastern Region electric services. They would need to be re-wound at the company's expense.
- June 1961: Further reports of problems with GEC transformers and English Electric motors. These continuing defects were having serious repercussions on services.
- September 1961: Supply committee report recommended claims against contractors for delay in delivering locos & rolling stock. Committee chairman is meeting North British Locomotive Co. to discuss claims which may bankrupt them. (see page 59). Failures in service of electrical equipment - transformers and rectifiers from General Electric. Pressure on manufacturers to expedite replacement of English Electric motors on LT&S - could not be completed before May 1962.
- September 1961: Delays in delivery of new locos and rolling stock.

BRB Minutes (PRO: AN167/1 to AN167/7)

- December 1965, BR Chairman [Dr. R. Beeching] had met the Chairmen of the three companies responsible for the production of Brush/Sulzer type 4 locos and left them in no doubt about the seriousness of the position. They promised to provide BR with reliable engines.
- November 1966, noted with concern, a high level of failure in electric locos.
- Repetitive failure of suspension tubes in Brush type 4 diesel locos. Being addressed by supplier.
- Due to failures in 1967, North British locos need to be re-engined.
- In 1967, Sulzer company told that it was held responsible for defects in cylinder blocks

Eastern Region Area Board minutes (PRO: AN118/6 to AN118/8):

- February 1961: On North London services, Westinghouse battery chargers gave trouble before the full service was introduced. They designed modifications, but still had failures. Immediately the new service began traction motors burned out on 71 units. GEC carried out Modification "A", which reduced motor defects but increased rectifier defects. New Modification "B" now being carried out though at a slow rate. Delivery of Clacton units will be delayed three months.
- May: Modification "B" has virtually eliminated traction faults. Rectifier faults remain. It is hoped new Modification "C" will resolve them.
- June: 37% of EMU out of service for modification or repair. North London lines have only 24 of 71 units in service, and had to use LT&S stock in lieu. LT&S units supplied by English Electric were experiencing serious difficulty with motors - 27 failed in May. The main cause is a fault in design - motors will have to be rewound. Utmost pressure being put on the manufacturer to improve the situation. Shenfield EMU - being converted from dc to ac by AEI - 73 converted and in service whereas all 92 were programmed to be completed by 10th June; partly due to diversion of the contractor's staff to urgent modification on units already converted. Problems with circuit breakers - not satisfactory needs a programme.

---

[22] An HMRI Inquiry was held into defects on trains and service breakdowns. An independent expert said transformers supplied did not have secondary winding assembly strong enough to support the conditions to which they have been subjected in service: *"No evidence had been submitted to indicate that the failure was due to any special conditions arising from the dual voltage system"*.

- July: Further [unclassified] modifications to North East London EMU after "C" Modifications, as they failed to operate in very hot weather[23]. Some EMU failed immediately they were brought into service. The defect rate of some EMU was 3-4 times as bad as the Eastern Region overall average - *which itself was not impressive.*
- September: 42 units have had Modification "C", many failures still occur. Cannot restore full service on North East London peak. Must postpone introduction of new LT&S electric service
- February 1962: A further report analysing causes of Deltic loco failures was tabled.
- August: Due to difficulties in manufacture of silicon rectifiers, GEC has deferred major modifications for GN Suburban and LT&S, so the first unit will not be sent until September. Completion of 71 units now due end of May 1963 - 2 weeks before the start of the summer service. In view of past experience of the unreliability of the contractor's programme - prospects are extremely doubtful. To be reviewed in January 1963 - the latest date for a decision on the timetable. Dr. Beeching is acquainted with the problem and is writing to GEC.
- September: In March, GEC forecast completion of deliveries of traction motors for Clacton stock by November. In August they gave revised delivery dates with completion February 1963.
- October: EMU average car miles per defect, March-September - All stock: 5,295;   GEC 1,382. EMU average car miles per casualty[24] March-September   All stock: 31,000;   GEC 9,000.
- November: Only two thirds of Clacton stock have been delivered.
- December: New and converted EMU are behind schedule. GEC failed to deliver rehabilitated traction motors in agreed quantities for Enfield-Chingford-Hertford-Bishop Stortford services

London Midland Region, Regional Control Log :

1981: Advanced Passenger Train gearboxes seized up on the main line, south of Rugby. All Up trains diverted for hours via the longer Northampton route, incurring 20 minutes delay. To reach a depot with an inspection pit, it had to be skidded along with locked wheels. To minimise damage it was moved at 20 mph, on a 100 mph line. This did not warm the hearts of staff who had to inspect sixteen miles of track and replace damaged rails. Rolling Stock Engineers were not pleased either.

BTC/BRB Annual Reports :

- 1961: New EMU services north of the Clyde were suspended in November 1960 and restored in October 1961, after rectification of technical faults by the manufacturers.
- 1963: Technical faults that developed during the year adversely affected the availability of certain main line diesel locos. In the main, these were design weaknesses and vigorous action has been taken by manufacturers to find effective solutions.
- 1967: In addition to late delivery of propulsion units, troubles with rolling stock caused considerable difficulties. Liverpool Street-Enfield/Chingford/Hertford/Bishops Stortford electric services, inaugurated in 1960, continued to be affected by faults in electric equipment of rolling stock. Some LT&S stock had to be used temporarily on these routes.
- 1973: There was a serious shortage of steel rails.
- 1979: Service from some contractors & suppliers was poor. A strike in the engineering industry caused problems and the reliability of delivery and quality left much to be desired. This was reflected in the quality of day-to-day performance and in the delay in introducing new equipment.
- 1989/90 Delays in delivery of over 400 class 158s due to manufacturer's difficulties.
- 1991/2: The new class 158 trains which came into service in 1990 had technical problems in their first year. Manufacturers carried out modifications. Late delivery of rolling stock was reported.

Examples of Media Reports:

- 21% of steam locos, average age of 25-30 years were under repair compared to 17% of diesels, which had an average age of *three* years. (Railway Gazette, 24.11.61).

---

[23] The media missed the classic line: "the wrong kind of sunshine".

[24] A "Casualty" was a train delayed for 5 minutes or more. *General Electric stock was three times the average.*

- In December, BR withdrew 50% of diesel trains operating between Nottingham, Leicester and Birmingham due to axle faults, and re-introduced steam trains. (Railway Magazine, February 1962).
- A lot of teething troubles with diesels in the winter - oil freezing and mechanical difficulties. (Times, 19.2.63).
- The most powerful Western Region diesel hydraulics - 2700 hp were out of service to repair transmission faults which developed after only 75,000 miles. Less powerful diesels - 1700 hp and 2200 hp - had to be substituted with consequential effect on punctuality. Transmission equipment had to be returned to the manufacturers for urgent modification. (Times, 6.11.63).
- Poor performance on Eastern and Western Regions due to problems of High Speed Trains [HST] over the past four years resulted in severe unpunctuality and cancellation. (CTCC 1983 Report, Page 5). BR reported that the problems led to a £7m penalty on suppliers[25]. (Times 19.10.80).

Authors:

A very useful and comprehensive survey of BR diesel traction by R.M. Tufnell (*"The Diesel Impact on British Rail"*), whilst praising successes, catalogues a substantial list of failures[26]. These include guarantees of availability that were not achieved, unimpressive hours in use between overhauls, failures of diesel engines, transmission, electrics; and track damage caused by wheelslip on Deltics.

Joy argued that UK loco builders did not produce reliable diesels after 1955 because they had no home market and that diesel loco orders were forced on an "ill-prepared loco building industry". (Joy, Pages 38,50). That only serves to underline the complacency of UK industry. Whereas, American manufacturers went round the world knocking on doors, UK manufacturers sat waiting for customers to come to them. They had not researched the market to find what was needed.

Gavin Morrison (*"Class 47s"*), reveals that this - the main class of locos - suffered many problems.

Other problem areas:

Supply delays and ill-fitting uniforms were a serious problem. Suppliers claimed "a cause of ill-fitting uniforms was inaccuracy of measurements which staff had to provide - garments may be tight if staff indulged in wishful thinking about waist lines", but baggy garments caused more concern. In 1985, I investigated uniform supply, then costing £8m pa, and found one supplier was 35 weeks in arrears with issues to new or promoted staff, and thirteen weeks with replacements to other staff. The Preston Area Manager reported that of 438 uniforms due to be supplied in one month, 50 were the wrong size - about half too large, others too small - five were incomplete and 53 had not been despatched. My Report had 27 recommendations to improve reliability of supply, staff appearance, and financial control. The remark about wishful thinking was arrogant, implying that staff bought no clothing. Most, if not all, had a suit or casual clothes bought from shops with facilities to try on clothes and be measured. Hence, they would know what size of uniform was required. In 1986, consultants, MVA carried out an investigation, and found that "the majority of staff experienced delay when returning uniforms for replacement - the time range for replacements was 1-2 months for a shirt and 7-12 months for a full uniform; 18 months was an average wait for replacement of misfits; 32% said trousers were too baggy; women prefer to buy their own trousers - uniform ones are too baggy and masculine". *Uniform costs quadrupled from 1938 to 1950.* (see page 167)

Drivers were wearing their own clothing because of poor quality uniforms, some had come from Poland. BR could not confirm this, as uniforms were supplied by a UK company. (Times 18.6.63).

Freightliner had problems with crane failures. Delay in erection and handing over by contractors of new installations. Delivery times were lengthened considerably. (BRB 1969 Report, Pages 15,47).

"BR placed an order for 60 Class 56 locos, 30 in Romania. The constraint in Britain appears to be difficulty of getting design facilities. Even allowing for the unsatisfactory state of the British Industry, it seems surprising that the task of adapting existing design work could not be completed here". (Select Committee Report, 1976-7, Page 108).

---

[25] There are few such reports, although defects listed in Minutes & Reports show just cause for recompense.
[26] Heavy training costs were incurred for footplate and maintenance staff on new locos and multiple units. Costs were not refunded by suppliers of unreliable units or locos, some of which had to be prematurely scrapped.

BR has been criticised, especially since privatisation, because modern trains on the East Coast line required attention to resolve air conditioning and other problems. Criticism should surely be levelled at the private sector suppliers, not BR.

Privatised Railways

Privatisation was described by the late Robert Adley, MP, as "*A Poll Tax on wheels*". Like the Poll Tax, not all who should pay, do so, due to ending checks at stations, which as joint costs, create disputes as to shares, leaving on train staff to check tickets. Due to frequent calling points, some fares are missed. Often, no ticket check is made. Inevitably, this will lead to calls for more subsidy.

GNER Chief Executive said Railtrack and train companies made the mistake of assuming BR had been inefficient on costs, but found it was bloody efficient and had it down to a fine art. (Rail N° 466). Newcomers have found that standards demanded of rail transport eclipse those tolerated for air, sea and road. Punctuality and reliability targets have never been published by operators in those fields. One must admire the ingenuity of some in presenting poor performance in a favourable light.

Benchmarks should have been specified to compare with BR: closely defined investment[27], safety, punctuality (see page 164), average fare, information, connections broken, service frequencies, train miles *actually* run (excluding trains replaced by buses), complaints, manpower, track and asset maintenance frequencies and standing passengers. Regrettably, almost all of these benchmarks have been overlooked or not publicised. As BR was not privatised on one day, track comparisons should date from April 1994, and train services should compare post-April 1997 with pre-April 1994.

Closures

OPRAF expected dozens of applications to close lines, as 'It is inevitable that companies will try to remove services *they see* as unnecessary and unprofitable'. One such line is the Stockport-Stalybridge line. North West Trains has to keep it open, so it runs a one-way service on Fridays only. Services have been similarly cut on other lines. The ATOC argued: "Many lines inherited from BR may be uneconomic". *That is why BR had a subsidy*! BR was directed not to close those lines. Some companies stated that closures may be made if they are not given more subsidy. All were given more subsidy than BR (see pages 162-164). Some companies had licence to cut services from the BR level by 20%, which Ministers claimed would not happen. Only nine of the 25 train companies undertook to run, at least the same number of trains as BR[28]. An assurance that trains would not be cut in a franchise period should preclude closures, (see page 41). In 2003, the SRA introduced a discreet way of effecting closures: "bustitution" - where franchisees are invited to submit bids for services in which some trains are replaced by buses! Some stations were opened by local authorities or Passenger Transport Executives, continuing the trend of the last 20 years.

Complaints

It is claimed that **only** 1% of passengers complain. Under BR, it was 0.009%. (see page 105). Passengers are thanked for *comments* or *invited feedback*. TUCCs initiated feedback 50 years ago!

71% more complaints. The Network Railcard was subject to swingeing cuts and prices increased by up to 135%. (South RUCC 1997/8). Delays in getting replies to complaints[29]. (Midlands RUCC 1998/9). Complaints tripled. (RUCC Reports, 1998/9). Standard letters from companies did not deal with issues raised[30]. (Scottish RUCC 1997/8, South RUCC 1998/9). Punctuality was worse than under BR. Twenty minute wait for tickets. South West Trains told a passenger to get a taxi when a train was late, and then offered to refund the taxi fare with vouchers. (South RUCC 1998/9). Passengers and

---

[27] Comparing infrastructure investment, not total investment which includes shops and property.

[28] OPRAF letter to the author 5.12.96. Some companies boast of running more trains than BR with the same rolling stock. As train mileage rose much faster than passenger mileage, they will have to backtrack. Whilst industry may manufacture more than it can currently sell, placing the balance in a warehouse - railways do not have that luxury.

[29] LRPC took 13 months to resolve my complaint about misinformation. They were much busier with complaints now

[30] In reply to a complaint about replacement of BR's long-line Public Address at an unstaffed station, by a press button "Information Point", which gave none on delays, Central Trains apologised for the unreliability of inherited trains!

the RUCC were treated in a cavalier fashion by train companies. (N.E. RUCC 1998/9). In 1998/9, there were 1.073m complaints - 8% up on last year. In the next six months, they rose 25% on the same period last year. (Daily Telegraph 26.8.99 & 17.2.99). Companies claimed that complaints were up because BR did not reply to them. CTCC Reports contain no such criticism as they would, had that been the case. Moreover, BR statistics were inflated. (see Table 6). Letters to the media complain of station tracks soiled with excrement and stinking in hot weather, and weeds in main lines.

Fares

The Rail Passengers Council say companies are deceiving passengers by advertising heavily discounted fares but fail to admit that only a few seats are available. (Times 13.12.02). Train companies claim that the number is not disclosed as it is *sensitive information* which may be of use to a competitor. This is nonsense. They said at the outset that they were competing with *cars*. Franchisees said fares would be simpler, but offer a wider range, which can only be obtained by making more than one phone call! "There are 19 different fares between York and London, excluding special offers". (North East RUCC 1997/8). The CTCC called on BR to state the number of tickets it plans to sell at reduced fares. (see page 94). Noticeably, they do not make the same demand now.

In 1998, a TV report compared BR fare increases since 1985 with *one year* under the private sector. No comparison can be so meaningless. With bigger subsidies, there should have had no increase! As a start point, 1985 was a non-year for comparisons. It was a year when the BR fare index was allowed to rise more than the *current* RPI, but was still below the 1948 RPI base, (see Appendix A). Despite those rises, by privatisation, BR had not recouped sums lost by fares held below inflation, as a result of inept Government policies and interference. "*In the previous 40 years, well above inflation fare rises were the norm*". (Daily Telegraph, 12.2.99). BR fares trailed inflation from 1948, through 1959 - i.e. 40 years earlier, (see Appendix A).

"*As a safeguard, at least **one fare** will be regulated on every line in the country*", (OPRAF letter 5.12.96). "In June 1997, Super Savers on Cross Country increased 32%, and Anglo-Scottish 15%", (North West RUCC 1997/8 Report). "Long distance passenger fares rose twice as fast as inflation since 1995, and are likely to rise further. Only 44% of fares are regulated. The London-Manchester standard class single is £92, it was £50 under BR". (Times 30.6.02). BR received no subsidy for this route! So much for capping. OPRAF believed that "*where effective competition is provided by other transport, market forces are more efficient than regulation in keeping fares at a reasonable level*". BR managers had said for decades, that effective competition was provided by car, coach and air!

The Franchise Director said: "Historically, BR has increased fares considerably more than inflation". (Public Accounts Committee 15th Report 5.3.97, Page 6). He was misinformed. (see Appendix A)

Media reports in October 1995 revealed private sector fare increases of 56% "to dampen demand". BR was criticised because fares rose in 1984 above inflation - so it is claimed - "to dampen demand". Private sector businesses impose increases, when demand exceeds supply - hotels, air, sea, package tours - due to *market forces* which also dampens demand!

Freight

The freight companies are headed by professionals. Expansion continues in traffics that BR had been building up, and for which it had negotiated contracts: aggregates, cars and car parts, coal, containers, household waste, oil, steel, etc., (see pages 126-127), and from the Channel Tunnel. Given Government's desire to transfer traffic from road, it is surprising that army tanks for Catterick were on the M1 in June 2003, causing death and disruption. In 2000, a loading dock was built and track improved on the Wensleydale freight line. It cost £0.75m, paid for the MoD to load or unload tanks between southern England and Catterick military depot. The MoD failed to put a *penny* into facilities in BR days, despite pleas by MPs that it would keep rural routes open. Amateurs seeking to restore passenger trains to the line will benefit from this gratuitous handout of taxpayers' money.

Competition was not a cost problem, once BR was freed from Government's anti-rail rates structure. A "European Working Time Directive to cut road drivers hours will add *at least* 18% on transport rates". (R.F. Boughton, Institute of Transport Journal "Focus", April 2003). Perhaps Government will listen to private sector complaints about an unlevel playing field, where they didn't with BR These costs and steps to improve safety will benefit railways and would have benefited BR.

Information

Visual displays and announcers proclaim that First Class will be at the rear, when it is at the front. Visual displays break down, as they did in the past - as the private sector has yet to invent 100% reliable equipment. BR had staff at ticket barriers to direct passengers.

It is claimed that NRES answer calls more quickly; but as they give *less* information[31], calls should be answered more quickly, leading to fewer engaged signals. In November 2000, it was stated that under BR: "about 60% callers found phone inquiries were engaged or calls unanswered". (Lords Hansard vol. 618, col. 1530). A request to the DoT for the source, produced a reply from the SRA - presumably the source - who "*understood that BR commissioned reports from British Telecom, that showed over 60% of callers found BR call centre lines engaged or calls unanswered*". A request for details: when Reports were published and to which BRB *manager* they were addressed, brought the reply that the source was a "colleague who was manager of Tonbridge TEB[32] under BR". The period, was "1995/6, going back indefinitely. There is no published source". It could not be *indefinitely*, implying from nationalisation in 1948, as Telephone Enquiry Bureaux [TEBx] did not exist then. They later wrote: "the Authority has documents referring to studies when barely 40% were answered", and said "we are not going to reach agreement on interpretation of past events". It is *impossible* to misinterpret documents one has not seen. They had "documentary evidence referring to *various studies*, indicating that before NRES ramped up its capacity and switched to the 0345 number *over 50%* of calls *may* have received the engaged tone nation-wide, and barely 40% were answered. Records of high incidence of engaged signals took place in late 1995 when sample BT data was *extrapolated* to produce an estimated over 50% incidence of engaged signals, with up to 70% at some West Coast centres". A request for access to the documents was not granted.

A review of West Coast centres in 1985 showed none answered less than 67% - most were 85-94%. Standards worsened when the new boys introduced new technology at fewer centres. 60% unanswered was out of line with independent research in 1993/4, i.e. before privatisation. (see page 105). Figures of 40% would have been repeatedly criticised by "Watchdogs". There is no mention of such a figure in their Annual Reports. The CRUCC 1993/4 Report shows calls answered by Tonbridge, which seems to be at the centre of criticism now made of BR, as 68.1%. Advances have been made, because industry got around to developing systems recommended in my 1985 Report.

There have been reverses. NRES does not give Eurostar or European train times. Another call. is needed. Fares often require a call to a train operator - or two or more - to see "*if there any seats left*". There, one suffers interrogation by answerphone, the duration of which is much longer than to BR, and the caller pays for additional calls. These offices are not manned continuously, hence, night calls are unanswered. Statistics for these "off-shoots" are not included in NRES data, voiding the claim that enquiries are dealt with quicker. Some calls are diverted "off-line" to the "Support Team", and thence to a "Supervisor", taking up to ten minutes. They deal with fairly mundane queries, e.g. addresses of NRES and the Rail Passengers Council - which they didn't know existed - when wishing to complain. Callers cannot now identify which NRES office answered the call.

Unprecedented number of complaints about inaccuracy of information supplied since the inception of the new system. (North West TUCC 1997/8 Report). There were nearly four times as many complaints about the accuracy of information provided by NRES in 1997/8. (CRUCC 1997/8 Report). Consumer Association research exposed 60% inaccuracies with fares. (Sunday Telegraph 18.8.03).

---

[31] They regard information on carparks as an "extra facility". (*Rail*, N° 464). With BR, it was basic information. After NRES was set up, I asked for parking charges at a station, to see if a taxi was cheaper. NRES, based at four centres, did not know, and would not give the number of the station's Travel Centre or supervisor who *would* have known.

[32] As a Regional Chief Officer with access to information at Board level, a member of the Inter Regional *Customer First* Group, which examined problems and developed measures to improve these and allied issues, I would not accept a *junior* manager as a national authority on Enquiries, or any other subject. Tonbridge was a small two shift unit.

Investment

Comparisons must exclude profits to contractors, sub contractors and Railtrack, and must exclude like-for-like renewals which were *working expenses*, not *Investment*. "Track renewal in Railtrack's plan is reduced to 0.8% of the network each year, suggesting rails have a 125 year life - clearly a nonsense. In the BR period, it was 2.1%, in Europe, 2.7%". (*Railway World*, Apl 1996, Page 22). The BBC told a Minister (3.1.97): "£410m had been spent on rolling stock over the past five years [under BR], is now £143m, and that Railtrack maintenance backlog is £277m". Railtrack's ten year Investment Plan has words such as "possibly" or "proposed", and does not imply it has approval by Railtrack. (RUCC South 1997/8 Report).

A much bigger subsidy will be paid to enable new trains to be leased by South West Trains to re-place BR coaches. (SRA press release 11.7.03). To secure £1bn investment in new trains and service improvements, South Central Trains will get £670m subsidy - almost twice that in the previous agreement. (SRA press release 8.7.03 & Daily Telegraph 12.7.03). Privatisation was justified on grounds that the private sector would deliver *more* investment *and* improved services for *less* subsidy.

Electric interaction problems between trains and signalling were not helped by a poor record of equipment inherited from BR. (Scottish RUCC 2001/2). *Seven* years after Railtrack inherited infra-structure, they were still making this pathetic excuse. Perhaps they sacked the wrong people.

In January 2003, it was reported that due to rising costs, plans for improvements had been de-ferred or dropped. So much for assurances that the private sector would fund investment. The tax-payer has been giving cash to them to modernise - when they were not supposed to get any.

The Rail Regulator said upgrading the west coast line has risen from £2bn to £10bn.[33] From Sep-tember 2004 the line from Euston to Birmingham/Manchester/Liverpool will lift from 110 to 125 mph, not the 140 mph forecast by 2005. Work north of Manchester will be deferred at least a year, before it is lifted to 125 mph. (BBC Radio 24.7.03). Improving power supplies will cost £1bn to permit new trains to run at full speed as the present supply is insufficient[34]. (Daily Telegraph 5.1.03.)

Passenger Services

More trains are facilitated by shorter trains even in the peak (*"Modern Railways"* Apl 2002, Page 77). Reduced track renewals create extra paths. A reversal of renewal policy will cut paths and services, to, or below, BR levels. Commuter operators plan to remove toilets to create more standing room!

"In most of our Region, competition does not exist. Some are reluctant to hold a train for a few minutes so passengers from a late running connection can make it. Missing out stops to avoid a train being late at destination is not unknown. Who is going to pay for big investment suggested by train companies? Are they prepared to gamble on there not being a downturn in the economy in the next 20 years? Not one of the toilets was working - they stank to high heaven, and are a health risk. In some cases, companies are adamant that they would not compensate. Off peak fares are not regu-lated and have been raised by Connex to double the inflation rate. There is a trend for smaller seats in new rolling stock, even though people are getting fatter". (RUCC South 1998/9 Report, Page 39).

Punctuality

An overall private sector standard is derived by applying each company's standard to the trains it runs, as shown in the 2001/2 SRA Report. A comparative figure is derived by applying BR's stan-dard for the Business Sector (see BRB 1993/4 Report - BR's last year as an entity), from which the franchise was drawn, to those trains. These give BR 91.2% and the private sector 77.9%, (see Ap-pendix E). They hope to get back to pre-Hatfield standards. Unfortunately, these were worse than BR. Using the OPRAF 1998/9 Report, calculated in the same way, produces 90.4% for the private sector to compare with BR's 91.2%. Given the policy of breaking connections, lengthening journey times, missing calls to recover delays[35] and not making extra calls to replace a cancelled train, punc-

---

[33] A Government appointed study estimated £400-600m. (North West TUCC 1993/4 Report). See page 76.

[34] 1,000 carriages were idle, as the SRA found out too late that new trains required more power for airconditioning and power doors. Some trains were too wide for stations. These problems are a consequence of fragmentation.

[35] Operators said, we are entitled to do so, to make up time! (Sunday Telegraph 13.1.02).

tuality should eclipse BR's. Some blame decrepit assets, but had not warned that standards may fall. If stock cannot be economically replaced in 15, instead of 30 years, future franchisees will complain of *inherited decrepit stock*. On "*Any Questions*" (1.6.02), an MP said that an arrival 15" late was satisfactory. In many contacts with MPs, *none* conceded *one* minute late as acceptable. Watchdogs told BR that five minutes late and a target below 100% was unacceptable, (see page 104), but call for neither now. Late arrivals for the ten worst companies were 21% to 43%. (Daily Telegraph 26.11.02).

Long distance train operators have increased train km by 60% whilst passengers have only increased by 10%. (SRA Rail Capacity Study). The effect is to congest the system and cause delays.

Safety has not improved. (see Chapter 16).

Subsidy was doubled in the year before privatisation. (see Chapter 15). In addition to the overt subsidies, the SRA launched a £400m Fund in 2002 to improve rail performance!

Privatised Utilities

Among claimed justifications for rail privatisation, was the past success of other privatisations:

Buses "Quality and geographical coverage reduced. Competition limited by mergers. Bus station closures. Impossible to know which company runs which service, or find a timetable. Fleet ages have increased". (CTCC "*New Opportunities for Rail Passengers?*"). "No real reduction in fares". (Scottish TUCC 1993/4 Report). Conditions of service give less protection than rail passengers.

BT soon began to charge for Inquiries. The Inquiry service has now been fragmented in a user-non-friendly way. BT said (CTCC 1987/8 Report, Page 16), where there was no phone at a station they would erect direction signs. They have not done so locally, after moving one from the station, where it stood for decades. Many stations have no sign. Ex-BT managers say that new technology to cut staff was already being introduced. Correction of errors in bills is a slower process.

Electricity cuts persist but they are not liable, and *never* apologise. Power lines cut by weather are an *Act of God*, but due to incompetence on BR lines. British Energy is an example of successful privatisation! Lower prices are offered by "competitors", which the "host" supplier is not allowed to match! British Gas offered a lower rate to nPower than to Manweb customers in the same street

Gas is not liable for supply failures. A maintenance contract increased by six times the RPI. In an attempt at consolation, they said that new customers given the same service pay more.

Water suppliers have no liability for supply failures. Failure to meet peak demand was due to the *wrong kind of weather*, but it is not sarcastically trawled up like "leaves on the line".

Personal misfortunes

Personal misfortunes led to complaints to airlines, airports, banks, building societies, bus companies, credit card companies, garages, hotels, insurance companies, manufacturers, restaurants, retailers, stockbrokers, supermarkets and utilities. They cover increased prices, unreliable deliveries, items out of stock, defective products and poor service. They include mechanics in ostensibly respectable garages stabbing around in the dark, and finding a "loose connection", later found by the AA to be a worn petrol pump connection, located in the boot of a Wolseley 1500. Mechanics had only looked under the bonnet! Other cases include failure to tighten joints causing oil leaks, new cars returned within 12 months with paint peeling off, one year old cars which could not be converted to lead free petrol; manufacturers who said a part made by them, costing a few pence, was not available when it was; tradesmen who failed to keep to agreed dates, or whose quality of work is poor; banks which fail to make scheduled payments, make payments twice, transfer money out of an account without authority and misspell names on bank cards. All were due to human error or circumstances beyond their control. Analogous failings on BR were attributed to incompetence

A private sector *guarantee* is one tenth of expected life expectancy of a product. Five minutes after 12 months the "*piece of paper*" is worthless. It is analogous to BR guaranteeing punctuality for 10% of a journey. One guarantee was for two weeks *under 12 months*, because delivery was two weeks after paying a deposit! It was only resolved by acrimonious faxes to the company chairman.

It is a popular myth that BR was subsidised from Day One to cover losses and that the subsidy paid to the new boys was less than to BR. Cabinet papers, public records and other sources prove that Government caused the deficits, that BR was not subsidised for the first 21 years and the subsidy to BR was doubled for one year before privatisation due solely to splitting three passenger businesses into 25 companies. Each needed administration, advertising, insurance, and legal services. Government then tried to show that the ensuing record breaking subsidy to the newcomers was reduced as a result of selling off rolling stock to three companies to lease to train companies. This confuses revenue and capital. Government prevented BR leasing stock in the 1970s. (see page 71)

Pre-nationalisation
Pre-war privately owned railways received *no* Government help, even during the world's worst recession. In 1939, Lord Stamp, LMSR President told the Glasgow Chamber of Commerce: In subsidy-ridden Europe, only Britain's railways *"have not taken a penny out of the public pocket"*. It has been stated that pre-war railways were given £60m subsidy when it was found that the expectation of maintaining 1913 profits in perpetuity (see page 6), failed to materialise[1]. The £60m was in lieu of £150m which its own lapdog Committee said was due to *Pre-Grouping* companies, for six years' [1914-20] sequestration of railways, that carried every item connected with war, *free of charge*, and everything else by Government decree, *at pre-war prices,* whilst inflation rocketed by 240%! It was much less than was forecast, (see page 5), and paid *before* loss to road began.

In 1921, Government created a law court to limit railway profits to 1913 levels - "Standard Revenue". Loss of traffic to unregulated road haulage, was facilitated by Government inertia, preventing achievement of statutory profits, despite economies[2]. Government, having long known that war was likely, set up an Inquiry to deal with claims - which the MoT accepted - of unfair treatment. When war came in 1939, and railways were poised to achieve Standard Revenue, the law was suspended.

In 1929, Government offered an interest free loan for railway capital works which would ease acute unemployment. In 1935, another loan was made for the same purpose at a low interest rate. (see page 11). Government demanded and was repaid those loans by BR. (BTC 1951 Report, Page 65). During the 1939-45 War, a few assets were funded by Government, mainly to counter air damage. They demanded, and were paid - indeed *overpaid* - for those assets by BR. (see page 12).

In contrast, subsidies for 1931-38 were - agriculture: £47.2m, shipping & shipbuilding: £4m, civil aviation: £3.6m, mechanical transport: £0.013m. (Keesings 3148A). Railways were, effectively a negative figure, as they were subsidising industry - via their controlled rates and freight rebates, (see pages 7,11) - which Government would otherwise have had to fund.

An AA spokesman said that "Churchill diverted money to the railways from roads". (BBC Radio 4, 17.1.96). Asked for their source, the AA quoted a British Road Federation booklet which stated that in his 1926 budget speech, Churchill "wanted to protect railways". I told the AA that he did not use the word "protect", (Hansard vol. 194, col. 1710), nor allocate a penny to railways, as their accounts confirm; and informed the BBC of the facts. They did not undertake to broadcast a correction.

The BTC Era: 1948-62
When the BTC took control, railways were heading for a loss, due to Government's war-time policy having created losses in a situation in which making a profit was child's play, by freezing rail fares and charges from 1940 to 1946, whilst other industry was allowed to match prices to rising costs. In July 1946, the MoT authorised increases in fares and freight charges (see pages 17,18), after

---

[1] *"Broken Rails"* by C. Wolmar. In 1951, an MP said, that after World War 1, railways were given £30m subsidy. He was told that it was part of the £60m payment for free use of railways during that war. (Hansard vol. 493, col. 306).
[2] Stamp put them at £20m for the LMS alone. The Railway Rates Tribunal confirmed railways were run efficiently.

six years of no change, lifting prices to 55% above pre-war, which was justified in 1941. The Wholesale Price Index was 116.2% above pre-war. BR's inherited price base was well below inflation, with 1941 prices and 1948 costs. Other industry had 1948 prices and 1948 costs. The requirement to submit Charges Schemes to a court of law delayed increases to match inflation.

The BTC repeatedly pointed, in Annual Reports and correspondence, to the inevitability of insolvency under the unique conditions of external control of fares, freight charges and closures. After twelve years, Grants were made to cover losses caused by inept Government policies, but in such a way as to imply managerial incompetence. Real overt subsidies only began after 21 years.

"It is clear the present level of charges will not enable the BTC to comply with the directive to pay its way. It is not possible that any undertaking which is to pay its way should submit to constant increases in the costs of commodities which it needs and yet refrain indefinitely from raising prices to its customers. Higher prices of commodities above pre-war ranged from steel: 80% to linseed oil: 633%". (BTC 1948 Report,Pages 27,125). "Prices continue an upward trend, without pause or warning. By contrast, charges made by the BTC can only be altered after formal and public hearings which involve preparations and investigation over a considerable period of time". (BTC 1949 Report, Page 38). "No system can absorb shocks of this nature without increase in charges. Increases do not come into effect until long after the need for them has become manifest". (BTC 1950 Report, Page 39).

"The BTC began without reserves and has not secured any margin to accumulate them. It is alone in having little latitude for adjusting charges. Any organisation working under these limitations - price control and no reserves - *is bound to be chronically in deficit*. Delay in increasing freight charges cost £11m and of fares increases, cost £0.5m. Even after freight rate increases, there was no change in volume. The BTC asked for a method of effecting quicker changes in prices to avoid deficits. By December 1950, BR freight rates were 81% and BR fares 75% above pre-war levels, whereas, prices for steel rails had doubled, copper plates and tubes trebled, sleepers quadrupled, brass and tin quintupled, general timber was up 3.5 times, oil had tripled, motor spirit and diesel was up $2^{1}/_{2}$ times, uniform clothing had quadrupled and coal tripled. London Area fare increases had been reduced from BTC proposals by a Tribunal decision, reducing income by £1m - from £3m budgeted due to lower increases on Season and Day tickets". (BTC 1950 Report, Pages 39,42,57,95,96)

"The working surplus in the first four years was £166m. Costs include £13.6m capital redemption charges for 1948-51. Compared to 1939, BR fares were up 77%, goods rates 99%, overall 93%. Costs, excluding interest and remuneration of capital, had risen 150%. The price of coal was 340% above 1938, having started 1951 at 280% above 1938 levels[3]. Oil was 296% above 1938". (BTC 1951 Report, Pages 16,27,45). See Table 2 for price increases of key materials.

"BR which are paying their way are having to subsidise London Transport. The Railway Executive had saved £15m pa since 1947". (Railway Gazette 1953, Page 583). £15m was about 5% of costs.

"The fall in working surplus is because fares and freight charges were never able to catch up quickly enough with rising price levels. When there are no margins in charges to meet rising costs until a readjustment is possible, a deficit is inevitable". (BTC 1954 Report, Page 2).

The media clearly saw the cause of the deficit: "*If time lags were avoided, the BTC could be profitable at a level of charges which has risen less than the general price level*". (Times 29.6.55).

"The explanation for £70m deficit is persistent inflation. On seven dates from 1949 to 1955, the BTC could see an increase in charges was inevitable to preserve its position in real terms and took action to secure approval. Delays on each occasion before modified increases were sanctioned produced a loss of over £50m. The BTC are prevented from keeping any margin in newly adjusted charges to provide against further price movements against them in the period ahead. Thus in the intervals before an application became inevitable, the BTC were carrying increased and uncovered charges totalling £50m. Hence it is apparent that inflation has cost £100m. This compares and more than explains accumulated deficits of £70m. BR wages and charges compared to wage and price

---

[3] Coal Board increases were not controlled. In December 1951, they announced increased prices. (Keesings,12128A).

levels in manufacturing industry prove that far from themselves starting an inflationary process, public transport has, from the beginning, been dragged into the spiral. Receipts per passenger mile are well below pre-war allowing for the fall in money values. Another factor is the unequal terms on which BR is expected to meet the competition of privately owned transport, being hedged about with restrictions and obligations not shared by competitors, leaving the BTC providing services at controlled charges that fall short of the cost of providing them. (BTC 1955 Report, Pages 11-12)

In 1956, the BTC Chairman told the Royal United Services Institution: "The 1947 Act enjoined the BTC to integrate transport. The 1953 Act reversed that and the work of those years and directed a return to competition. The BTC were promised freedom of charging on railways and release from restrictions on the rates which they may quote. Because of the cumbersome procedure which has to be followed before approval can be had to a new railway freight charges scheme, railways have not yet achieved the flexibility in charging which the Act promised[4], meanwhile competition grows daily. The country must make up its mind whether public transport should be run as a commercial enterprise, self supporting financially, and as free to run its affairs as any commercial enterprise under private ownership, or as a service bound to minister to every want of the community, however uneconomic. That inevitably means subsidising it from taxation." (Chairman's Paper, Pages 6,18,19).

"The deficit is due to the policy of deficit financing deliberately introduced in 1956 and the decline in the coal and steel industries which mainly affected railways. BTC had never been allowed to build reserves necessary to absorb fluctuations of this kind. £55m was due to deficit financing, the rest was due to a decline in heavy traffic. Fares are still well below pre-war levels in real terms with average earnings keeping ahead of fares". (BTC 1958 Report Pages 2,57).

"The CTCC is impressed by the handicap of the BTC in adjusting charges where supplementary charges might help to put a service on a paying basis. It seems to the CTCC that procedures to obtain additional charges should be freed as much as possible, subject to such safeguards as may be considered necessary". (CTCC 1958 Report, Pages 4,5). "Fares were 115% above 1938, retail prices were 165% higher. Public transport should be able to alter fares". (Railway Gazette, September, 1958).

The BTC asked Government to "reconsider the structure of fixed interest charges which are large in relation to the working surplus. BR rates for coal and steel had risen 24% and 13% against coal price increases of 39%, and steel of 26%". (BTC 1959 Report Pages 4,72).

The MoT's Special Advisory Group - the Stedeford Committee - said in 1961 that: "Fare changes, even after the 1953 Act, were taking 2-3 months. No procedure could cater for retrospective wage increases. The BTC was eager to charge different fares in different areas, but this had been blocked[5]. Part of the deficit is due to delays in obtaining authority for fare increases. The level of fares is inordinately low in relation to the general movement of prices since the war. Recently, the Tribunal agreed a 5% increase, delayed for six months, when 20% was justified. There is no case, even for post facto justification, even in the London area". They urged ending the Tribunal's role. *Government did not implement their recommendations, and locked their Report away for 30 years.*

The Government didn't listen to Beeching, who stated, both in secret - as a member of the Stedeford Committee - and publicly in BTC/BRB Accounts, that the underlying cause of deficits was underpricing of fares, because they neither granted BR equal commercial freedom with the private sector, nor offered to pick up the tab for their social policies. He came from that much praised sector that the MoT claimed should be a beacon to BR. His former company was, doubtless, familiar with the *Principles of Enlightened Private Enterprise*[6]. (see page 171).

A Select Committee reported in July 1960: "The effect of the Minister's intervention in 1952 and 1956 was £15-£23.5m, and the BTC say the effect spread to later years. They should be compen-

---

[4] That promise was not implemented for freight till 1962, enabling road haulage to consolidate an unassailable position. The MoT interfered in fares up to 1993, and freight rates until 1980 to protect shipping. (see pages 35,117).
[5] Refuting claims in 1967, that BR only turned to selective prices due to NBPI pressure. (see page 178).
[6] In 1956, the MoT froze fares - then trailing inflation by 43 points (see Appx A) "to show BR how to make a profit". No business was named that applied this peculiar pricing & financial policy. (see "*Blueprints for Bankruptcy*").

sated from public funds. By delay and its decisions, the Tribunal has severely cut BTC earnings. If the Tribunal is kept in being, the criteria which should govern its decisions should be clearly laid down". (Report Paras. 407,408,410,412). *It had been functioning for 12 years without criteria*!

Besides losses caused by charges held below inflation by external control, closure of uneconomic lines was delayed and often blocked by the Minister, who refused to fund his decisions, but left BR with a rising burden which translated into losses to be temporarily alleviated by interest bearing loans. Other factors included the burden of bridges and level crossings. (see page 128).

The Transport Tribunal - a court of law - to decide rail charges [7]

During the BTC era, fares and freight rates were determined by a Court of Law, and involved the Court of Appeal. Local authorities, industry, agriculture and competitors were empowered to object to increases in fares or charges, whilst they, increased prices without let or hindrance. Objectors were inflationary pace-setters. Some 59 local authorities contributed to BR bankruptcy by objecting at legal hearings to increases, whilst their Rates pursued an unrelenting upward spiral. They expected BR to do what they did not do - hold charges below inflation. Municipal rates rose much faster than fares. (see "*The Railway Closure Controversy*", Appendix C). BTC applications to increase fares and freight charges were routinely delayed by this unique court of law. Delays in obtaining authority to increase charges to catch up on inflation, coupled with reductions imposed by the Tribunal or Minister, were a major factor in the creation of a deficit. (see Appendix B).

In the 1953 Charges Scheme, the BTC proposed increasing Seasons[8] as "they were much lower than Ordinary fares, but for which services were no less costly to provide". (BTC 1952 Report, Page 56). The LCC challenged the Scheme in the Court of Appeal, who put it back to the Tribunal, which confirmed and authorised it from 16th August. BR will be free to quote freely and competitively for traffic provided they do not exceed maximum charges[9]. The delay cost £3m. In each case, the rise in fares has been about a year behind the rise in costs. (BTC 1953 Report, Pages. 2,8,45).

"BTC put a new Freight Charges Scheme to the Tribunal in March 1955 following months of consultation with representatives of rail users and other interested parties". *Despite this*, "28 objections were lodged with the Tribunal whose Public Inquiry opened 10th October and after 44 days of hearings adjourned to 7th March 1956. BTC is still without that greater freedom to charge, and hence to compete, which Parliament intended them to have". (BTC 1955 Report, Page 7).

The 1947 and 1953 Acts specified that the Tribunal should do nothing to impede the BTC paying its way, but the Tribunal did exactly that. Its President told the Stedeford Committee that "delays arising from Hearings cost the BTC money, and that they took social considerations into account in reaching decisions. No formula was applied and no attempt made to quantify the social element".[10]

Political failure and interference

In March 1951, the Cabinet was told: "The MoT and Chancellor met the BTC Chairman who agreed not to pursue monthly return fare increases. Hopes of the BTC to balance accounts in 1950 had been falsified by increased wages granted under Government pressure and in excess of what BR was prepared to give on commercial grounds. Many economies had been made, e.g. 50,000 staff. When the 1947 Act was passed, it was widely recognised that BR would be unable to pay its way[11]. Fares and charges had not risen as much as other charges. As the public would link Government and

---

[7] Hearings and Reports of the Tribunal cover 6,000 pages. They ruled over freight rates until 1962, and fares until 1968. (see Appendix B). See also "*Blueprints for Bankruptcy*" for a record of each of the 27 Hearings.
[8] Which were held down by Government during the Control period, and continued to be until 1968. Beneficiaries were professional classes: office workers, civil servants - working classes mainly used workmen's tickets.
[9] This was not freedom. Road transport, including that controlled by the BTC was totally free.
[10] Acts made no provision for social considerations - their remit was not to impede BTC paying its way.
[11] By those who opposed wartime freezing of charges, and those who knew BR would be denied materials to renovate war worn assets for ten years (see pages 52-54), and denied a right to match inflation.

Tribunal, the BTC to be persuaded to make minimum demands to the Tribunal. They should be authorised to put to the Tribunal[12], proposals to yield £4m-£5m in London fares instead of £11m contemplated, similarly scaled down elsewhere". The Chancellor said "The Act did not contemplate the MoT coming between the Tribunal and the BTC". *Nevertheless he did so*. Fares and charges had not risen as much as other charges. Some Ministers said "it was a mistake to assume that increases would drive traffic off BR, as was borne out by an increase in freight charges in 1950". The Cabinet authorised the MoT to authorise the BTC to increase BR freight charges by 10%.

Having asked the CTCC in 1952, to review a Decision by the Transport Tribunal - a law court - the MoT ignored their approval, enforced yet lower increases than the Tribunal had decreed, and delayed all increases. (see *"Blueprints for Bankruptcy"*, Pages 100-104). He said he was not bound by their recommendations, which begs the question: Why involve them? He said his role was to see that anomalies did not persist - but the Tribunal had done that, he *perpetuated* anomalies. He said the matter was discussed with the BTC - as required by the Act *before* intervention. In fact, meetings took place on **5th, 6th & 10th June**. (PRO: AN85/5: minute 5/453; AN85/5: Memo 35). His Direction was made on **15th April,** and on **28th April** he had assured MPs that consultations had taken place. That this action was unjustified and ultra vires, is borne out by media reports, a secret ruling by the Government's own top legal advisor - the Attorney General - and by the Speaker:

- The Times pointed out that when the proposed 1947 Act was being debated, the Tory opposition wanted to prevent interference with railway charges by the Minister, and voted for an amendment to block him from giving Directions that may lead to the BTC operating at a deficit. "Yet operation at a deficit seems likely to be the effect of the Direction now given. Recently, BR had been doing better and there was a real prospect that the increase of fares would turn the scale and make them self supporting". Government's action ended that prospect. "The road is opened to continuing deficit and subsidy". By bowing to political pressure, it will become "more difficult to permit future increases in fares, however necessary they may be". Rail fares are low compared to the general increase in prices and against pre-war fares. Under the Act, "the MoT has no power to negative decisions made by the Tribunal". (Times 17.4.52).
- The Times warned that BTC's viability was under threat unless Government climb down. BTC viability will be seriously threatened by the difficulty of obtaining any increases in the face of popular objection in the future. The sub standard fares at the heart of the issue, are subsidised by other passengers. The Tribunal decided - and the CTCC agreed - that this was unjustified. Railway charges should be realistic, not the reverse. All those who examined the issue, have agreed that "sub standard workmen's and season tickets are unjustifiable, and 1883 [Act] workmen's tickets are an anachronism". (Times 28.4.52).
- The Attorney-General stated: "The MoT does not have power under the 1947 Transport to give a Direction which relieves the BTC of the duty to conduct their undertaking as to secure that income is sufficient to meet expenditure taking one year with another. He has powers to delay or prohibit increased fares if, the national interest would be affected and if such a duty would not necessarily result in breach of the BTC duty under the Act. A Direction may be in order if the burden of increased costs could be met in other ways such as economies"[13]. (Cabinet Minutes 22.3.55).
- The Speaker of the House of Commons ruled that fares could not be discussed as there was no Ministerial responsibility. (Hansard 28.4.52 vol. 499, col. 1022). He had earlier ruled that "final responsibility for a Charges Scheme rests on the Transport Tribunal, and during the transitional period, on the Minister. In neither case is the BTC the responsible body". (Hansard 3.3.52 vol. 497, col. 106). The transitional period - provided for in the 1947 Act - was to cover the situation until a Scheme was prepared by the BTC and submitted to the Tribunal. A Scheme had been prepared,

---

[12] The Acts did not require the authority of the Cabinet or Ministers before submitting applications to the Tribunal.

[13] The 1952 Direction was "to avoid hardship", not for economies. If the MoT said economies could be made, but the BTC disagreed, it would be difficult for him to specify *his* economies. The Cabinet knew economies had been made.

submitted and the Tribunal had handed down its Judicial Decision. Therefore, it follows, that the Minister had exercised powers that were *specifically* excluded by legislation.

"On 15th April 1952 the MoT directed BTC not to increase charges beyond those in force on that day - the BTC had to implement the Tribunal's 28% reduction in Ordinary fares[14] - which the BTC had not planned to change - at a cost of £1m from 1st May. Increases, worth a further £2.3m authorised by the Tribunal must not be introduced. Increased costs added £18m to BTC costs". (BTC 1952 Report, Page 55). On 19th April, the Prime Minister argued that Government needed the power of Sec. 4 of the 1947 Act "because the policy of the BTC may be wrong and contrary to the national interest" - but they were overruling the Tribunal - a Court of Law - not the BTC. Government could have appealed to the Court of Appeal - the LCC did so in 1953. (see page 93).

Harold Wilson, Leader of the Opposition, speaking in London said: "The Minister's Directive is a stunt to avoid disaster in the local elections. It is at variance with the line Tories took when in Opposition. In the debates on the Bill, they said they wanted to protect rail charges from Ministerial interference and that Ministers should be prevented from giving Direction to the BTC which would lead to a deficit in the Accounts. It must lead to heavy losses in the railway system. If Mr. Churchill wants to keep rail charges down the only way is to introduce a system of subsidies". (Times. 21.4.52), *Instead, the Government imposed interest bearing loans.*

On 22nd April 1952, Prime Minister Winston Churchill told the Cabinet that he "would not accept that the BTC should be free, even with the approval of the Tribunal[15] to adjust railway rates without any intervention by Government or Parliament, and *he did not consider that railways should be obliged to recover from revenue all their costs including capital invested in them*". *Despite this, Government retained the concept of the BTC paying its way in the 1953 Act*, which in the circumstances was ludicrous and impossible. Cabinet was discussing a draft White Paper for the 1953 Act to denationalise road haulage, which envisaged that "the BTC would be free to decide its own passenger and freight charges". Cabinet decided that "words should be added to make it clear that the BTC would remain subject to the overriding power of the MoT to give such directions in this matter as the National Interest might require". The White Paper was duly amended.

"A freight rates increase was authorised 5th June, but freight rates were still below the index of wholesale prices. BTC road haulage rates are varied according to circumstances. It would benefit BR if they had equal liberty to adjust charges, and would assist in attracting to rail, goods for which that medium is suitable, whilst transferring the unsuitable to road". (BTC 1955 Report, Page 6).

The MoT said, in July, 1955: "By applying ordinary principles of enlightened private enterprise, I am hopeful that we are going to show how they [BR] can make a profit". (Hansard, vol. 555, col. 1320). Managers who believed he would free BR to act commercially on prices and closures like the private sector, were disappointed. What he imposed on BR, had no parallel in the private nor public sector. He said that the "most important principle of enlightened private enterprise was competition using up to date methods". (Hansard, vol. 556, col. 1191). When industry had lost a world lead in *every* field, they closed factories or re-opened in the Far East. His predecessor blocked full competition.

In March 1956, the MoT "asked" the BTC to defer fares increases "to stop continually passing on this sort of charge to the public". An Opposition MP said "fares and freight charges had risen less than the RPI or Wholesale Indices". As these were *averages* it was *impossible* for fares and freight rates which were below the indices to be the cause of inflation. (see Tables 4,8). Published data proved that rail charges had been anti-inflationary since 1940. BR was the *only* industry that had not *continually passed on increases*. His action prevented BR from increasing Ordinary fares to a level below 1947 in money terms - below pre-war in real terms having not reverted to the level from which his predecessor and the Tribunal had reduced them in 1952. "In deference to MoT wishes,

---

[14] The BTC had applied to the Tribunal on 7.4.51 for increases in seasons, reduced & sub standard fare. Ten months later they ruled that fares could not be increased by the amounts sought and also directed that Ordinary Standard fares be reduced below pre-war levels. The MoT made further cuts. Increases were delayed 17 months.

[15] That was free? It was a strange definition of commercial freedom from the Party of businessmen.

the BTC postponed for six months an Application to the Tribunal and would not increase Ordinary fares within existing powers". (BTC Minutes 15.3.56). The MoT was not interested in facts, claiming that he was going to show BR how to make a profit with prices held further below inflation, with the insecure prop of an interest bearing loan. He did not name *one* business using this policy.

The MoT 1956 Paper: *Proposals for Railways*, [Cmd 9880], stated: "The BTC applied to increase freight charges on 21st February. The MoT said on 19th March: As an essential part of that decision - upon the Application - a reassessment of the economic and financial future of the BTC would be undertaken in the next six months. The BTC have not and never have had a complete monopoly of traffics for which their services are provided. It remains Government's view that every effort to avoid continued cycles of price increases in basic industries is essential to break the spiral of infla-tion - any general increase in railway charges should be avoided. The MoT advocated carrying substantial deficits until 1961-2. This does not mean that the BTC will not impose selective increases in charges in the next 5-6 years. It *may well involve adjustments* in fares in certain areas from time to time. Government will - as the price of preventing increases in fares & charges - loan £250m on which BTC will pay interest. The BTC will be empowered to borrow to cover the first three years' interest"[16]. (Cmd 9880 Pages 3,5,6,7). The MoT stated that "£250m loan was to finance the deficit". (Hansard 2.4.58, vol. 585, cols. 1201-2). BR was clearly not the source of inflation.

This policy was not devised by someone proficient in arithmetic. The inflation rate was an aver-age. The logical way to reduce an average is to pull down all figures *above* average - not the one *below*: viz. BR fares and charges. (see Tables 2,4 & Appendix A). BR could not pay the interest, so they were authorised to borrow to pay it. Picture it: BR was loaned £55m on which they had to pay £2.75m interest pa, which they borrowed. On £2.75m, they paid £0.14m interest, which they borrowed. In due course, they had to repay the loan, so they borrowed and borrowed, leading to the huge losses criticised by Governments whose own policies created the deficit!

The Paper included a Memo from the BTC: "It is Government policy that Nationalised Industries should seek fully to reflect their costs, but Government was asking the BTC, in the national interest, to follow a course which would involve an exception to this policy. Increases for which they had applied, were reduced or postponed for six months, during which, a fresh assessment would be un-dertaken, followed by such special action as seemed appropriate at the end of that period. It was on this clear understanding that the BTC agreed to the course proposed. The BTC earned a working surplus in every year since they began operations, on the other hand, in several years the surplus was not sufficient to meet financial charges on fixed interest borrowings[17], which constitute the sole source of external capital. They started without reserves and never obtained increases in fares and charges large enough to permit their creation. There was a lapse of several months in putting up charges which cost £10m in 1955. The accumulated deficit at end of 1955 was £70m, due mainly to time lags in putting up fares and charges, largely on traffic such as London passengers rather than weakness in the competitive field. First among statutory restrictions and obligations which have fettered BR must rank restrictions on freedom to fix fares & charges. The Freight Charges Scheme has, after lengthy public enquiry been amended by the Tribunal's Decision, viz.: while agreeing the principle of maximum charges for conveyance of traffic, they decided that there should be two ex-ceptions: [a] any consignment weighing 100 tons or more; [b] goods carried in owners' wagons. In these instances, charges made must be 'reasonable', which would on application be settled by them. The Tribunal not only rejected the BTC proposal for a single series of scales, but lowered the pro-posed maximum charges and provided a separate series of named commodities normally carried in bulk; and they also introduced in each series, alternative and lower maximum charges for goods

---

[16] Inevitably suppliers' prices would rise. The word **'may'**, infers that he may block future increases. The policy would have brought a blush of shame to the cheeks of a loan shark. BR had to keep charges below inflation and "pay its way" with interest bearing loans. It is difficult to conceive a more inept policy. Other industry was not subjected to a freeze.
[17] In November 1991, the Financial Times claimed that in 1948, the cost of assets was written off and interest met from taxes. This Cmd Paper, and regular references to the annual interest burden in Annual Reports refute the claim

consigned to and/or from a private siding. The Freight Charges Scheme was appreciably restricted[18] by the Tribunal. The standstill on charges was conditioned by an expectation that Government would implement action to enable the BTC to meet statutory obligations. The BTC forecast that this policy would cost £6m pa rising to £20m pa in 1961 in interest charges, and these would continue to at least 1970". (Cmnd 9880, Pages 11-13,24,26,29). *Subsequent events disappointed the BTC.*

The MoT, in his White Paper, did not contradict these comments. Doubts expressed in the Paper by the MoT, regarding the risks of increasing prices do not sit easily with BTC views communicated to him. The BTC was unconvinced about restraint. (see BTC Minutes on pages 171-172).

A Dept. of Transport file (PRO: MT132/32) deals with this plan to freeze rail charges, with disastrous consequences. It cannot be claimed that the consequences were unforeseen, the relevant 1941 file in which the Chancellor and others had accurately forecast ruin from the same policy, (see page 14), having been referred to several times between 1950 and 1960, by DoT staff, some of whom had been in the Department in 1941 when the policy was last tried. (see Imperial Calendar). Not content with making the same mistake in 1956, their successors in 1971, repeated it. (see page 179).

The BTC Memo sent for inclusion in Section D of the White Paper, added: "*The effect of changes in the Freight Charges Scheme imposed by the Tribunal means a greater proportion of traffic will be carried at unremunerative rates. The rates system will be more difficult to administer and means a lower effective ceiling of charges. Where charges are subject to a test of reasonableness, the threat of legal action is bound to inhibit the pursuit of a businesslike policy. The Tribunal has retained jurisdiction over an important sector of traffic - a third - which will be subject to reasonable charges*". The paragraph was left out. The Treasury told the DoT "it was anxious to avoid emphasising the prices issue, and preferred an implication that the BTC was working on a plan of this sort as a matter of course". *The BTC had said it was at Government request.* (see page 174).

The file reveals that the BTC opposed the Chancellor's plan to make loans "to the nationalised industries over the next two years" as an anti inflationary measure, in lieu of price increases. The BTC told the MoT that "losses arising from delays implicit in the granting of price increases since 1949 by the Transport Tribunal totalled £56m". *This excluded interest and costs of lawyers and executives employed on this activity.* The file shows that in May, the MoT became aware of a coal price increase, which would add £4m to BR costs, but did not object, and had not warned the BTC. The Treasury argued "an increase in gas prices arising directly from the coal increase was allowable as it was the end of a cycle"! *This was nonsense, it fed straight into price indices.*

On 13th June 1956, the Financial Times stated that transport was given close direction by the MoT, whilst three Fuel & Power industries were left by their Minister to run their own affairs. "That BR was technically backward, was not the result of too little political interference. No one can run an industry subject to the degree of interference which exists already".

On 29th June 1956, the Guardian said that the BTC feels it has been bullied and tricked long enough. The promise in the 1953 Act that railways would be set free to compete on commercial terms with hauliers has not been kept. Time after time, applications for higher charges made necessary by higher costs were refused and delayed. No honest observer can deny they have borne more than a fair share of Government efforts to muffle inflation. The real reason for pushing them into deficit was political convenience. They were not allowed to displease the electorate by putting up charges in line with increased costs. There are no secret reserves in BTC Accounts which could absorb rising costs without raising charges. Yet the Government prevented the BTC in March from adjusting charges to costs and has now bullied them into promising a further freeze. The deficit frustrates the Budget because it puts more money into circulation than it takes out.

In contrast to his rail policy, vague responses were accepted from industry: "The British Employers Federation will make every effort to avoid increasing prices; The National Union of Manufacturers had an uncontrollable element in manufacturing costs". (Keesings 14977). With BR rates frozen

---

[18] *The Charges Scheme was supposed to give BR commercial freedom. A unique form of freedom.* (see page 114)

this confirms that BR was not the source of inflation. An MP told the MoT: Even after a recent freight rates increase, rates were only up 184% over pre-war, compared to 244% in Wholesale Prices. Fares were 100% over pre-war - the RPI was up 146%. (Hansard, vol. 552, col. 2341, 17.5.56).

The BTC has not been allowed, as the Coal Board has, to recover cost increases from price rises. For nine months, BR will have held charges constant whilst other industries have been able to increase theirs. Governments have been largely responsible for deficits caused by stabilisation and delayed increases. There are two ways forward: modernisation or the greater commercial freedom which still has to be delivered. (Economist 30.6.56). By influencing changes for the sake of political expediency the MoT has aggravated the BR wages problem and by indicating lines of settlement in disputes has usurped the authority of the BTC". (Times 10.12.56).

"Financial worsenment is due to freezing fares and charges to combat inflation. The BTC abstained *at MoT request* from increases in 1956 although prices of coal, electricity, steel and other commodities had risen considerably. In agreeing to make no increase, the BTC had hoped that suppliers would exercise restraint ..... but were perhaps over optimistic". (BTC 1956 Report, Page 11). The MoT had powers in the 1953 Act to give a "Direction", but - perhaps wisely - failed to use them. This way, if BTC finances worsened, they could be blamed for not opposing his 'request'.

The Transport [Railway Finances] Act 1957 enabled the BTC to meet interest and other revenue charges by borrowing and modifying the 1947 Act as to the sufficiency of BTC revenue to meet revenue charges. Government set aside £250m - *a loan to cover Government created deficits. With total freedom, losses would have been avoided, instead of forcing them to borrow and shackling them indefinitely as debtors to the Treasury.* In October 1956 the MoT said the "£250m loan to cover deficits was a Tough bargain". It was no *bargain* for BR. "Alternatives were to carry deficits or impose heavy increases on bulk traffic, which may drive traffic away, and would be a serious addition to industrial costs, and it was against the national interest to do the latter[19]". Having claimed an excuse to hold down freight costs, he 'requested' the BTC not to apply to increase **fares** for the rest of the year, when had they gone to the Tribunal, it would have taken that length of time anyway. Implausibly, he claimed: "It is vital the BTC should take advantage of freedom Government have given them to vary charges in accordance with sound principles, and that the Government view was that passenger services should be run at remunerative rates", when the Tribunal and Ministers had held fares below the RPI. Statutory, but not political, freedom on freight charges and fares was given respectively six and twelve years later. The MoT said the BTC could not be expected to keep down prices if faced with further large increases in costs, not balanced by a corresponding improvement in efficiency. *The BTC was required to further improve efficiency to contain higher costs which industry failed to contain by efficiency! How much further did he want rail charges to fall below inflation where they had languished since 1940? Hence, BR had deficits and the private sector didn't. The first step to put BR in line with the private sector was pricing freedom.*

Fares could not be inflationary, when they were 4% above 1948, against the RPI which was 47% higher. (see Table 4). The MoT authorised freight increases in 1956, when the 1955 level of freight rates was 54% above 1948, albeit, still below industrial price indices, (see Table 8). Government policy lacked logic. Had fares been tied to the Retail Price Index which others exceeded, by the end of 1956, BR would have been £336m better off. (see Table 4). Freight rates tied to the Wholesale Price Index would have produced £212m more. (see Table 8). Freedom on prices and closures would have created reserves and led to modernised assets, generating more revenue.

In the years 1957-60, the BTC borrowed £264m - at 1956 prices - to cover revenue deficits and paid £58m interest on the loan. It would have been unnecessary had fares and charges been linked to inflation. They also borrowed from, Government - by Treasury decision - instead of, as hitherto, on the market, sums to finance investment and modernisation. (see page 61).

---

[19] Freight increases had not lost traffic (see page 170). The MoT clearly intended to preserve the BR subsidy to inefficient industry (see pages 28,113,115).

Finally realising that the mess into which BR finances had been propelled by Government policy, could not be helped by interest bearing loans to cover revenue deficits, the Chancellor broke new ground and *gave* £90m to the BTC in his 1960 Budget. (Hansard vol. 621, col. 48). This charade perpetuated the myth that losses were due to managerial incompetence, when they were due to inept Government policies. Some of the Grant was used to repay interest on Government loans. Grants were continued for a few years, rather than face the reality that BR should have commercial freedom and not be used to subsidise industry, commuter and rural travel to keep electors happy. Loans for modernisation and investment were unaffected and were required to be repaid over 25 years.

Dr. Joy (Page 67), referred to the BTC "defying the expressed wishes of the Government to break even". On the contrary, it was the Government *itself* which took the momentous and conscious decision to undermine the principle of breaking even, and Cabinet minutes and other Papers show that they did not accept that BR should recover all costs from revenue. (see page 171).

The BTC 1960 Report recalled "In 1956 when Government introduced deficit financing the BTC did not increase prices to levels contemplated. The 1958 recession, in coal and steel, cut revenue by £30m in 1958 and 1959. Steel has recovered, but not coal". The Report referred to a "drift of staff away in London and Midlands where industrial wages have risen sharply[20]. Fares are still not at parity with pre-war. The long drawn out process of public enquiry and argument has given this [fares] a special significance in the mind of the public and has affected the willingness of the public to pay reasonable fares. The Government stated that people must be prepared to pay more for rail travel. Increases are needed not only to offset changes in the value of money but to compensate for costly trends in patterns of traffic. Earnings - over double 1948, are racing away faster than fares which were 20% up". (Report Pages 1,5,61,63,65).

The MoT Paper, "Reorganisation of Nationalised Transport Undertakings", December 1960 (Cmnd 1248), stated: "There is confusion between what is economically right and socially desirable. The commercial capability of BR is circumscribed by outmoded statutory obligations and restrictions on trading operations. The present restriction on the ability of BR to adjust, quickly and adequately freight charges and fares are, in the Government view, no longer justified in present competitive conditions[21]. Statutory restrictions on the development of BR property will be suitably *relaxed*". (Cmnd 1248, Pages 4,13). *Relaxed, not abolished - giving less freedom than industry*

In March 1961, a Select Committee reported "The comparatively small deficit at that time [1955] could be attributed to inflation and delay in securing authority for adjustment of fares and charges".

The 1962 Transport Act retained the Tribunal with powers over London Area fares which had risen less than provincial fares[22]. It was beneficial to Government employees and commuters in the south east. "The BTC will be dissolved, finances reconstructed, and maximum *practicable* freedom given to BR[23]. Railways will be freed from statutory control over charges - except for the London Passenger Transport Area", *which included BR lines.* "BR shall not be regarded as common carriers[24], nor bound by enactments which authorise revision of freight charges on complaint by competitors or traders. The effect is to reduce the functions of the Tribunal which now concerns itself with rail and road fares in the London Passenger Transport Area. Coastwise shipping retained protection against BR".[25] (BTC Review, April 1963, Pages 106,114,115).

---

[20] In 1961, Roy Salt, Station Master, Coventry said that two men applied to be trainee guards at Coventry. One was illiterate and was not recruited, the other was. A week later, he resigned as his illiterate friend had got an unskilled job at a motor company at twice the wages!

[21] They were never justified. BR did not get freedom, like suppliers or competitors. Conditions were the same as 1953

[22] London Area fares per mile were 6% above 1961, outside London were up by 9%. (BTC 1962 Report, Page 52).

[23] Real freedom was promised in 1952 - "maximum practicable freedom" was meaningless.

[24] "The last vestiges of the common carrier obligation will have to be abandoned". (1977, Cmnd 6836, Para. 188).

[25] The Transport Act 1980 abolished the Railways & Coastal Shipping Committee, ending protection eighteen years after the Stedeford Committee recommended it.

BRB Era 1963-1968

When the British Railways Board was created, BR deficits before interest totalled **£147m** at 1963 prices, 1.6% of turnover. (see BTC Reports). From 1948 to 1962, BR had been denied, at 1963 prices, **£1115m** revenue - passenger: £779m freight: £336m - by prices held below inflation. (see Table 12).

	fares loss £m	freight loss £m	freight loss £m	RPI	fares loss £m	freight loss £m
	see Appdx A	see Table 8	see page 114	1948 = 100	1963 prices	1963 prices
1949	15	18		105	25	31
1950	20	29		108	33	48
1951	29	62		113	46	98
1952	41	39		127	57	55
1953	44	32		133	59	43
1954	48	8		135	63	11
1955	47	2		140	60	3
1956	53			147	64	
1957	63		7	154	73	8
1958	69		7	159	77	8
1959	71		7	163	78	8
1960	53		7	162	58	8
1961	44		7	165	47	8
1962	38		7	173	39	7
Totals					779	336

Table 12 - Revenue losses due to external interferences & lack of freedom 1948-1962

The BTC paid £635.2m interest on Loan Stock issued by Government to buy assets from previous owners, over 25-30 years and repaid £45.6m of that Loan. BR's share of the Stock was 70%. Interest on the 1957 Act loans to cover BR 'losses' was £65.5m (see BTC Reports). On these items, at 1963 prices, BR paid **£690m**. (see below).

	Interest on Loan Stock	Capital repaid	BR share 70%	1957 Loan	Total BR	RPI	Totals at 1963 prices
1948	35.3	2.5	26.4		26.4	100	47.1
1949	36.3	2.6	27.2		27.2	105	46.1
1950	38.0	2.6	28.4		28.4	108	46.9
1951	37.0	2.9	27.9		27.9	113	44.0
1952	37.8	2.8	28.4		28.4	127	39.8
1953	41.6	3.0	31.2		31.2	133	41.8
1954	44.2	3.0	33.0		33.0	135	43.5
1955	45.2	3.2	33.9		33.9	140	43.1
1956	45.6	3.3	34.2		34.2	147	41.4
1957	45.7	3.3	34.3	2.6	36.9	154	42.7
1958	45.7	3.3	34.3	7.2	41.5	159	46.5
1959	45.7	3.3	34.3	11.5	45.8	163	50.0
1960	45.7	3.3	34.3	14.6	48.9	162	53.7
1961	45.7	3.3	34.3	14.8	49.1	165	53.0
1962	45.7	3.3	34.3	14.8	49.1	173	50.5
Totals	635.2	45.6	476.6	65.5	542.1		690.0

Table 13 - Interest & Capital Burden

These exclude £117m interest paid on modernisation loans, of which £131m of those loans was redeemed. The total **£1805m** (£1115m + £690m), were political - not managerial losses - and explain the 1963 debt of **£1560m**. Grants paid before 1963 (see BTC Reports), amounted to **£411m** at 1963 prices. Against this, traffic worth £41m pa was lost by the archaic rates structure, (see page 112), worth **£493m** at 1963 prices, whilst blocked or delayed closures and bus subsidies cost millions more. BR had to fund the Transport Tribunal and Watchdogs[26]. Before Beeching, BR would have had a surplus instead of a loss, given freedom to manage, even if - unlike industry - its charges had been pegged to inflation.

Government would not pay for uneconomic routes kept open by the MoT- but head in sand - maintained the illusion that such lines need not be unprofitable, and hence needed no Government subsidy, unlike rural buses, agriculture and industry in the same areas!

BR complained that expenses include items from which BR derives no benefit: maintaining and manning crossings, overbridges and CTCC/TUCC costs of £60,000 pa. (BRB 1963 Report, Page 27). BR funded them, and museums (see page 131) until 1969 when Government took over funding.

The Transport Tribunal

Despite the recommendation of the MoT's Advisory Group that Tribunal fare powers be ended, the MoT retained it to rule over London Area fares. The level of those fares had a knock-on effect on other fares, as there could not be a huge disparity between the fare to the last station within the Area and the first outside it. The Tribunal was not finally laid to rest until 1969, having caused enormous losses in revenue, as its President admitted. (see page 29 and Appendices A & B).

Political interference continues

BR must give early warning of changes in fares and freight charges. In November, BR did so in respect of increases to be introduced in early 1966. BR deferred an application for a fare increase at Government request worth £1.4m pa. The delay cost £0.5m. (BRB 1965 Report, Pages 11,21).

The MoT's 1966 *Transport Policy Review*, (Cmnd 3057) finally admitted: "BR is struggling to reconcile two mutually contradictory objectives: to provide an adequate service for the public and to pay their way. Commercial viability is important but secondary. Government must decide now the role for BR. A Joint review will be set up to study the issues". (Cmnd 3057, Pages 2,3,7). Eighteen years after nationalising railways, Government was *beginning* to think about the BR role! DoT files must have bulged with 38 years of data. Further bureaucratic study delayed action.

"Government restraint prevented implementation of increases in fares and charges, some of which had either been approved by the Transport Tribunal or were provided for in commercial agreements". (BRB 1966 Report Page 1). Most were delayed long enough to be frozen.

"Government refused, because of the freeze to allow increases in fares and charges, including some approved by the Tribunal as long ago as July 1966. Government referred proposals to the NBPI from whom a decision was awaited at the year end. This highlights the perennial problem of fares and charges always lagging behind increases in costs - agreement to any increases comes too late and allows too little margin to build up reserves to combat the next cost increases. There is an urgent need for headroom to be granted in advance to enable costs and charges to be kept in step. Government accepts the point made in the BRB 1966 Report that under existing legislation, the deficit is not a true reflection of the achievements of the Board". (BRB 1967 Report, Pages 1,2).

In March, "the MoT gave sanction for modified fare increases". But not for long: "The MoT would not agree to fare increases previously agreed to, nor to certain workshop rationalisation proposals previously agreed to. The BRB view was that BR was being discriminated against compared to other nationalised industries e.g. Electricity and Air". (BRB minutes 23.3.67, 10.8.67).

---

[26] At 1993/4 prices, funding of the Transport Tribunal cost £5.9m and of CTCC/TUCCs £6.7m. Museums cost about 1.25 times as much pa as the latter - see page 131 and above - so, at similar prices they had cost BR about £8.4m.

In 1968, the BRB referred to a new policy - "of pricing not on mileage, but according to market conditions. While research was being completed, BR applied for an increase to ensure a flow of revenue, and powers of headroom for future rises", which "in September 1967, the MoT had referred to the NBPI, who approved 10% increase in Ordinary fares, and 7.5% in Season fares in the London Area. The 10% was later reduced by the Transport Tribunal. The NBPI rejected a general increase for the rest of country telling BR to pursue the BR plan for variable fares[27] which would take months. BR accelerated its research and the first stage was ready by September 1968, gaining £70m in a full year. Considerable revenue was lost by nearly a year's delay". (BRB 1968 Report, Pages 16,17). *The delay would cost about £50m.* "The impression was given that BR was trying to hang onto a sterile system of standard tariffs. BR had asked for headroom to make selective price increases but it was rejected by the NBPI". (BR Management Quarterly, October 1968, Page 16)

The NBPI Report in May 1968, (Cmnd 3656) stated: "In the spring of 1967 the BRB informed the MoT of a wish to raise fares outside London. Following the Prime Minister's announcement on 7th September that all future price increases in nationalised industries would be referred to the NBPI[28], these proposals were referred to us on 3rd October. The proposed increases would raise the RPI by less than 0.04%. In the event of our approving the London proposals they would then be submitted to the Transport Tribunal, which considers fares in the London area". (Pages 1,12).

"Tribunal duties for London fares should be abolished. Subject to *financial objectives*, BR should determine fares on the network. They will consult the Greater London Council annually, and inform them in advance of proposals. Proposals for major increases should be referred to the NBPI. No one has succeeded in defining 'adequacy of service'. It is unlikely that any community, even a prosperous one, would be willing to pay for a service so adequate that hardly anyone complained. The concepts of viability and adequacy of service are irreconcilable, though they remain desirable objectives. Lack of viability is because of the financial structure, control, and external intervention in fares in the face of rising costs. There is no reason why future travellers should pay so that today's passengers can travel at less than the cost of the services provided[29]. In these circumstances relating charges to costs seems not unreasonable. The Board should develop pricing based on peak costs - when they have the freedom". (*"Transport in London"* 1968, Cmnd 3686, Pages 13,14,34,38,57,61).

The NBPI stated in 1969 (Cmnd 4250): "The Minister issued guidelines to BR limiting the amount by which London Area fares should rise - reducing the proposed increase by 28.8%, which the NBPI had to consider - as he expected fare increases to worsen road congestion. This assumption [of transfer from rail to car] is not founded on market research". (Cmnd 4250, Pages 4,5).

BRB Era 1969-1974

From 1969, under the 1968 Act, Government introduced *subsidies* for the *first time* to avoid electorally sensitive closures. They "are not charity but provide the community with services which appropriate authority has ascertained are required. It is not a subsidy to BR but to travellers using these services. Unprecedented inflation caused steep cost increases". (BRB 1970 Report, Page 2) They were not automatic, nor indefinite. BR had first to submit proposed closures to TUCC scrutiny, and only after they decided that a closure would cause hardship, did the Minister agree a subsidy. Periodically, these line subsidies were reviewed, and some were withdrawn, precipitating closure. Loans of £15m were made to BR by the MoT at 9.75% interest. (BRB 1970 Report, Page 54).

"Early in 1970, the MoT agreed to BR raising Season ticket rates in the London Area to start from 26th April". (CTCC 1970 Report, Page 11). *Freedom, belatedly conceded to BR in 1968, to act commercially like other businesses was short lived - BR now required political approval.*

---

[27] Variable fares was another term for selective pricing, which the Tribunal and objectors had prevented years ago.

[28] When all prices were supposed to be controlled by the NBPI, their power with hauliers was less than with BR, who dare not fail to co-operate. In contrast, the NBPI Report - Cmd 2968 - in April 1966, said that it had sought from the road haulage industry "information on costs and charges, but the poor response made firm conclusions impossible"

[29] Government policies had enforced this situation from 1940.

"A CBI initiative to keep price rises at 5% within 12 months of the last increase was endorsed by Government. BR had to accept the directive and would have to borrow at 8-9%. Government advanced BR £27m to cover overdue rises they were not allowed to make. The effects of artificial restraint can never be recovered". (BRB 1971 Report, Page 2). It would increase losses. Eventually prices would have to reflect that 8-9%. *It was not a problem in the private sector which had not had price control and for whom it was voluntary. It would cut their profits, but increase BR losses.* Was borrowing to keep prices down a "*Principle of enlightened private enterprise*"? (see page 171)

An obituary to Sir Campbell Adamson, former Director-General of the CBI, stated his biggest achievement was to get 900 member firms of the CBI to agree to limit price rises in 1971 to 5%, which may have helped to cut inflation. (Daily Telegraph, 24.8.00). In 1971, there were 577,228 separate businesses registered with Companies House, 900 seems to be a drop in the ocean. Inflation was industry led: "Materials and supplies costs were 17.4% and rail wages 6% higher than 1970". (BRB 1971 Report, Table 4-B). Industrial wages rose 12-13% in this period, (CSO: Annual Abstract of Statistics), contradicting the belief that BR increased wages faster than the private sector, which clearly was *not* exercising restraint. The evidence is that his initiative didn't cut inflation.

"Although BR was compensated for price restraint during the year, restrictions on price increases will inevitably have an effect for years ahead making further compensatory payments necessary". (BRB 1972 Report, Page 2). "BR still suffers from and is bound to suffer *in perpetuity from the effects of past price restraint*. The adverse effect on finances of restraint on the levels and timings of increases has been considerable. The effects of this restraint are in present circumstances permanent for BR is, as a result handicapped to a place behind the start line for increases made necessary by the rising cost of materials and living. A year of unprecedented inflation". (BRB 1973 Report, Page 3).

"1972 costs rose by 10%, we were allowed to increase prices by 8%. In 1973 costs rose by 6%, we were allowed to increase by 3%. In 1974, the Chancellor gave BR the freedom to price up, but by then the price base was so low that the market could not take the increase needed - costs rose by 33%" - *5% had also been lost in the preceding two years* - "and we were able to price up only 16%. At constant prices, present earnings per passenger mile are in fact slightly lower than they were in 1969. Unpleasant economic facts do not go away if you ignore them, they always get worse. BRB foresaw financial problems stemming from the arrangement adopted by the Government and gave early warning of their forebodings. In Spring 1975, these forebodings are being realised at a higher level than they were first seen because like all such problems they are aggravated and distorted by inflation and by the rolling effect of past pricing restraints". (BRB 1974 Report, Pages 3,4).

BRB Era 1975-1980

Grants for specific lines retained for social reasons, were replaced under the 1974 Act by a Public Service Obligation grant [PSO]. EEC Regulation 1191/69 directed that financial burdens devolving on transport undertakings by reason of maintaining obligations, shall be subject to compensation. The 1974 Act specified that BRB shall from 1st January 1975 operate its passenger system so as to provide a public service comparable with that provided at present. PSO payments cover activities which BR would not assume, if it considered only its own commercial obligations. The Minister may impose obligations on BR but will compensate them for those obligations. Payments under the PSO are subject to a pre-determined cash limit. (BRB 1982 Report, Pages 16,17). Before the start of each year, the amount of payment required to meet the PSO is calculated on the basis of BR's budget. (see page 34). The price is discussed and agreed annually with the DoT. Once agreed, the predetermined price may only be varied for specific reasons: national emergencies or major disasters, or Government intervention on pricing or changes in the obligation. (BRB 1980 Report, Page 20).

Statements in the DoT's 1976 Consultation Document *Transport Policy* proved they were out of touch with reality: "The peak has been a *factor* in keeping unit costs high". *was the definitive understatement.* "The trend of growing losses has continued since the 1950s despite revenue and capital grants. Subsidies were going to the better-off, rather than the less well-off. It is the higher income groups who use railways the most regularly for travel to work and business journeys, those on lower incomes travel by rail more sporadically. Passengers should be asked whether they prefer a slightly faster journey or a better buffet[30]. There is no evidence the real fare increases that occurred 1970-72 were accompanied by any significant change in the pattern of rail use. A reduction in fares without an increase in subsidies would be unlikely to pay for itself through increased ridership[31]. Since the 1950s railways have experienced successive financial crises and been rescued by subventions from the taxpayer[32]. Costs have risen much faster than revenue particularly during the period when fares were held down as part of a counter inflation policy from early 1971 until early 1974. Fares rose less than the RPI. There were substantial rises in the cost of energy and other resources[33]. The key to success lies in identifying areas where specific tasks can be dispensed with[34]. Recent increases have had remarkably little effect on traffic volume. BR earnings increased by £90m, with a further £30m expected. Seasons were under-priced" (Vol. 1, Pages 6,13,17,20,49,53, 54,55)

A Select Committee Report in 1976-7, [305], stated: "BR say from 1971-74, BR rates were constrained by severe price restraint. London & South East passengers benefit disproportionately from Government support, about £16 per head of population compared to £8 elsewhere. Fare increases lagged behind inflation in the early 1970s[34]. Taking an index of 1972 = 100, the RPI at the end of 1974, was 127, and rail fares 120, but at end of 1976 were equal at 184.[35] BR becomes dependent on Government for further loans - **£63m** in 1975 alone.[36] Fares should not increase for at least five years by more than average RPI".[37] (Pages 78,90,96,111,117).

Our 1978 proposals for fare increases were referred to the Price Commission who recommended there should be no restrictions on the notified increases. (BRB 1977 Report, Page 6). *A unique event.*

Transport Policy, 1977 (Cmnd 6836): "Fare increases have fallen well short of amounts needed to cover the full impact of inflation since 1971. Travel at peak times is often very expensive in resources which has little or no use at other times. Management must design fares to cover costs". *When they tried to do, the Tribunal and Government had held fares down.* "Government believes that commuters should have a period of years to adjust to fares which are bound to rise to cover higher costs of assets. The more successful BR is in other parts of its business, the less the burden on commuters will be. Government welcomes selective fare reductions to encourage travel at off peak times"[38]. (Cmnd 6836 Pages 11,14,29,37). *Transport Policy* "Recognised that the BRB is obliged to provide a passenger service which costs more than it can earn". (BRB 1978 Report, Page 4).

The Price Commission reported in 1978: "Fares were artificially held down in the early seventies[33]. BR should ensure divergence from average rates per mile for comparable journeys are kept within moderate limits". *Freedom was again deferred.* "Past experience of resistance to increases shows it is usually temporary. Over the past decade fares have been market oriented and BR estimates it produces 6-10% more revenue. It is clear to us from the wide ranging studies by both the Board and outside bodies that there is no prospect that general reductions in fares as distinct from the BR practice of making selective reductions might increase revenue. BR has successfully developed pricing techniques for this purpose i.e. filling off peak seats". (1978 Report, Pages 2-3). .

---

[30] He didn't advise what to do when they didn't agree. BR carried out more market research than most realise.

[31] The BTC had said so in 1950 - (see BTC 1950 Report, Page 49).

[32] Crises did not *happen*, but were caused by Government. Their rescue was as helpful as a colander thrown to a non swimmer, pushed in at the deep end. The problem began because interest bearing loans were enforced to block fare increases. Given freedom in 1948, deficits would not have arisen. Deficit financing was Government policy from 1956. The policy was not beneficial to BR which was branded as a loss maker.

[33] The penny may have dropped, but not far enough - for 1971 read 1940! The cost of energy & other resources were allowed to rise - rail fares alone were held down. Fares were below the RPI for 39 of BR's 46 years! (see Appendix A)

[34] Managers had done so since 1948 and replied to ensuing criticism, not least from MPs.

[35] This is meaningless, the 7% margin is never regained; related to 1972-4 revenue it equalled £63m

[36] The loss due to the RPI-fares gap was £63m, and could be calculated earlier in the Report, that did not see the link.

[37] Unless the private sector did likewise, history would repeat itself.

[38] Commuters had been subsidised for 23 years. Why should it continue? Off peak tickets were available for decades.

BRB Era 1980-1994

The External Financing Limit [EFL] covers all external finance requirements, including PSO payments, borrowing and leasing. It is an absolute constraint on the funds which the Board can raise externally and is the overall finance control on the business. (BRB 1982 Report, Page 5).

Fares held steady for a full year. 9.5% increase applied in November was 2% below inflation. (BRB 1981 Report, Page 24). Not until 2011, will it be known if *BR was leaned on, to hold fares down*

Under Robert Reid's Business Sector structure, and with slightly less interference, BR began to turn the tide, and to move towards standing on its own feet, as extracts from Annual Reports reveal:

- We have built up revenue & cut taxpayer support by 14% in real terms. (1980 Report, Page 10)
- The key Government objective for BR is to reduce the requirement for PSO grant to £635m at 1983 prices in 1986. (1983 Report, Page 10).
- InterCity revenue is up in real terms. Other sectors improved on budget. (1984/5 Report, Page 1).
- Reduced costs led to a reduction in PSO for Provincial Services by £12m more than its target. InterCity will be ineligible for PSO after 1987/8. The subsidy is 14% less than 1983. The Government objective is to reduce the PSO by 25% between 1983-7. The key result is to reduce the PSO while embarking on the biggest investment programme for 25 years. (1985/6 Report, Pages 3,4).
- Subsidy reduced by £110m; reduction £260m in real terms over three years. (1986/7 Report, Page 3).
- Objectives require us to reduce the Grant by a further 25% by March 1990. From April 1988, InterCity is a fully commercial business with no Government support and expected to contribute to other railway services. (1987/8 Report, Pages 4,16).
- Reduced subsidy by £33m and repaid £64.5m of subsidy paid in previous years. The principal existing objective set by the Government was to reduce the subsidy by 25% by 1989/90, this was met a year early. In its first year as a commercial business InterCity received no subsidy, income rose by 10% and volume by 4%, and turned in a profit of £57.4m. (1988/9 Report, Pages 3,12).
- BR beat the objective by £91m. The principal objective set three years ago was to reduce the subsidy to £665m by March 1990. By that date it had fallen to £574m. Revenue earned in Provincial Sector enabled a reduction in subsidy. (1989/90 Report, Pages 1,4,16).
- Our objective us to reduce the NSE [Network SouthEast] subsidy to nil[39], and Regional Railways [formerly called Provincial Sector], by 21% to £350m by March 1993. (1990/1 Report, Page 3).
- InterCity remained in profit for the fourth year. (1991/2 Report, Page 3).
- Subsidy increased by 29% to facilitate voluntary redundancy of 6% of staff. (1992/3 Report, Page 4)
- BR's duty is to provide a service comparable with that in 1988. The subsidy was reduced by 20%. NSE increased its profit without revenue support from Government. (1993/4 Report[40] Pages 1,5,19)

The CTCC drew attention to Government's eight year policy of reducing the PSO. (CTCC 1990/1 Report, Page 9). Government recognises that economic benefits such as the relief of road congestion justify the provision of Grants. (BRB 1988/9 Report, Page 6). Since road congestion was worsening, a reduction was, arguably, illogical. The MoT had told the CTCC the PSO was given:

- To alleviate road congestion in the South East.
- To sustain loss making parts of the network, to maintain minimum levels of accessibility to areas where people have come to rely on rail for essential local journeys, and local communities are economically dependent on them. (CTCC 1989/90 Report, Page 9).

An overview of the nationalised era

Whilst Government claimed to subsidise BR, in reality, they "gave" with one hand, *some* of that taken - directly or indirectly - with the other. Yesterday's passengers, especially south east commut-

---

[39] Government was working to eliminate the NSE grant, (CTCC 1989/90 Report, Page 10). NSE could only be made profitable with substantial & rapid real fare increases. (*New Opportunities for Railways*, Cm 2012, 1992, Page 3). The MoT stated: fares could only be reduced if subsidies increased. (Hansard, vol. 216, col. 532, 11.1.93).

[40] The last full year in which BR was responsible for all train operations.

ers, gained from lower fares, at the expense of today's. BR was, like its privately owned prede-cessors, forced by Government to subsidise industry and sections of the public: notably commuters, rural passengers, and the armed forces, through below inflation charges. (see pages 92,112,118).

Requiring charges to be decided by a court of law, widened the gap to inflation. Objectors sought to delay and reduce *every* increase. BR was pressured to avoid passing on increased costs which they faced, and pay regard to social implications, which was Government's role. Ministers were aware of the consequences of *covertly* subsidising passengers. Taxpayers subsidised commuters and others via BR "losses". Government gained from low fares and sub standard freight charges, (see pages 92,114). The country has had far more than "a pound of flesh" from British Railways.

Reductions of some freight charges in the late 1950s and early 1960s to recover or retain traffic until modernisation could improve the service, was used by Dr. Joy, (Page 24), to dismiss complaints that Tribunal and Ministerial control prevented pricing up. In fact, the Tribunal actually reduced some charges against the wishes of the BTC, (see pages 114,172). Had Government given equal freedom, equal allocation of controlled materials and an independent identity to BR, railways would not have lost so much traffic to have had to cut prices to recover it. Low rated captive traffic could have been priced up, thereby, creating reserves. Government policy gave hauliers more than a head start until 1962. Hauliers still enjoy competitive advantages even today, (see page 187).

It is incredible that a Government, whose Ministers boasted of business expertise, expected BR to avoid losses if they could not fix their own prices. They were warned of the effect before the war by railway Chairmen, during the war by Ministers, and later by Stedeford. The demise of the Tribunal gave BR some freedom. From 1980, BR steadily reduced the subsidy. From 1988, InterCity had no subsidy; NSE required none in the year before privatisation, whilst the third Sector, Regional Railways' rural and secondary routes got lower subsidies. These facts are in BR Annual Reports. BR could have continued to operate InterCity and NSE without subsidy, and have further reduced that for the third arm of passenger services, which was carrying increased numbers of passengers on its improving services. "BR subsidies were tiny in comparison with Europe" (Economist 30.3.91 Page 28)

Dr. Joy said (Page 81), that had subsidies been made for loss making lines from 1948, instead of 1968, it would not have solved BR problems. That is because making up losses on loss making lines does not create profits. Nor would it enhance profits on profitable routes, as higher charges would have done. Nor would it have provided funds for interest payments and redemption of capital. Nor would it have affected freight traffic, whose viability was blocked by rates control and legal re-straints.

In 1952, Government took the decision that undermined the principle of the BTC paying its way, by deciding that the BTC's principal subsidiary - BR - need not recover all costs from revenue, whilst at the same time maintaining the charade that the BTC must break even. (see page 171).

More generous subsidies to the private sector

Subsidies to the private sector are unjustified. They were supposed to show how to manage with-out a subsidy *and* keep fares below inflation! BR fares were below inflation for 39 years. In April 1996, the MoT stated that "two thirds of services were franchised for one third of the subsidy paid to BR". Unable to get a reply from the Dept of Transport, inquiries of Tory Central Office estab-lished that "two thirds was calculated on the basis of passenger revenue". OPRAF data showed, that as at October 1996, on that basis, *one-half* had *by then* been franchised. The subsidy to franchisees of £567m was 4.9% *more* than the net subsidy BR was paid in 1994/5, after deducting the unwar-ranted *administrative profit* of 20.3%, which had never been paid before[41]. (see Appendix C). The average BR fare was 12p per mile, franchised fares averaged 12.5p per mile - 9.6% higher than un-franchised at 11.4p per mile. (see Appendix C). This higher fare level called for initial subsidies to be 10% *less* than BR! Attractive services were hived off first rather than the challenging rural areas.

---

[41] The introduction of a "profit" element was revealed in letters to the author from OPRAF and the BRB.

Eleven of the thirteen services, which received 84% of the total subsidy, were profitable under BR! When all services were franchised, the total subsidy was double that paid to BR in 1993/4:

"Railtrack plc was created 1st April 1994. Within BR, 70 business units were created with responsibility for train operations, rolling stock, and other services. Each business unit charges prices calculated to enable it to be a self sustaining commercial enterprise, earning profits to fund investment and a return for shareholders. This led to much higher charges attributed to them than while BR was a single entity. Most notable was the price paid by operators to Railtrack for access to the infrastructure and rolling stock companies for leasing trains. *As a result, Government paid much higher grants.* Previously, the PSO was paid for the statutory obligation to provide loss-making services for social reasons. In 1994/5, the payment was **£1,748m** in place of the former PSO of **£930m**. In addition, grants from PTEs increased to £342m, **more than double** the previous year's payments. (BRB Report, 1994/5, Page 5).

"The industry starts off with a much greater level of funding than provided to BR in the final years of the previous financial system. Government has specified much more clearly than ever before what non commercial services it requires the industry to provide". (BRB 1995/6 Report, Page 6).

Had BR not been about to be privatised, Government would *not* have doubled the PSO to facilitate a split into 70, even had BR argued that it would improve services and increase traffic. The 1994/5 subsidy would have fallen below that of 1993/4. The theory was that the average for the franchise period would be less than the hugely increased and artificial subsidy to BR. £1 paid now is worth more than £1 paid in 15 years time! There was an assumption that anyone bidding for a lapsed franchise would make a bargain bid, when they would want to start back at "GO", and collect *their* £200m. In 1993, I forecast ("*Blueprints for Bankruptcy*"), that, if franchisees cannot operate profitably with a reduced subsidy, or are wound up, the state will be called on to run trains, or a higher subsidy paid. This has happened - Arriva had an increase of £60m in the subsidy; ScotRail[42] and Central got an extra £56m between them; Connex SouthEast was given an extra £58m to stave off bankruptcy for one year. GB Railways received an extra £24m subsidy in 2002 to keep it afloat until the franchise ends in 2004. Other companies seek "re-negotiation of subsidies". "Railtrack received £732m in Grants from Government, in the first year of its funding cycle with four more to go. Its profit for the year was £292m. It cannot survive without Government handouts". (Times 19.12.01). Prior to privatisation, it was stated that Railtrack would receive *no* subsidy, but would be financed by access charges paid by train companies. (Select Committee on Transport, 4th Report, March 1995). "The new railway has had to receive twice the subsidy of the old one, despite business rising by more than a third". (Times 16.1.02). "All former Regional Railways franchises have now received extra funding compared to the original deal". ("*Modern Railways*", April 2002, Page 5).

The Franchise Director told MPs: "over the first seven years, savings of £2bn *should* be achieved compared with operation by BR. Even if BR had achieved 3% savings, it would only cut the cost by £1.7bn.[43] If OPRAF had extra money to spend, he would consider extra station staff in agreements!" (Public Accounts Committee 15th Report 5.3.97, Pages viii, xi). This means that where a management buyout bid was higher, managers who had been realistic about staffing were squeezed out, and the outsider could now get a higher subsidy to provide staffing that managers had deemed essential!

As if the bigger subsidy was not enough, rolling stock and infrastructure were sold for less than their value. The sale of rolling stock was completed in early 1996 for £1.8bn. Some was re-sold for a 56% profit within eight months. By the end of 1997, all had been re-sold for £2.7bn - a 50% profit on a depreciated asset, as no new stock had been acquired, proving that stock was not "decrepit". Some media reports claimed that assets were under priced due to fear of re-nationalisation, which

---

[42] They won the franchise in 1997 with a subsidy of £288m pa, to fall to £202m by the end of the contract. They said the franchise is not a commercial operation, unless you strip out a whole lot of routes. They cannot operate on the present subsidy if the current service is to be maintained. (Sunday Times 20.1.02). The subsidy covered all services.
[43] This conclusion is only valid if BR only achieved a 3% cut *and* started from the unjustifiable higher subsidy level.

pre-supposes that the Tories expected to lose an election in four years' time, of which the media carried no such forecast. The flotation of Railtrack cost the taxpayer £6bn. A Select Committee criticised the last Tory Government and its civil servants. The Treasury raised £2bn from the sale. Railtrack's share value quadrupled to £8bn. Government made the mistake of selling 100% of the shares in one sale, instead of testing the market value by selling them in stages. Advisors said that it was the first time a Government had sold a company dependent on a subsidy of around £1.8bn a year. (Public Accounts Committee Report No 24, 1999).

Government claimed it cut the subsidy paid to BR, by offsetting against subsidies, capital from the sale of rolling stock companies. This seems to be the classic error of mixing capital and revenue. They had stopped BR from leasing stock in 1971, or there would have been less stock to sell.

The Institute of Directors said that "3,000 miles of branch lines should be closed, diverting subsidies to main lines". Audited BR Accounts show that InterCity received no subsidy from 1988, and NSE none in the year before privatisation. Only rural and provincial commuter routes had subsidies. Had 3,000 miles of branch lines not existed, BR would have had no subsidy. In the last year under BR, Government - without precedent - changed the basis and doubled the subsidy. No main lines should have had a subsidy! The SRA said some [subsidised] services are of "dubious economic value", (Policy Statement, Page 9), signalling an intention to close them. Clearly the goalposts have been moved. BR, with a lower subsidy, was directed not to reduce the system (see page 34).

A Minister stated (BBC TV, 11.5.03) that Government gives railways £73m per week - equating to £3.8 billion pa. This is more than *double* the inflated subsidy which Government paid during BR's last year, having *doubled* the previous year's subsidy solely because of fragmentation. (see page 183). An ex-Minister had forecast it would be one third of the BR subsidy by 2003. (Economist 21.9.96).

The SRA issued a Franchising Policy Statement which shows that the subsidy has been above the contracted figure from 1998 onwards, and whereas it was reducing, but not to the extent planned, after 2001, it began to rise. It had fallen to a low of about £1300m - still way above the realistic BR 1993/4 subsidy of £930m - before rising by about 25% above the original forecast for 2002.

One Chief Executive said that the days of declining subsidies are over. (Daily Telegraph 12.7.03). A claim that some companies are now "paying a premium" is nonsense. Those that had a subsidy for 5-6 years will not be paying a premium, until they have repaid subsidies plus interest.

In December 2002, the Scottish Executive announced an investment package for ScotRail, for 22 three-car trains, estimated to be worth £70m of taxpayers' money. New rolling stock was supposed to be funded by the private sector! In July 2003, the SRA said that huge increases in subsidy were to deliver real improvements: reliability, new or *refurbished* cleaner trains. The MoT said in 1993, that these improvements - and more - would arise from privatisation and with declining subsidies!

How subsidies could have been avoided

Had fares kept pace with the RPI from 1948 to 1994, BR would have earned, at 1994 prices, an extra **£11.8 bn**, (see Appendix A). Sales resistance may have reduced the yield, although, the Tribunal thought the BTC pessimistic in expecting a 1% loss of yield. Deducting 1% - the much trumpeted margin by which fares are *supposed* to be held below inflation in the privatised era - cuts the loss to £11.6 bn. When BR obtained statutory freedom after 1968 and were occasionally permitted *real* fare rises, independent reports showed that resistance was short lived, (see page 95), despite increasing competition. Losses were escalated by delays in the procedure. (see Appendix B). Add compound interest, and little imagination is required to see how much improvement to services and revenue would have been generated by such an enormous sum. In addition to these BR fares losses, the BTC lost on LT fares for similar reasons. There were no front page protests that BR had not kept to the rate of inflation from 1948. In 2003, the SRA announced that even its cap of 1% below inflation on Seasons is to be dropped, and replaced by 1% above inflation! Most fares were not capped anyway.

In July 1992, the MoT said on BBC TV, that, unlike road transport, BR pay no taxes. Acts did not require BR to make a profit, but to break even, and not even that 1948-62, when it was the BTC -

not its subsidiaries - that was required to break even. Indeed, the Cabinet decided that BR should not be required to cover all its costs from revenue. It could not therefore be in a position to pay taxes! Even after 1962, Government policy never allowed BR to earn profits from which to pay tax.

Subsidies would have been avoided, had infrastructure been funded by Government as advocated by the LNER and BRB, (see page 38). Had BR paid fuel duty and road tax licences, they would have saved by laying up vehicles in a recession - as hauliers do. As it is impractical to make a fair assessment of such a saving, it is appropriate to use pre-recession data, hence, costs are based on 1989/90.

1. **Vehicle Excise Duty** - on similar basis to road transport	£m pa
Locos, freight & parcels: 901 at £3,100 each pa - the top scale for road tractive units	2.79
Locos, passenger: duty levied on seating capacity of coaches, as for road transport	0.00
Wagons: 21,970 at £355 each pa - as for road trailers	7.80
Non passenger carrying vehicles: 1,319 at £355 each pa	0.47
Passenger coaches, on the same basis as PSVs	
- 9,606 coaches with 60 or more seats at £450 each pa	4.32
- 2,879 coaches with less than 60 seats at £300 each pa	0.86
Deduct licences surrendered when "off the road", in main works undergoing major maintenance & repairs - estimated 10%	-1.62
Total vehicle licences	14.62
2. **Duty on diesel fuel**	
Gas oil for traction was 628.5m litres pa. 17.5% of locos are on track maintenance or depot duties. The former would be debited to infrastructure costs. Fuel used in depot duties is analogous to unlicensed road vehicles on depot work that pay gas oil duty. In 1989/90, duty on derv was 19.02p and gas oil 1.18p per litre = 17.84p more per litre. Dutiable fuel would be 628.5m litres less 17.5% = 518.5m litres costing 17.84p more.	92.50
Total licences & duty	107.12
3. **Infrastructure costs, 1989/90**	
To be funded by Government (Costs shown in BRB 1989/90 Report, Page 41)	758.60
Deduct Government Grant or "Subsidy", (BRB 1989/90 Report, Page 1)	-500.80
Deduct Duty to be paid by BR (see above)	-107.12
Net BR Profit on which taxes would then be levied	150.68
Table 14 - Devised by the Author. Data sources: BRB Annual Report 1989/90; HM Customs & Excise	

Had infrastructure been financed thus from 1948, no subsidy would have been paid. In addition to annual profits therefrom, (see above), had charges matched inflation, it would have produced over £11 bn more in fares, (see Appendix A) and cut freight losses (see Table 12). With commercial freedom, many loss making routes would have been quickly closed or pruned, and others retained by pricing up - standard private sector practice. It would have been for others to fund unprofitable services for strategic, social or political reasons. BR would have had huge reserves. Taxes would have been paid

"The BR solution was to seek support for the infrastructure over which they, in most cases would run passenger and freight services on a commercial basis. Both outgoing and incoming Governments rejected this in favour of a totally supported passenger railway with commercial freight superimposed on the passenger system". (BRB 1974 Report, Page 4). Under the BR plan, instead of grants for loss making lines, Government would pay for rail infrastructure, as they did for road. As a result, Government, not BR, would fund bridges required for road transport. (see "*Square Deal Denied*").

Dr. Joy argued that a Rail Track Authority would not be doing its job if it did not close surplus capacity. (Joy Page 106). In contrast, the Highways Authority does not close roads when motorways are built, despite the fact that there are 22 times as much road mileage - perhaps 80 times as much acreage - for ten times as much traffic. At best, they turn them into lay-bys: parking areas for lorries.

Chapter 16   Safety

"Safety" in railway terms has two meanings: "safety of the line" - operating a railway that is made as safe as is humanly possible, and "personal safety" which relates to the safety of all staff - not merely those on the track. On BR, the former was part of the documented duty of thousands of managers and staff in operating and engineering functions. Other managers and staff, who did not have a documented safety role, were expected to draw attention to any potential hazard that they encountered that *may* jeopardise safety. "Safety is and always will be the first priority in the management and operation of the railway. Nothing in the system of financing or selecting investment gets in the way of this prime objective". (BRB 1988/9 Report, Page 8). "The importance attached to safety is underlined by the decision to withdraw all 42 of class 155 multiple units for modification after a fault was found with the door mechanism on one door". (BRB 1988/9 Report, Page 16).

100% safety target for BR only

Governments were obsessed that railways - and only railways - should be 100% safe. Road carnage was 500 times - and is now about 400 times as great - but the spotlight rarely wavered from BR, an Everest of safety among anthills, but required to spend ever more to produce marginal improvements. Had Government made clear that it would fund such enhancements, all well and good. However, their role was confined to the touchlines - seeing the solution as something to be financed internally, whilst blocking any measures to provide the means to finance it. BR practices which may have seemed restrictive ensured higher standards of safety.

Following fatalities in a 1986 motorway coach crash, an operator said that seat belts would be too costly! In 1993, two disasters led to calls for seat belts. It was *1998* when regulations were imposed to provide belts in *some* vehicles. Even where they are provided, there is no requirement for drivers to ensure that they are worn. Airlines would not introduce smoke hoods. Ferry companies decried the need for measures to prevent capsizing and prevent hundreds of deaths. Road competitors should be compelled to catch up on BR standards: effective speeding checks, brakes actuated by traffic lights and deadman's pedals. If these are impractical, cabs should be double manned instead of relying on children to wrestle with the wheel when a coach driver collapses or falls asleep. Roads would be much safer if the principles of separation of dangerous consignments, as practised on railways, (see page 193), was transmitted into road practice and law. In addition, vehicles carrying hazardous goods should park when roads are affected by fog, snow or ice. Roads would be safer if HGV and PSV drivers were prevented from driving excessive hours. On a TV programme about the Selby collision, HGV drivers *admitted* to driving when over-tired. Had Selby occurred in the BR era, there would have been demands for BR to provide safety barriers without delay. Now that railways are privatised, barriers are seen as a taxpayer' responsibility. Without doubt, equal treatment on safety matters would have led to a transfer of traffic from road to rail.

In 1967, the MoT Paper "*Public Transport and Traffic*" examined PSV drivers' hours. "Legal limits on hours of PSV drivers have been unaltered since the 1930s[1]. The maximum length of the working day will be reduced from 14 to 11, except stage services which may spread 11 hours work over $12^1/_2$ hours; not more than 9 hours at the wheel. The rest period before work will be increased from 10 to 11. On one day per week, it may be $9^1/_2$ instead of the present eight hours. There will not be more than 60 hours per week. Many bus and coach drivers are working hours substantially in excess of these limits". (Cmnd 3481, Pages, 23-24). *Even the proposed hours were unsafe*. In comparison, BR drivers, signalmen and others had an 8 hour day, with a 12 hour rest period since 1919.

The 1967 White Paper "*Transport of Freight*", (Cmnd 3470, Appendix 2), proposed a working day for an HGV driver be cut from 14 to 11 hours with not more than 9 at the wheel - 11 hitherto - and 60 hours per week.

---

[1] Prior to that there was no legal limit whatsoever to the hours of drivers of road passenger and goods transport.

The 1968 Transport Act was less severe, reducing hours at the wheel to 10, with a $12^1/_2$ hour working day for an HGV or PSV driver - 50% longer than Government enforced on railways - for *all* railway staff, not merely drivers - *49 years earlier*, (see page 5). If road drivers' hours had also been limited to eight hours per day and comparable safety conditions imposed, road transport costs would rise significantly, and rail would be more competitive. With competitors:

- allowed longer working hours by law,
- overloading their vehicles and exceeding statutory speed limits;
- using vehicles whose cost is kept low by a lack of safety devices similar to BR's;
- able to cut costs in recessions by de-licensing, suspending insurance, and laying off drivers, whose training period is a fraction of that of BR drivers; it is no surprise that BR lost so much traffic[2].

In 1976-7, a Select Committee stated: "One argument about competition is that Government is not taking an impartial attitude towards European Economic Community Regulations in respect of road and rail freight. It is phasing out rail subsidies and not implementing regulations on drivers hours and tachographs. The Secretary of State saw neither as affecting competition"! (Report Pages 72,73).

If the hours of haulage drivers were cut to rail levels, they would need 50% more drivers, who would want higher basic wage levels than tolerated now, to compensate for lost overtime. These, plus add-ons: national health, administration costs, would increase hauliers' costs. (see page 162). Perhaps, now that the beneficiaries are in the private sector, Ministers may be brave enough to act.

BR managers welcomed practical developments to make railways more safe and did not need politicians nor others - who would not know where to *begin* to tackle rail safety - to pressure them to take action. In my day, the current concept of having a target of an *acceptable* level of fatalities of passengers or staff, was unthinkable - and it remains unthinkable in retirement. BR's target was zero. Government has been far too complacent and have turned the blind eye for too long to the serious and well-known malpractices in competing road transport. The legally permitted working hours of professional drivers is insanely excessive - and even these are exceeded. No self respecting BR manager would have allowed train drivers nor other rail staff in the front line of safety to work as long, and with as little off duty rest between shifts, as the road industry has tolerated for 80 years. If a BR manager ignored or condoned such practices, he would - on inevitable discovery or leak - be looking in some other industry for employment. Of that, there is *no* doubt! Moreover, it is significant that among the first questions in an inquiry into a rail accident - first by BR managers and then by the HMRI - were the length of time staff involved had been on duty, the period of rest before duty, and data covering hours on duty and rest periods during preceding days and weeks.

Extensive reports of rare rail accidents made no comparison with road fatalities, which were 400 times as great, despite the comment in November 1988, by a Tory MoT that there are "*three Clapham[3] accidents on the roads every week*". Ultra brief reports on fatal road accidents were on inside pages, whilst non fatal rail accidents were on front pages. Rail accidents were called *disasters*, road disasters were *tragic accidents*.

In January 1991 the Daily Telegraph had 578 col. cms on the Cannon Street crash, in which one fatality was reported, and 5 col. cms for an M4 crash which killed five - 500 times as much per fatality. They listed rail accidents from 1952: 294 fatalities equal to eight pa - but did not compare them to thousands killed *annually* on roads - and the age of railway coaches, "which had twice per week examinations". I wrote pointing out that the M4 disaster, by comparison, warranted 2,890 column cms. In road accidents neither the frequency of examinations - *annually* after the first three years for cars, nor the age of vehicles, nor car maintenance which has been found seriously

---

[2] Unlike BR, hauliers also had uncontrolled pricing freedom, and were empowered to refuse unprofitable traffic.

[3] The last accident comparable with Clapham was 20 years ago. The basic cause was quickly established as a wiring fault during re-signalling work - checks were made throughout BR immediately. (BRB 1988/9 Report, Page 8). BR's Chairman immediately accepted responsibility and undertook to pay compensation - in contrast to current practice.

wanting by consumer surveys[4], are mentioned. When they did not publish the letter, I wrote to the Press Complaints Commission. They informed the Telegraph, who wrote that they *"did not think the coverage excessive given the particularly public circumstances and the very great number of commuters involved, although fortunately the death toll was very small"*.

Is there no interest in road deaths? If as much prominence was given to road, as to rail accidents, some effective action may follow. Whilst many were injured, doubtless they were happier being injured than killed in a road accident. The death toll was low because of the strength of rail vehicles, as is usually the case. For example, in September 1986, a 100mph train collided at Colwich[5] near Stafford, with another, causing one fatality - a BR driver. A similar collision on roads leaves scores dead. Commuters were delayed by the Cannon Street accident, but no one establishes road commuter delays, which are much greater, e.g.: the BBC reported (15.9.51), an overturned lorry - a common occurrence - blocking the M4 for nine hours. Delays, which must have been horrendous, were not revealed. In November 1993, a Daily Telegraph report devoted 581 col. cms to the M40 disaster, 48 col. cms per fatality, whilst on 23rd December 1993, they reported, in four col. cms, three killed in a crash when an articulated lorry crossed the central reservation on the M5.

Now, all is changed. The media has highlighted that road safety standards are far worse than rail, despite attempts by the road lobby to distort the statistics. This comparison is not due to rail safety being better than it was under BR, because it is worse. (see pages 195-197).

That professional drivers tamper with safety devices[6], or wedge an accelerator to save leg strain is an abuse of the word *professional*. The discovery of anything similar on railways would have seen the offender suspended immediately, and facing a disciplinary hearing accompanied by a union official or fellow employee, neither of whom would condone the malpractice and have no defence against removal from driving. That, managers of haulage drivers should be failing to carry out checks to prevent such malpractices is reprehensible - yet there must have been failures. That road transport vehicles are permitted to take to the road with faulty brakes and badly worn tyres - whose evidence litters our roadsides - is a sign that the industry is less alert to safety risks. Analogous material on tracksides would lead to rigorous investigation. Some drivers do not even stop after losing a tyre. (see *"Blueprints for Bankruptcy"*, Page 86).

It is reprehensible that company employees drive in such a way as to put others at risk - excessive hours and speeds and without the skill to spot defects. Yet this is a major factor in the competitiveness of a car. It is obvious that distances of which many boast, cannot be covered except by taking risks with their own lives - for which managers have a duty at law - and lives of other road users. Such practices are an indictment and disqualifies them to be called *managers*. Their disinterest contrasts with BR managers pro-active attitude. For instance, in the early days of seat belts, when use was widely ignored and not a legal requirement, it was made clear to Stoke Division Operating staff authorised to drive BR cars, that anyone who did not use a belt would have authority withdrawn, which, if use of a car was essential to carry out their duties, would result in loss of job!

In 1946, the MoT stated that the provision of guard rails between front and rear lorry wheels had been fully reviewed in 1938 by the Transport Advisory Council which said that they were not likely to contribute to safety. (Hansard, vol. 218 col. 181).They did not become mandatory on articulated vehicles until 1983; and even later, on rigid vehicles! Provision had been recommended as early as 1919. (see *"Square Deal Denied"*, Page 60).

---

[4] A recent newspaper report states that 86% of garage servicing is inferior.

[5] A flyover at this location in the 1955 Plan was cancelled by MoT directive to cut spending on modernisation, for which BR, not the MoT was paying. The compensation cost of the fatality, plus costs of breakdown and engineering staff attending this one accident, and costs of repairing tracks and rolling stock would, coupled with train delay costs have gone some way towards paying for the flyover.

[6] The scope for tampering is confirmed by a Report: "The digital tachograph will make it more difficult to cheat the system". (Institute of Logistics & Transport, Freight Transport newsletter 2002). NB -"more difficult", not impossible!

No time limit was placed on alterations to ships, aircraft, or motor vehicles despite heavier fatalities. Replying to calls for seat belt law in July 1994, a Minister said that hundreds of thousands are conveyed safely in mini buses, and after a RoRo catastrophe, that 40m passengers are carried safely each year across the Channel. Safety improvements at sea called for in 1990 were not expected to be implemented until 2000[7], yet experts said they were inadequate. BR conveyed 790m safely each year, but this did not prevent calls for action to prevent rare fatalities. Government's intention to limit coach speeds produced protests because "coaches will share lanes with lorries", but lorries do not have separate lanes. A media report in December 1994 said: "Limiters on PSVs will operate in a similar way to existing restrictions on lorries, which are fitted with limiters". In other words, a non event. Limiters cannot prevent limits below 60 mph being exceeded. Whilst rail drivers were subject to speed checks by hidden cameras and other equipment, road users have to be given warnings of cameras! Occasional overspeeding by BR drivers was usually due to an error, rather than a deliberate act as applies on roads. BR drivers did not have the advantage of illuminated speed restriction signs, except for temporary speed restrictions. The more widespread permanent speed restrictions are not illuminated - the driver has to memorise their location - and yet can keep to speed limits.

"Laws covering railwaymen under the influence of alcohol and drugs should be brought into line with road. ("WHICH?" June 1986). *Any* BR employee, especially train drivers, signalmen, etc., have an alcohol and drug limit which is **zero**; contravention risks loss of job. Road transport should adopt BR's zero limit. Government has rejected a recommendation to cut alcohol limits on motorists.

In 1990-94, under the motor industry's voluntary recall system, 3.6m vehicles were recalled for rectification of problems - an average of 720,000 pa, or about 3% of cars on the road. *("Vehicle Safety Bulletin"* published by the MoT Vehicle Inspectorate Executive Agency). 3% of dissatisfied motorists compares unfavourably with 0.009% dissatisfied railway passengers. (see page 105). A motor industry spokesman said on radio on 26th June 2001, that now they have improved safety of car occupants, they will improve design to reduce pedestrian fatalities. These two aspects of safety did not have to be addressed consecutively, but could, and should have been addressed simultaneously.

Research carried out by the Metropolitan Transport Research Unit, and Earth Resources Research was published by Transport 2000 in its 1993 Report, *"Taming the Truck"*: "HGVs are substantially more dangerous than cars in relation to fatalities - per mile travelled, lorries are up to eight times more likely to be involved in fatal accidents". The Report drew attention to risks of damage to underground services, particularly gas, where serious explosions can occur. "One lorry does as much damage to the roads as 10,000 cars. They also bash bridges (see page 102), and damage services such as gas mains. Spot checks on motorways showed up to 24% of lorries were overloaded. Lorries produce diesel particulates, which can cause or worsen bronchitis and asthma. They produce a quarter of all UK emissions, which contribute to urban smog, acid rain and global warming. On some main roads it is more common for HGVs to break the speed limit than to comply with it".

HGVs cause accidents in rain with a Niagara like spray, which ought to have been resolved by manufacturers, long ago. They intimidate motorists by inadequate braking distance and pull out as cars are alongside. All open lorries should be sheeted to prevent material falling off and after unloading, thoroughly cleaned to avoid broken windscreens and ensuing accidents.

To show that air travel is safer than rail, distance travelled per fatality, on *scheduled* services - excluding Charter flights - has been compared by the air industry to *all* rail travel - which includes *excursion and charter travel*. Life expectancy is based on time, not distance; on three score and ten years, not three score and ten thousand miles. Moreover, it is evident that the greatest dangers are on take-off, when zero miles have been travelled. Books on air safety by Laurie Taylor, Stanley Stewart, Michael Prince; and a report on the Comet, (Channel 4, 13.6.02), present a worrying picture.

---

[7] SOLAS 90 - "Safety at Sea 1990". Despite inquiries at the DoT and elsewhere, it has not been possible to ascertain whether even these modest measures have been 100% implemented.

Safety of the Line

Before taking up an appointment as station master [later Area Manager], inspector, supervisor, signalman, guard, etc., a selected person was examined in his/her knowledge of Rules & Regulations - instructions relating to safe operation of the line - not, as some Ministers appeared to believe, a union Rule Book of demarcation practices. Staff who failed to pass did not get the job, as it was essential that they could implement safe procedures instantaneously, without reference to a book. They were re-examined annually, or in some cases, biennially. Failure to pass meant loss of job[8].

HMRI[9] 1948 Report on safety, stated that "two major accidents would not have occurred with modern signalling, which but for the war would now be in operation". Shortage of materials and labour have resulted in a further deterioration in safety. For ten years after the war, railways were denied authority to order materials - especially steel[10] - in quantities required to restore railway infrastructure and rolling stock to pre-war standards, much less to modern standards arising from advances in knowledge. The motor industry was able to acquire such materials in excess of quantities prescribed by Government economic plans. (see pages 54,55). That industry repaid Government's "blind eye" by losing the post-war export race, due to the inferior quality and over-pricing of cars.

Four elements of railway modernisation that did most to improve safety from 1955 onwards, were:
- Improved signalling, including extensive colour lights, track circuits and warning systems.
- Renewal of track as continuous welded rail, with improved quality steels.
- Modern steel construction coaches capable of withstanding collisions.
- Mechanised track maintenance.

The delay in progressing these improvements undoubtedly contributed to many serious accidents. It is a matter of record that fatalities in rail accidents were less if steel coaches were involved. Pre-war Governments, by favouring road transport at the expense of railway viability (see "*Square Deal Denied*"), ensured that railways lacked the capital required for large scale modernisation. Post-war Governments maintained the same policy towards BR. In the years 1948-51, due to Government restraint, BR built 50% fewer coaches than planned (see page 53), to make up for 4,000 destroyed or worn out in the war, and to replace life expired coaches. In 1952, there occurred the worst railway accident in BR history - which remained the worst. At Harrow & Wealdstone, 112 people were killed in a collision, ten died later of injuries. It occurred in thick fog, and the recorded cause was that a driver passed a distant signal at caution [a warning], followed by two semaphore stop signals at danger and ran into a stationary commuter train of nine wooden coaches, carrying 800 passengers. A third train from the opposite direction ran into the wreckage almost immediately before it could be stopped. The MoT's Inspecting Officer "praised the way that the coaches of the third train, *which were all of steel construction* had stood up to the shock". It was the worst accident since 1915. There can be no doubt, that had BR been allowed sufficient steel by Government to replace this old rolling stock, the casualty list would have been much lower. There can be no doubt that had all signals been colour light, the driver's view would have been better. Had lines been track circuited, the signalman would have been aware that the train was not stopping, and may have been able to take protective action. Track circuits would automatically have reversed signals to danger, when derailed vehicles fell on to the track of the approaching third train. When BR was allowed to begin investing its own money in modernisation, colour lights contributed hugely to improved safety.

On these two counts - delays to replacement of old rolling stock and signals - the Government stand indicted. Had BR or unions employed lawyers, as applies in the current regime, the driver might have been, at least, partially exonerated. The Harrow accident pressured Government into allowing BR to obtain - with their own money - essential materials and commission new equipment to improve safety. Among these was a system of Automatic Train Control, later termed AWS

---

[8] e.g. During my time at Rugby, a station master was removed and demoted to a clerk for failing re-examination.
[9] HMRI - Her Majesty's Railway Inspectorate - were known as the MoT's Railway Inspectorate until the 1990s
[10] The supply of steel was subject to licence control by Government 1939-50, but supplies to BR were cut until 1955.

[Automatic Warning System], on which they had been working since 1948. It differed from the existing GWR system, in that it could be used on third rail routes. It is certain that its introduction reduced rail fatalities and injuries. "After lengthy experience over 105 route miles, BR has obtained the approval of the MoT, and it is now to go ahead. The cost of £20m had been included in the [1955] Modernisation Plan". (BTC 1957 Report, Page 28).

The general trend of rail accidents has been steadily downwards - before nationalisation and during BR days. Despite claims to the contrary, the years since privatisation reveal a worse record. (see Appendix D). It is completely illogical to go far back to make comparisons - usually to the Harrow & Wealdstone accident in 1952 - before multiple aspect colour lights and the automatic warning system, before disc brakes and sundry other improvements. But then, logic has no place when trying to prove that the private sector is safer than the public sector.

Improved safety did not arise as a result of chance or some benign influence. It came about because most staff were acutely alive to their duty to maintain and operate a safe railway, because managers, supervisors and Inspectors - operating, signalling, track, etc. - monitored day-to-day activity. Many of those with these skills found that they were no longer needed after 1995. Belatedly, some steps are being taken to re-recruit such people. (see page 47). The need for human supervision of human conduct did not cease with modern equipment and techniques. Computers fail, signals fail - because the private sector has yet to invent 100% reliable equipment. At such times, the human hand has to act alone, and then the need to monitor is vital. Our experience showed that one had to be pro-active with safety - looking ahead for the risk areas, not acting after accidents. The time of greatest risk is when equipment fails, and train control reverts to the human.

Station Masters [SMs] had a vital safety role. Their duties included visiting signalboxes within a mile daily and others weekly; and out-of-hours visits to all boxes monthly. The purpose was to ensure that the box was worked safely. The objective would be foiled if he had to seek permission to enter[11]. As an SM, and in senior positions, I entered hundreds and *never* asked permission. Had I, as a Divisional Officer, found that an SM was doing so, he would have been found a job suited to his limited competence. When someone acted as Pilotman in single line working, no train could enter a line without his permission, and he was *required* to enter a box for that purpose. Others had *right of entry* to carry out duties specified in the [Safety] Rules Book, e.g. traincrew, inspectors, technicians. SMs were also required to visit level crossings regularly to ensure that they were operated safely.

From time immemorial, Joint Inquiries[12] were held by railway managers from the Operating and such Engineering Departments as were involved. At these Inquiries, no union official, much less a lawyer - both of whom figure prominently now and advise involved employees which questions they may answer - were present. Call-outs to accidents were initiated by the Control Office[13] based on a list which began with the On-Call Operating manager, who would check on actions being taken, and go to the site where he would assume the role of Mishap Controller. As "Safety of the line", and particularly keeping trains apart, was primarily an Operating responsibility, all at the site would work under his control. With cranes, machines and engineering trains and hundreds of staff on site, care was necessary to organise work areas to avoid the risk of another accident, and restrict the approach of other trains. He would ascertain the cause, and forecast when a line would open for trains, facilitating information to the public. Lawyers, accountants, insurance loss adjusters were not called out - as seems important now. There was no question of having police, lawyers or insurance adjusters second guessing the cause and its *parochial* implications. Preliminary advice would be given as soon as possible, throughout BR on any unusual or newly experienced cause. Whether the cause was an Operating or Engineering one, there was no parochial attempt to delay this crucial advice. A full Joint Inquiry Report would be made, within days, by the District or Division to

---

[11] "Not even the Station Master would enter without permission". ("*Scenes from a signalbox*", Page 57).

[12] As a trainee in 1954, the Author attended one and in 1961, chaired his first Joint Inquiry.

[13] Fragmentation of Control (see pages 38,46), has contributed to fatalities and delayed restoration of services.

Region, Board and Ministry, with verbatim evidence of all witnesses and an *agreed* conclusion between those who conducted the Inquiry. HMRI conducted their own Inquiry, in public, within a week or two. They had powers to require attendance of BR and non-railway persons whose evidence may be germane. Any recommendations, although these might simply reiterate what BR had already implemented, followed quickly, although publication of the HMRI Report may not be immediate.

Whilst it was important to be re-active following accidents and quickly disseminate information on causes to prevent recurrence elsewhere, it was more important to be *pro-active*. During public trials, the APT tilt system sometimes failed, and had to be isolated because of the discomfort factor, limiting trains to line speed - then 100 mph. In December 1980[14], I was told that the APT was having *two* types of tilt failure. The aforementioned was a "soft" failure, when it failed to tilt where it should. The new variety - a "hard" failure - was when a train tilted where no tilt was required. This appeared to pose a risk of a train, with such a failure, striking a train on an adjoining line. I called a meeting and asked which sections of the route might pose a risk. The Chief Civil Engineer would not clear any section of line, and said that the whole route must be treated as posing a hazard if a train had a "hard" tilt failure. He said that, pending investigation, the APT would need to be treated as out-of-gauge and other trains not allowed to pass, when the APT was running through junctions or connections. That was not a practical option. In view of the risk, I directed that, until the problem was resolved, the train must run with tilt isolated, and hence, at line speed. It was not a popular decision, but pro-active action is the best way to avoid fatalities. There were critics - none of whom would share responsibility for safety on the Region if the worst happened. The decision received the full support of the General Manager of the London Midland Region.

In 1970, the functions involved in investigating accidents - operating and engineering - were offered assistance by BR's Derby based R&D department. "Site assistance by R&D staff was given at all the more serious incidents to enable the cause of derailments to be pinpointed more quickly". (BRB 1970 Report, Page 50). Initially, some doubted the need for their help. Despite having investigated derailments since 1961, I was among the first to call for their help with an unusual plain line derailment in 1970. They had particular skills - including engineering - and had been amassing considerable trend data from Accident Reports. In contrast, no help was sought from the BT Police - as evolved after my retirement - since they had *no* data and *no* experience. To glean from a TV programme that a police officer had been given instruction in the operation of AWS so that he could conduct the Southall investigation was unbelievable. Any Operating Department manager or inspector who did not understand AWS, signalling and related operations, and failed to get a line re-opened quickly, would have been found a post suited to his limited talents. Managers had wondered whom the police would call on to test a train's brakes, had it been held for examination after hitting a person on the line - which they usually weren't, having gone on its way unknowingly. The role of police at rail accidents has *seriously* delayed resumption of services. Noticeably, such prolonged delays do not follow road accidents. The R&D Department was abolished after privatisation..

Fragmentation and the dismissal of experienced managers and engineers, has led to the creation of a new body to investigate accidents. Government is setting up a "new Rail Accident Investigation Branch to ensure that remedial action is taken as soon as possible". (Hansard, 28.1.03, vol. 398, col. 764). Prior to privatisation, there was no problem. The face saving excuse, is that "unlike air and marine accidents, there is no one body for railways, whose sole responsibility was to find out quickly what went wrong". As one whose duties included such a role, the fulfilment of which was never subject to criticism - internal nor external - we found causes, mostly, within hours. To put forward *marine* accident investigation as an example is not justified by post-*Herald of Free Enterprise* culture. Nor is *air* accident investigation an example in view of inaction on post-Ringway smoke-hoods. BR managers were never impressed with what seemed to happen after air accidents - a haste to exclude causes before an Inquiry began: "it cannot be the aircraft/pilot/maintenance/air

---

[14] The APT had been derailed at 125 mph eight months earlier, when bolts securing some wheels sheared off.

traffic control, etc". BR managers neither identified a cause, nor excluded one, before investigations were complete - often to the annoyance of reporters.

BR Chairman Reid accepted BR's legal liability at once, and did not try to avoid responsibility for the Clapham accident. (Daily Telegraph Obituary 18.12.93).This is in sharp contrast to current practice.

When TOPS was being introduced to monitor and control freight traffic, a Divisional Operating Manager was required - "as a front line Operator" - to address the well-run supervisors' training courses on the use of TOPS. As the Training School for all BR supervisors was located at Crewe, which was within the Stoke Division - the task fell to me. The theory was that a talk on the benefits of TOPS to operating staff, would be more readily accepted from such managers, rather than those running the courses, although they would have got the same message over. More probably, it was to let the supervisors hear a different voice than those of Jack Jones and his instructors, who were all career railwaymen of considerable practical experience. A valuable contribution to safety, that had not been considered, occurred to me and without prior authority, was included in the talk. The make up of freight trains was a complex exercise, requiring guards to ensure that:

- train loads did not exceed those permitted over a route nor the power of the allocated loco,
- there was sufficient wagon brake power to assist the diesel or electric loco on falling gradients,
- many other conditions were observed, including the quantity of explosives on a train,
- a load of steel bars was not next to an oil or chemical tanker,
- explosives were not with flammable liquids[15], and so on.

These conditions were in the Working Manual, Freight Train Loading Guide, Handling of Dangerous Goods and Freight Train Loads Books - which guards were required to learn. They were examined annually on their knowledge of these books and on safety Rules, etc. It was onerous, and no BR critics would have been comfortable with the task. Computer printed train consists were planned as part of TOPS to show the actual weight and braking power of a train. If TOPS was also loaded with this data, and included in the consists, it would cut the risk of human error. The enhancement would include *maximum* permitted weight/length/braking of the allocated loco and all details affecting train safety, so that the train would conform to all freight instructions. The idea was adopted.

The CTCC is alarmed that the cost of new safety standards for platforms may cause closures, and approached the HMRI who will adopt a flexible attitude. (CTCC 1990/1 Report, Page 12). *Former managers with safety responsibilities were amazed. Who would be responsible if a passenger was injured or killed by deferring improvements? The CTCC was putting a lower priority on safety.*

In May 1992 - after the decision was made to privatise - BR was directed by the MoT to fit locks within *six months*[16] to all slam doors, to resolve complaints that coach handles *may* have caused deaths. This loaded accounts with these costs. "Locks will cost £16.5m". [RailNews June 1992]. The benefit accrues to privatised railways which claim credit for reduced fatalities of passengers falling from trains. They also gained from paying less compensation. "An H&SE investigation found that most falls from trains showed that alcohol or misbehaviour was a factor in one degree or another". (BRB 1990/1 Report, Page 7). In 1992, the Executive confirmed that alcohol and misbehaviour *were significant factors*. (BRB 1992/3 Report, Page 9). BRB Annual Reports chart the progress:

- 1991/2: Work began on a locking system that automatically locks doors when a train reaches 9 mph. It is planned to replace slam door coaches [by new coaches with power controlled doors] on Kent Link trains by 1993.
- 1992/3: Secondary locks are being fitted on InterCity slam-door trains over the next three years, ensuring that doors can only be opened when a train is at a station. Elsewhere on BR, trains with

---

[15] The juxtaposition of such loads on roads is commonplace, and it is a common practice for them to drive with inadequate braking distance. Roads would become safer, if authorities took preventative action.

[16] Hauliers should be given six months notice to resolve unsafe practices. (see pages 186-189).

power operated doors will have replaced 35% of the slam door fleet by 1995, and modified locks are being developed for the remaining units.

- 1993/4: Secondary locking fitted to all InterCity slam door rolling stock will be completed in 1996
- 1994/5: We are now seeing the benefit of fitting locks to slam-door stock. Since 1992, a programme for fitting locks to slam-door stock is virtually complete [on InterCity stock]. Falls from trains reduced to seven pa, compared to twenty-four in 1990/1.

The task was well advanced by 1994/5, so that the newcomers can claim credit for fewer deaths, without spending a penny. Door locks improve punctuality, as departures will not be delayed by passengers arriving at the last second, and opening the door of a moving train, which then has to be stopped for safety checks. Again, the private sector will get the brownie points.

Three other developments took place in the years preceding privatisation that would enhance the safety of the line: radios in cabs, black boxes and cab simulators. All will benefit privatised railways - improving safety and cutting training costs - without spending a penny. They can bask in the glory of the benefit of measures begun or decisions taken before their organisations even existed.

Again BRB Annual Reports chart the progress:

- 1988/9: Fitting data recorders on all NSE commuter trains. Fitting radios to cabs to enable drivers to contact signalmen. Cab simulators were designed and constructed to improve driver training.
- 1989/90: The work of fitting radios to locos is almost complete and it is planned to complete the programme for all traction units within five years.
- 1990/1: Radios have been fitted to all InterCity locos and 60% of freight locos; all traction units to be equipped by 1995. Fitting of black box data recorders into all new and recently built trains has begun. Black box data recorders are proving useful in expediting maintenance
- 1991/2: Over 5,000 train based mobile radios enable InterCity and Freight drivers to contact control centres. It is intended to equip all trains by 1995.

BR costs were increased by level crossing improvements to cut accidents caused by motorists and pedestrians, (see pages 66,67,129). In contrast, provision of safe pedestrian road crossings is based on a restrictive formula[17], which means that local demands for crossings are often dismissed as being outside the criteria. The phobia about modern level crossings is impossible to comprehend since independent reports show they are safer than manned crossings. Some fear "automatic signals", the like of which have been used on roads since 1930. No one can deny that rail crossing safety is light years ahead of road crossings, where it seems that one in ten disregard red lights. (Road survey 2003). Critics must believe that one will be dead longer if hit by a train instead of a car. Some may have hoped that level crossings would be replaced by bridges at BR expense, ignoring that the mass of road traffic arose after railways were built - by 100 years or so. Any logical person would concede that those who created the problem - motor vehicle owners - should pay for the solution.

To give access between fields, some farms have "Accommodation" level crossings, at which accidents occur when users do not carry out operating instructions, leading to collisions and delay or cancellation of trains. At similar - "Occupation" - crossings giving access to a few houses, some residents fail to close gates or lower barriers, in accordance with notices displayed at the crossings, leading to others crossing without stopping and looking both ways. BR staff checked crossings when in the locality, closing them if open, recording in a signal box train register book, details of any found open, and writing to offenders. In the event of an accident, the standard excuse was to claim equipment was faulty. By creating a record of malpractice, BR was able to pre-empt that excuse.

In 1966, in a typical scenario, BR proposed to convert two manned crossings into Open Crossings on the very lightly used Haltwhistle-Alston line. This type of crossing had been in use in Europe and the USA for decades! Trains would stop at a distance from them. "Halt" signs would be placed on

---

[17] The road lobby claims there are more deaths because of the pedestrian-vehicle interface. It can be resolved by fencing and automatic barriers - the cost borne by vehicle licences, since pedestrians used roads long before motor vehicles.

roads. There would be no lighting, they would be like rural cross-roads. Councillors said that there should be some indication to show that a person was going to cross, because drivers may not stop. One said he was "not worried about expenditure when it comes to human life". (Hexham Courant, 16.10.64). There are *millions* of locations where pedestrians cross and walk on roads which have neither pavements nor lighting nor any "indication" of approaching vehicles that may not stop, because most councils do *not* put human life before expenditure limits. When BR was criticised in a letter in the *Cambrian News* for modernising a crossing near a playground, my reply stated that if children were too young to cross the line safely, they were too young to walk along the road with no footpath on the playground side, to get to the playground beyond the crossing. The frequency of motor vehicles, which leave one just as dead, is many times greater than the frequency of trains on branch lines

BR is developing a computerised safety information system BRIMS [BR Incident Monitoring System] to identify trends in safety standards. and log all incidents which put the public and staff at risk. (BRB 1989/90 Report, Page 7).

In the four years 1997-2000 inclusive, there were three very serious accidents[18] - in which 35 passengers lost their lives: Southall in 1997, Ladbroke Grove in 1999 and Hatfield in 2000. The latter would have been avoided in the BR regime, and, in all probability, so would, the first two.

In October, 2000, there were claims that the number of broken rails had been reduced and that railways had been made safer under Railtrack. Reports by the H&SE show that broken rails have *increased*. In eight years from 1994, when Railtrack became responsible for track, the annual average was 751. In the last eight years before Railtrack took over, it was 678. (see Table 15).

Broken & Buckled Rails								
BR era [19]					Privatised era			
year	broken	buckled	total		year	broken	buckled	total
1986	847		847		1994/95	656	46	702
1987	670		670		1995/96	752	133	885
1988	632		632		1996/97	709	45	754
1989	626	81	707		1997/98	755	34	789
1990	582	72	654		1998/99	952	18	970
1991/92	684	12	696		1999/00	917	60	977
1992/93	681	33	714		2000/01	709	27	736
1993/94	699	25	724		2001/02	561	49	610
Total	5421	223	5644		Total	6011	412	6423
Average	678	45	723		Average	751	52	803
Table 15 Source: HMRI Annual Reports - changed from calendar to fiscal year after 1990								

It is of interest to note that the H&SE had "difficulty in obtaining data on broken rails". (H&SE 1994/5,1995/6,1996/7 Reports). When 1995/6 figures were reported, they were later revised upwards

---

[18] **Southall** - As the AWS was working at the rear, we would turn a train to get the operational AWS to the front. A triangular junction was available to do so in this case. Delay was a small price for safety. Fragmentation imposes extra track access and delay charges for such movements. We did not delay an express for a freight to cross its path.

Ladbroke Grove - Using inexperienced drivers on such a busy line was not a BR practice. He had 20 weeks training - less than for a man without a car licence to become a PSV driver, and a train driver has more to learn.

Hatfield - Replacement of track would not have been delayed whether it affected punctuality or not. An Engineers Dept patrolman would have imposed an immediate speed restriction. Operating managers responsible for punctuality would not have argued. BR Civil Engineers and staff had the last word on such matters.

[19] As buckled rails were not reported before 1989, the BR average is based on 5 years. The annual average of broken and buckled rails is the sum of the averages for broken and buckled rails and not an average of the total of 5644.

Railtrack's Chief Executive stated "*1998 was the first year since 1902 when there was not a single passenger fatality*". (Sunday Telegraph, 8.10.00). It was not. None were killed *in train accidents*, but 19 were killed in 1998 in "Movement" and "Non-Movement" accidents. None were killed in *train accidents* in eleven years of the BR era! Train accident fatalities in 1997/8 and the following four years* total **46**; whilst in 1993/4 and four preceding years*, they total **5**. (see Appendix D).

There have been many reports of post-privatisation failures that put safety at risk including signals not replaced and track machines left on lines that had been declared safe for trains. H&SE stated (BBC Radio File on Four), that after Railtrack extended the life of rails in Severn Tunnel by 50%, there were four rail breaks in seven months compared with none in the past 20 years. (see also page 44).

Some try to prove privatised railways are safer *now* by dredging up the 1952 Harrow & Wealdstone disaster. One could equally prove that BR was safer than privately owned railways by dredging up the Quintinshill disaster in 1915! There is no doubt that, had railways returned to their owners after the war, the 1952 disaster would not have been avoided, unless they had been allowed unrestricted access to essential steel and raw materials. (see page 52 & footnote[8] on that page).

Some call for seat belts in trains. Belts in cars are effective because drivers are responsible for seeing that passengers wear them. In coaches the only requirement is to provide them - wearing them is not monitored. The value of lap straps is highly questionable. In aircraft, belts are mandatory on take off and landing - equivalent in rail terms to starting or stopping. Critics have not addressed the implications of instructing passengers standing in a buffet or elsewhere, to find a seat and put a belt on because a train is about to make an emergency stop. When PSVs are equipped with a Device similar to those on trains to stop them when drivers collapse or fall asleep, and motorways have multiple aspect signalling would be a good time to consider belts in trains.

Despite the unchanged disparity between rail and road safety, questions are raised as to whether millions are justified on rail safety or ought to be spent on road safety. The obsession of comparing the cost of safety improvements to the value of a life ignores financial losses arising from accidents:

- manpower, resources, trains and equipment deployed in clearing derailments,
- damaged track, overhead or third rail electric equipment, locos, rolling stock, bridges, stations, etc. The introduction of more sophisticated equipment increases the cost of repairs.
- extra costs of re-routing trains and providing replacement buses until the line is restored
- costs incurred for injured staff and others made unfit for work
- loss of revenue and refunds due to cancelled, delayed or re-routed trains
- compensation payments to delayed and injured passengers.
- and, not least, lawyers' fees.

The Annual Report on Railway Safety by HMRI for 1996/7 stated that some [rail] employers *were using quantified risk assessment to justify taking no action to improve safety, or worse still, to justify reducing the level of safety already provided. Some railway managers think that they need make no changes to improve safety and take umbrage if a* [HMRI] *Inspector asks for action to make a situation less dangerous.* No remotely similar report was published in the preceding 50 years. Such attitudes were unheard of in the BR *culture*. Had a BR manager taken either stance, he would find himself unemployed. BR managers were better versed in safety techniques and practices than today's managers. The Report lists six prosecutions by HMRI, compared with three in 1995/6, four Prohibition Notices and 20 Improvement Notices - including one relating to Forth Bridge maintenance - were issued to rail companies, which undermine claims that the industry is safer now. A 60% increase in train miles (see page 165), required more track renewals and maintenance - not less.

A study by consultants reveals a failure to manage repair and maintenance costs and poor investment decisions. Railtrack has lost understanding of repair and maintenance and had a belief in

---

*These periods represent the five years in which railways have been fully privatised, and for which statistics have been published, and the last five years in which all railway operations were under BR.

a Government bail-out. (Sunday Times, 3.2.02). The cost of maintaining the railway soared under Railtrack, but has been paid by the taxpayer. (Times 30.6.02). The Rail Regulator said that Network Rail inherited a mess from Railtrack who panicked after Hatfield and put on 1,200 speed restrictions. (BBC Radio 24.7.03). Railtrack boasted of reducing delay to trains to 6m minutes. (BBC Radio 22.7.03). Had the line at Hatfield been subject to a 20 mph speed restriction - as it would under BR if renewal was delayed - the eleven month delay in replacing the defective rail would have cost about 4-500,000 minutes. Had the ensuing 1,200 speed restrictions been imposed earlier, the minutes of delay would have been millions more.

Personal Safety

On BR, personal safety - i.e. the duty of management for the safety of staff - was a subject for *negotiation* with staff representatives, and had been since 1919. In contrast, when the rest of industry was compelled to begin to take a meaningful interest in the safe working conditions of their employees, they were enjoined to make it a matter for *consultation*. There is a world of difference. The former requires joint management/employee *agreement*; the latter relates to discussing a management plan, leaving a final decision to management. When the Health & Safety at Work Act was passed in 1974, Government organised a "road show", led by representatives of the TUC and CBI. They appeared in 1976 at Stoke-on-Trent, before an assembly drawn from local industry. On behalf of BR, I accepted an invitation and took along, a couple of managers and four staff representatives. None of us were impressed with the advice. One of the staff representatives - a goods guard - said "we've been doing all this for donkey's years, and with us, its negotiation".

Among subjects discussed and agreed were the selection of safe walking routes on or near tracks, methods of working, provision of and use of helmets, protective clothing, ear defenders for men working near noisy equipment and in engine compartments, high visibility clothing [HVC] - fluorescent jackets were useless on the track where there were no headlights to illuminate such clothing - provision of look-out men for staff working on the line, and many other allied matters. BR managers took very seriously, the organisation of Accident Prevention campaigns to increase awareness, offering prizes in competitions. Joint workplace inspections were made by managers and staff. A member of staff reported as working in an unsafe manner was subject to disciplinary procedures. In one case, a guard was so reported by a driver at Leicester for a dangerous practice, in which he endangered himself. He was severely reprimanded and warned that a recurrence of anything similar would require him to be found a less responsible post, and at correspondingly less pay. He received no sympathy from his own colleagues or union. There were no further problems.

When on safety inspections with staff, any potentially dangerous practice was stopped at once, in such a way as to ensure that staff representatives, some of whom were prone to see every safety risk as a managerial failing, got the message that some of *their* colleagues were too casual about personal safety - their own, and that of others. Any situation that could be improved by personal management action was done publicly - to impress staff of one's commitment to safety. Examples include warning BR civil engineers that immediate action - not some long term plan - was needed to improve slippery underfoot conditions in Chester carriage sidings, or the sidings would be closed and the engineers asked to answer for unserviced coaches. The effect was electric. Similar action to accelerate repairs to signal box steps, and items too numerous to mention, had a double effect. First and foremost was the removal of a risk of death or injury, second a boost to morale - making it clear that managers were as committed to staff safety as to making economies.

Industry seemed less committed to staff safety. During a visit around a factory with the manager, I drew his attention to workers using machines, on which hung undisturbed protective goggles, employees being unaware that you only get issued with one pair of eyes. He said that he kept telling them. My practice was not to ignore breaches of safety instructions. That makes a manager culpable.

Chapter 17   The way forward

Railways have now experienced "enlightened private enterprise" (see page 171), and it is not a pretty sight. A recent SRA Franchising Policy Statement (Page 5), says that franchisees failed to achieve what was promised under privatisation, that several have not been viable and have been given extra subsidy. "The extent to which risk has transferred to the private sector is questionable".

BR had many faults, but delivered the most cost effective railway of its kind in the world. There is much to be learnt from its history and little to be gained by dismissing comparisons between then and now. If franchisees fail, Government should stop bailing them out. (*Modern Railways* Jan 2003).

There are calls for re-nationalisation. (see Times 16.1.02, Daily Telegraph 28.10.02). The Tories say they will not privatise railways if they are nationalised. Clearly, they have realised that it is a vote loser - it is, as predicted a poll tax on wheels - and that taxpayers' money is going into a bottomless pit. Too late, they discovered that BR was not inefficient. Labour is between a rock and a hard place. If they nationalise, it may be some time before benefits emerge. If they do not re-nationalise, services will be cut, lines will close, subsidies *and* fares will rise, and hope of transferring traffic from road to rail will vanish. Either option will consign them to the opposition benches for decades

There is opposition to re-nationalisation, backed by anecdote rather than researched facts. This book catalogues the documented facts on fares, performance and safety. One newspaper, asked for the source of their criticism said it was in the Public Record Office, which has nine million files!

Re-Nationalisation

It does not require vast capital - railways were nationalised without laying out a penny. (see page 23). Infrastructure maintenance and renewal must be in-house - monitoring contractors will be costly and ineffective. Rolling stock could be re-nationalised but should continue to be leased, as BR began to do in 1971, until the Treasury stopped it. New stock could be acquired by a State railway, and used as a base to pull down leasing costs. When railways were nationalised, the State acquired expert managers and trained manpower at salaries and wages below industrial levels, due to Government's discriminatory wartime policies. (see page 23). Since 1994, much expertise has been lost, as new brooms came in, believing that their miscellaneous business skills were equal to the task of running a unique industry - and have proved *unequal* to the task. Bringing track maintenance *staff* back in-house - due to fragmentation among sundry companies - may be difficult. Many skilled track staff were replaced by construction workers. The problem could be eased by recruiting former track supervisors to train staff. Current wage rates cannot be reversed, but leap-frogging will be avoided, and with it many disputes. Managers with equal dedication and innovative skills as earlier generations of BR managers will not be willing to work again for sub-industrial salaries. They have tasted the fruits of capitalism - high salaries, share options, perks - and will require comparable packages. There will be no takers if the Treasury and Transport Ministry want to keep poking their clumsy oar in and second guessing *qualified* professionals, who must have freedom to manage.

Returning train companies to the State, would be done in stages, and later re-grouped, as before in Business Sectors. A State owned plc should be established, with professional railway management, poached from selected companies and by re-employing BR managers who became consultants, set up subsidiary businesses or have been discreetly re-engaged on projects. They will then have an opportunity for continued gainful employment. They can then begin to develop the next generation of managers, re-instating management schools and an effective management trainee scheme. Comparable salaries, freedom to manage and an opportunity to put the railways back on their feet would motivate many former managers to demonstrate their skills. There is no practical reason, therefore, that railways should not return to state ownership. The Government would be paying less because there would be no dividends, no cumulative profits and no golden pay-offs. A return to the public sector offers the only hope of cutting the subsidy which is out of control.

Control organisations would be re-integrated, ending interface cock-ups between companies.

Persevere with privatisation whatever the cost

There must be changes. Fragmented Control organisations for signalling, maintenance, train operations, etc., must be re-integrated to avoid cock-ups with accidents and expedite the introduction of alternative services when lines are blocked by accident or other causes. The SRA Policy Statement admits that the existing concept has failed. Large scale mergers must be enforced to *try* to revert more nearly to an integrated system. It may be necessary to re-introduce a *legal* Tribunal to control fares and charges and limit profits, whilst withdrawing subsidies on all but socially necessary rural and secondary routes, after subjecting them to close financial scrutiny. All services previously in the InterCity and Network SouthEast sectors ought to revert immediately to zero subsidy. If the much denigrated BR managers in those sectors could manage without subsidy, the new boys should have been paying a premium from Day One. Some profits should be reclaimed. Mergers should reduce the disruptive consequences of poaching trained staff, pay leaf-frogging and ensuing disputes.

Current SRA plans will lead to a **rise** in subsidies, and a **fall** in route mileage and train services. "The principle was that franchises would go to the lowest bid. This has not delivered the outcomes contemplated. New contracts direct management towards reliable performance and meeting passenger needs. The SRA is looking at benchmarks to compare with international operators[1]. The SRA should specify service levels and quality standards. The objective is to ensure that operators are not financially harmed as a result of poor performance by others. Better value may be obtained if the SRA takes some of the risk". (SRA Franchising Policy Statement Pages 3,7,8,9,12,15).

If franchises do not go to the lowest bid, there must be *subjective* selection. Ministers had an implicit belief that the original concept would ensure reliability and subsidies would fall. That the SRA, or rather taxpayers, will take *some of the risk* - which means *more of the risk* in view of rising subsidies - from *enlightened private enterprise* is an admission that the experiment has failed.

The SRA expects to pay more than its current £1.5bn pa to franchisees. Network Rail needs £5.4bn pa to get standards back to those enjoyed under BR. The total is seven times BR's subsidy!

It is all too clear that, whereas BR knew that it must reduce demands on the public purse, the new boys believe that the purse is bottomless. In no other field of enterprise is anyone protected from others. Neither BR nor their predecessors were protected from others. Protecting operators from poor performance by others will create more jobs to ascertain supportive data and make claims.

The middle, or interim, way

An option is to create a State owned company with its own infrastructure to compete with the private sector. It will be easy to find fault to justify taking over services before franchises end. Some companies may be happy to surrender them. Selective head hunting former BR managers from existing companies or from retirement would provide the leadership. Some, sacked - by arrogant newcomers who knew nothing of the industry - may welcome the opportunity. Swift action is needed to recover the expertise and skill of BR trained managers and engineers before they are too old to want to be involved in setting the railway back on track and training the next generation. If it is successful, it can be expanded in stages. Should it fail, it could revert to the private sector, and let the system contract. It was an option in 1994, but Government must have been afraid to risk comparison.

The way forward

The Way Forward is the Way Back - and without delay. If change is left too long, it will be too late, and railways will be consigned to history within a decade or two - except for cities, when commuters will learn how costly peak travel can really be.

The test of a great general, Wellington said, is to know when to retreat and to dare to do it. It must surely be the test of a great politician. Hopefully, it may not be too long before we see one.

---

[1] BR made such comparisons. but Government was not impressed that subsidy per head was lower on BR.

Comparison of fares & RPI (1948 = 100)

year	index of average fare		receipts £m		lost revenue £m		
	actual	RPI based	actual	RPI based	in year	1994 prices	cumulative
1949	93	105	114	129	15	259	259
1950	91	108	107	127	20	342	601
1951	89	113	107	136	29	472	1073
1952	93	127	112	153	41	596	1669
1953	96	133	115	159	44	617	2286
1954	96	135	117	165	48	651	2937
1955	100	140	118	165	47	624	3561
1956	104	147	128	181	53	666	4227
1957	106	154	139	202	63	756	4983
1958	106	159	138	207	69	803	5786
1959	108	163	140	211	71	809	6595
1960	120	162	151	204	53	604	7199
1961	129	165	158	202	44	494	7693
1962	140	173	161	199	38	406	8099
1963	141	178	162	205	43	442	8541
1964	143	181	167	211	44	454	8995
1965	159	190	174	208	34	330	9325
1966	165	198	179	215	36	334	9659
1967	177	205	180	208	28	257	9916
1968	169	210	185	230	45	395	10311
1969	190	223	205	241	36	295	10606
1970	205	234	228	260	32	255	10861
1971	238	254	261	279	18	128	10989
1972	259	275	274	291	17	114	11103
1973	274	296	297	321	24	149	11252
1974	291	332	329	375	46	258	11510
1975	390	398	429	438	9	41	11551
1976	490	491	505	506	1	4	11555
1977	559	572	593	607	4	45	11600
1978	631	629	702	700	(2)	(7)	11593
1979	690	688	800	798	(2)	(6)	11587
1980	831	814	954	934	(20)	(44)	11543
1981	919	920	1023	1024	1	2	11545
1982	931	1031	924	1023	99	178	11723
1983	1041	1082	1150	1195	45	77	11800
1984/85	1133	1194	1227	1293	66	102	11902
1985/86	1207	1260	1331	1389	58	86	11988
1986/87	1279	1309	1428	1461	33	47	12035
1987/88	1345	1352	1604	1612	8	11	12046
1988/89	1431	1453	1780	1807	27	35	12081
1989/90	1569	1564	1883	1877	(6)	(7)	12074
1990/91	1698	1705	2033	2041	8	9	12083
1991/92	1810	1775	2093	2052	(40)	(42)	12041
1992/93	1862	1805	2129	2064	(65)	(67)	11974
1993/94	1966	1850	2166	2038	(128)	(128)	11846

Summary of delays in raising fares & charges

scope of submission	submitted on	revised	date of decision	effect of decison	implement from	weeks delay	charges[1] index	RPI/WPI
London fares	23.2.50	twice	23.8.50	reduced	1.10.50	27	91	108
all fares	7.4.51		16.5.52	reduced	1.9.52	72	93	127
all fares	5.1.53		20.7.53	reduced	16.8.53	31	96	133
London fares	1.4.54	twice	23.8.54	reduced	26.9.54	25	96	135
all fares	7.3.55		28.4.55	approved	5.6.55	12	100	140
London fares	30.11.55		2.12.55	approved	8.1.56	5	100	140
all fares	20.2.56	submitted twice & withdrawn twice					104	147
police fares	17.4.56		12.2.57	approved	12.2.57	42	106	154
all fares	11.4.57		6.8.57	amended	8.8.57	17	106	154
all fares	1.9.58	once	8.7.59	reduced	1.8.59	47	108	163
all fares	1.3.60		14.4.60	reduced	14.4.60	6	120	162
all fares	1.11.60		14.6.61	reduced	1.1.62	61	129	165
London fares	16.3.62		26.3.62	approved	2.6.62	11	140	173
London fares	7.3.63		19.12.63	reduced	19.12.63	41	141	178
London fares	12.3.64		12.7.64	approved	19.7.64	16	143	181
London fares	10.7.64		22.1.65	reduced	22.1.65	23	159	190
London fares	4.1.66		18.7.66	approved[2]	1.8.66	29	165	198
London fares	30.5.68		16.8.68	reduced	1.9.68	13	169	210
BR freight[3]	28.11.49		6.2.50	approved	15.5.50	24	97	105
BR freight[3]	20.3.51		6.4.51	approved	16.4.51	4	119	146
BR freight[3]	17.11.51		3.12.51	reduced	31.12.51	6	119	146
BR freight[3]	29.10.52		13.11.52	approved[4]	1.12.52	4	134	149
BR freight[3]	30.12.53		10.2.54	approved	1.3.54	10	138	150
BR freight[3]	7.3.55		26.4.55	approved	5.6.55	13	148	151
BR freight	21.3.55		31.12.56	reduced	1.7.57	118	154	155
BR freight[3]	1.3.56		3.4.56	reduced	23.4.56	7	154	155
BR freight	12.7.57		30.7.57	approved	1.8.57	3		
					Total weeks =	667	= 12³/₄ years	

Delay of fares applications = 9¹/₄ years, of freight rates = 3¹/₂ years

[1] BR fares or freight rates respectively, 1948 = 100; RPI/WPI also taking 1948 = 100

[2] Not implemented on 1.8.66 - held up by NBPI for a further year, then reduced by the Tribunal.

[3] Made to the MoT, who asked the advice of the Tribunal. All others made direct to the Tribunal

[4] The Tribunal advocated a higher increase than sought, but the MoT held it to that requested.

Appendix C **Comparison of BR & Franchisees' subsidies - October 1996**

Franchisee/ BR Business Sector	Data supplied by OPRAF			BR subsidy 1995/6	
	revenue	passenger miles	subsidy	Total	"Profit"
	£m [1]	(millions) [1]	£m	£m	£m [2]
Anglia	34.0	300.0			
Cross Country	102.0	1,128.0			
East Coast *	217.0	1,900.0	64.6	66.2	18.4
Gatwick Express	27.0	96.0	-4.6	-3.1	3.1
Great Western *	156.0	1,200.0	53.2	61.8	14.5
Midland Mainline *	58.0	442.0	16.5	14.5	5.9
West Coast	216.0	1,815.0			
InterCity [3]	*810.0*	*6,881.0*	*129.7*	*139.4*	*41.9*
Chiltern	22.0	161.0	16.5	17.3	2.3
Great Eastern	109.0	855.0			
Island	0.8	4.0	2.0	2.5	0.1
LTS *	53.0	423.0	29.5	32.1	4.1
Network South Cen *	158.0	1,300.0	85.3	94.5	13.7
North London	55.0	439.0			
South East	215.0	1,548.0	125.4	142.9	18.0
South West	221.0	1,800.0	54.7	83.4	19.9
Thameslink	65.0	455.0			
Thames Trains	46.0	376.0	33.2	42.0	4.7
West Anglia	107.0	729.0			
Network SouthEast [3]	*1,051.8*	*8,090.0*	*346.6*	*414.7*	*62.8*
Cardiff	5.7	52.0	19.9	21.4	0.7
Central	60.0	601.0			
Merseyrail	19.0	147.0			
North East	61.0	692.0			
North West	44.0	377.0			
Scotrail	86.0	851.0			
Wales & West	40.0	412.0	70.9	74.9	4.4
Regional Railways	*315.7*	*3,132.0*	*90.8*	*96.3*	*5.1*
Totals	2,177.5	18,103.0	567.1	650.4	109.8
Less "Profit"				-109.8	
Net			567.1	540.6	
Franchised	1,219.5	9,714.0			
% franchised	56.0	53.7			

This is the halfway house - with about half of the train companies privatised.

[1] Revenue & passenger miles are 1994/5 except where shown * which were 1993-4

[2] A "profit" was new. Hitherto, a subsidy was the forecast deficit. (see page 34). Before privatisation the subsidy to BR was doubled as a result of fragmentation. (see page 183)

[3] Inter City received no subsidy after 1988. NSE received no subsidy in 1993/4

Appendix D   Rail passenger fatalities

year	train[1]	movement[2]	other[3]	total	year *	train	movement	other	total
1948	39	48	5	92	1975	47	22	0	69
1949	0	44	7	51	1976	0	29	1	30
1950	11	49	3	63	1977	0	27	3	30
1951	43	54	7	104	1978	13	32	2	47
1952	111	49	3	163	1979	8	42	2	52
1953	22	44	6	72	1980	0	25	1	26
1954	0	40	4	44	1981	4	31	4	39
1955	40	49	4	93	1982	0	18	2	20
1956	0	49	1	50	1983	2	25	2	29
1957	92	46	1	139	1984	18	21	0	39
1958	18	33	2	53	1985	0	31	2	33
1959	1	34	0	35	1986	8	23	1	32
1960	6	37	1	44	1987	3	36	29	68
1961	9	37	4	50	1988	34	34	1	69
1962	20	35	2	57	1989	6	25	2	33
1963	1	33	5	39	1990	0	37	2	39
1964	5	37	3	45	1991/92	2	53	3	58
1965	2	25	1	28	1992/93	0	16	2	18
1966	0	22	3	25	1993/94	0	15	2	17
1967	71	25	2	98	1994/95	3	12	2	17
1968	10	24	5	39	1995/96	1	8	2	11
1969	10	31	5	46	1996/97	1	13	3	17
1970	2	47	6	55	1997/98	7	15	4	26
1971	3	42	2	47	1998/99	0	16	3	19
1972	6	21	3	30	1999/00	29	14	4	47
1973	14	28	0	42	2000/01	10	7	3	20
1974	1	24	1	26	2001/02	0	9	3	12

[1] Train accidents: derailments, collisions with other trains or with road vehicles, etc.

[2] Movement: entering or alighting from trains, falling from moving trains.

[3] Non-movement: slipping on platforms, stairs, escalators.

* Calendar years up to1990; 1991/2 was 15 months (1.1.91 to 31.3.92); fiscal years thereafter.

Source: Annual Reports of HMRI who uses the above categories. 2001/2 Report later increased

Railtrack took over 1.4.94; Train operations 1.4.94 to 31.3.97 partly BR, partly franchisees.

Train Operating Company [TOC]	BR Business Sector	% within target		trains pa	trains within target	
		TOC	BR		TOC	BR
Anglia - inter city	InterCity	77.3	90.6	23321	18027	21129
Anglia - local	Regional Rlys	85.7	90.3	70076	60055	63279
Central	Regional Rlys	74.2	90.3	404114	299853	364915
Chiltern	NSE	89.4	92.0	90654	81045	83402
Cross Country	InterCity	62.5	90.6	44742	27964	40536
GNER	InterCity	70.0	90.6	39065	27346	35393
Gatwick Express	InterCity	81.1	90.6	54035	43822	48956
Great Eastern	NSE	85.2	92.0	257937	219762	237302
Great Western	InterCity	71.6	90.6	63994	45820	57979
Island	NSE	96.7	92.0	23734	22951	21835
LTS	NSE	82.1	92.0	99518	81704	91557
Merseyrail	Regional Rlys	81.3	90.3	204157	165980	184354
Midland Mainline	InterCity	74.2	90.6	44771	33220	40563
Northern Spirit	Regional Rlys	75.7	90.3	452033	342189	408186
North Western	Regional Rlys	78.6	90.3	474776	373174	428723
Scotrail	Regional Rlys	82.2	90.3	602449	495213	544011
Silverlink	NSE	82.9	92.0	202961	168255	186724
South Central	NSE	77.6	92.0	575226	446375	529208
South East	NSE	80.2	92.0	558866	448211	514157
South West	NSE	69.9	92.0	546583	382062	502856
Thameslink	NSE	71.8	92.0	156308	112229	143803
Thames Trains	NSE	80.2	92.0	267686	214684	246271
Wales & Borders	Regional Rlys	78.6	90.3	83494	65626	75395
WAGN	NSE	74.8	92.0	328148	245455	301896
West Coast	InterCity	68.7	90.6	59237	40696	53669
Totals				5727885	4461718	5226099
% punctuality					77.9	91.2

Punctuality targets are on the same basis. Inter City within ten minutes, the rest within five.
The number of trains pa are those shown for the companies in the SRA Report
The targets and actual percentage of trains within target are from the BRB & SRA Reports
Sources: BRB 1993/4 Report & SRA 2001/2 Report

INDEX

The Author

In 1946, Ted Gibbins joined the LMS Railway, as a junior and ended as a Chief Officer with BR. A Station Master at 21 years old, his 40 year career took him to various locations in three Regions and to BR Headquarters, serving in several Operating and General Management positions, before taking early retirement. His previous books were:

"*Blueprints for Bankruptcy*" 2nd edition, 0-9521039-2-3 [Leisure Products]. The first book to expose the myth that BR fares exceeded inflation and the first to catalogue the powerful role of the Transport Tribunal - a court of law - that determined fares and charges for 20 years and admitted its decisions had cut railway revenue. Their Reports and Proceedings of Court Hearings covered 6,000 pages. The book included extracts from Government papers closed to the public for 30-50 years. It also revealed the extent of external interference in day to day working, such that no industry however skilled its managers could have avoided bankruptcy.

"*Square Deal Denied*", 0-9521039-3-1, [Leisure Products]. The first comprehensive account of the pre-war demands, by Britain's privately owned railways for a "Square Deal" - equality of treatment under the law to that given to road transport and to coastal shipping. Reveals the circumstances leading to their demand for 18 years, through three public inquiries, and to a fourth and final equally ineffective inquiry. Disproves the claim that the Government was about to concede equality, when it was deferred by the start of World War II. Exposes the iniquitous treatment of railways which were sequestrated, by Government, in two World Wars, and for which there was no parallel in transport or industry. It discloses the content of related Government and railway papers - held, inaccessible to the public, for up to 50 years in the closed storerooms of the Public Record Office.

"*The Railway Closure Controversy*", 0-9521039-4-X, [Leisure Products]. New research into Public Records and those of Transport Consultative Committees - rail "watchdogs" - which conducted public hearings into closures. Examines popular fallacies and beliefs propounded by critics and objectors to closures, and reviews hitherto undisclosed details relating to ten closures which hit the headlines. Examines the basis for objections and criticisms, and completely disproves - with fact and figure - claims by amateurs and even those designated as "experts", that viability could be achieved by the adoption of their plans. A comprehensive answer to closure conspiracy theories.